P9-BHT-829

PENGUIN BOOKS

NANCY CUNARD

Anne Chisholm studied history at Oxford University and then went into journalism. After a year with *Private Eye* she spent two years in the United States, mainly in New York City, working on *Time* magazine. Since then she has worked for the *Telegraph Magazine* and the *Observer* and written for *The Times Educational Supplement* and the *New Statesman*. She has also worked in publishing in England and Australia. Her previous book was *Philosophers of the Earth: Conversations with Ecologists* (1972). Her home is in London with her husband, Michael Davie, and her nephew, Jesse. *Nancy Cunard* was awarded the Silver Pen Award in England for the outstanding book published in England in 1979.

N·A·N·C·Y CUNARD

—a biography by—

Anne Chisholm

PENGUIN BOOKS

Penguin Books Ltd, Harmondsworth,
Middlesex, England
Penguin Books, 625 Madison Avenue,
New York, New York 10022, U.S.A.
Penguin Books Australia Ltd, Ringwood,
Victoria, Australia
Penguin Books Canada Limited, 2801 John Street,
Markham, Ontario, Canada L3R 1B4
Penguin Books (N.Z.) Ltd, 182–190 Wairau Road,
Auckland 10, New Zealand

First published in the United States of America by
Alfred A. Knopf, Inc., 1979
First published in Great Britain by
Sidgwick & Jackson 1979
Published in Penguin Books 1981

LIBRARY OF CONGRESS CATALOGING IN PUBLICATION DATA
Chisholm, Anne.
Nancy Cunard, a biography.

Reprint of the 1979 ed. published by Knopf, New York.
Includes bibliographical references and index.
1. Cunard, Nancy, 1896–1965—Biography. 2. Authors,
English—20th century—Biography. I. Title.
[PR6053.U447Z6 1981]   828′.91409 [B]   80-28952
ISBN 0 14 00.5572 X

Printed in the United States of America by
Offset Paperback Mfrs., Inc., Dallas, Pennsylvania
Set in Bembo

Letter from Ezra Pound to Nancy Cunard copyright © the Trustees of
the Ezra Pound Literary Property Trust, 1979. Published by permission of New Directions and Faber & Faber Ltd, agents.

Since this page cannot legibly accommodate all permissions, ac-
knowledgments to reproduce previously published material appear on
page 450.

FOR CLARE

1945–1975

Contents

	List of Illustrations	9
	Foreword	13
1	The Cunard Inheritance	19
2	Growing Up at Nevill Holt *1896–1910*	31
3	The End of Childhood *1910–1911*	41
4	Girlhood *1911–1914*	49
5	Marriage *1915–1919*	58
6	A Year in Close-up *1919*	70
7	Michael Arlen *the early 1920s*	91
8	Aldous Huxley *the early 1920s*	110
9	Travels and Poetry *the early 1920s*	121
10	Paris and New Friendships *1923–1925*	130
11	Louis Aragon *1926–1928*	146
12	A House in the Country *1927–1928*	153
13	Venice and Henry Crowder *1928*	162
14	Return to Paris *1928–1929*	175
15	The Hours Press (I) *1928–1929*	189
16	The Hours Press (II) *1930*	200
17	The Breach with Lady Cunard *1930–1931*	212

18	The Black Cause *1931*	230
19	*Black Man and White Ladyship* *1931*	245
20	The Making of *Negro* *1932–1933*	255
21	The Publication of *Negro* *1934*	275
22	A Visit to Moscow *1935*	296
23	The Spanish Civil War (I) *1936–1938*	308
24	The Spanish Civil War (II) *1938–1939*	325
25	The War: Chile, Mexico, London *1940–1945*	340
26	Return to France *1945–1948*	360
27	Looking Back: Norman Douglas *1952–1954*	384
28	Looking Back: George Moore *1954–1956*	395
29	Return to Spain *1957–1959*	405
30	Breakdown *1960*	411
31	Last Years *1961–1965*	424
32	The Last Journey	433
	Epilogue	441
	Appendix 1 Nancy *and* The Waste Land	443
	Appendix 2 *Bibliography of Hours Press Publications*	445
	Appendix 3 *Nancy Cunard's Writings*	449
	Permission Acknowledgments	450
	Notes	452
	Index	465

List of Illustrations

Section 1 following page 120

page 1 Nevill Holt, Leicestershire (*National Monuments Record, London*).

2–3 Sir Bache Cunard in a *Spy* cartoon (*Radio Times Hulton Picture Library*); Bache Cunard as a boy (*HRC*); Sir Bache and Lady Cunard (*HRC*).

4–5 George Moore painted by J. B. Yeats (*courtesy of the National Gallery of Ireland*); drawing by Max Beerbohm of Nancy with George Moore (*reproduced from G. M.: Memories of George Moore, in the British Library*); Sir Thomas Beecham (*Radio Times Hulton Picture Library*); Lady Emerald Cunard (*Cecil Beaton, Sotheby's Belgravia*).

6–7 Nancy with her father, 1912; with E. W. Tennant, 1914; with two friends, 1914 (*all HRC*).

8–9 Nancy with Lady Diana Manners; Nancy's wedding day (*from a newspaper clipping*); Sydney Fairbairn about 1914; Sydney and a brother officer (*HRC*); Nancy with Lady Diana Manners and others; with three friends in a musical tableau.

10–11 Portrait of Nancy by Alvaro Guevara (*the National Gallery of Victoria, Melbourne, Australia*);

portrait by Eugene MacCown (*Hugh Ford*); Janet Flanner in fancy dress (*Library of Congress*).

12–13 Drawing of Nancy by Wyndham Lewis (*the British Council*); photograph by Curtis Moffat (*Sotheby's Belgravia*).

14–15 Michael Arlen (*HRC*); Aldous Huxley (*Popperfoto*); Edith and Osbert Sitwell (*Radio Times Hulton Picture Library*).

16 Nancy at Sanary in the south of France, 1921; with George Moore at Sanary (*both HRC*).

Section 2 following page 274

page 17 Photograph of Nancy by Cecil Beaton (*HRC*).

18–19 Photograph of Nancy by Cecil Beaton; photographs of Nancy and Louis Aragon by Curtis Moffat (*all Sotheby's Belgravia*).

20–21 Portrait of Nancy by John Banting (*from a photograph of the painting, Library of Congress*); photograph of Nancy by Cecil Beaton (*Sotheby's Belgravia*).

22–23 Henry Crowder in the late 1920s; Nancy with her Hours Press books (*all HRC*).

24–25 Nancy with Henry Crowder and a friend (*HRC*); cover for *Henry-Music*, designed by Man Ray (*British Library*).

26–27 Nancy and Henry at the Hours Press (*HRC*). List of new works from the Hours Press; cover by Len Lye for Laura Riding's *Four Unposted Letters to Catherine;* cover by John Banting for Brian Howard's *First Poems;* cover by Elliot Seabrooke for Harold Acton's *This Chaos* (*all British Library*).

28–29 Nancy with Henry Crowder and friends in
       Austria; George Padmore; Bob Scanlon; Chris
       Jones and Kwesi Oku; Marcus Garvey; Lady
       Emerald Cunard and an Indian rajah (*all from
       Negro, in the London Library*).

30–31 Nancy in Barcelona, 1937; with Edward Cunard,
       mid-1930s; Tristan Tzara at Réanville, 1935;
       Nancy at Giverny, 1948; in Capri, 1949 (*all
       HRC*).

   32 Nancy with Clyde Robinson in Majorca, 1959
       (*Hugh Ford*).

*All pictures credited HRC are from Nancy Cunard's
scrapbooks, which are in the collection of the
Humanities Research Center, the University of Texas
at Austin.*

Foreword

In every generation, a few people appear to be especially characteristic of their times. They stand for the age even during their lifetimes, and still more after they are dead. Something in their style of behavior catches the attention of the image makers, the commentators, novelists, or diarists, and they are singled out and fixed forever as the embodiment of a certain period or mood. Nancy Cunard was one of these; or so I thought when I began this book, and so, to some extent, I still think.

Nancy did indeed live through a series of what have become stereotyped episodes from the recent past. She had a childhood of Edwardian luxury and privilege, a girlhood overshadowed and disrupted by the First World War, she made a sensational plunge into gaiety and high bohemia in the 1920s, and she eagerly embraced political causes in the 1930s. At a more private level, too, her turbulent life possesses a resonance. Her notorious revolt against her background and family, her rejection of social and sexual conformity, and the price she paid for her boldness acquire a special interest now that many women question and reject accepted patterns of thought and behavior.

Yet no one is a stereotype. The truth about any single life is complex and subtle, and all labels demean and distort. Nancy's temperament was unusually volatile and her life was full of dramatic extremes; her behavior was loaded with ironies and inconsistencies. The useful labels seem especially inappropriate to what she really was.

Several of the people closest to Nancy at different times in her life have said to me that they never began to understand her. Moreover, all her life she was surrounded by rumor and exaggeration. I have tried in this book to be factual and objective. Had I known her, detachment would have been difficult; her impact on people was always dramatic. In her youth few could altogether resist her, even if they disapproved of her. Later, people often deplored her conduct and what they thought she stood for—wild living, wild art, wild politics. Her association with a black man and the black cause did not help to make her liked or respected in the world she had left.

In exploring Nancy's life, I have come to feel that because she broke the rules of her class and her sex, she was punished in a way that she did not altogether deserve. She was not always taken seriously. Partly this was her own fault. She was incapable of restraint or discretion, and she liked to shock. But as I hope this book will show, she cared greatly about things worth caring about, and she did her utmost for the people and ideas she believed in.

Nancy herself shied away from the prospect of biography or autobiography. She tried and failed to write an account of her own life, and she was irritated by most references to her in books by other people. She had a large ego but little vanity; and objectivity never interested her at all, either about people or issues. She would probably not have cared much for this book. However, it is largely based on what she wrote, in books, pamphlets, articles, diaries, and private notes, and letters to her friends.

First therefore I must thank Nancy Cunard's relations and heirs for permission to quote from her published and unpublished writings and for granting me access to her papers. I am also most grateful to: the staff of the Humanities Research Center at the University of Texas at Austin, who made these papers available to me, and especially to Mrs. Carolyn Harris; the Manuscript Division of the Library of Congress, Washington, D.C.; and the Morris Library (special collection) of Southern Illinois University. I owe a particular debt to Dr.

Ernest B. Speck of Sul Ross State University, Alpine, Texas, who allowed me to read Henry Crowder's unpublished auto-biography, and to Mrs. Dolores Finch and Mrs. Doris Hargrove for permission to quote from it.

The following people gave me invaluable help: the late Sir Robert Abdy, Sir Harold Acton, Lady Ashton, Mrs. Deirdre Bair, Miss Géraldine Balayé, Mr. Samuel Beckett, Mrs. Sybille Bedford, Lady Beecham, Miss Myriam Benkovitz, Miss Kay Boyle, the late Baroness Budberg, Professor Charles Burkhart, Mr. and Mrs. A. H. T. Chisholm, Miss Susannah Clapp, Mrs. Elizabeth Clark, Lady Diana Cooper, the late Mr. Michael Dawson, Mrs. Margot de Noblet, the late Mrs. Thomas Deuchar, Mr. John Fairbairn, the Honorable Mrs. Daphne Fielding, Mr. William Finley, the late Miss Janet Flanner, Professor and Mrs. Hugh Ford, Miss Martha Gelhorn, Mr. Milton Gendel, Mr. John Gilbert, Mr. and Mrs. Vere Gosling, Mr. John Guenther, Miss Allanah Harper, Sir Rupert Hart-Davis, the late Mrs. Wyn Henderson, Mr. Anthony Hobson, Miss Diana Holman Hunt, Mr. Michael Holroyd, Professor J. R. Hooker, Lady Jones, Mr. Alister Kershaw, Professor Harry Keyishian, Mr. Jean Lambert, Mr. John Lehmann, the late Mr. Walter Lowenfels, Mr. Alastair MacAlpine, Miss Cecily Mackworth, Mr. Michael McManus, Mrs. Basil Marsden Smedley, Mr. Raymond Michelet, Mr. Raymond Mortimer, Mr. and Mrs. William Patterson, Mr. D. C. S. Phillips, Mr. Edgell Rickword, Mr. Norman Sims, Mr. Sacheverell Sitwell, the late Miss Solita Solano, Dame Freya Stark, Mr. and Mrs. James Stern, Mr. Walter Strachan, Mr. André Thirion, the late Miss Sylvia Townsend Warner, and Mr. and the Honorable Mrs. Robert Treuhaft.

I also gratefully acknowledge the help of the Phoenix Trust.

Above all, I want to thank my editor, Charles Elliott, for his support and his helpful comments; and my husband, Michael Davie, for his encouragement and his patience.

N·A·N·C·Y
CUNARD

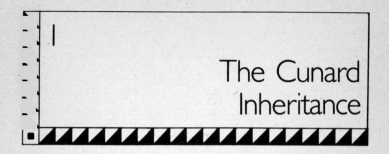

The Cunard Inheritance

Nancy Cunard's childhood could be a story by Henry James. At the end of the nineteenth century, in a vast, ancient house in the remote Leicestershire countryside, a daughter is born to a middle-aged English baronet of sporting and conventional tastes and a young American woman, twenty years his junior, pretty, intellectually and musically inclined and with a passion for social life. They are both rich, though the wife is richer than her husband; the name he has given her, however, is synonymous with commercial success and international glamor. Their daughter, an only child, grows up feeling lonely and unloved, left in the charge of servants except when the house is filled with her mother's dazzling guests, who include many of the most celebrated artists and politicians of the day. The daughter is herself strikingly pretty and gifted; she is also observant. She soon notices that her parents have little in common and that male guests in the house are often romantically attached to her mother. One of these guests becomes deeply fond of the child, and she of him. An idea, not without foundation in the gossip of the house, lodges in her mind: that this guest, a famous writer of bohemian reputation, may be her real father.

When she is on the threshold of adolescence, her mother's affections turn elsewhere, and life changes utterly. She and her mother leave the house and go to London. By the time the daughter enters society, her mother has begun to realize that her daughter does not love her. She tries to plan her future and repair the breach; but it is too late. Her daughter's life, in future, is to be molded by two instincts: to escape from her mother's orbit and to make her life as different from her mother's as she can contrive.

Even today the great house of Nevill Holt in Leicestershire, where Nancy Cunard was born in 1896, seems remote and mysterious. The house retains an aura of detachment, self-sufficiency, and power derived from seven centuries of history, although it is now a boys' preparatory school and the Corby steelworks is visible on a clear day from the terrace. It is a vast complicated structure of golden gray stone and stucco, looking from the back like a small village and from the front like a grand country mansion. Nancy Cunard was never nostalgic about her childhood, which she regarded as unhappy and, despite its grandeur and luxury, unfair; but the effect on her of the peculiarly strong beauty of the house was profound and permanent. Although she left the house for good at the age of fifteen, and lived to be sixty-nine, she never had as settled a home again; and she kept pictures of the house near her all her life.

Nevill Holt stands on top of a slope of misleading gradualness, so that the visitor is surprised by the dominance of the house over the surrounding countryside and the span of the views across the valley of the Welland and the broad fields and dense woods of the best hunting country in England. The structure is long, low and irregular, the unity of the facade barely maintained by the crenellations, some medieval, some Georgian, some Victorian, which link the rooftops together. The spire of the fifteenth-century chapel, now the Church of Saint Mary's, Holt, dominates the building and adjoins its western end. The intricacy of the house, which reveals that it was not built as one imposing structure, but grew like shells around a central rock, is calmed by the gravel sweep, the smooth grass and the formal balustrade overlooking the park. Traces still survive of the first manor built on the site, probably around 1250; and for four centuries, from 1476 until the middle of the nineteenth century, it belonged to one family, the Nevills. They expanded and steadily altered it during the fifteenth and sixteenth centuries; and in the seventeenth century they added cloisters and an elegant stable block. In the early eighteenth century, the Nevills smoothed over the Tudor structures with a Georgian veneer and replaced the Elizabethan gardens with classical landscaping, terraces and lawns.

The house and estate of some thirteen thousand acres were acquired by the Cunard family in 1876. It was bought by Edward Cunard, a twenty-two-year-old officer in the 10th Hussars, who was killed the following year playing polo. When Sir Bache Cunard inherited the house in 1877, it was a remarkable mixture of styles, intricate but not confused, large but not massive, a peculiarly English combination of grandeur and domesticity.

The house has been a preparatory school for boys since 1926, but even in term time there is little sign of their presence at first. School trunks are piled in the stables and sports gear in the entrance hall, but the front door still opens directly into the Great Hall, the heart of the house for five centuries; two stories high, with a steeply pointed, beamed roof, a vast sixteenth-century fireplace, and stone-flagstoned floor. The hall is dimly lit by a fine fifteenth-century carved bay window, and has dark paneling halfway up the walls. A brocade curtain falls from a high medieval arch leading to the first floor. A glass-fronted box on the wall in the servants' quarters still lists the bells of the Cunard household: "Sir Bache's room," "Lady Cunard's room," "Miss Nancy," "Schoolroom," "Governess."

Sir Bache Cunard, Nancy's father, possessed all the attributes and tastes of an English landowner and conducted himself like a man whose forebears had lived in such a house for generations. In fact, as his un-English names revealed, he was a comparative newcomer. His grandfather was the civil engineer Samuel Cunard, founder of the Cunard line of steamships. Born in Philadelphia in 1787, Samuel Cunard moved to Halifax, Nova Scotia, and started the first transatlantic steam-vessel mail service in 1840. In that year his ship *Britannia* traveled from Boston to Liverpool in fifteen days, cutting a month off the sailing time. When, in 1859, he settled in England, Queen Victoria created him a baronet in acknowledgment of his energetic services. He died in London in 1865. His son, Edward, the second baronet, married an American, Mary McEvers, daughter of Bache McEvers of New York; they had three sons—Bache, born in 1851, Edward, in 1855, Gordon, in 1857—and four daughters.

Despite their American background, the Cunard boys were brought up in conventional English style. Bache was educated at Rugby and Trinity College, Cambridge. His father died suddenly on a visit to New York in 1869, aged fifty-three, so that Bache, at eighteen, became the third baronet. His passion in life was sport; he took no part in the immensely prosperous family business, and he was always happiest in the English countryside with his horses, dogs, guns, and fishing rods. Like his grandfather, he had a strong streak of the craftsman in him; but the interest in machinery which had led Sir Samuel to found a shipping empire emerged in Sir Bache as a mild eccentricity. He became a skilled metalworker, whose hobby was making ornamental and decorative objects.

With his American connections it was not surprising that Sir Bache should find an American wife. The 1870s and 1880s were the heyday of the Anglo–American society marriage; the most notable and influential was the wedding of Jennie Jerome (who was to become a great friend of Lady Cunard) to Lord Randolph Churchill in 1874. But there were many others, including that of Consuelo Iznaga to Viscount Mandeville, the Duke of Manchester's heir, in New York in 1876. Sir Bache Cunard was among the guests. The usual arrangement was that an impecunious but impeccably aristocratic Englishman would trade his social standing for the wealth of an American girl; American gossip columnists uninhibitedly published lists of bachelor dukes and earls, and totted up the money that might be available to them if they captured particular American heiresses. Sir Bache's marriage at the comparatively late age of forty-three to Miss Maud Alice Burke of San Francisco did not quite fit this pattern. She was certainly rich, but so at the time was he; and his baronetcy was unimposing in comparison with some of the titles being hawked round the American market by European fortune hunters. Also Maud Burke was a Californian, and Californian society, though it had its higher echelons, was still comparatively new, and crude. Nevertheless, Sir Bache did not escape American sneers. In his *Diary of Society As It Really Is,* a Californian named William H. Chambliss wrote:

> A complete list of all the marriages of American women to titled men, for the past thirty-five years, shows that at least two hundred million dollars have gone away from this country in that period. . . . California has had more than her share of this burden to bear. Seven Californian girls have taken away from this state alone nearly twenty millions of dollars, or 10 per cent of the entire amount, in exchange for seven titles most of which are both shabby and shopworn.
>
> Prince Colonna has probably cost, up to date, in the neighbourhood of five million dollars. Prince Hatzieldt an equal if not larger sum. Prince Poniatowski came cheaper: a quarter of a million was about his price. The *dot* of Lord Wolseley's California bride was probably something under a million, but with moderate luck Sir Bache Cunard will get some two millions of old man Carpentier's accumulation of dollars, as his bride, Miss Burke, is the Outland Capitalist's favourite niece and should come in for a large slice of his estate.

Maud Burke had plenty of money; but socially her background was precarious in comparison with that of some of the East Coast girls who had married titled Englishmen. She herself always avoided inquiries about her family or early life, more probably because she liked to encourage the rumors of exotic irregularities that circulated around her origins than because she was conscious of any social inferiority. Her father, James Burke of San Francisco, was of Irish descent and claimed to be related to Robert Emmet, the great Irish patriot; her mother was half French. One of her father's friends was William O'Brien, one of the four partners who opened up the Great Bonanza Mine in the Comstock Lode, the vastly profitable Nevada silver mine, in the 1870s. One of the exotic rumors was that this good looking, fair, blue-eyed millionaire was her father, and that he left her a lot of money.

Maud Burke was born in San Francisco in 1872. Among the few facts she let fall about her childhood were that she had an older brother who died in infancy, and that she was looked after by Chinese servants. Her father died when she was in her early teens, whereupon her mother acquired a succession of rich admirers and protectors. One of these was Horace Carpentier, a southerner and former general in the American Civil War, who had made an enormous fortune out of real estate and adopted young girls as "nieces." Whatever his precise relation may have been with her mother, Carpentier certainly made Maud Burke one of his special favorites. She was small, fair and pretty, and grew up with an eager interest in literature and music. It was Carpentier who encouraged her to read Greek and Latin poetry, Balzac, and Shakespeare; she first read her favorite English novel, Richardson's *Pamela,* in his library. She remembered hearing her first opera in New York at the age of twelve and feeling "as if a new world had opened out." She made several trips to Europe with her mother and was stirred by France and French literature; after her mother's remarriage to a New York stockbroker called Frederick Tichenor, she found, at the age of eighteen, "a second home" with Carpentier, whom she referred to as her "guardian."

Then, on one of her visits to London, almost certainly in the spring of 1894, when she was twenty-one, she met a man who was twice her age, wholly captivated him and inspired him to write a series of descriptions of her that suddenly bring her appearance and character to life. This was George Moore, the Anglo-Irish writer, who was then in his early forties and at the height of his fame. His novel, *Esther Waters,* giving a sympathetic account of a servant girl who has a child without being married, had just been published, strengthening his reputation as an enemy of tradition and prudery and a critic of orthodox morality and religion. He had lived in Paris and was a patron of Manet and Degas; and the friend of Mallarmé, Huysmans, and Zola. He also cultivated—too assiduously, some thought, to be convincing—the notion of himself as a great lover. His appearance was not exactly romantic: he had a pale oval face, sloping shoulders, a drooping moustache and a small red mouth. According to one of Moore's versions of his first encounter with Maud Burke, she was wearing a pink and gray shot-silk dress and changed the place cards at a luncheon at the Savoy Hotel so that she might sit next to him.

Elsewhere he recalled "a brilliant young lady; destined to become one of the principal figures in society, who listened delightedly to his sallies, and with a sudden inspiration called out to him, 'George Moore, you have a soul of fire!' It was the compliment of his life, the remembrance of which he constantly cherished. . . ." He fell in love with her at their first meeting and remained devoted to her for forty years.

Moore wrote about what is recognizably his romance with Maud Burke in his novels as well as in his volumes of autobiography. He always allowed himself wide poetic license, but at the same time he was restricted by convention; his love for Maud was increasingly public knowledge in both their circles, but he had to handle it carefully in print for fear of overstepping the bounds of discretion. But Moore seldom invented things altogether. It is therefore possible to piece together a picture of the early stages of their romance.

Moore was bowled over. "The body envelopes the soul, and a shot silk shimmered in the May sunlight when she came forward and put her little hand, like a fern and white as a lily, into mine." He was more than usually in a mood to fall in love, having recently come to the end of an awkward liaison with Pearl Craigie, also a novelist, who wrote under the name of John Oliver Hobbes; with the touch of absurdity often present in Moore's love affairs, the relationship had apparently ended after he kicked her in the backside in a fit of irritation during a walk in Hyde Park. From the start, he felt, he knew that this love for the Californian girl was different. "All the partial loves of my youth seemed to find expression at last in a passion that would know no change. . . . She had the indispensable quality of making me feel I was more intensely alive when she was by me than I was when she was away."

At first, his feelings seemed to be reciprocated. They spent idyllic days traveling together in France and Germany; castles were visited in Provence and paintings examined in Holland and Paris. But Moore's account of their early raptures is tempered by his awareness of the steel in Maud's character; she was young and beautiful and she may have been in love, but she was not carried away.

> Her courage, independence, her intellectual audacity, no doubt captured my admiration . . . I admired her cold sensuality, cold because it was divorced from tenderness and passion . . . I loved but an immortal goddess descended once more among men. Her sensuality was so serene and so sure of its divine character that it never seemed to become trivial or foolish. While walking in the woods with one, she would say "Let us sit here," and after looking steadily at one for a few seconds, her pale marmoreal eyes glowing, she would say, "You can make love to me now, if you like."

Moore wrote a poignant description of how he knew from the beginning that "Elizabeth" was not the kind of woman to marry him. " 'If we were married,' she says, 'we should be very happy—for six months.' "

" 'Only for six months?' I answered, admiring her lawlessness. 'Is it then decreed that I shall lose you? It is not then your destiny to watch my back broadening as I lean over a desk writing novels. You have come into this life to shine in society, to be a light, to form a salon and to gather clever men round you.' "

He knew, he wrote, that "wiser by far it would be to seek a husband for her, a springboard from which she could leap." For a while they were together in London discussing which of her admirers would form her "springboard," and then they parted, Maud returning with her mother to America, and George Moore to Ireland. They were not to meet again for two years.

Back in New York, Maud Burke encountered another man who seemed for a while—unlike George Moore—to be the ideal marriage partner. He was a Polish prince, André Poniatowski, the grandson of the late king of Poland, and he was handsome, rich and cultivated, as well as energetically determined to become a success as a businessman in the New World. They wrote to each other after he returned to Europe and Maud to San Francisco in the winter of 1894; and when Maud heard he was returning to America, she seems to have convinced herself that he was going to ask her to marry him. The newspapers got hold of the story, and by the time the prince reached San Francisco he was widely considered to be Maud Burke's fiancé. This was not what he had in mind; he was hoping to marry another girl, and moreover a girl from a much grander San Francisco family: Beth Sperry, sister of Mrs. Harry Crocker, one of the leaders of West Coast society.

At Poniatowski's request, Maud Burke made a public denial of their engagement; she gave as the reason the opposition of her "guardian," Horace Carpentier, to the match. Poniatowski married Miss Sperry, the couple settled in San Francisco, and Maud and her mother moved to New York. The whole episode must have been painful and humiliating for Maud and helps to explain why she decided to marry the prosaic Sir Bache so soon after she met him in New York. Though not a prince, and old enough to be her father, Sir Bache could at least offer her a title and a new life far from any gloating rivals.

Courtship and marriage were rapid; there is no reason to believe that Sir Bache, an imposing figure, tall, well built, and dark, with a drooping walrus moustache, was not as bowled

over as Moore had been by the small, golden-haired, sparkling girl, whose charm rarely failed when she chose to exert
it. There is a story that one of Sir Bache's sisters begged
Maud to break the engagement, for she knew her brother
could only be happy leading a quiet country life, whereas it
was quite plain that Maud needed the stimulus of town life
and society; but Maud had made up her mind. "I like Sir
Bache better than any man I know," she said. They were
married in a simple ceremony at a church in New York on
April 17, 1895. Maud wore "a tailor-made gown of grey cloth
and a bonnet to match." Three days after the wedding, Sir
Bache and Lady Cunard sailed for Europe.

When Maud first saw Nevill Holt, now her home, she may
have felt excited at her new status, but it must also have
seemed oppressive and daunting. She must soon have realized, too, how little she had in common with her husband. Sir
Bache had two great interests: his country sporting pursuits,
in particular the pack of hounds he kept at Medbourne, the
village nearest to Nevill Holt, and his metalwork, for which
he had built himself a workroom in one of the towers and a
forge at a nearby farm. He was not enthusiastic about artistic
or intellectual matters, nor about social life apart from ritual
sporting occasions. He loved Nevill Holt and had embarked
on several improvements, as he saw them, designed to add a
touch of Victorian gothic to its generally medieval and Georgian gothic aspect; he liked the house darkly paneled and full
of armor, old swords, hunting prints and trophies and stuffed
heads, and he liked life there to be conducted in a formal
old-fashioned manner. All this must have seemed gloomy to a
high-spirited and intellectually and socially ambitious young
American of twenty-three. Lady Cunard was notorious later
in life for her distaste for the country and her refusal to mod-
ify either her dress or her behavior to fit in with country
ways. Nor was she likely to think highly of her husband's
metalwork, the stable signs and weathercocks he made for
Holt and the tower of Medbourne church, the elaborate
ostrich-egg holders, the vine leaf covering for the electric bell

at the dining table, the candelabras for wedding presents. Sir Bache also took a keen interest in the garden, particularly in the yew hedges which the gardeners clipped to his careful designs and fed regularly with a substance known as bullock's blood. A favorite family story told of Lady Cunard's chilly reaction when she returned one day to Holt to find that her husband had constructed for her an elaborate new present, an outdoor ornamental gate with the message "Come into the Garden Maud" worked around the arch in horseshoes.

Lady Cunard had her own ideas about the decoration of the house. On one occasion she took advantage of Sir Bache's absence to order some local workmen to cover a particularly fine room, paneled in Tudor oak, with white paint. He arrived home after the household had retired; as soon as he entered the house, he smelled the paint and knew something was up. He kept his carriage waiting, and when he found the newly painted room, he was so angry that he sent the carriage to fetch the workmen back from the village, to stay until every speck of white paint had been removed. This incident passed into local lore and is still talked about in the village seventy years later; so is the incompatibility of the couple's tastes and ways and the coincidences between Sir Bache's departures and the arrival of Lady Cunard's friends and admirers.

Medbourne still shows traces of Sir Bache's time as the local squire. The Victorian brick stables and kennels he built for his horses and hounds are still there, with the monogram BC and a round hole where the clock was meant to go (the villagers say he ran out of money before it could be installed). His plans to build a fountain on the village green outside the pub, with a basin for the village women to use for washing and troughs for horses and dogs to drink at, are still remembered. Lady Cunard made little effort to develop country tastes. She rode to hounds a few times, but she soon became pregnant and gave it up. Sir Bache's family recognized that his wife, though charming and spirited, was not going to try to fit in. Few of them liked her. As for the neighbors, Lady Cunard made the required calls on them, but they did not meet her idea of society. Nor were all the local people polite to her. One elderly eccentric, Lord Mexborough, who had been wheeled into the drawing room wearing a top hat, his white beard reaching down to his knees, shouted as soon as he saw her, "Take her away! Take her away!"

The Cunards' first and only child was born at Nevill Holt on
March 10, 1896, and christened Nancy Clara. Lady Cunard's
maternal instincts were not strong. She would later profess a
deep distaste for motherhood, which she called "a low
thing—the lowest." She displayed mock horror when she
heard that a friend had borne a child. After Nancy's birth she
had no hesitation in following the accepted social pattern,
handing over her child to the care of nursemaids, nannies, and
governesses and allowing the child to disrupt the lives of her
parents as little as possible. Nancy was to resent this aspect of
her childhood.

It was a curious upbringing. Some forty servants were employed in and around the house, including gardeners, coach-
men and grooms, yet Nancy's parents were seldom in residence, Sir Bache on his sporting round and Lady Cunard in
London, or abroad, or on visits to other country houses. For
the child, periods of isolation and solitude at the apex of this
social pyramid would be suddenly and arbitrarily interrupted
when, the visiting season having begun, her mother would
return, the carriages would jingle up the drive bringing ladies
in sable furs, Parma violets pinned to their shoulders, and the
Morning Room would fill with huge bowls of azaleas and
gentlemen endlessly playing bridge.

"My picture of Holt," wrote Nancy fifty years later, "is
one of constant arrivals and departures during half the year, of
elaborate long teas on the lawn with tennis and croquet going

on, of great winter logs blazing all day in the Hall and Morning Room, with people playing bridge there for hours on end. Beautiful and exciting ladies move about in smart tailor mades. . . . Summer-long in shot silk and striped taffeta they stroll laughing and chatting across the lawns."

She remembered the house as always filled with flowers.

Flowers were everywhere, including hothouse blooms and sometimes orchids brought by somebody from London or his own conservatory, and a glory of azaleas filled the great Chinese bronze incense burner, in the Hall. . . . It was in the Morning Room they sat most, in that long, low, harmonious place with a stone floor and many oriental rugs strewn across it, that grew yearly more luxurious because of an increasing number of Italian damasks, cushions, and brocades. Every ray of sun seemed concentrated on the four windowseats decked with old Chinese bowls of potpourri. The two oak writing tables, one at each end, were elaborately appointed with everything to hand for the distinguished calligraphy of those times. Art books and new novels lay about in profusion; here a great box of candy, there a box full of aromatic Russian cigarettes.

The arrival of guests was a great excitement for Nancy. She would be allowed to put flowers in the guests' bedrooms, and to help check that the writing desks were stocked with pens, ink, and paper. She always recalled the sense of amazement and indignation she felt when one day the gardener from whom she was fetching flowers for the house declined her offer of a bunch for his own small daughter, telling her that they had no right to their employers' flowers.

The Cunards, though they could have well afforded it, did not own a town house; but in any case the young Lady Cunard was clever enough to realize, as she embarked on a career as a hostess that was to last for fifty years, that she would be well advised to entertain first at Nevill Holt rather than tackle London society head-on. By comparison with members of the old families that dominated the London scene, she and her husband were outsiders and newcomers. In the country, where English upper-class life was still based, established social rank was of less significance, and her new friends soon showed themselves glad to spend a weekend in a remarkable house where the food and furnishings were the best, and they were cosseted and entertained by a hostess of exceptional charm, spirit, and originality. Social conventions eased with the accession of Edward VII in 1901, especially for pretty young hostesses, even if they were American. Initially, though, it must have required nerve for Lady Cunard to take on English society. She wanted social success; and she achieved it by the encouragement above all of good conversation. She seldom cultivated bores simply because they were grand.

The impressive Nevill Holt visitors' book for the first decade of the century demonstrates that most of her guests had something to offer apart from social acceptability. Many of them were titled or came from distinguished old families, such as Harry Cust, George Wyndham, or Lord Basil Blackwood, but they were also talented and original. Gradually, Lady Cunard began to know the leading politicians: A.J. Balfour, H.H. Asquith, F.E. Smith. She invited writers and journalists, including Edward Marsh, the poet laureate Alfred Austin, Francis Meynell, Somerset Maugham.

Increasingly, she invited guests with musical gifts, like the pianist Ethel Leginska, and the singer Reinhold von Warlich. She made several women friends who became frequent visitors: the duchess of Rutland, the beautiful and artistic mother of Lady Diana Manners, who was to become a girlhood friend of Nancy's; Cynthia Charteris, Asquith's clever daughter-in-law; Jennie Cornwallis-West, formerly Jennie Churchill née Jerome, the wife of Lord Randolph. She exchanged visits with another American-born hostess, Mrs. Charles Hunter, Henry James's friend, who had been painted by Sargent and was a patron of George Moore.

Romantic undercurrents, frequently with Lady Cunard at the center, were very much part of the atmosphere at Nevill Holt in its heyday. Nancy later recalled an evening when the house party played a truth game, and one of the guests, a dashing Slav prince, was asked whom he was in love with. The true answer would have been "my hostess," but the host was present and the victim neatly evaded the question with a joke about his passion for the pageboy at the St. James's Club. Another of Lady Cunard's admirers was Lord Alexander Thynne, second son of the fourth marquess of Bath and Conservative MP for Frome, a handsome, popular man-about-town; after he died in the First World War, love letters from Lady Cunard were found among his papers.

In later years Lady Cunard herself would tell a story that indicates that Sir Bache was not entirely unaware of what was going on. He returned to Holt on one occasion in midsummer, to find the house full of musicians and music lovers; one hot night, Maud recalled, one of the guests had thrown open his bedroom window and had given the Valkyries' cry, and from window after window other voices had answered until the whole place resounded with Wagnerian melodies. "When my husband came back," Lady Cunard once told Cecil Beaton, "he noticed an atmosphere of *love*. 'I don't understand what is going on in this house,' he said, 'but I don't like it.' "

Especially in the early years after her marriage, George Moore was one of Lady Cunard's favorite and most frequent guests. He was living in Dublin, having decided in 1899 that he must go back there and join his old friends W.B. Yeats and Lady Gregory in their efforts to reinvigorate Irish culture; but he often came over to England, and on one of these visits he again met Lady Cunard. George Moore reappeared in her mother's life when Nancy was about two years old. He describes in *Memoirs of My Dead Life* how he met his true love once when she was "four months gone, as the saying is" at a country house party to which she had arranged his invitation, but where she rejected his advances; "every night she locked her door when her maid left her, and the sound is and will be ever in my ears." Then two years later, they met by chance in Kensington. "She came towards me in another hansom, young and joyous, tremulous and slight, having regained her figure completely—her baby was then two years old, and her hair seemed thicker and more brilliant, more like real gold than ever. . . ." After this encounter, Moore began to be invited regularly to Nevill Holt for house parties; and occasionally, though not as often as he would have liked, on his own for a longer stay.

One of his happiest visits occupied the summer of 1904, when he coincided with Lady Cunard's mother, now Mrs. Frederick Tichenor. For several weeks he had Maud and her mother and Nancy, aged eight, virtually to himself; and in the following year when, to Lady Cunard's great distress her mother died, Moore wrote her a sympathetic, nostalgic letter recalling the enchanted summer they had spent together. "That happy, happy summertime—was god or mortal ever favoured as I was, living between you two women for one whole month in that beautiful house. . . . Do you remember our laughter? That part of our life is over and done—how intensely one remembers—my room hung with Italian engravings, and the round table at which I used to sit writing, and your ringing voice calling me away, or your mother's, or dear Nancy's. . . ."Although his adoration for Lady Cunard never flagged, it is clear from his subsequent letters to her that she moved him slowly but inexorably to the fringe of her life. She had many other admirers and flirtations, for she believed in romance and intrigue as the spices of society, and romantic friendship rather than a passionate or exclusive love affair was what she came to want from Moore, to his growing sadness. Meanwhile, as his letters and Nancy's own account show, he became very fond of Lady Cunard's small daughter. There was a deep bond between Nancy and George Moore; she always remembered him as a source of warmth and affection in her childhood.

It may have been partly this unusual bond that led to the suggestion that Nancy was George Moore's daughter, not Sir Bache Cunard's. It is possible, but not likely, given Moore's own accounts of the progress and timing of the relationship and the nature of the people concerned. Moore never exactly denied it; but then it was just the sort of rumor that, while having to be handled with discretion, would enhance his slightly precarious reputation as a daring lover. What is of great importance for an understanding of Nancy's character and relationship with her mother is that the question existed, and that it remained open.

"I suppose I was about four years old when I first remember G.M., and I suppose I may, in some sort, even call him 'my first friend,' " Nancy wrote, forty years later. "He came so often to Holt, generally on lengthy visits, and appeared then to be so much part of the place, talking to me always in a manner beyond my years and taking so much interest in all that concerned me, that he is the central figure of childhood. . . ." She remembered Moore calling her a romantic child, and thought that the first time, perhaps, he talked to her was when he found her curled up near the huge fireplace in the Great Hall reading Andrew Lang's *Violet Fairy Book*.

It sounds, from Nancy's account, as if what most endeared Moore to her was that he was always prepared to talk to her, listen to her, and keep her company. They would wander around the gardens together, inspecting the fountains; Nancy would drag him to the rubbish heap in the orchard, where she liked to pick out bits of broken china, or sit with him in the shade of the cloisters, where there was a plaque to her alleged forebear, Robert Emmet; or she would try to tempt him to climb into her favorite cedar tree, where she kept a store of beechnuts in a stone bottle. She was fascinated by the sight of the occasional tramp passing on the road under the terrace: "those tramps excited me and I told GM I wanted to run away and be a vagabond." Sometimes they would walk to local churches and look at the inscriptions on the gravestones; or pick wild flowers, with Nancy instructing Moore on their names. When Nancy discovered a particularly deep secluded ditch and decided to make it her "house," filling it with her treasures—"some oddly curved root, and a stick stripped of its bark, fierce sea green flints, and a small blue empty medicine bottle"—she kept it a secret from everyone except

Moore. On long walks the governess would accompany them, to Nancy's disgust; she would run on ahead leaving Moore holding his bowler hat and politely discussing French poetry. When he was away from Holt, they would exchange affectionate letters.

Nancy instinctively felt that Moore was on her side against rules and authority, and she loved him for it. On at least one occasion he took her part against her mother and her governess. A guest had brought down a copy of Elinor Glyn's romantic novel, *Three Weeks,* which was considered immensely daring and provocative, and a parody, *Too Weak* by a current wit, Montague Eliot. Nancy, aged eleven, found them and read them. "My week with *Three Weeks* in bed in the clandestine hours of dawn was a very great enjoyment. So that was an adventuress—beautiful, perfidious, dashing. She blazed awhile across the repressions of my childhood. It also chanced that *Three Weeks* was the first novel I read." She told George Moore and he asked her, "with real interest," her opinion. "I told him it had thrilled me, but that *Too Weak,* though very unkind, had made me wonder if there were not, well, some exaggeration in it. . . . We must have talked for twenty minutes, while I asked myself how severely punished I would be if the matter were discovered." Unluckily, her governess overheard their discussion and the matter was reported to Lady Cunard.

"Astonishment and annoyance soon turned into uproar because GM came out firmly on my side, and as I stood there crimson with defiance, saying, 'Why not? Why not?' there was an increasing vehemence in all his words: 'What is the *harm* in that, will you kindly tell me? Why should she not read *Three Weeks*? It may not be good literature, but what possible *harm* can come to her from reading it?' "

On another occasion Moore inadvertently got Nancy into trouble. He was demonstrating how well he could waltz and by mistake kicked Nancy's terrier, Buster, who howled piteously. Nancy flew at GM and slapped his face; GM was horrified, Lady Cunard angry, and Nancy confined to the schoolroom in disgrace for two days.

Although most of Nancy's early childhood was spent at Nevill Holt, there were occasions when Lady Cunard took her daughter with her to London, or abroad. Nancy made two or three trips to America when she was very small; she vaguely recalled both traveling in great luxury on a Cunard liner, and staying in a grand New York hotel where she would help a maid arrange the huge bouquets of red roses sent by her mother's admirers. In the winter of 1906 she visited her mother's "guardian," Carpentier, who by this time was old and ill and living in a modest wooden house in Saratoga, New York. Nancy was presented to another of the "nieces"—a fat old woman with heavily jeweled hands who lived nearby. In London she would sometimes be taken to the opera, her mother's great passion. Her precocity was striking; Edward Marsh wrote in a letter to a friend:

"Do you know Lady Cunard's little girl aged eleven? I went to Figaro the other day with them and between the acts Nancy said in her high little squeaky toneless voice, 'The Count is exactly like George the Second. The Countess I should put a little later—about 1790.' What are children coming to?"

It was the governess who reported the Elinor Glyn affair whom Nancy specially hated. Miss Scarth seems to have been an intelligent but unsympathetic woman, although Nancy may well have been exaggerating when she later recalled "her detestable temper, her punishments and outrageous discipline." She had been Vita Sackville-West's governess, with success; she must have been in charge of Nancy for three or four years, because she was still at Holt in 1909 and 1910, when Nancy kept a diary, which has survived among her papers. Miss Scarth did not allow Nancy to keep her diary private; she read it and even occasionally wrote in it herself, which Nancy resented. Nancy's childhood diaries of life at Holt consist of brief entries about lessons, riding her pony— she was taught to ride as early as possible by her father, and blooded, out hunting, at six—children's parties, playing charades, picking mushrooms and blackberries. Among the few children she was allowed to play with were her cousins on her father's side. She grew closest to her uncle Gordon Cunard's sons, Victor and Edward, both near to her in age, who lived not far away. Another cousin, however, remembers that visits to Nevill Holt were not all that popular in the family, although the children enjoyed hiding in the suits of armor on the stairs. Nancy was a fierce little girl; Sir Bache was huge, silent and alarming; and Lady Cunard, though very pretty, was not sympathetic to children.

When she was just thirteen, she kept a rather fuller account of a journey to France and Italy with her parents. In Paris her mother tried on dresses while her father took her to the Louvre or Versailles with a cup of chocolate in a café afterward; in Rome she fell ill and had to stay in bed for a few days: "What is the use of coming to Rome to be ill? . . . *Dig* my pencil in the paper. . . . I was in such a temper at being ill." All through her life illness or weakness made Nancy furious with herself. When she recovered, she saw all the sights of Rome, and she went to see Pope Pius perform a beatification, accompanied by the duchess of Rutland and her daughters, Marjorie and Diana. In Florence on their way home, to Nancy's embarrassment, Lady Cunard became ill and had to be "carried about like a queen . . . people stare so."

During 1910 the diary shows that Nancy was spending more time in London, attending classes at Miss Woolf's exclusive school in South Audley Street and going to museums and the opera. She wrote part of this diary in a quaint mixture of invented Old English and French. "Fathere dyde leave todaye forre Ye Holte. . . . *GM et moys allames fayre une promenade a Sohoe.*"

At the back of her 1910 diary Nancy listed the books she claimed to be reading that summer and early autumn: an impressive collection for a fourteen-year-old girl. The list includes Walter Scott, Shelley, *Paul et Virginie*, Schiller, Goldsmith, Molière, Shakespeare, Ouïda, *Lavengro* and *Romany Rye*, Daudet, Dickens, Corneille, the Book of Job, Aeschylus, and *The Canterbury Tales*.

One thing above all emerges strongly from these diaries; when Lady Cunard was away, Nancy missed her. In 1909 she writes: "Mother has gone to Belvoir today by train. Things have begun their usual course again and lessons recommence. Therefore during this period . . . things will not be very bright and nothing much happens." A little later: "I am not going to write a diary while Mother is in America as nothing amusing or interesting happens."

In the summer of 1910 Lady Cunard went to Munich with George Moore and a woman friend to listen to Wagner. Sir Bache had returned to Nevill Holt from Scotland; "We shall soon be quite alone but notte for very long, I hope." A few days later: "I have not yet heard from Mother and GM." And again: "When Mothere ysse awaye ytte ysse allerwayes most quyette heer."

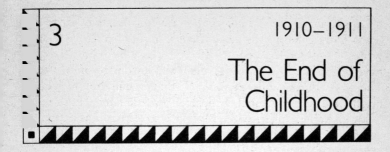

Fifty years later, Nancy was to give a considered appraisal of
her parents and her attitude to them during her childhood. Of
her mother she wrote:

> Her tastes were musical, literary and artistic, she loved and
> promoted good conversation by her own sporadic outbursts of
> airy, fantastic wit, and developed a remarkable gift for enter-
> taining on a grand scale. Later on all of this went *con brio
> furioso,* but the times at Holt evoke words like "spacious, com-
> fortable and leisurely." . . . Chopin's Third Ballade and Bee-
> thoven Sonatas were played with skill and feeling by my
> mother, who would be reading the classics and contemporary
> French literature half the night.

When Sir Bache was indoors, he was not likely to join in
either the music or the literary conversation:

> It was in the tower room above the porch that my father spent
> most of his time, hammering silver, carving coconuts elabo-
> rately to mount them into cups, and making other things with
> his able hands. Thoroughly conservative in his ideas, he was
> manually an ingenious, gifted man in all his manipulations of
> wood and iron. . . . Somehow I felt—and was—entirely de-
> tached from both, admiring and critical of them by my own
> standards, those of a solitary child wondering much in silence
> how life was going to be. It seems fantastic now to think of
> the scale of our existence then, with its numerous servants,
> gardeners, horses and motorcars.

It was indeed an extraordinary upbringing, as another relic of those days at Nevill Holt, Nancy's autograph album, shows. Many of the guests in 1909 and 1910 wrote something amusing or sentimental in the small brown suede book or drew a quick sketch for their hostess's thirteen-year-old daughter. The first, and longest, entry is appropriately by George Moore: an ill-punctuated and melancholy four-page effusion on the theme of the age gap between himself and Nancy. His entry is dated June 30, 1909, and he is on the point of leaving Holt until August.

It is harder to write a page for a little girl than volumes for the great anonymous public.

It seems impossible to keep my thoughts out of sentimentality—I keep remembering that when you are a beautiful young woman in society I shall be a very old man—if I have ten years more. On this theme one can write for ever for of course you will get old as well as another, that is an unpleasant thought for me, you have not arrived at the age when such thoughts assail you. It is better not to think that the moment is always going by. It is better to enjoy it. That present moment may not be enjoyed by me—I am utterly tired and despondent—but I can look forward to walks in August—we will go through the woods to the old wells where people used to go to take the washing long ago; and I have not forgotten the great hedges—the blackberries will not be ripe in August so we shall not gather them this year. I haven't forgotten your little house in the dry ditch—we'll visit it together. We will visit all those places together Nancy, and at the bottom of the hill you will tell me just as you did in February, "now you won't mind but I'm going to run up the hill." I've been writing for many months and am looking forward to these walks with you, to seeing the squirrel in the porch again and the dog whose name I can't remember. . . . the little dog with the lame leg who is afraid of the hounds . . . ah, the hounds . . . we shall go to see them together. . . . Goodby Nancy till August 7th.

Always affectionately yours,
George Moore

After this gloomy opening, the entries become more light-hearted and predictable, with several drawings of the guests (including Moore) by Pansy Cotton, and an endearing sketch entitled "The Mildewed Poet and the engaging Nancy" by Montague Eliot, the author of the *Three Weeks* parody, showing a man at a desk and a little girl with an untidy mop of hair and very long thin legs. Eliot added:

> One does not need some aid divine
> Or any necromancy
> To write some semi-idiot line
> Which seems to rhyme to Nancy.

A few pages later Max Beerbohm contributes a few sharp lines mocking George Moore's earlier entry: "Let us not be cowards, you and I. Let us steadfastly, hand in hand, envisage Moore as a very old man." Then there is a caricature of a bent old figure captioned "Gaffer Garge." "Aye, aye!" he is saying. "My memory is not what it was; but I do mind me o' them blackberries, and the squirrel in the porch! Aye!"

The volume is powerfully evocative of an Edwardian house party, when the daughter of the house briefly becomes the pet of the gathering, passing around her precious book, suddenly the focus of attention, compliments, and laughter. The duchess of Rutland sketched Lady Cunard and wrote underneath, "To Nancy from Violet Rutland, of her sweet little mother Maud," and Lady Diana Manners, then seventeen, contributed a romantic poem by Browning in beautiful elaborate writing with illuminated capitals. Lord Howard de Walden sketched Nancy in a short frilly dress, with long hair and ballet slippers, and wrote, "I have no advice to give you but to take no advice from anyone." Frank Swettenham, the Oriental scholar and colonial governor, wrote firmly, "Do something; make interests for yourself, not one but many." (He cannot have imagined how dramatically his advice was to be followed.) Miss Scarth's old pupil, Vita Sackville-West, copied out one of her own poems in French.

There is also a touching, if stilted, poem signed "Father." It does not read like his own composition, but rather as if it were part of a stock of suitable verses for inscription in young ladies' autograph books.

> Dear Nancy—if you wish to know
> What fate reserves in store for you,
> Ask not the idle cards to show—
> I'll tell as wisely—and as true.
>
> For I will take a magic book
> Of characters divinely fair—
> Upon thy lovely self I'll look
> And read—dear girl—thy fortune there . . .

The verses continue in a vein more appropriate to a mild flirtation than to fatherly advice and end:

> Now shall I look into your heart
> And see what heart is favoured there—
> No—be that fatal truth suppressed
> Lest I should sink in my despair.

Jennie Cornwallis-West (Churchill) scrawled a gloomy aphorism in French: "La vie n'est possible qu'avec beaucoup d'oubli et encore plus d'indifférence," and added, "My mood today!" One of the nicest entries is a sketch entitled "The Vampire of Holt," which shows a huge spider's web with the figure of Nancy, long hair dangling, in the center, with six thin arms holding out her book, ink and pens, and the tiny figures of her victims struggling in the web around her. There are several verses, but the one most particularly written for Nancy and her book is by F. E. Smith (the future Lord Chancellor and first Baron Birkenhead), dated January 1910:

> The song and the dance and the charm of romance
> Are everywhere found in these pages.
> Conventional scope has been found for the trope
> Which verse gives to youth through the ages.

Profound Mr Moore has developed a tour-
de-force of illegible wisdom!
The Pencil of Max scribbles age on our backs
Not even the diplomat is dumb.

A humbler refrain, very much to my pain,
Is mine than your sonnets and easels;
No muses give ear; 'tis contagion they fear
For poor little Nancy has measles!

The days at Holt recorded in Nancy's album were almost
the last she was to spend there. One of the entries in the book
is a plain, strong scrawl with no accompanying message:
Thomas Beecham. The signature prefigured the end of Nancy's childhood. Sometime in 1909 or early 1910 Lady Cunard
met and fell in love with Thomas Beecham, the conductor.
Beecham was a protégé of Mrs. Charles Hunter, and it is
possible Lady Cunard first met him at her house in Essex. At
Holt their relationship rapidly came to a head. Anecdotes still
told in Medbourne show that the locals were well aware of
what was going on; one story has it that Beecham and Lady
Cunard were spied upon in her bedroom by men working on
the clocktower above the stables. By 1911 Lady Cunard had
decided to leave her husband and Holt and move to London,
taking Nancy with her. For the next thirty years she was
devoted to Beecham and his career, which she fostered and
supported in any way she could, not least financially. He was
to become the dominant figure on the English musical scene,
not only a great conductor but a great impresario, whose
efforts kept opera alive in England. He also became a great
character, renowned for his quick wit and fiery temper, his
dandified wardrobe and liking for pretty women.

In 1911 Beecham was thirty-two; Lady Cunard was thirty-
eight. His grandfather was the Beecham who made a fortune
out of liver pills, and his father, Joseph, was a rich Lancashire
businessman with a strong interest in music. Thomas originally intended to become a concert pianist, but after hearing
the Hallé Orchestra play at his school, he determined to be-

come a conductor. Under pressure from his father he joined the family firm, but he also started an orchestra of his own, the St. Helens Orchestral Society. In 1889 his father became mayor of St. Helens and arranged a concert by the Hallé, under Hans Richter, to celebrate the occasion. When Richter dropped out at the last minute, Beecham offered to step in. The Hallé players were not pleased, but Joseph Beecham supported his son, and Thomas conducted with great success.

In attaching herself to this rising star, Lady Cunard was taking on someone far more erratic and strong willed than the lugubrious and malleable George Moore. By the time she and Beecham met, his mother was in a mental asylum and he had quarreled violently with his father for putting her there; he was married to an American and had fathered two sons.

Soon after she met him, he became involved in a divorce case that made him notorious. He had taken up with a pretty blonde married woman called Maud Foster, an amateur painter and singer, who became determined to heal the rift between Beecham and his father so that Beecham's career would have the support of the family fortune. When a reconciliation was eventually brought about, not by Mrs. Foster but by the composer Ethel Smyth (who invited the king and queen to a performance of her Cornish opera *The Wreckers* and arranged to have both Thomas and Joseph Beecham presented to the royal couple afterward), Thomas wrote a happy, indiscreet account of the occasion to his mistress. Mrs. Foster left the letter in a stocking, and it was discovered by her housekeeper, who took it to Mr. Foster. Soon afterward, Foster intercepted another even more indiscreet letter; and in October 1911 he sued his wife for divorce, naming Thomas Beecham as corespondent. Against the odds and the evidence, for the letters were read out in court, Maud Foster and Beecham denied that they had had more than a friendly relationship; but neither the judge nor the jury were convinced. Adultery, they found, had been committed, and the divorce was granted with costs against Beecham.

Lady Cunard was undeterred by the scandal. At the same

time she took care to maintain the proprieties. There was to be no Cunard divorce case; she simply decided to separate from her husband and set up her own establishment in London. By this time Nancy was regularly attending classes there and would shortly be ready to come out into society. Although the relationship between Lady Cunard and Beecham was increasingly well known, she had many other friends and activities, as did he; they never lived together, and she never even called him by his Christian name in public. Apart from everything else, he was still married and did not get a divorce from his wife till 1942; he stated then that they had not lived together since 1909.

It is not hard to imagine why Nancy's relationship with her mother became difficult as she started to grow up. She must have come to resent the way that after a whirl of gaiety and activity at Nevill Holt, when her pretty, energetic, admired mother was the center of attention and Nancy shared in her success, she would be left behind with her governess and the servants. She began to show her resentment; when Lady Cunard offered her a chocolate from one of the lavish boxes lying around at Holt, she would refuse; but later, when she could do so unobserved, she would creep downstairs and help herself. She shocked George Moore once by telling him, calmly, that she did not very much like Lady Cunard. He felt, rightly, that it would have been more normal had she passionately declared that she hated her mother.

But above all, just as Nancy was changing from a child into an adolescent, her life was transformed as a result of her mother's feeling for Thomas Beecham. Not only did they leave Holt, her home since she was born, and her father, for whom she seems to have had an inarticulate, rather baffled but genuine affection, but it must have been obvious to her that her beloved George Moore was also suffering as a result of Lady Cunard's new relationship. Moore moved back to London from Ireland permanently in 1911; the Celtic revival seemed to him to have lost its momentum, and he may well have thought that he should see more of Lady Cunard now that she was apart from Sir Bache and living in London by herself. But Thomas Beecham and her social ambitions on the London scene took up most of her attention; Moore's letters show that he found himself more and more often begging her not merely to include him in her parties but to visit him quietly in Ebury Street or to take a drive with him *à deux*. She seldom did so.

So by the time that Nancy would anyway have been starting to regard her mother with a critical adolescent eye, there were additional reasons why the natural tensions between a young, pretty, and ambitious mother bent on refashioning her life and a growing daughter should have become deeper and more lasting than usual. Lady Cunard was probably not a dramatically worse mother than most women of her class; Nancy was not ill treated. But she had a sensitive, spirited nature, and she grew up feeling that she had been deprived of something; she felt she had not been loved. And from her earliest childhood her mother's relationships with the men around her, and most of all with Sir Bache and George Moore, must have made Nancy confused and wary about the stability and permanence of love.

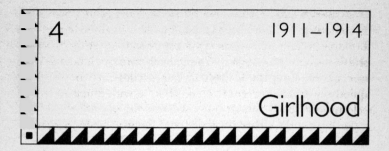

After the move to London Nancy's life and education followed the conventional pattern. She became a regular pupil at Miss Woolf's School, where her intelligence and originality won her attention and several prizes. After Nancy left, Miss Woolf used to say that Nancy Cunard was one of the nicest, as well as the cleverest, pupils she had had; but that Lady Cunard was quite another matter, and likely to ruin her promising daughter.

While Nancy was still a schoolgirl, her mother moved into a large house at 20 Cavendish Square; she rented it from the Asquiths, who had moved to Number 10 Downing Street when Asquith became prime minister in 1908. Lady Cunard was already a friend of Asquith and his second wife, Margot, and now became a frequent guest at Downing Street. Margot Asquith was already renowned for her social energies and her teasing manner with the important people she loved to entertain. Asquith's biographer writes of her that "her forte, especially on a first meeting, was the unexpected provocative remark . . . she liked particularly to know the great and famous, and if possible to be more in their confidence than anyone else." She and Lady Cunard must have had much in common, which explains the hint of rivalry that marked their acquaintance.

Lady Cunard rapidly imposed her own style on the house in Cavendish Square. It was a spacious, comfortable house but inconvenient and expensive to run; the kitchens were across a courtyard at the back of the house. The Asquiths had found fourteen servants, including a butler and two footmen, necessary to keep the house going on the grand scale. Though Sir Bache, once his wife and her fortune had withdrawn from Nevill Holt, found himself compelled to retrench, Lady Cunard, at this time and for many years to come, could afford to live as she pleased.

The decor Lady Cunard devised was heavily influenced by Sergei Diaghilev's Russian Ballet and the designs executed for it by L.N. Bakst, which had great fashionable success in London that year. Beecham was one of the chief supporters of the Russian Ballet, and his orchestra played for them on their first appearance in London in 1911. Lady Cunard covered her dining room walls with arsenic green lamé, and a cloth hanging painted with dappled giraffes. Her table was lapis lazuli. Her favorite furniture was always delicate, gold, and French; she bought furniture and paintings as casually as she bought clothes. From Cavendish Square she embarked on the entertaining that was to make her rapidly into one of the best-known and most sought-after hostesses in London. She liked to mix the arts and politics, as she had done at Nevill Holt, and she enjoyed mixing ages too. But Nancy was still too young to be involved in formal social life.

In the autumn of 1912 Nancy was sent to Munich to continue her German and music studies. She stayed in the home of a suitable German family and, despite the presence of a governess, to her surprise she found herself comparatively independent. It was in Munich, she afterward wrote, that she first "tasted of adult life" even though to one observer who met her there, the Chinese scholar Arthur Waley, she seemed very young and innocent: "a raw, Scotch-looking girl of about sixteen . . . dowdily dressed, simple, straightforward and quite unconscious of herself and her alert governess." She told him she intended to be a poet, and that George Moore had recently praised one of her poems.

By the spring of 1913 she was staying in Paris at a girls' finishing school and finding it dull and restricting. The school was run by three unmarried French sisters named Ozanne, the daughters of a Protestant clergyman from Calais, who had made friends with many English visitors. The family knew the headmistress of Heathfield, and it was on her advice that the Ozanne sisters started their own establishment in Paris. It was to become the best-known place of its kind; Nancy was one of the earliest pupils.

Nancy was bored for the first three months. She already knew French too well to find the language classes a challenge, and the Ozanne pupils were carefully chaperoned everywhere. But she enjoyed reading Scandinavian and Russian literature, expecially Turgenev, and she made great friends with one of the Ozanne sisters, Marie, who was only slightly older than she was; they went to three concerts a week and the opera too, when they could.

George Moore visited her at the Ozannes' and thought she looked discontented. He asked whether she was having some sort of religious crisis, such as many adolescents experienced. Nancy felt that this was not her problem; although she loved some of the old churches in Paris, she was more moved and excited by exploring old streets in the Quartier Latin. "My mysticism was in those streets."

In the summer of 1913 Lady Cunard took a *palazzo* in Venice and invited several friends to stay. They included the Asquiths and the duchess of Rutland, and her daughter Lady Diana. A group of friends were staying in another *palazzo* nearby: the Raymond Asquiths, Billy Grenfell, Duff Cooper and his sister Sybil, Denis Anson, and Felicity Tree. Lady Diana was three years older than Nancy and so was already "out" and officially grown up. She was dazzlingly beautiful, clever, and funny, hugely admired not only by her contemporaries, and with a reputation for being, if not exactly rebellious, certainly more independent of convention than her mother would like her to be. She was the center of a glamorous, talented group, the sons and daughters of the Souls who were her mother's friends—Asquiths, Grenfells, Tennants, and Herberts. Their adventures were not really very wicked, but they set their own style and called themselves, daringly, the Corrupt Coterie. They wrote each other witty, romantic letters and verses, they made secret assignations, they arranged all-night masquerades, they went swimming by moonlight. Nancy longed to be one of them; she felt a bond with Lady Diana when the older girl grumbled at her mother's protectiveness and fear of scandal, and in gentle mockery referred to the duchess as "Her Grace." Nancy started to call Lady Cunard "Her Ladyship," but it seemed to Lady Diana that Nancy's tone had a sharper edge to it. Lady Diana was, and remained, an appreciative and affectionate daughter; she also became very fond of Lady Cunard. On the prime minister's birthday in August the whole party celebrated; Lady Diana remembered how they made him dress up as a Venetian doge and how he sat beaming happily, surrounded by presents and admiration, and pretty girls.

In 1914, during the last season before the war, Nancy came out. She looked back on this episode with amusement and scorn. She was presented at court wearing a pink dress with a train of tulle and rose petals and endured the round of parties; "one ball succeeded another until there were three or four a week, and the faces of the revolving guardsmen seemed as silly as their vapid conversation among the hydrangeas at supper."

But by this time Nancy had found a friend in her own circle whom she perceived as a kindred spirit. This was Iris Tree, the younger daughter of Sir Herbert Beerbohm Tree, the great actor-manager. Her sister Viola was married to Alan Parsons; they were part of the core of the Coterie. Nancy and Iris had met as children at London tea parties; Iris always remembered how furious Nancy had been with her when she criticized another little girl. Nancy turned on her and told her sharply: "If you don't like my friends, you ought not to come here." When they met again, Iris was seventeen and studying painting at the Slade. She was romantic and bohemian by temperament, a charming, small girl with thick fair hair and a snub nose, original, clever, and as bored as Nancy with grand parties and stuffy conventions. They became close friends and allies. "We were bandits," Iris wrote, escaping environment by tunnelling deceptions to emerge in forbidden artifice, chalk-white face powder, scarlet lip rouge, cigarette smoke, among roisterers of our own choosing: Augustus John and his gypsy models at the Café Royal; Horace Cole, genius of practical jokes; Osbert Sitwell, happy fantasist, who later brought our poems to "Wheels" anthology; studio attics with the then young wise owls of the Bloomsbury clique; stray Tommies who proffered rides on motor bikes; and the coterie, crowned by Diana Manners, which included the most brilliant and exuberant spirits united at the various inns and outings: Cavendish Hotel, Cheshire Cheese, pubs in Limehouse, river barges, cab shelters and a secret studio which Nancy and I shared for secret meetings with the favourites, or poems by ourselves.

Iris and Nancy were intoxicated with their new-found freedom. On the eve of the war there was a curious atmosphere of excitement, especially in the arts and writing. The Victorian and Edwardian certainties were breaking up; already, there were signs of experiment and discord. "Transition and danger were in the air," Iris remembered romantically.

We responded like chameleons to ever changing colour, turning from Meredith to Proust to Dostoievsky, slightly tinged by the Yellow Book, an occasional absinthe left by Baudelaire and Wilde, flushed by Liberalism, sombered by nihilistic pessimism, challenged by Shaw, inspired by young Rupert Brooke, T.S. Eliot, Yeats, D.H. Lawrence; jolted by Wyndham Lewis's *Blast* into cubism and the Modern French Masters, "Significant Form," Epstein's sculptures; Stravinsky's music (booed and cheered); the first Russian ballets and American jazz. . . .

The first black jazz bands played at all-night parties like those given by a mysterious rich American, George Gordon Moore, who was infatuated with Lady Diana Manners; when she left, the parties stopped. Nancy loved the new music; her favorite tune was "Oh, You Beautiful Doll," which she would sing in a surprisingly deep contralto voice.

Sometimes Nancy and Iris would go to the country together. Iris's parents had taken a house in Kent, Glottenham Manor; Nancy went there often, and she and Iris would go for long walks in the fields or spend a day by the sea. Once, she took Iris with her to visit Sir Bache, who was no longer living at Nevill Holt. After Lady Cunard left, he found he could not afford to manage the big house; he moved to Wansford, a small village beside a huge bridge over the river Nene about twenty miles east of Holt, just off the Great North Road, where he rented a substantial house on the main street called the Haycock. It was an ancient inn that had been turned into a private house by previous owners, with a large courtyard at the back, stables, and a formal garden down to the river where he could practice his topiary. It must have seemed modest after Holt, but it was still an imposing place to live and he was able to run it in some style. Iris found that since Nancy had abandoned country pursuits, she and Sir Bache had little to say to each other anymore.

Nancy at eighteen had become a beauty. She was fair, but more tawny blonde than her pink and white mother, and she was tall and slim, with elegant long legs and fine, slender hands. She had a distinctive light, swaying way of walking; Iris Tree recalled "the delicate dance of her walk through London Streets" and an even more distinctive voice.

> She spoke in high piping notes, punctuated by odd stresses and pouncing exclamations of jubilance or rejection: "Ohh!" "Ahh!" The obstinate, staccato "No!" An inward mirth simmered through sentences which revealed by hint or sudden swoop some peculiar detail which for her was key to an obvious situation. She was both delicate and shocking. Not exactly witty, but perceptive and always surprising—no dull dinginess obscured the quality of crystal, neatly crisp, gracefully turbulent, arrogantly disruptive, brave.

She had great physical allure. David Garnett saw her come into the Café Royal one evening and was amazed. "She was very slim with a skin as white as bleached almonds, the bluest eyes one has ever seen and very fair hair. She was marvel-lous." For the first time, she was able to escape occasionally from her mother's world. The room she had rented with Iris was in Fitzroy Place, at the top of Charlotte Street, near Bloomsbury and the Slade. They could escape there to meet their admirers unchaperoned, or to write and paint, or design their costumes for a ball; they both loved dressing up. Once they were arrested for swimming in the Serpentine at dawn after a party; after this, their mothers tried to keep a stricter eye on them, but without much success. It was already begin-ning to seem clear that Nancy had a stronger streak of wild-ness in her than most of her contemporaries. Lady Diana Cooper remembers that the Fitzroy studio was always in chaos and seemed to her squalid; she also remembers Nancy saying defiantly, during some conversation about maternal prohibitions and anxieties, "My mother's having an affair with Thomas Beecham; I can do as I like." For all Lady Cunard's care not to flout conventions, her relationship with Beecham was no secret and gave Nancy an easy weapon against her. What seemed like discretion to her mother looked more like hypocrisy to Nancy.

It seems that Nancy's hostile feelings toward her mother were beginning to be public knowledge. One ominous inci-dent was related in a 1914 letter from one of Lady Cunard's friends, Lady Desborough, to her son Julian Grenfell. Lady Desborough was describing an evening of parlor games at Windsor Castle, where she had recently been staying as lady-in-waiting. "They were playing the game one night of who they would like to see best come into the room and Nancy Cunard said in that high voice 'Lady Cunard *dead*.' " Margot Asquith later sent for Nancy to reprove her, "but of course Nancy was smart enough to deny the mot and Margot was left in an abject situation of apology."

Although Nancy did not care for most of the men she met at formal parties, she made several friends and conquests, es-pecially among the more unusual young men. One was Os-bert Sitwell, whom she found herself sitting next to at a dinner party of her mother's; another was Evan Morgan, Lord Tredegar's son and heir; another was Tommy Earp. She was also fond of a brilliant and eminently suitable young man called Edward Wyndham Tennant, nicknamed "Bimbo," son of Lord Glenconner and nephew of Margot Asquith. Tennant was also, like Nancy, a budding poet. Once Nancy was officially launched into society, her friends and her mother's friends frequently overlapped. Partly on her daughter's account, partly because she never liked to restrict her guests by age or interests, Lady Cunard took up several young men or women of Nancy's generation, many of whom became as much, sometimes more, her friends as they were Nancy's. Diana Manners and the Sitwell brothers were often her guests, and she particularly liked a young Chilean painter, poet and amateur boxer called Alvaro "Chile" Guevara, who soon became infatuated with Nancy. Ezra Pound, who was already beginning to make a name for himself as a poet and critic, met Nancy at her mother's house. Nancy was astonished by his appearance, his thick red hair, pointed beard, "lynx-like" green eyes, sweeping black cape, and large black hat. Wyndham Lewis came there too. Clearly, it was not simply by choosing friends for their talent rather than their social acceptability that Nancy could make a world for herself separate from her mother's. She could, and did, make gestures to prove that she wanted to live her own life, such as renting the studio with Iris Tree, spending as much time as she could in the Café Royal or other places where artists and writers gathered, or alarming her mother by turning up for a dinner party before a ball wearing a man's black evening waistcoat. She would rather have been a poet than a society beauty, but her mother approved of literary ambitions and had the connections to help her daughter's poetry, if it was any good at all, be recognized and published.

Nancy had been writing poetry since her early teens; this had been a bond between herself and George Moore at Nevill Holt. He had encouraged her and given her a sense of the beauty of words and the nobility of a poet's calling, but he also submerged her in the Victorian writers he admired and confused her with talk of "objective" or "pure" poetry, by which he meant poetry that seemed to him uncontaminated by sentimentality or ideas. Writing poetry was still, for Nancy's generation, something of an accomplishment to be learned and practiced like playing the piano; her admired Coterie showered romantic or witty sonnets and verses on each other. Her first published poem appeared in the Eton *College Chronicle* in 1915, when her cousin Victor Cunard was editor. At the same time, at the age of seventeen or eighteen, she was beginning to meet people for whom poetry and the other arts were something potentially subversive. The Sitwells were beginning their campaign to open English poetry to European influences and to break away from constricting forms and vocabulary; Wyndham Lewis, Ezra Pound, and other energetic young writers and artists were in a ferment of activity, looking to such foreign groups as the Futurists, who linked experiment in the arts with the urge to transform society. They started the Vorticist movement, with its satirical magazine *Blast*—which included in its list of hate objects "Beecham (Pills, Opera, Thomas)"—dedicated to dragging English culture out of smug Victorian insularity. It is easy to see why Nancy should have been drawn to the idea that art could be subversive and that the drawing room and social acceptability could be stultifying. She loved experiment and risk, and she began to see a way to outmaneuver her mother on her own ground.

But in the summer of 1914 the world Nancy had grown up in was sliding toward destruction faster than anyone of eighteen, no matter how sensitive and rebellious, could possibly have realized.

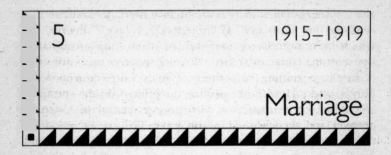

At first, after war broke out in August of 1914, life in England for girls like Nancy went on very much as before. The war began as a romantic adventure; it was to be some time before its full horror became clear.

The first of Nancy's surviving scrapbooks illustrates the transition poignantly. The early pages show her and her friends playing croquet on the lawns of Nevill Holt, enchantingly pretty in long muslin dresses, with soft, round, girlish faces. There are photographs of Nancy with one young man in particular, Bimbo Tennant, and sketches and funny poems by anonymous admirers. Then the mood changes. There is a picture of Lady Diana Manners as a nurse. Bimbo Tennant reappears in uniform. Then suddenly there is a picture of a young man asleep on a hospital bed, blood showing on a bandaged leg. Underneath, in Nancy's hand, is the caption "Sydney asleep in Cairo, 1915."

In 1915, Sydney Fairbairn was twenty-three. Although his background was Australian, he had lived in England since the age of four and had had the education and upbringing of a rich young Englishman. His grandfather had left Scotland for Australia in the 1830s and had made a considerable fortune. He had also bred a family of brilliant athletes, including Sydney's father, Steve Fairbairn, who became one of the most famous sportsmen of his day and revolutionized English rowing. His two sons, Sydney and Sydney's younger brother Ian, were brought up in a country house in Buckinghamshire and on grouse moors in Scotland. Sydney went to Eton and to university in Germany. The pictures in Nancy's album show him to have been handsome—tall and dark, with a moustache and a strong rectangular face with a cheerful, open expression.

At the beginning of the war Sydney Fairbairn joined the Royal Bucks Hussars, a yeomanry regiment. In the spring of 1915, he was wounded at Gallipoli, evacuated to Cairo to recover and then sent home on leave. Gallant wounded officers were the center of attention in the drawing rooms and hotel ballrooms and theaters where Nancy and her friends were selling programs for war benefit occasions and dressing up for tableaux. They were also much admired guests at fashionable country house weekends.

According to Mrs. Alfred Duggan, the beautiful, rich American widow who had recently become secretly engaged to Lord Curzon, it was during a weekend with her in Hertfordshire in 1916 that Nancy Cunard and Sydney Fairbairn became engaged to be married. Nancy's mother, a close friend of the future Lady Curzon, was also there, and her feelings about the engagement were plain.

"Maud did not approve of the engagement," her hostess later wrote. "Unhappily we—the house party and the children—were unwilling listeners to a rather acrimonious dispute one afternoon at tea. Maud, who had little self-control when annoyed, started to find fault with the newly engaged couple, who were there too. It became so heated that I finally said to the children (who were having tea at a separate table with their tutor) 'I think you will have finished your tea and you can go.' "

Lady Cunard presumably had higher ambitions for her beautiful, original daughter. Sydney Fairbairn, while in no way unsuitable, seemed to several of Nancy's friends, as well as to her mother, an unlikely choice for her to have made. He was handsome and agreeable, a first-class cricketer and a gallant soldier, but he was more conventional than most of Nancy's chosen companions. Later on, the story would get about that the marriage was somehow Lady Cunard's doing; but in fact she seems to have done her best to dissuade Nancy, and even called in Sir Bache to intervene. Probably, such opposition simply consolidated the affair. Nancy herself never suggested that her mother had pushed her into marriage with Sydney Fairbairn, though she blamed her for it in another way; she maintained that her one motive had been to get away from her mother's house and live her own life. Marriage was the simplest way for her to achieve a measure of independence.

The wedding was announced with a burst of more or less inaccurate trivia in the social pages. "Miss Cunard, who is extremely pretty, has helped at most of the big charity affairs of the last few months." "Nancy Cunard is a valiant member of the programme selling, anything-for-charity-brigade." References were made to Sir Bache's connection with the Cunard Line and his preference for rural life: "He has been a famous hunting man." Lady Cunard was already well known on such pages. There were references to her "huge fortune" inherited from her mother. On the eve of her wedding Nancy was compared with her mother and her best-known friend. "Nancy Cunard is one of the best-known girls in town, and, as far as publicity is concerned, runs her bosom friend, Lady Diana Manners, very close indeed. She is fair and fresh-complexioned, and looks but little younger than her mother. . . . Pretty in a dollish way, she is yet as piquant and clever as you please."

The wedding was set for Wednesday, November 15, and announced as a "quiet wedding." The choice of date was unfortunate; November 15 had been chosen, as Lady Cunard must have been disconcerted to discover, for a big royal wedding—between Countess Nada Torby and Prince George of Battenberg, at Saint Margaret's Westminster. As the day approached, the social pages (clipped and pasted into Nancy's album, they fill fourteen sheets) described the bride's "unconventional" plans: no bridesmaids, no bouquet, no gloves, and a dress of cloth of gold instead of white. Just before the wedding Nancy was described as "an exquisite specimen of English girlhood. Fresh, sweet to look at, sweet in disposition and full of fun, she also possesses a strong capacity for deep feeling. . . . Her hobby in life will probably be dogs."

The photographs of the wedding day show Nancy looking very young and wistful; Sydney Fairbairn looks gallant and confident. The list of wedding guests, despite royal competition, was impressive: it included the French, Italian, and Spanish ambassadors, the duke of Rutland, Lady Diana Manners, the marchioness of Dufferin, and Ava, Lady Randolph Churchill, George Moore, Sir Thomas Beecham (he was knighted in 1916), and Mr. Ivor Novello. Sir Bache, who had been busy running a munitions factory at the Haycock since early in the war, came to London for the occasion. To his intense embarrassment, he was required by Lady Cunard, in rose-colored velvet and sables, to throw handfuls of silver coins to the crowds. Instead of a full formal reception, after the ceremony, the paper reported, Nancy went around the church and simply asked about thirty guests to call at her mother's house. At the party Nancy encountered Evan Morgan, whereupon in an odd but prophetic gesture she tore off the wreath of gold flowers around her head and flung it to the ground. Later, she left for a honeymoon in Cornwall wearing a dress of green velour trimmed with beaver. "Originality was expected of Nancy Cunard," wrote one paper, afterward, adding confidently, "She will be one of the leaders of society after the war."

The marriage was foundering well before the war was over. Nancy, whose memory for dates was usually precise, wrote much later of "the whole twenty months of my married life . . . a caesura between many good things past and further good things to come." This bleak public summary of the marriage is moderate, almost kindly, compared with the deep bitterness she would express afterward in private. She remembered her marriage as one of the unhappiest times of her life.

During the short time they spent together, Nancy and Sydney Fairbairn had a house of their own in London, 5 Montagu Square, a present from Lady Cunard. They also moved around the country a good deal, staying with friends or briefly taking a house by the sea. Nancy's album contains two or three pages of photographs showing the couple together in a country garden at Tadworth, in Cornwall, with Sydney in a deck chair smoking a pipe while Nancy sits reading on the grass, or walking together at Epsom, Brighton, and Aldershot. One newspaper cutting shows them walking side by side down a street in London, Sydney handsome and confident in uniform, Nancy dressed in what looks like pale muslin, pretty enough but unsmiling. The series ends with a handful of seaside pictures, dated Bognor, June 1918. The twenty months had run out. Sydney Fairbairn, who, when he recovered from his wounds after Gallipoli had joined the Grenadier Guards, left for France at the beginning of July of that year. By her own account Nancy's main emotion was relief.

Why was the marriage a failure? It is tempting, looking back, to see it as doomed from the start. Under the strain of war, many people have made hasty emotional decisions. Nancy and Sydney, though by no means from different worlds, had very different temperaments and interests. The picture Nancy would draw, later, was the one that suited her best and showed her in her chosen light. She was intellectual; Sydney was philistine. She wanted to read or write poetry; he liked sports and bridge. A difference of interests, though, is not in itself enough to explain why the marriage so rapidly went wrong. Even discounting some of Nancy's vehemence as exaggerated, there is a note of revulsion in her references to her husband that indicates that she may have found the sexual side of her marriage difficult. It is hard to imagine any other specific reason for the violence of her reaction. More generally, she made it plain in all her later references to her marriage that she felt, very strongly and very soon, that she had exchanged one trap for another. She had longed to escape from her mother; but found marriage to be equally smothering and claustrophobic. Whatever it was she was looking for, whatever she was struggling to be, she could not find in marriage.

writers and artists to that of her straightforward husband's friends. Augustus John and Wyndham Lewis were both great admirers of hers. She was in her early thirties, eleven years older than Nancy, and had two children, Rupert and Deirdre. She was a vivid, unusual, slightly troubled personality. Nancy was drawn to her.

Looking back many years later, Nancy felt that Sybil Hart-Davis had been a very strong influence on her. She called her "my liberator." Their close friendship made some of their friends and relations uneasy; they were said to be not a good influence on each other, usually a bond in friendship. They went around London together, with and without their husbands; they visited undergraduate friends at Oxford. They had long talks about life and love and books; Nancy had been much impressed by a novel just published by Norman Douglas, who was later to become part of her life. *South Wind* seemed highly daring and subversive in 1917. The conversations and eccentricities of a group of expatriates on Capri dabbling in intellectual and sexual experiment may not seem powerful enough to help liberate someone today, but it had a distinct impact on Nancy. She began to feel certain that life was full of possibilities, and that her marriage need not confine her forever.

When both their husbands returned to the front, Nancy and Sybil decided to share a house in the country for the summer of 1918.

After a final evening out in London at the Queen's Restaurant in Sloane Square, when Nancy and Sybil, Augustus John, and Chile Guevara sat drinking and laughing while John sketched them all on the tablecloth (Nancy kept the cut-out drawing of herself all her life), the two women set up house near Kingston Bagpuize in Oxfordshire, with Sybil's two children, Nancy's maid, and a cook.

That summer at Bagpuize Nancy was happy—or as happy as it was possible for her to be, with a failing marriage and the war dragging into its fourth year. She and Sybil were free to invite whomever they wanted for dinner or a weekend. At last she really felt she had an establishment of her own choosing. She enjoyed the company of Sybil's children (who were so much more reasonably treated by their mother, she felt, than she had been by hers), the struggles of the cook to produce edible meals with wartime materials, long walks on windy afternoons, and the books the two women read and discussed together—Meredith, Swinburne, de Maupassant, and Havelock Ellis's *Psychology of Sex* ("gaily referred to as 'the six brown books' "). On weekdays the children did their lessons and Nancy shut herself away to work on her poetry. Rupert Hart-Davis has recalled the impression her efforts made on him.

> Between the wild parties there were quiet days, without visitors, when Nancy would spend all day in the drawing room writing. "Shh," we were told. "Nancy's writing a poem," and at intervals one of us would tiptoe in with a cup of tea, put it quietly down on the writing table, where Nancy, smoking continuously, sat locked in battle with her Muse . . . and tiptoe out again. Those days gave me an impressive and romantic view of the poet's calling that I have never quite lost.

Neither Sybil nor Nancy seem to have felt any need to live as if they were pining anxiously for their husbands in the trenches. Young men poured in from Oxford, or London, or on leave from France. As Rupert Hart-Davis recalls,

> My sister and I spent the long daylight hours playing outside, while inside the house there seemed to be a perpetual party. The guests were variegated—young officers, wounded and whole, artists and writers, Augustus John in the uniform of a war artist, "Chile" Guevara the poet, St. John Hutchinson the lawyer . . . Henry Mond (later the second Lord Melchett), the courtly and magnificent Lord Ribblesdale, the Sitwell brothers, over from some camp or barracks, and a forgotten crowd of others. Drink (I suppose some form of fairly potent cup) was dispensed from huge glass jugs, and there always seemed to be plenty.

During that summer, Nancy fell in love. Sometime in the autumn of 1917 she had met one of Sydney Fairbairn's brother officers, a man called Peter Broughton Adderley. According to Nancy, they knew each other for only five days before he had to go back to the front. In the summer of 1918 he came home on leave and went down to Bagpuize. Rupert Hart-Davis remembers Broughton Adderley as a charming, good-looking young man who taught him to play cricket on the lawn. He and Nancy read romantic poetry and novels to each other all day, in the long grass under the trees—including George Moore's latest book, *A Story Teller's Holiday,* which Nancy associated ever afterward with her love for Peter.

Inevitably Broughton Adderley had to return to the war. As the autumn drew on, Nancy and Sybil found themselves leading a quieter life at Bagpuize. With the war in its fourth winter, they felt constantly menaced and overshadowed. So many of their friends and contemporaries had been killed, many of them the most beloved and gifted—Bimbo Tennant, Raymond Asquith, Julian Grenfell. The two women talked about death and waited for news. One cold morning in October at Kingston Bagpuize Nancy woke to find Sybil standing by her bed. Peter Broughton Adderley had been killed.

The next few weeks were among the worst in Nancy's life. She felt utterly obsessed and crushed by misery. When at last the war came to an end a few weeks later, she could feel no sense of triumph or relief, and went for a long walk by herself.

Several of Nancy's friends think to this day that she might have had a happier life had Peter Broughton Adderley lived and had they married after the war. To some, he represented her one real chance of living calmly and normally. Nancy herself was never one to express regrets or discuss what might have been; but she always remembeed her love for Peter.

Someone else was deeply shaken by the death of Peter Broughton Adderley in October 1918. Sydney Fairbairn wrote to his mother on October 18: "This last battle has been too long drawn out to attempt to describe; it has been most successful but hideously fatiguing and I am in rather a state of mental chaos at the moment. These damned Germans killed poor Peter, at least he got badly hit and died of his wound (stomach), it's dreadfully sad, his poor mother will be completely heart-broken . . . they always kill the very best, don't they?"

In Fairbairn's letters home, among the accounts of battles, the names of friends wounded or killed, the optimistic predictions, and the requests and thanks for the extras that the gentleman soldier enjoyed—whiskey, port, foie gras, Curiously Strong Peppermints, and even, once, a brace of grouse—are a handful of references to Nancy that hardly read as if from his point of view the marriage was virtually over. She was apparently writing to him frequently even after the move to Bagpuize; he asks after her, worries about her, and is generally solicitous and protective about her. It sounds, not surprisingly, as if his parents were writing him determinedly cheerful accounts of her.

After the armistice, there is a reference to Nancy having sent him some oysters, which, to his annoyance, had not arrived when expected. In the immediate aftermath of the war, then, Nancy was perhaps less determined to end her marriage than she liked to recall. She was certainly deeply unhappy; but she was still in close touch with her husband. On December 27, 1918, still in France, Sydney wrote to his mother, "What a lot of bridge you seem to be playing. I am very glad Nancy looks so well, she seemed very depressed by her letters to me, says everything is so dull and life rather empty. However we will liven things up considerably when I get my leave, or better still, demobilised."

But although one may question the details of Nancy's later account of the end of her marriage, there is no reason to question the broad outline. Two people played a crucial part in her decision: Peter Broughton Adderley, whom she was convinced she truly loved, and Sybil Hart-Davis, who seemed to Nancy to stand for independence of spirit. With Sybil, Nancy felt she was the person she wanted to be; their friendship gave her a sense of her own worth and some confidence in the future.

Nancy thought she recognized something else in Sybil: the soul of an artist, unsuited for the mundane tasks of being a wife. This is very much how Nancy came to think of herself. Partly from genuine conviction, partly in self-justification as she struggled to use the talent and energy she felt she had, Nancy became determined to reject marriage and all it stood for. It is hard to escape the conclusion that some of Nancy's vehement hostility toward her husband derived from guilt. Guilt and anger are often linked, especially in people of Nancy's temperament, who never question their right to behave exactly as they please. Nancy was never able to look back at her marriage calmly, to regard it with any tolerance for two young people at a time of great strain who simply made a mistake. Instead, she referred to Sydney Fairbairn with increasing hatred and contempt, alluding darkly to his conduct and character. She succeeded in convincing many of her friends that he was a monster, and that their marriage had been a dreadful experience.

It seems more likely they were fundamentally ill suited for each other and that Nancy simply could not stand being tied to someone she did not love. If by marrying Sydney Fairbairn she was trying to behave like other girls of her age and circle at that time, then one of the few conventional acts of her life was a resounding failure.

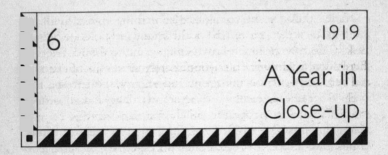

Early in 1919 Nancy caught the Spanish flu, which flared
through Europe in the wake of the war and killed 150,000 in
England alone. She developed pneumonia and lay in bed,
weak and furious, in her mother's house (Lady Cunard had
recently moved to Grosvenor Square), for most of January,
February and March. When she eventually recovered she was
physically and emotionally exhausted. She had told Sydney
Fairbairn soon after his return from France in January that she
could not go on with their marriage; but there were still decisions and plans to be made that she could not face. It was
decided that she should make the traditional long journey of
convalescence to the south of France, accompanied by the
watchful, devoted Marie Ozanne.

At this point in her life Nancy can be seen in close-up. She
kept a regular diary during 1919, beginning with her departure for France in April. This is the only year of her life for
which such a record exists: three fat, old-fashioned volumes,
two with locks, page after page covered with Nancy's pen-
ciled scrawl.

Catching Nancy at a moment of transition, the diary is of
interest not just because it is often lively and amusing, but
because it contains many clues to Nancy's later attitudes and
behavior. Many of the attributes that were to make her extraordinary—her urge to shock, her need to keep on the move,
her compulsion to keep her emotional options open—are rec-
ognizable in her diary as the ordinary willfulness of a high-

spirited, spoiled young woman. She was dissatisfied with her life but had no idea what to do about it; she hardly ever looked outside herself. She mentioned her own poetry, but there is no evidence of a serious interest in writing or the arts, and her comments on society were restricted to her own tiny circle. In 1919, according to her diary, Nancy was restless, emotionally and physically vulnerable, and driven to submerge her doubts about herself in a hectic round of travel, flirtations and social occasions. Her life lacked sense and purpose, and she knew it, and sometimes she hated it; but at the same time she had an enormous capacity for enjoying herself.

Nancy was in poor spirits as she and Marie Ozanne passed through Paris, but she was not particularly looking forward to the south either. As she and Marie moved from one expensive hotel to another along the coast—Ezes, Beaulieu, Cannes—Nancy had a series of interviews with doctors, all of whom murmured to her about being "delicate" and "suffering from nerves" and looked her over with what she described as "those erotic persistent eyes always cast up to heaven so numerous in France." She was told to rest, to take gentle exercise, to have massage. She was idle, bored and irritated with herself. "Oh God, shall I ever get into any mood here, and not be finding it forever incomplete?"

She missed her London friends, but when one of the most devoted, the sociable barrister St. John Hutchinson, turned up in pursuit of her and took her for long drives in the hills, she found him irritating too.

Then suddenly her mood would change and she would feel a wild need to be gay. A gala evening at a hotel put her into "an immense jolly Rabelaisian mood, strung up to any vulgarity to outdo them all." She would flirt with mysterious foreign strangers over cocktails and embrace whomever she pleased behind palm trees in the moonlight, while Marie Ozanne clucked reprovingly in the background. But the mood never lasted. "Oh these reactions and after-effects when the mind is so clear and yet so agitated, flimsy and unstable."

Nancy was discovering the old truth, which she was never

perhaps to take in completely, that travel cannot solve problems, though it may distract from them. She put it well herself. "There's a vague promise of excitement in the air and nothing ever happens. C'est le mal des voyageurs."

She read, went for long walks alone, became more and more low and nervous. She was afraid to go into the casino and hated herself for occasionally flirting with some stranger met out walking or in the hotel lobby. She felt the doctor was spying on her. She scrawled desperately in the diary an ominous message to doctors, to Marie Ozanne, to anyone looking at her with curiosity or concern: "Leave me alone, leave me alone, or I may become too wicked."

Toward the end of May she started thinking about the return to London. She wrote a long "soul-searching" letter to one of her American admirers. She tried writing poetry again.

In the train to Paris on her way home she picked up drinking companions, something she was to do with relish all her life. Marie Ozanne greatly disliked this habit. Nancy commented defiantly, "I shall certainly always drink with anyone, as indeed will I, do I, talk with any stranger."

By June 6 she was back in London. "My first impression of return—everyone dead—Denny, Edward, Patrick, Raymond, George, Billy and the later, more personal and acute people, the lovers of last year."

Once back in her mother's house, the familiar problems swooped down again. "This terrible enforced idleness—what shall I do? Enter mother in shining yellow satin and Thomas Beecham. They change not, and I can see many battles over the going or not going to the opera—and so ends the journey."

June and early July Nancy spent at 44 Grosvenor Square. The diary reflects the mounting tension she felt as the strong undertow of her mother's social life drew Nancy's fragile independence closer. It was hard to live in the same city, let alone the same house, as her mother, without feeling that inexorable pull. Nancy's reaction was to plan once again for a summer establishment of her own, and to spend as much time as possible out of her mother's immediate orbit. Her mother, after all, could not compete with Nancy over romantic entanglements with young men, and would not wish to spend long evenings in raffish company at the Tower, or at East End nightclubs.

The Tower in particular became Nancy's refuge. A small French restaurant (properly called the Eiffel Tower) in a house in Percy Street, just north of Soho, it had flourished since before the war under the inspiration of an Austrian proprietor, Rudolf Stulik, who made friends with his customers, encouraged them to stay late, and allowed them limitless drink and credit. It had been a favorite haunt of Wyndham Lewis and the Vorticists, who decorated a couple of rooms. Like the Café Royal in the 1890s, the Tower became known as the place where the artistic and literary met the fashionable. After the war it was a cross between a club and a continental café-restaurant where like-minded people could expect to meet without prior arrangement. For Nancy it was to be for ten years a second home, at a time when she was not at all sure where her home really was.

The weekend of June 7, 1919, was the Whitsun holiday, and Nancy was furious to find that many of the people she wanted to see were out of town. She lunched at the Ritz with one friend, dined at the Tower with two more, searched for Sybil Hart-Davis ("I have a frantic desire to see Sybil"), planned a new wardrobe, commented acidly on two of London's most prominent hostesses, Mrs. Hwfa and Mrs. Corey, and found society generally rather pointless. "God keep one from getting too bored," she wrote despairingly—the perennial plea of the spoiled, rich girl.

She saw something of George Moore, whom she described in her diary with mingled affection and exasperation. "GM . . . is extremely wearying, grown very deaf and slow and exacting, but says I have become far more defined a character and am coming into my own—also likes several poems."

She kept reminding herself that she must sort out her marriage: "God, I must see Sydney." As she felt more and more resistant to the round of lunch parties and dinner parties and parties for the opera organized by her mother, so the idea of finding a house again for the summer seemed a means of escape. "I must find a country house—the one refuge and place of content—the only possible life." Her friend Marjorie Trefusis wanted to find a place too, so they decided to look together. Lady Cunard, who hated the country, failed to understand this obsession of her daughter's, and Nancy noted one typical comment: "Mother with a word about houses. 'Only the *banal* need a home.' "

In the intervals of house hunting with Marjorie, she spent a weekend by the sea with Mary and St. John Hutchinson at Wittering. She loved it—the long walks on the beach, the private jokes. She and Hutchinson had a special game involving imitating George Moore's way of talking. They would walk for hours "doing GM." Back in London things did not go so well. She and her mother were getting on each other's nerves. One night, after a typical evening out there was an explosion. "I went to bed cross—had a scene with Mother and told her practically everyone was stupid, ugly and wicked—(she rather upset)—cried for an hour—and got that awful feeling very strongly that nobody likes one really."

Next day, the diary reveals Nancy's reaction to having for once let down her guard with her mother. "After last night's fiasco found her as usual very intelligent, falsely understanding and very wicked." Clearly, if Lady Cunard did try to comfort her daughter or advise her about her life on such occasions, she did not meet with much success.

As for Nancy's romantic life at this time, she was going around with several admirers simultaneously, for whom she occasionally records a flash of real interest or affection but with whom she did not seem remotely to be in love. The pattern of Nancy's evenings was repetitive. One she describes as "perfect"; it consisted of cocktails and dinner at the Hyde Park Hotel with St. John Hutchinson and another friend, then the ballet, then a rendezvous with another young man, and a late-night session of sweet champagne at the Tower, where they rocked with laughter and generally made a nuisance of themselves. Nancy described it all with gusto: "Presently Joe came in and whispered to us that we were making so much noise they had complained of not being able to sleep—we laughed the louder and hoped there would be a 'case' out of it that Hutchy would defend. Finally rolled out of Tower."

Next day her good mood continued. "One of those large lunches at 44—I a little dazed after last night. Sat between Maynard Caines [sic] and Lytton Strachey, loved both."

On June 20 an American admirer arrived from the States on the *Mauretania*. Nancy was wildly excited at the prospect and met him off the boat with a taxi. "Frightfully happy—but it doesn't last."

Upset by her own emotions, Nancy wrote in her diary of her "shocking super-sensitiveness. Oh how often indeed have I cursed that, and now more than ever—it stands in the way of everything, distorts my life and makes me almost impossible to live, get on with I should say. Hidden, it's even worse, this gnawing and probing and exaggerating and lacerating state of mind. I seem to want too much, hence a mountain of unhappiness."

But Nancy's spirits easily picked up again at this stage of her life. She may have been spoiled, confused and not very happy with herself, but she managed to have a lot of fun. For someone who was to become famously uninterested in food, and eccentric in dress, she took, at the age of twenty-three, a healthy interest in both. One day she wrote enthusiastically, "I was beautifully dressed in a tight blue and white skirt, eke jersey top and straw hat, jolly cape and parasol." And soon after: "My god, what a help and moral support clothes are." She wondered continually what to do with her life, and her friends wondered with her, to varying receptions.

"John [Craigie] waxed slightly tiresome, said we [Marjorie and I] ought to have an occupation, suggested a hat shop! Then turned to me and said—of course I think you ought to have children. . . . (God!) I laughed, there being no answer."

Not all her speculations about what to do were earnest or

poetical. Over lunch with a favorite American admirer Beale Davis at the Ritz: "We got frightfully excited and thrilled about an idea of dancing together on the stage, masked, beautifully dressed, original and very professional—and we both meant it most seriously."

There were lots of parties, lots of admirers, lots of drink. The word used by Nancy and her friends for tight was "buffy," and it features in the diary a good deal. Sometimes the parties involved Lady Cunard, and on one rare occasion Nancy gave some sign of appreciating her mother's style and wit. After one party she wrote of her friends: "They all adored her—and my mood went up."

Some of Nancy's confusion and aimlessness, and her wild swings of mood can be ascribed to the conflicting emotions that swept her generation in the aftermath of the war. Relief and the urge to celebrate were mixed with pain and anger and a feeling that nothing could ever be the same again. But also Nancy had an unusually volatile nature, as, in some moods, she recognized. "I find life quite impossible, as I cannot enjoy a thing without carrying it to all the extremes and then nearly dying of the reaction—it is weak-minded, certainly it is."

When the peace was finally signed at Versailles on June 28, 1919, Nancy, like millions of others, had very mixed feelings and one particular grief.

"Oh Peter, it's too cruel, all the associations of this place and the waves of thought of last year . . . and some being dead and others not . . . got very sad and hated the demonstrations."

But a few days later she was off to the races and pasting her escort's tribute into her diary:

> Two little lips, a trifle rouged
> The breath of life impart
> Whilst fingers slim and manicured
> Are tugging at my heart
> Large grey blue eyes, a boyish form,
> High heels, french frock and hat,
> A well-shaped head and fair short hair
> And . . . quite enough! That's that!

Early in July Nancy went down for a weekend at the Wharf, the house on the Thames at Sutton Courteney, Oxford, where H.H. Asquith, the former prime minister, and his wife, Margot, lived after the war ended. Weekends at the Wharf were serious social occasions, and Nancy's diary shows her tackling this one with a mixture of nervousness and irreverence.

They were a party of thirteen, an odd mixture of foreign diplomats, literary and sporting figures, and pretty socialite women, Clifford Sharp (then editor of *Drama*), Mr. J. A. Spender (editor of the *Westminster Gazette*), "Satterthwaite the tennis man," and an ambassador to one of the Scandinavian countries. At dinner on Saturday, "Margot sat at a side table with Spender who was never seen to speak," wrote Nancy dryly. She also recorded with distaste finding a book by her bed containing first sayings of Margot's children and "a huge book of Margot's feelings—terrible." Next day, things got worse, "Dreaded lunch terribly and it was bad. I thought that Clifford Sharp was Satterthwaite and talked accordingly of tennis. He got very restive. . . . Margot meanwhile was very brilliant and very full of old anecdotes of Tennyson and her early contemporaries. They paucity of drink is appalling, both at lunch and dinner." As a finishing touch Margot told Nancy that she always looked "ghastly ill."

When she returned to London, Nancy found that her mother had not enjoyed the weekend either. Lady Cunard had been down to Montacute, Lord Curzon's house in Somerset. "She said she could not bear 'these terrible *intimacies* one has in the country.' "

On July 10 Nancy, Marjorie Trefusis and a cook moved into Turks Croft, near Crawley, Surrey, for the summer. Instantly Nancy's mood seemed to lighten, and for the next seven weeks the diary sounds less tense and frenzied, although the note of discontent and aimlessness persists. Her admirers came and went, bringing poems, drink and gossip from London. Private jokes and private language built up. "Hutchy to lunch—bringing some poems of Iris—Talked of an amazing new poem by Eliot—concocted new names for ourselves, he

the 'religious arithmetician' and I the 'romantic weevil'. . . .
Idle days and I love them—free of names of people and of
people themselves . . . my country mood develops." Nancy
began to write poetry again, most of it highly personal. One
long poem was called "In Answer to a Reproof"—adminis-
tered by one of her admirers who told her one day that she
was "too impetuous and contemptuous of opinion."

Though from time to time she felt romantic about Jim or
Ted or Eddie, Nancy was more in love with summer, poetry,
friendship, and independence than with anyone in particular.
She and a young man lay on the lawn the whole of one bright
day reading George Moore's *The Lovers of Aurelay* aloud to
each other. A couple of days later she records "a five mile talk
with Hutchy who was perfect—most of the time discoursed
on GM and kept on coming to the conclusion that he must be
my father and then saying 'But what of my long limbs and
general shape of body?' " Then come some of the most interesting lines in the whole diary: "Shall we ever know? It
seemed to me that if it were true I should become quite a
different personality and a much more contented one."

What did Nancy mean by those brief, wistful lines? If she
was beginning to feel out of place in conventional society then
clearly she could identify with a father like Moore much more
easily than with a father like Sir Bache, fond though she was
of him in a puzzled way. George Moore today is a half-
forgotten figure; but in Nancy's youth he stood for many of
the things she aspired to; he was regarded as a great writer
and a man who had lived dangerously and romantically, as a
great writer should.

These few lines in Nancy's diary prove that she was genuinely in some doubt about who her father was. Often, later,
she was unable to resist the temptation to toy with the possibility that Moore was her real father in a way that made many
of her friends think that underneath she was not serious, that
it was just an irresistible opportunity for a tease at her
mother's expense. But if she really did not know, and did
discuss the question with her close friends, then it is likely

that she had been thinking about it for some time. When we search for reasons for Nancy's difficulties with her mother, and even for some of her difficulties with herself, it is hard not to place this uncertainty about her father near the top of the list—especially as, so far as we know, Nancy never confronted her mother with the question.

As July moved on, Nancy made one or two expeditions to London to go to the ballet and catch up with her friends there. She found her mother still relentlessly pursuing the theme of where and how Nancy would live now, quite unable to allow her daughter to drift through the summer as she pleased. "Mother . . . was a little difficult with many questions as to how long one would *stay* there." Her mother's box at the ballet was, as usual, visited by everyone. Nancy, "exhilarated and buffy" kept looking out for Tommy Earp and T. S. Eliot, whom she had recently met and longed to see again, but instead was confronted with a lowering Chile Guevara and bumped into her husband escorting another girl. She escaped thankfully back to Turks Croft.

Ted Ralli seems to have emerged as the favored admirer around this time, and Nancy wrote that one day she "suddenly told him a good deal about the Haycock and Sir Bache"—as if it was a subject she did not usually discuss. She sums up her mood thus: "Very happy days these, but there is always the restlessness of wanting more of them, the longing for happiness to be ratified and enduring."

It is striking how seldom in this diary Nancy looked outside herself and her immediate surroundings. Once, dreamily, she wrote, "How hidden and remote one is from the obscure vortex of England's revolutionary troubles, coal strikes, etc. So much newspaper talk does it seem to me, and yet—is it going to be always so?" Mostly, Nancy was interested in herself.

Marie Ozanne paid a visit to Turks Croft one day and told Nancy something that delighted her about "some awful woman having said that my name and reputation were so bad that I should never go to Court again, but that the King was going to send for me to have a talk! Adored that." Later in the same visit: "We did the cards and foresaw great journeys for me and a 'complete change' of existence, which I hoped would be true." It was not at all a bad forecast.

The late summer drifted on, with life at Turks Croft punctuated by Nancy's emotional entanglements and one or two visits from her mother. One weekend in August, which Nancy described as "the best weekend of all"—a round of cocktails in the garden, dancing after dinner, long walks in the moonlight, singing and laughing—one of her suitors told her that she "wasn't at all physical . . . he has a somewhat cruel theory that 'the lover' can never be 'the friend,' that directly a friendship becomes sensual it's ruined—and the worst of this is that it's so terribly true." They lay around in the heat reading lurid Sunday newspapers, gossiping, and Nancy heard once again how bad her reputation was becoming. She was delighted.

On August 20, the diary records Lady Cunard and George Moore visiting Turks Croft together. Moore, in a tightly buttoned gray suit and brown buttoned boots, was restless; Nancy's mother was "in a furious temper, which I did not notice at first, although the others did." After tea, Nancy took Moore around the garden. "He was suave but ponderous, still harping on why I should wish to publish poems now—in his eye a roguish gleam when he spoke of his journey to France, detailing several adventures with women!" St. John Hutchinson was left to deal with Lady Cunard.

Meanwhile, mother was working herself up still more. First, over the tea, which she said was so bad that she "wouldn't offer it to a horsethief" for it was "muck." Secondly, over my supposed friends—"Americans!" All this was said to Hutchy, who was terrified and replied "Yes, yes, quite, quite" to everything. Then came a flare-up about S's mother having taken my linen and china from Montagu Square which ended in an outburst to me: "You have no sense, knowledge or experience and no plan of life."

By the time the visitors left, Nancy was herself in a rage and Hutchinson had a headache. "We stamped round fields at a great pace, disclaiming against them, laughing but irritated, wondering whether GM was at that moment on his old hobby horse, asking her Ladyship if I was possibly in love with Hutchy."

Nancy continued to speculate on what she would do with her life. Sometimes she enjoyed discussing this crucial question with friends; at other times the whole subject irritated her intensely. "Hutchy very ponderous at lunch with an irritating and stupid theory—saying I ought to know more intellectual people and see them frequently to improve and develop my brain—logical enough but a silly remark—the names cited were: Lytton Strachey, Eliot and Earp! I said I loathed the idea of this." Another time, lunching in London with Eddie: "We elaborated an amusing new scheme of life for me, ie. to become the mistress of a millionaire rajah (such as the Shah of Persia) and be very ostentatious, therefore annoying the whole world." Nancy even cut out a photograph of a fat, young Oriental prince from a newspaper and tucked it into the pages of her diary, to reinforce the joke.

She also, reluctantly, had one or two meetings with her husband. In late August she mentions a visit to Montagu Square "to collect things," and "a short and perfectly futile interview with Sydney which made me very tired." On the first of September she went again to the house to sort furniture with her mother. Afterward they went shopping. The day was not a success. Nancy could not bear her mother's solicitude and wrote angrily of her mother "saying all the time how ill I looked and observing me with a maddening persistency. . . . I was furious and more wretched than ever before at not having a home of my own—I must, I must and sacrifice everything else to it—not drag on as I have done for so vastly too long now. . . . I detest that room at Grosvenor—it reminds me of the appalling days when I was ill and mad, it reminds me of the worst days of my life."

By September 3 the lease on Turks Croft was up. Nancy

wrote in her diary of "leaving without looking back at all, as
is my habit." She then described another visit to Montagu
Square and an interview with Sydney Fairbairn. When she got
to the house, she found and destroyed her early letters to him.
Then

> at 5 Sydney arrived . . . he was very dreary . . . he asked me
> to make mother consent to annulling the marriage settlements!
> We then talked of divorce and he had the most absurd views,
> saying his mother was the person he now had to think of, that
> she would never agree to my divorcing him, etc. that this
> would hurt his "career" (God). Once in the street it occurred
> to me to say "Have you ever thought how much more it
> would prejudice people against you if you divorced me?"
> which he could not answer—smug and very self-contented and
> arrogant he was (however his mother has returned the linen)!

It seems plain that Nancy now felt nothing but a bored contempt for her husband, but she could write of him calmly
enough. (Eventually a legal separation was arranged; Nancy
and Fairbairn were not divorced until 1925.)

The next day, Nancy saw a doctor. She was still rundown
after her illness, and he advised a rest cure of a least a month.
Nancy, between leaving a selection of her latest poems at
Duckworth and taking Sybil Hart-Davis on a flat hunt, was
planning a trip to Paris and had no intention of following his
advice. However, she did try to rest.

> Sunday September 7:
> All of a long morning in bed. Sent for GM. He came at once
> in a superlative mood, wanted to go to Richmond to Lady
> Donega's But that was stopped. . . . He stayed till 7, and
> talked and talked—of love, or erotic adventures, of his adven-
> tures, citing a very recent one of a woman who came to see
> him about a play, lay on a sofa and said "shall I, shall I?" . . .
> (apparently they did! I could hardly believe this). GM very
> gross but most lovable—never have I liked him so well—he

was very human and sympathetic, he also talked of Sydney, said how awful he had always thought him and how well he understood my point of view. . . . I have never got on with him so well, which leads one to the conclusion that he does take a vast amount of time.

Later that evening she got up, went out and visited the Coopers and Alan Parsons. "Ah, the Coterie—that takes one back five years—too—my god, we are all that's left of it."

Her last couple of days before leaving for Paris were hectic. She dropped into the Tower "for a minute where we saw Stulik, who has returned from internment shrivelled, tiny, pitiable and very, very humble. . . . I was horrified. . . . How that place is bound up in and with my life—I dare not think of last year there at all." She bumped into Sydney Fairbairn at a party. Nancy reproached herself with being "too nice to him . . . but finding him stupid. All through the night I kept on thinking of Paris and feeling glad at leaving England where such people exist."

On September 9 she was off: "Mother's farewell was good: 'I know I shall find you in the Rat Mort, but it is better than to find you with Le Cochon Vivant.' " She took the night train to Dover and felt her spirits lift as she observed "the land all white with mist and moon . . . and life beginning, as at the beginning of all travel . . . "

Next day, on the boat, she met the Craigies, beginning their honeymoon. On arrival Nancy found herself to be cross "at knowing no-one in Paris and having to be a constant third with the Craigies." But things soon picked up. Although Nancy already regarded Paris as an escape from London, she was far from being able to lead a different sort of life there. On September 12 her cousin Edward Cunard "suddenly rushed me into a dress and off to Poiret's to dance."

Poiret, the immensely successful and influential designer, would organize costume balls for Paris society around a chosen theme. Nancy recorded a

large obscure garden, full of coloured gravels, trees and mysterious lights—sweet champagne and a general confusion in the
dark. This time it was huntsmen—English huntsmen that Poiret had dressed his retainers and himself in a huge scarlet
coat—they likewise with great curling gilt cornet de chasse
wound round them, blowing a fanfare between each dance,
each tango! Sublime mixture—we were then given a long pole
on top of which was a stag's head supporting a cross which
had an electric light inside it! All this in the semi dark, procession of mannequins and procession of "tigress women"—Poiret's reason for his very justifiable love of red is that he has
seen so much blood in the trenches he can think of no other
colour!

Among the keen socialites Nancy met in Paris were Elsa
Maxwell ("a monstrous woman") and the young Chips Channon ("an odious little snob, American"). Within a few days
she moved to the Ritz, which she dismissed as "terrible—the
whole of the front passage lined with gaping people and
Channon hanging about."

Many of her evenings were spent with her cousin Edward,
who was then with the Foreign Office, and his friends,
among whom was Harold Nicolson, in Paris for the Peace
Conference. Nancy and Harold Nicolson never cared much
for each other later on, and the diary indicates the antipathy
went some way back. "Dined with Edward who brought
Harold Nicolson—this made my heart sink, more so when he
insisted on going to Montmartre in search of filthy little restaurants when the only possible place that night seemed to be
a very expensive and high-class one." After dinner they went
to a gala at the Apollo, which Nancy describes gleefully as "a
low place" and recounts how Harold Nicolson fell on the
floor, to the amusement of the tarts, and she herself managed
to be picked up by a strange man. She was feeling the lack of
an attendant admirer by this time. "I swore constantly never
to go to Paris again without a chap or even several."

She then went off to spend the weekend with Mrs. Mabel
Corey, the American society hostess, a friend and rival of her

mother's, who had moved to France and entertained at the Château de Villegenis, not far from Paris. Nancy was reluctant to go and could not restrain her malice in her diary. She found the opulent setting preposterous, the company unappealing and her hostess absurd. "Mabel Gilman the light opera star married to an impotent steel king—a curious world this." At lunch on the first day, described by Nancy as "IMPOSSIBLE," were "Melba, Lady Randolph Churchill with her awful husband Porch, two little nameless dagoes, very dull . . . Mrs Corey, or 'Mabelle,' who kept on saying, 'Where is Mr Channon' . . . there was less wine than at the Wharf." Nancy spent most of her time hiding in her room, except for mealtimes, when she had to face the company. Evenings were worse than lunchtimes: "After we heard Mrs Corey sing the Rosary (Oh God!) we were finally allowed to go to bed."

Back in Paris Nancy continued to go to parties, spend evenings in the Café de Paris and go shopping for clothes. St. John Hutchinson turned up in Paris, which pleased her, and she dragged him, protesting, around with her. On September 22 she heard from Austin Harrison, the editor of the *Week-end Review*, that he had accepted one of her poems. She was tremendously pleased. Meanwhile she was dallying with a new American admirer. Nancy loved the initial stages of a romance and would fling herself wholeheartedly into it. But she found it difficult to sustain a relationship; above all, she found it difficult to accept the independent reality of the other person. She knew this of herself: "How odd I am in the way I pick up with people, and get to know them terribly well seemingly, and really do also, very quickly, and then jump every time the mechanism works of itself, and the doll speaks."

She went to another Poiret gala, "Under the Sea" this time ("ghastly"), and went on afterward to what she described as "some curious and obscure sort of brothel." On October 2 St. John Hutchinson produced a copy of the *Week-end Review* with her poem in it. On October 4 she left for England, accompanied by Hutchinson, who proved useful with the formalities, which always made Nancy highly impatient. "Whisked through the diplomatic office in front of everyone, Hutchy being very pompous and saying 'I am the Peace Conference.' " Once on board, they shut themselves in a cabin and had sweets, biscuits, peaches and champagne. Nancy was not pleased to get home. "I loathe England, one ought never to return to it." Back she went to Grosvenor Square "to find Mother very pleased over my poem."

The last two months of 1919 found Nancy resuming her London life without much enthusiasm. The more passionate and demanding her admirers became, the more she despised them. Chile Guevara was very much in love with her at this time, but according to the diary, she found him simply tiresome. "Dined with Chile at the Tower. Went to his studio where he became too appalling and very violent—I hysterical actually." Within a week after her return Nancy had decided to follow the doctor's advice and take a month's "rest cure" at Hindhead. At least this meant she could escape from her mother. But before she retreated to bed, Nancy had one encounter which pleased her very much. Iris Tree had recently returned from America with her new husband, Curtis Moffat, an artist, Nancy was delighted to see Iris again and liked Curtis immediately.

From October 12 until November 10 Nancy was in seclusion at Hindhead. She spent two weeks in bed, reading Hardy, Gauguin's letters, GM's *Confessions*, "which made me laugh with delight" and his *Mummer's Wife* "on the subject of which I wrote him a new kind of letter, which he was pleased to call my 'first woman's letter.' " She corresponded with Hutchinson and Beale Davis, and had visits from her mother, Sybil Hart-Davis, and Marie Ozanne. She wrote of this quiet time (slightly unconvincingly): "How strange it would be to think of one's life being spent entirely in the country with never a rendezvous at Ritz or Tower. How much nicer."

When she emerged, she saw a lot of Iris; they had some long talks, and it sounds as if Iris, happy in her marriage, made

Nancy a little jealous. She told her one day "that my capacity for happiness was starved." Iris was also wary. "I loved the Moffats, but am forever annoyed at this ridiculous idea that Iris has that Curtis will fall in love with one." A certain amount of gossip and advice about Sydney Fairbairn came her way, including a rumor that he was having her followed by detectives. She started sitting for her portrait by Guevara, which kept her around Grosvenor Square. "Lunched in . . . a funny mixture of the Loughboroughs, Mrs Dudley Ward, Alastair McIntosh, Bertram [sic] Russell and wife and Clifford Sharp . . . really an absurd contrast."

On November 21 she went for a weekend visit to Sir Bache at the Haycock. It was a mixed success. "One feels more and more neurotic after an hour or two with Sir Bache, as if no kind of existence were left one at all—and what's more I believe no-one would come to look for one here no matter how long one disappeared for . . . I love the bridge and the street, river, meadows, outlook and house itself—but Sir Bache with his eternal patiences and small talk (when any) sap one's energy and patience a good deal." Nancy went for long walks and wrote to Robert Nichols, a young poet who was showing signs of falling in love with her. Sir Bache did not mention her marriage or divorce.

Back in London, she began to find Nichols tiresome too. "At the Tower came Nicholls [sic]. (Lord had I but known what I was starting, when I got hold of that young man . . . He is mad, no doubt of it, and very, very common, but thinks he is a genius instead of which he is really a shocking poet)."

For all Nancy's scorn, Nichols had published some striking war poems and was generally regarded at the time as a promising new talent. He poured his infatuated love for Nancy into a sonnet sequence entitled "Sonnets to Aurelia," which was published by Chatto and Windus in 1920. The sonnets (whose quality as poetry tends to support Nancy's opinion) resound with descriptions of Nancy's beauty and hard-heartedness, her "terrible eyes," her "sunflower hair," and "air of ease and delicate pride":

The slenderness, purity and magnificence
Of the magnolia's alabaster flower
Are yours, and from you floats as effluence
Of a like cloistered and voluptuous power:
Thus limn I you, knowing, alas, too well
That outward heaven hides an inward hell.

The poems were dedicated to Nancy, and Nichols sent her the full manuscript, complete with drafts and corrections, bound in crimson, with a large golden *N* and his own name surrounded by a wreath of bay leaves on the cover. Far from being flattered, Nancy was, and remained, annoyed by the implications of the poems, which, she later wrote, "tell of every kind of lurid occasion that never arose at all between us—poetic license, if ever there was."

She was not much happier with Guevara. "Chile comes to paint me every day at 2. Early nights and temperate make one feel not so ill, but certainly very dull and witless." Neither Guevara's absorption in her portrait nor Nichols's frenzied letters and poems cheered Nancy at all as the year drew to an end.

November 28:
Terrible letters from Nicholls [*sic*], and sonnets that don't scan, every morning on the breakfast tray!

December 1:
London is so vile, with the sky falling and the mud rising in steam about one, nor can I remember anything of the long afternoons that go as Chile paints background and the shadow of my boot. This diary is tedious now, and I write it two weeks late.

In 1955, when Nancy was living in France, she came upon the three 1919 diaries. They were locked, and the keys lost, so Nancy took them down to the village blacksmith who broke them open.

When she had reread them, she wrote a long entry in the

third book, giving her reactions, at the age of fifty-nine, to reading herself at the age of twenty-three. She was moved not to nostalgia but to anger.

I read . . . all that night and was, in the end, outraged—an impression that lasted all the next day. To think that so many of these people around me, and Her Ladyship, should have been telling me constantly "Do something! Make good! You're wasting your life!" etc. What were the facts? I was then 23—I had married a foul man, Sydney Fairbairn, at the age of 20, in 1916, after breaking off the marriage one day (unfortunately not sticking to that!); I loathed him, knew it was an idiotic thing to do, but did it, went through with it all so as to get away from Her Ladyship and have a home of my own. It was wartime—the many young men I loved were all dead. I was always in love—sometimes with two or three at the same time. In July 1918, Sydney Fairbairn went to the war for the second time. and I shared a house at Kingston Bagpuize with Sybil Hart-Davis and Rupert and Deirdre.

Then comes something which shows how, once she realized that she could not live with her husband, she bitterly resented her renewed dependence on her mother.

At this time I had not one penny of my own: Her Ladyship gave me, voluntarily, what she might have settled on me; I felt I could not count on it and how rightly felt that she could and would have cut it off had she so wished—therefore the condition and circumstances I was in all of this diary year 1919 were:

1 Separated but not yet legally so, or divorced—(to be separated was perfection).
2 Still extremely unhappy and "lost" after the death of Peter.
3 Still very ill, weak and exhausted by the influenza and pneumonia—hence all the references to feeling like hell— all of which was made worse by the incessant drink— (drink, drink, drink, repetitive—god).
4 I longed to be really on my own—have a flat, a house somewhere, and . . .
5 Of course—it was Ted Ralli I loved, up to a point—and Jim

McVickar, the American—both of them pretty awful, with considerable charm—All the rest of the names were friends, companions, etc. and in this press of people that reads to me now like a rushing welter—a diary can read like that— there were singularly few lovers.

So—instead of holding out a helping hand, those who criticised went on criticising. What a fiddle-faddling lot of people; Her Ladyship was often maddening. . . . By the end of 1919, after Chile (Alvaro Guevara) had finished his unending, his blockish (?) his awful portrait of me (now in the Melbourne Museum, Australia) I had determined to leave England—and leave I did—on January 7th 1920, I went to France—alone "for ever." And here I am—to this day September 1955.

A few weeks later, again writing in the old diary, Nancy returned to the attack: "Damn all those footling, boring, stupid people of 1919, and Her Ladyship most, for the total lack of sympathy about her!"

There is one more later entry in the diary. The tone is quite different.

"I wish there had been ME now with ME of then—we should have gotten on very well. We should have gone off together. The ME of now and the ME of then. But when did the ME of now begin? Begin is not the word—but when was there a leap out of the uncertainty about self nearly all the time? In Paris in 1923, I should say, but progressively a little sooner."

Michael Arlen

Although Nancy would always refer to her departure for Paris in January 1920 as a watershed, as the definitive moment when she started to live her life in her own way, she remained very much part of the London scene for several more years. In England it was the time when the legend of the twenties was being formed; and the legend of Nancy as an archetypal twenties girl took shape simultaneously. Indeed, the style and behavior of girls such as Nancy were a basic ingredient of twenties mythology, both at the time and afterward.

They were supposed to be a new kind of woman: independent, unconventional, and free-living. They were much more dashing than the rather earnest "New Woman" of the prewar period, who set her heart on bicycling and mixed study groups; the war, inevitably, was blamed by the censorious for what seemed a tendency to recklessness and immorality. The war did indeed contribute to a new attitude toward women; but in fact, though there were real changes taking place in the position of all classes of women during the 1920s—when they finally won the vote, began to take up careers, and to control their fertility—the fascination of the public with the antics of fashionable upper-class young women had the most tenuous links with such practicalities.

Nancy was never exactly a "Bright Young Person"; by their heyday, the late 1920s, she was over thirty and spending most of her time in Paris. But at the beginning of the decade, she certainly behaved in ways that fitted the popular notion of the twenties girl; she cut her hair, wore short skirts, smoked and drank a great deal in public and earned a reputation for having a great many casual affairs.

Nancy always hated the cult of the twenties and the notion of her role in it; and yet images of a period, or a person, are not powerful and enduring without some reason, and one of the reasons why the mood of the early twenties has become fixed in the imagination is because of the way novelists of the time captured and popularized it. Nancy, because of the world she moved in, the people she knew and the relationships she had, and because something in her temperament, behavior and style seemed particularly of the times, found her way, in various disguises and distortions, into the bloodstream of fiction.

At this time Nancy was at her most devastating. People who knew her in the early twenties describe her with a breathless amazement, even when writing years later. Raymond Mortimer, the writer and critic, who met her on a Channel crossing, put it like this: "Everybody old, it is hoped, can look back to one person who was incomparably bewitching; and I have never met anyone to equal Nancy Cunard when first I met her." He described her physical impact:

> What first struck one was her *regard* (there is no English word meaning not only the eyes—hers were an arctic blue—but the way in which they confront the visible world). Next came the mixture of delicacy and steel in her build, hips, legs and ankles all of the slenderest. Her walk also enchanted, the head held high with its short fair hair, and one foot placed exactly in front of the other, not with mannequin languor, but spontaneously, briskly, boldly, skimming the pavement. Never in her life, I believe, was she frightened of anything.

Certain details recur in descriptions of Nancy: her eyes (usually recalled as startlingly blue, though sometimes as green), her short fair hair, her white skin, her extreme slimness and her extraordinary dancing walk. Her voice, too, was special. Harold Acton, whom she first met at this time, wrote: "She was slim to the point of evanescence, and her voice evanesced in conversation to revive, surprisingly sharp and pointed, in a disarming query. Her small head, so gracefully poised, might have been carved in crystal with green jade for eyes, and this crystalline quality made some people think she was cold to the core."

Several of those struck by her beauty and style were troubled by intimations of complexity, even desperation, beneath the dazzling exterior. William Carlos Williams, the American poet, who met her in Paris, evidently found her disquieting. "Nancy Cunard, straight as any stick, emaciated, holding her head erect, not particularly animated, her blue eyes completely untroubled, inviolable in her virginity of pure act. I never saw her drunk; I can imagine that she was never quite sober." He saw her and Iris Tree, whom he met at the same time, as "young, detached from reality, without passion. They, young as they were, had had bitter early experiences without emotional response. There was nothing left in either of them. They were completely empty, and yet they were young, appealing and unassailable." Mary Hutchinson, who knew Nancy nearly as well as her husband did, has described the beauty and the melancholy that struck so many observers.

She seemed always to be on the move—buffeted by storms—agitated—dissatisfied—unsatisfied—always attended by a different companion. What was she seeking? A victory? Or stability somewhere? It is true that whenever I saw Nancy I was struck by her appearance. In some early letters I described her as she seemed to me then. . . . In 1919: "Miss Nancy Cunard is wonderful, made of alabaster and gold and scarlet, with a face like Donatello's Saint George; a lady who would fit into the early court of Louis XIV or Boccaccio's world . . ." In 1924: "I met Nancy. She kept up perfectly her facade, behind which one seems to see a shadow moving—an independent, romantic and melancholy shadow which one can never approach. The facade was exquisite, made of gold leaf, lacquer, verdigris and ivory."

So Nancy in the twenties was strikingly beautiful, and mysteriously sad. In some of these accounts she already sounds like a novelist's invention. Since several of the men who fell in love with her at this time were novelists, and since one of the preoccupations of the day was the new sexual freedom, particularly for women, it is hardly surprising that this aspect of her behavior interested them more than, say, her poetry.

In the spring of 1920 Nancy met a young man in London who was deeply determined to do two things: become a writer and achieve fame, fortune, and social power. He was something of an oddity, especially when he was still struggling, before success had won him the aura of easy acceptability. For one thing, he was Armenian, although educated at an English public school, and he not only looked extremely foreign—small, dark, and intense—but he had a peculiar name of virtually impenetrable foreignness: Dikran Kouyoumdjian. Before his first book was published, he sensibly changed his name to something more manageable: Michael Arlen.

The basic facts about their relationship are simple. Nancy, with her taste for outsiders and the exotic, saw quite a lot of Michael in the early twenties. He was twenty-three; she was a year older. He fell in love with her. They met in Paris as well as London over the next couple of years and during the summers in the holiday houses Nancy would take in France.

Arlen's first book, a collection of stories called *The London Venture,* was quite well received; his first novel, published in 1922 and called *Piracy,* was more successful and contained two characters—the heroine, Virginia, and her mother, Lady Carnal—who had overtones of Nancy and her mother. Then in 1924 he published *The Green Hat,* one of the most famous best sellers of the century. The heroine of that novel, Iris March, seized the imagination of a generation, and Nancy Cunard, it was said then and has been said ever since, was the "real" Iris March.

Arlen's novels are not much read today, except as curiosities or for camp amusement; bracketed with Elinor Glyn or Ouida, they are not considered literature. They fall into the category of high-class, stylish trash. They are intensely romantic, wildly overwritten, almost embarrassingly effusive; and yet the writer's sheer energy, his absolute determination against all the odds to make his fictional world convincing, and the care with which he constructs his absurd tales of love and betrayal give him a certain impressiveness.

The presence of Nancy in Arlen's work is powerful, which is not to say that she was his only inspiration. Many of the characteristics of his first heroine, Virginia Tracy, fit Nancy; but they would also fit many other young women in the world Arlen longed to join. The places as well as the people in the early Arlen were taken from life. Many of the crucial scenes in *Piracy* happen in a restaurant called the Mont Agel, which is the Eiffel Tower in thin disguise. Its proprietor, "the polite and amiable M. Stutz," is a portrait of the long-suffering Stulik; "the bearded and significant figure of M. Stutz's most considerable patron" is Augustus John. Arlen described the impact the "Mont Agel" might be expected to make on "stout yeomen from Wimbledon and honest burghers from Kensington Gore, gallants from Holland Park and beaux from Golders Green" especially the impact of

> the vivid entrance of those tawny haired women of almost barbaric fairness, whose faces the men of Putney recognised from the illustrated papers with a thrill of disapproval. . . . Those young women of patrician and careless intelligence, whom it is the pet mistake of bishops, diarists, press photographers and Americans, to take as representing the "state" of modern society (whereas, God knows, they represent nothing but themselves, and that too rarely) and who, by some law of sympathy, have found refuge at this Mont Agel from their tedious parentage or tiresome duties roundabout, say, Grosvenor Square. . . . And on many nights will come the toughs and roughs and bravoes of the town, to press their ill-favoured noses against the windows of the Mont Agel and watch the leading beauties toying with their food and their poets.

As Nancy remembered it, decades later, she met Arlen at the Tower, though she was not quite sure. "It may well have been at the Eiffel Tower, both of us being assiduous frequenters, though never together till then. After that we were there very frequently together, God bless the place and dear sophisticated, generous, drunken Rudolf Stulik." There was an incident with a brooch:

> The first meeting with the Baron—Dikran Kouyoumdjian was his authentic name—contained an orchid (or did that come next morning?) and a large diamond brooch set in platinum with a reconstructed ruby in the centre—till recently my mother's. It fell to the floor in a London taxi, un-noticed of me. In no time the Baron perceived it under his feet. "Hallo, what's this? Ah! your bauble?" He retrieved it and returned it to me like a Cavalier. Yes, the orchid came next day, a classic Callia. . . . I must have been to a Ball that night.

In the 1950s, when Nancy was making a serious effort to write her memoirs, one of the first people she chose to describe was Arlen. Here, as well as in her scrapbooks—which are suddenly full of pictures of him—she called him "the Baron."

In explaining this nickname, she described the reaction of one of her old admirers to the latest recruit.

> Hutchinson . . . was the one, I am sure, who suffered most from the Baron, who, via myself, had suddenly come into his highbrow world like a menacing pirateer, at first a mere black sail on the horizon, all too soon a matter of daily, or almost daily occurrence. They used to glare at each other across the napery, until, unable to bear Hutchy's decreasingly veiled sarcasms any longer, the Baron, to the delight of all save Hutchy, would suddenly prick at him with some lordly rococo-esque quip. . . . Hutchy would complain to me later in a high voice: "I really can't see why you like this ghastly oriental rug-merchant; no, no, really, really . . . " He called him Krumjy-Jumjy—a fine example of xenophobic barrister mentality. "Well, if that's not his name," he would say, "what is his name?"—his voice, by then, in high falsetto.
> "Well, Hutchy dear, he tells me his name, as well you know

by now too, as we've heard it often together from him, is Dikran Kouyoumdjian—to my mind a wonderful name. He says that not only his three elder brothers but himself as well are all entitled to be called Barons—Armenian Barons, but somehow, they don't want to use their titles; they are businessmen, all, I think. Rupen, Krikor, Takvor—beautiful names. Dikran says he wouldn't think of using his title. He has chosen an English name, as well you know too, by now . . . Michael Arlen. Very British, isn't it?" Whereat Hutchy snorted, "I see, I see, all right—THE BARON." So that was the origin of the name. He was "The Baron" subsequently to a great, great many of us in the earliest Twenties.

There is a ring of authenticity about this exchange, as there is about Nancy's next remark. " 'Men' loathed the Baron—at least, then. Later, when entirely thanks to his own ingenious and properly rewarded literary efforts he was on a level with Noel Coward or at least in the Coward class, they loathed him less." However, she was not altogether right about the origin of the nickname. In Armenian the word for Mr. is "Bahr-rohn."

Piracy hangs a lot of breathless verbiage around a simple story of an intense young writer, Ivor Pelham Marlay, who falls in love with a married society woman, loses an arm in the war, falls in love with another married society woman, and lives with her in Paris. She develops a mysterious gynecological complaint, undergoes a serious operation, recovers, refuses to marry him, and eventually, after he has withdrawn from her in rage, dies. In this comparatively clumsy early novel Arlen introduced the themes he would continue to use with great success: social aspiration, sexual passion (preferably adulterous), and gallant death. "Virginia Tracy" reflects Nancy's early history—notably a socially powerful mother and entrance into society on the eve of the First World War. Arlen described Virginia and her friends as "young and cool and remote, and ever so faintly contemptuous of those whom their carelessness about things might shock."

The prewar Virginia is surrounded by beautiful, brilliant,

doomed young men. "They were clean and intricate and pagan and they were quick to believe in fine things; and they could both drink and think. In everything they were a denial of their fathers, for these young men were sceptical of generalisation in everything; they were a denial of the catchwords for which they were to fight; and in everything they were the finest expression of the paralytic civilisation for which they were to die." Virginia "loved one and then another, seldom alone, but always in a crowd." When the hero meets Virginia again after the war, she has had one disastrous marriage and is floundering in another. She has also become, as had Nancy by the time Arlen met her, a woman with a reputation. "No-one could deny that there was a glamour about her, certainly there was a glamour. But there was a rottenness in that glamour—now where did that come from? and Why? Quite decent men took faint license with her name, while lewd men who had never met Virginia, could never have met her, said that they had touched her, they chuckled at the mention of her name." And by this time Virginia, like Nancy, was showing signs of hostility to the society world she inhabited. "Virginia seemed not to be quite of the society which she graced so brilliantly; she seemed to despise it, she passed people swiftly. A queer provocative indifference there was about her." In a long, vivid passage describing Virginia's life during the war Arlen has her abruptly leave parties in grand houses to make her way to Soho.

"Suddenly, swiftly, silently, she leaves the room. She waits for no man. She leaves the house just like that, she leaves it. Maybe this departure offends—Virginia doesn't care. . . . Now, whither does this swift and secret passage take her? Sometimes to her house in Belgrave Square, a mausoleum of a house which Virginia bitterly hates; sometimes to meet someone in some place: more often to the Mont Agel."

Once there, Virginia-Nancy sits writing letters, attended by Stutz-Stulik, until very late. Unlike Nancy, Virginia drinks only Vichy water. Then she walks home, braving the approaches of men in the Soho streets. It all sounds very much as Nancy, in 1920, would have described her recent past to a new lover.

In the summer of 1920 Nancy took a villa, Les Mouettes, by the sea at Hardelot, near Boulogne. In her notes on Arlen she described the time they spent there: not in idyllic solitude (that was seldom Nancy's style) but with various others coming and going—her cousin Victor, Beale Davis, Marjorie Trefusis, "Chile" Guevara. Guevara can hardly have been a very comfortable presence, for he was still wildly in love with Nancy too; indeed he had made her, as his biographer says, "his female prototype." Nancy remembered some awkwardness. At one moment she was alone with five men. Then, worse, she found herself alone with Arlen and Guevara.

> By day the Baron worked. In the evening the three of us would settle down to drinking, after dinner. And then, at times, there would issue from Chile some remarkable remarks. One, in particular, though what led to it I can't imagine, made both the Baron and myself very cross (that must have been a very late night). "Huh," said Chile. "Don't you think Dostoevski is like a carthorse in a bowler hat." Neither of us thought so as we told him vehemently.

They played poker when it rained, and went for long walks along the sands. Nancy remembered Arlen's annoyance when he spoiled a pair of shoes. Nancy greatly admired Arlen's capacity for work, though she would criticize him for writing such trivial stuff.

" 'Why can't you write ever something serious? You have a beautiful gift of observation; you work like hell. . . . Yet you go on and on writing about Cocktails with a capital C and ladies and gentlemen of Mayfair the likes of whom never existed. Couldn't you try your hand at something serious, just for once?' The Baron smiled. 'It wouldn't sell. D'you see?' "

That autumn and winter in Paris, they were together much of the time, as Nancy recalled with mingled affection and irritation.

The Baron was not only good fun and a charming companion. He could be as sullen as distant thunder, as heavy as lead, brooding and brewing for hours. I admit that some of this (as he would point out) was my fault. God, how I loathed him then. It would pass . . . with champagne as like as not. Our Montmartre nights were a delight that same autumn and winter, my first winter in Paris on my own; the Baron's first taste of France as well. We would go generally to "La Perle"— a most reasonably priced tarts restaurant, where the obese yet buoyant Madame, dressed in very high, very tight laced boots, now of white, and now of black, usually in that astonishingly bright short green taffeta dress of hers, would leeringly whisper to us: "J'ai connu le Roi Édouard Sept." It seems to me that she sometimes carried a whip. . . . In any case, for twenty francs a head, one could enjoy delicious food while appraising the girls as they came in to eat about ten o'clock, before going off to their work. And then we would go and dance somewhere else in Montmartre. It was always champagne, and our heads were often swimming.

Their affair was at its height. By Nancy's own account, Arlen was putting her under pressure. He mentioned marriage—after a fashion.

This too was the time I saw him every day; now he was on my nerves, and now he was not. (That feverish cutting of the pages of paper novels, in one of his books, is perfectly exact; on one occasion he made me so frantic with nerves that it seemed the only thing to do for me while listening to his taunts and complaints.) About now, too, the Baron once said: "If I were rich, I should ask you to marry me—d'you see? But as I'm not, there seems no point in doing so—d'you see?" I did, Quite apart from the fact that I was married and had not yet got my divorce, as I reminded him. The vanity of some men! Marry the Baron indeed!

Arlen was very much a part of Nancy's life before, during and after the illness and the operations that Nancy had in the winter of 1920 and the early spring of 1921. He put a similar operation into vital scenes in at least two of his novels; *Piracy* and *The Green Hat,* and Nancy confirmed that some of the details he used were authentic. But if the operation was significant for Arlen's fictional heroines, it was of enormous importance to Nancy in real life.

The nature of Nancy's gynecological illness is obscure. What is clear is that in the winter of 1920 she had a hysterectomy in a clinic in Paris, that there were complications, and that she was very ill. Afterward, she would sometimes tell a new lover or a close woman friend that she had deliberately decided to have a hysterectomy because she wanted complete sexual freedom and knew that she would never wish to have a child. But this was not always her story. Occasionally she said that she had had to have her womb removed because she had contracted a venereal disease. One simple explanation—that at a time when contraception was still erratic she became pregnant and either miscarried or had an abortion followed by complications—she never seems to have mentioned. She may have been prone to gynecological problems; she once told a friend that her periods had always been very painful.

Conclusive evidence in such matters is hard to come by. But among Nancy's papers is a scribbled note outlining her medical history.

Dec, Jan, Feb. in the hospital in Paris.
   1st Op.   Curettage
   2nd Op.   Hysterectomy
   3rd Op.   Appendicitis, Peritonitis, Gangrene
                with "a two per cent chance of survival"

The implications are clear. A minor operation, curettage, was followed by the drastic operation removing the womb. This, a serious enough operation now, when surgery and gynecology are both far more advanced than they were in 1920, was followed by further complications and infections.

The whole experience must have had a profound effect on Nancy, psychologically as well as physically. She was only twenty-four and had never known a lasting, happy relationship. After this she had no fear of pregnancy; but such freedom often carries with it doubts about femininity and capacity for fulfillment. To some of her friends and lovers, it seemed clear that her operation had affected her capacity for deep feeling.

It was no secret that Nancy was ill, but the accounts that reached the gossip columns were, not surprisingly, reticent. In her scrapbooks, among the reviews of her first book of poems, *Outlaws,* which came out in April 1921, are two newspaper cuttings about her illness. "Nancy Cunard is much better now. She had, of course, been terribly ill in Paris, and underwent an operation from which a recovery is almost unprecedented. The surgeon's fee alone for this was, I have been told by an intimate friend of the family, 100,000 francs. Both Lady Cunard and Sir Bache Cunard were with her continuously." The other says: "Lady Cunard's charming and clever daughter, Nancy Fairbairn, has long been unwell from peritonitis and its accompanying complications."

Readers of Arlen's novels, then and now, who know of their connection and detect Nancy in his heroines could not help seeing the mysterious illness rather differently. In *Piracy* Virginia suffers from a "sick little pain" connected with a gynecological problem and has to be flown to London for an operation that has complications and is described, vividly, as hideously painful.

> Virginia wasn't asleep, she was in pain. In great pain. Her face was thin and gray and it was somehow screwed up, and her eyes were tightly screwed up. . . . "It hurts," she whispered. "Frightful. . . . There's things inside me," she said with a sob. "Steel things. They've left them in there . . . holding things together. . . . Oh, it hurts, Ivor. . . .
>
> "Look," she said pitifully. And she lifted up her hands under the clothes, and he saw that they were tied together with a handkerchief. "That's to stop me tearing the things out and

killing myself," she explained with amazing clarity. "There's things sticking in underneath."

Arlen also put Nancy's operation into *The Green Hat*. "Part of that novel," Nancy wrote, "was inspired by the only too real circumstances around me in a hospital in Paris in December 1920 and Jan–Feb 1921. I did nearly die there, and he did hear me scream. . . ."

In fact, although Nancy has always been taken to have been the model for Iris March and although Arlen certainly used something of her style, her looks and one or two actual incidents, the essential character of Iris is strikingly un-Nancy-like. Iris is a much misunderstood woman, who for gallant and quixotic motives allows her reputation to be far worse than her conduct deserves. The whole point about Iris is that beneath her dashing, modern exterior and her bold disregard for conventions like chastity, she is a romantic idealist. Nancy certainly had a strong romantic streak, but she was far more advanced in behavior and attitudes than the luckless Iris, who dies "for purity."

Part of the secret of *The Green Hat's* success was Arlen's skillful mixture of the trappings of racy, unconventional, modern behavior with veneration for the old standards of loyalty, chivalry, and romance. The story deals with daring subjects like adultery, casual sex, venereal disease, and miscarriages, but never for a moment abandons the idea that certain kinds of behavior are acceptable and some are not. Although Iris is presented as a woman who has affairs, it is made clear that neither the narrator nor Iris herself is particularly happy about this. Before they go to bed together, Iris says portentously: "I am a house of men . . . of their desires and defeats and deaths. . . . Ah me, ah me. Oh, dear." The next morning, Iris is detached, unself-conscious, and apparently unashamed of what she has done, to the narrator's bemused admiration. "She was untouched, unsoiled, impregnable to the grubby, truthful hand of lex femina. She was like a tower of beauty in the morning of the world. It was a sort of blasphemy in her to be beautiful now, to stand in such ordered loveliness, to be neither shameful like a maiden nor shameless like a mondaine, nor show any fussy aftertrill of womanhood, any dingy ember of desire." But, when the man tries to suggest that the night they have spent together may mean something, her assurance crumbles. "Not regret," she said, so calmly. "Shame." She goes on: "You see, I am not what you think. I am not of the women of your life. I am not the proud adventuress who touches men for pleasure, the silly lady who misbehaves for fun. I am the meanest of all, she who destroys her body because she must, she who hates the thing she is, who loathes the thing she does. . . . I would die for purity, in theory."

Though the ambivalence about sex may have a faint flavor of the real Nancy, the agonized tone is most unlike her, as is another remark Iris makes about herself. "It is not good to have a pagan body and a Chislehurst mind, as I have."

So, although Iris has Nancy's expiring voice, tawny hair curled on the cheeks, white skin and blazing blue eyes, she is far more conventional than Nancy, especially about sex. What is more like Nancy than Iris March's confused morality is the observation the narrator-author makes about her somehow being outside her class and her time. It is not hard to see how Arlen, who so passionately wanted to conquer Nancy's world, would be fascinated by her contempt for it and her determination to escape from it. This elusive quality of hers made a powerful impression on him. His narrator says of Iris:

> You had a conviction, a rather despairing one, that she didn't fit in anywhere, to any class, nay, to any nationality. She wasn't that ghastly thing called bohemian, she wasn't any of the ghastly things called "society," "county," upper, middle and lower class. She was, you see, some invention, ghastly or not, of her own. . . . You felt she had outlawed herself from somewhere, but where was that somewhere? You felt she was tremendously indifferent to whether she was outlawed or not.

The end of this passage sees Arlen at his most unbridled. "She was of all time. She was, when the first woman crawled out of the mud of the primeval world. She would be, when the last woman walks towards the unmentionable end."

In her notes on Arlen, Nancy referred in passing to the supposed link between herself and Iris March. She recalled the accuracy of his picture of the hospital and corrects his description of a doll she kept by her bed. Arlen had the doll large and white with a red silk handkerchief tied around her wrist. Nancy remembered something "small and sweet—a little manicure pouch. I have her yet." But at the time, some scraps of evidence show, she was extremely hostile to the suggestion that she "was" Iris. She remembered, though, writing her name in candle smoke on the ceiling of Arlen's flat in Shepherd's Market, an incident that appears at the start of *The Green Hat,* and there is a parallel too with the first meeting with Iris, who loses an emerald ring, and Nancy, who dropped a ruby brooch. There is no evidence, however, that Nancy ever read the one piece of Arlen's later writing that reads like a straight portrait of her. This is an openly autobiographical story called "Confessions of a Naturalised Englishman," published in 1929. Here Arlen wrote as himself, Dikran Kouyoumdjian, and described an episode "nearly ten years ago" when the ambitious young Armenian would-be writer had first met a beautiful, intelligent, strange girl with a bad reputation and a failing marriage to a handsome guards officer. On the first of May 1920 he sat over a cocktail at the Mont Agel waiting for his first date with her. "Yes, I have but to say the words 'The First of May' and there is conjured up before my eyes the tall, the fair, the desperate figure of Priscilla." The narrator, who tells the story as a reminiscence, wonders what has become of her. "In what land, in what house notable for its discomforts and inconveniences, for thou wert ever given to putting the spirit before the flesh—hast thou at last found peace?"

In the next passage, returning to that spring of 1920, Arlen slipped a dexterous further hint that links Priscilla with the heroine of *The Green Hat.*

And here at last she comes, swinging in through the narrow door of the Mont Agel, brightening the looking glasses, ensplendouring all Soho, a long-limbed unsmiling girl crowned with a small crimson hat. . . . But away with hats, black, green or crimson and let us get back to the delicious moment when Priscilla swept into the Mont Agel, bringing with her the gold of the sun and a profound contempt for the Conservative Party, the usages of society, rhymed verse and her mother.

The story contains an interesting impression of Lady Cunard's attitude to her daughter. Some of it reads as if it came from Nancy, but some sounds very much like Arlen's own observation. "As a 'patroness of the arts,' determined to dominate London society, Mrs Byrrh, preoccupied with the conquest of London, had entirely neglected Priscilla as a child and a young girl. Then awakening to Priscilla's beauty, she had made use of her." She encouraged her daughter to make friends with the children of the aristocracy, some of whom were rather "wild."

Then Mrs. Byrrh "found a nice sound husband," a guards officer, for her daughter. But something went wrong. To Mrs. Byrrh's bewilderment Priscilla turned against her and everything she stood for. It appeared that she "disapproved very strongly of the mother who had done so much for her, on the grounds that her mother was a snob, and a silly chatterbox of a snob at that."

Arlen made Mrs. Byrrh much more stupid than Lady Cunard ever could have been, but he gave her Lady Cunard's manner of speech (as imitated by Nancy all her life) and some significant remarks.

In one curious passage the mother discusses with the narrator her daughter's attitude to sex. "But her temperament is cold—decidedly cold. . . . Priscilla lives mentally, as I do— only, of course, I discriminate a little more about people. But as to what they call 'love'—she takes after me in thinking all that kind of thing exceedingly low." She praises her daughter's brilliance but hints at instability.

" 'That girl,' said Mrs Byrrh with a sigh, 'has a truly re-markable mind. If only it was not slightly deranged, she might achieve *un*usual fame.' "

This exchange sounds as if it is based on a conversation between Arlen and Lady Cunard. Lady Cunard certainly used to discuss Nancy with Nancy's friends, and she rather liked Arlen when he became successful; she was given to introducing him as "the only Armenian who has not been massacred." And as Nancy's behavior became—in her mother's eyes—more and more bizarre and inexplicable, Lady Cunard may well have fallen back on the explanation that Nancy must be a bit unbal-anced. It must have been infuriating for Nancy to have her behavior and choice of friends ascribed to mental instability.

The narrator shows himself as an ambitious, struggling young writer who wants to overcome his Armenian back-ground, longs for everything "Priscilla" stood for and is at once captivated and unnerved by her. He describes her as arrogantly independent—she spurns his offer to pay for their first lunch together—and disturbingly complicated underneath her stylish exterior. "Shall I say that there was something about her that seemed to be denying her own worth, that interwoven with her being there was something desperate and self-fatal?"

The narrator muses on this streak of self-destructiveness, the impression "Priscilla" gave that she could never settle for an ordinary existence. "For always we felt that she was not for the likes of us, that she was about to leave us at the call of crusades which we could not hear, that her swift feet were destined by the gods to adventure down dark and dolorous paths whither none but the loftiest spirits might dare to fol-low her."

"Priscilla" despises worldly success. "For of all God's crea-tures the most contemptible to Priscilla were ladies and gentlemen, and so she could not be at peace but with artists and writers, or failing them, with tarts and mashers." She attacks the narrator for writing romantic popular stuff, just as Nancy remembered attacking Arlen.

"What annoys me," Priscilla says, "is that you are out to entertain the sort of people I detest." The narrator admits to himself that he wants above all to be successful but maintains that fundamentally his writing is a form of protest "for at heart I was profoundly anti-social." He surprises Priscilla by envying her the background she so dislikes; she responds with enthusiasm to his semi-joking plan to write a history of Armenia. Then, over the liqueurs, after the plovers' eggs and strawberries, he rashly starts to compare her with her mother.

"Priscilla's face grew sombre, for where her mother was concerned she had a very sketchy sense of humour." He tells her that she is a much more "sinister" snob than her mother. "You absolutely insist on regarding everything that shines at all as second rate, and everything that's grubby as worthy of admiration."

Annoyed, Priscilla ignores her companion and starts to write a letter. Then her handsome guards officer husband appears. The narrator feels sorry for him.

> Why did Priscilla make him so miserable? Why did she not respect his love and devotion? The stories I had heard about her came back to my mind. Wanton and faithless, she was given over to regrettable pleasures with post-Impressionist poets, Bloomsbury intellectuals and athletic Americans. That was what I had heard, and no doubt it was true. What was more likely? I could see the "unbalanced girl" taking lovers as she had eaten the strawberries, with the absorbed ecstasy of an early Christian giving herself up to the pleasures of martyrdom.

To his astonishment, as she is leaving the restaurant, Priscilla makes a surreptitious date with him for dinner that night at the Carlton Grill. Later, he waits for her there and she does not come. Furious, he goes back to his flat off the Fulham Road. He finds Priscilla, dressed in silver, waiting for him.

> "You've got some good books in your sitting room," she said.
> I said nothing.
> "My poems, too, I see."

"Yes, your mother gave them to me."
"The poems of an *un*balanced girl," she mimicked, laughing.

Suddenly he understands how unhappy she is. At the time, she does not tell him why; later on, he hears that she had been driven to behave outrageously by her husband, who did not want an unconventional wife. "Naturally he did not want her to divorce him, for he had his career to think of. . . . He understood Priscilla's character. She had only to be sufficiently goaded and she would play into his hands by behaving stupidly."

The story ends with Priscilla falling asleep on her new friend's bed, while he holds her hand—a less thrilling, but possibly a more convincing ending to a first encounter than that described in *The Green Hat*.

According to Nancy's recollection, she saw much less of Michael Arlen after the summer of 1921, though she bumped into him in Berkeley Square after he had become rich and famous with *The Green Hat* and heard how he had turned himself into a corporation to make the most of his earnings. Nancy never grudged him his wealth and fame, though she never thought much of his writing. By the mid-twenties, when Nancy was becoming more and more involved in Paris life, Arlen was living mostly in America. *The Green Hat* was produced on Broadway in 1925, with Katharine Cornell in her first starring role as Iris, and in London the same year with Tallulah Bankhead. In 1928 Arlen married a beautiful and internationally aristocratic girl, the Countess Atalanta Mercati, and settled near Cannes, but his wish to "belong" was never altogether granted.

It was probably just this outsider quality that chiefly attracted Nancy; she always remembered with affection his naïve delight in the luxuries his industry won for him.

"The good things of life—caviare, plovers' eggs, champagne—it seemed to me it was all as if he had never heard of them, but had discovered them all by himself."

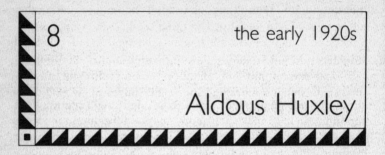

Aldous Huxley

If Michael Arlen stood for the style and romance of the early 1920s, Aldous Huxley was the writer who seemed to capture more sharply the mood of the time. Huxley's early novels were more complex, intelligent, and subversive than Arlen's tales of love and social aspiration, but he too found inspiration of a kind through a relationship with Nancy Cunard.

In 1922 Huxley was twenty-eight, two years older than Nancy. He had been married for two years to Maria Nys, a beautiful Belgian girl he met at Lady Ottoline Morrell's house, Garsington, and they had a baby son. Although he had had some success with his first novel, *Crome Yellow,* they were quite poor and living in a modest flat in Paddington. He was writing regularly for magazines and had signed a contract with Chatto and Windus calling for the delivery of four novels a year. Despite some financial strain, he was happy with his wife and his work.

Aldous Huxley and Nancy had known each other at least since the middle of the war. He made a passing and mildly sardonic reference to her in a letter of 1917, where he mentions contributing to "the well-known Society Anthology, *Wheels,* in company with illustrious young persons like Miss Nancy Cunard." Since then, they had shared several friends, even though Huxley's life was based in more intellectual, Bloomsbury-minded circles than was Nancy's; but Robert Nichols, Evan Morgan, and Tommy Earp became great friends of them both, as did the Hutchinsons, Marie Beerbohm and Iris Tree. They must have encountered each other often at the Café Royal or the Eiffel Tower.

So, as Huxley's friend and biographer, Sybille Bedford (who also became, later, a friend of Nancy's), has written, it is impossible to say exactly when Aldous Huxley fell in love with Nancy. "No records of this episode have emerged. Aldous did not speak of it; on Nancy it left small mark. What remains are his own transparent generalisations scattered through the novels, wisps of the gossip of the time, and what Maria told a few friends."

Huxley, it seems, became suddenly infatuated with Nancy; but she hardly noticed. She liked him and kept him dangling; he would wait miserably for her telephone calls or hang around her at parties or in nightclubs, which he detested. At one point she had a brief and, for her, unimportant affair with him, which left him more in love than ever; but his adoration bored her, and his jealousy irritated her. He once spent a whole night pacing the street below her window.

When Nancy went abroad in the winter of 1922, Huxley thought of following her, but she put him off. In April he joined his wife for two weeks in Italy; but when they returned, he was still miserably infatuated with Nancy.

Some time early in the summer of 1923 Maria Huxley issued an ultimatum. She would leave England the next morning, with Aldous or without him. She packed all night and in the morning they left together. They went again to Italy, where in two months Aldous wrote his second novel, *Antic Hay*. "He wrote it all down," Maria said, "he wrote it all out; it was over. He never looked back. The possession— that one descent of Ate—left a mark on his novel; not his marriage."

There is evidence in Nancy's papers, though, that the affair lingered on a little beyond that early morning departure. In her scrapbook there is a page of photographs taken in Florence and Siena, showing Aldous and Geoffrey Scott, dated 1923–24, and once, decades later, she recalled Huxley, in Italy, suddenly asking her to live with him. She refused because Huxley was already married and had a child. "I did nothing to excite or tempt him," she said. "We saw much of each other for two or three days, without sex, then drifted apart. I never saw him again." Sex, it seemed, though the essence of the affair for Huxley, was not for Nancy, who once told a friend that she found Huxley physically repellent; being in bed with him, she said, was like being crawled over by slugs.

Nancy's presence in several Huxley novels is powerful; but in a way, she may also have altered his life. During the rest of a long and remarkably successful marriage Huxley had other occasional romances; but they were taken lightly by all concerned. The attitude to fidelity adopted by both Huxleys might have been designed to prevent any recurrence of the traumatic Nancy episode.

Over and over again in Huxley's early novels the same situation recurs. An intelligent, imaginative, self-aware young man, usually poor or struggling, becomes physically obsessed with a woman he does not even like and suffers torments of jealousy and self-disgust. A beautiful, erratic, self-centered young woman, usually rich and upper class, toys for a while with her admirer before dismissing him with contempt. If it can be said to be good for a writer to experience extreme human emotions, Nancy was good for Huxley the novelist.

Antic Hay is the first book that Huxley wrote after his affair with Nancy, and is the book in which, according to Maria Huxley, he exorcised his violent passion. It is a deliberately plotless picture of a group of amusing, erratic, fundamentally desperate characters adrift in a chaos of emotions and ideas in the aftermath of the war. It was successfully published in November 1923, sold five thousand copies in its first year, and provoked alarm as well as praise. Though it is hard to imagine readers of the novel feeling that the author is recommending the way of life he describes, some thought that Huxley was advocating cynicism and promiscuity and denigrating the solid old virtues. Huxley's own father did not care for it; but Huxley wrote to him in its defense that it was "a

book written by a member of what I may call the war generation for others of his kind; and . . . it is intended to reflect—
fantastically, of course, but none the less faithfully—the life
and opinions of an age which has seen the violent disruption
of almost all the standards, conventions and values current in
the previous epoch."

It is not hard to find Nancy in *Antic Hay*. At the center of a
motley group of friends and rivals, bohemians, intellectuals
and aspiring socialites drifts the bleak, magnetic, destructive
Myra Viveash. Myra Viveash has Nancy's voice: "her voice,
as she spoke, seemed always on the point of expiring, as
though each word were the last, uttered faintly and break-
ingly from a death bed—the last, with all the profound and
nameless significance of the ultimate word." She also has
Nancy's look. "Mrs. Viveash . . . turned on him, without
speaking, her pale unwavering glance. Her eyes had a formidable capacity for looking and expressing nothing; they were
like the pale blue eyes which peer out of the Siamese cat's
black-velvet mask." And she has the walk. "He watched her
as she crossed the dirty street, placing her feet with meticu-
lous precision one after the other in the same straight line, as
though she were treading a knife edge between goodness only
knew what invisible gulfs. Floating she seemed to go, with a
little spring at every step."

Above all, she has Nancy's power over men; the power to
enslave, inspire, and torment. Apart from the hero of the
novel, Theodore Gumbril ("not Aldous's alter ego, but a
young man with a good infusion of Aldous all the same,"
remarks Sybille Bedford), who has been in love with her and
is still far from immune, she fascinates Lypiatt, the painter,
who struggles with a portrait of her (much as Chile Guevara
had struggled to paint Nancy), and Shearwater, the biologist,
who vainly fights against her power. In this novel Huxley
gave Myra-Nancy extraordinary allure; but he also made her
sad and empty, incapable of love, and contemptuous of the
passions she arouses in the men she gathers around her. The
most striking link with Huxley's own experience comes when

Gumbril, early in the novel, tries to warn Shearwater away from Myra by describing what he had been through on her account.

> "There was a time," he said in a tone that was quite unreally airy, off-hand and disengaged, "years ago, when I totally lost my head about her. Totally. . . . Towards the end of the war it was. I remember walking up this street one night, in the pitch darkness, writhing with jealousy." He was silent. Spectrally, like a dim, haunting ghost he had hung about her; dumbly, dumbly imploring, appealing. "The weak, silent man" she used to call him. And once, for two or three days, out of pity, out of affection, out of a mere desire, perhaps, to lay the tiresome ghost, she had given him what his mournful silence implored—only to take it back almost as soon as accorded.

Huxley's Myra is far from passionate. When Lypiatt asks if he may kiss her, "Mrs Viveash turned towards him. Smiling agonizedly, her eyebrows ironically lifted, her eyes steady and calm, and palely, brightly inexpressive. 'If it really gives you any pleasure,' she said. 'It won't, I may say, to me.' " But when Lypiatt protests that she likes to make men suffer, that she enjoys laughing at them, she denies it. " 'But I don't laugh,' said Mrs Viveash. On the contrary, she was very sorry for him; and what was more, he rather bored her. For a few days, once, she had thought she might be in love with him. His impetuosity had seemed a torrent strong enough to carry her away. She had found out her mistake very soon."

Mrs. Viveash has a past oddly like Nancy's. The reason for her heartlessness is that her true love (not, needless to say, her husband, who is fleetingly mentioned as being on an expedition in Africa, as Sydney Fairbairn was around this time) has been killed in the war. Huxley fills Mrs. Viveash's exquisite, empty head with random thoughts of this dead love, whose name is Tony Lamb. " 'I was very fond of him,' she said at last. 'That's all. He was killed in 1917, just about this time of the year. It seems a very long time ago, don't you think?' "

She tells Gumbril how she doesn't like anyone since Tony died; he says she should try.

" 'But I do try,' said Mrs Viveash. . . . It revolted her now to think how often she had tried; she had tried to like someone, anyone, as much as Tony. She had tried to recapture, to re-evoke, to revivify. And there had never been anything, really, but a disgust. 'I haven't succeeded,' she added, after a pause."

There is more poignancy in Huxley's portrait of Nancy as Myra Viveash than dislike, but all the same, as Sybille Bedford observed, "Mrs Viveash is not so much Nancy Cunard disguised, as Nancy disindividualised, turned into a type, a type, what is more, representing but a fragment of her personality." It is perhaps in the nature of sudden, unhappy and passing love affairs that those concerned never see each other as they really are; but it is also true that Huxley loved Nancy at a particularly uneasy, aimless time in her life.

When Huxley returned to his experience with Nancy in his next novel, *Those Barren Leaves,* which came out in 1925, he remembered still less of her, as a person, but still more vividly the humiliation he had endured. One of the members of Mrs. Aldwinkle's curious collection of guests at her castle in Italy is Francis Chelifer, a struggling poet who describes how he fell deeply in love with a girl called Barbara and how he came to realize, slowly and painfully, that she was not at all the creature of his dreams and fantasies. At one point he says: "I was learning that it is possible to be profoundly and slavishly in love with someone for whom one has no esteem, whom one does not like, whom one regards as a bad character and who finally, not only makes one unhappy but bores one." The way Huxley described Chelifer's role in Barbara's entourage recalls his own role in Nancy's.

> Her success so far had mostly been with genial young soldiers. She had counted few literary men among her slaves. And being infected with the queer snobbery of those who regard an artist, or anyone calling himself by that name, as

somehow superior to other beings—she was more impressed by a Café Royal loafer than by an efficient officer, and considered that it was a more arduous and finer thing to be able to paint, or even appreciate, a cubist picture or play a piece by Bartok on the piano than to run a business or plead in a court of law—being therefore deeply convinced of my mysterious importance and significance—she was flattered to have me abjectly gambolling round her.

The climax in Chelifer's wretched obsession with Barbara comes when he spends most of a night waiting outside her house, as Huxley once did outside Nancy's. He knows she has other admirers and is especially jealous of one in particular.

To Barbara, no doubt, I appeared as a kind of minor Aristotle. But what made the comparison somewhat less flattering to me was the fact that she was equally gratified by the attentions of another literary man, the swarthy Syrian with the blue jowl and the silver monocle. Even more gratified, I think; for he wrote poems which were frequently published in the monthly magazines (mine, alas, were not) and, what was more, he never lost an opportunity of telling people that he was a poet; he was for ever discussing the inconveniences and compensating advantages of possessing an artistic temperament.

It seems likely that Huxley here is writing about Michael Arlen, substituting Syrian for Armenian and poetry for novels.

Huxley's first novel to sell well, Point Counter Point, came out in the autumn of 1928. By the end of the year it had sold over ten thousand copies. Then and since, the novel seemed to represent Huxley's considered view of postwar intellectual, social, sexual, and political confusion. It is a witty, erudite, desperate novel. Huxley himself called it "a rather good, but also a rather frightful novel," and D. H. Lawrence wrote to him: "I think you've shown the truth, perhaps the last truth, about you and your generation, with really fine courage. It seems to me it would take ten times the courage to write Point Counter Point than it took to write Lady C."

Point Counter Point is full of "real" people. Part of its fascination has always been the element of *roman à clef* about it. Philip and Elinor Quarles are very close to Aldous and Maria Huxley. Rampion is akin to D. H. Lawrence, Burlap has a powerful whiff of John Middleton Murry, and it is impossible to read of Everard Webley without thinking of Oswald Mosley. Again Nancy Cunard is not hard to recognize. Lucy Tantamount (though dark-haired instead of fair) is rich, arrogant, sexually powerful, promiscuous, and destructive. Huxley gave Lucy a powerful social mother, Lady Edward, with a particular interest in music, an invisible husband, and a genial former lover, a grand old artist.

This time the Nancy character's chief victim is not the character closest to Huxley himself. But poor Walter Bidlake's abject passion for Lucy Tantamount, and the way she treats him, dragging him around London at all hours of the night while the agonized and pregnant Marjorie waits at home, recalls most powerfully the period of Huxley's subjection to Nancy. So does Walter's excruciating awareness of Lucy's limitations and reputation. "She was all the people enviously or disapprovingly called her, and yet the most exquisite and marvellous of beings." To Illidge, the outsider with unformed revolutionary ideas, Lucy Tantamount represents the worst of her type. "The consummate flower of this charming civilisation of ours—that's what she is. The logical conclusion, so far as most people are concerned, of having money and leisure."

The hallmarks of Huxley's experience with Nancy are all there. Walter knows Lucy does not love him, knows she is not really worthy of love, but cannot help himself. Lucy likes to have him in servile attendance, despises him for loving her so much, and sleeps with him casually once or twice. In *Point Counter Point* Huxley made Lucy harder, more vicious and emptier than Nancy, for all her selfishness, could ever have been; just as Walter is more stupidly abject than Huxley himself, for all his infatuation, could have been. But there is one particular episode that reads very much like an elaboration by Huxley on something he heard either from Nancy or about her. Lucy Tantamount is in Paris, and Walter is hoping desperately that she will allow him to join her. He makes the mistake of writing her a pleading, jealous, proprietary letter, which brings a devastating response. Lucy, to teach him a lesson, writes telling him how one day she has let herself be picked up in the street by a handsome dark-skinned young Italian. They go straight to a cheap hotel and make love. She describes the episode with excruciating vividness. "He came at me as though he were going to kill me, with clenched teeth. I shut my eyes, like a Christian martyr in front of a lion. Martyrdom's exciting. Letting oneself be hurt, humiliated, used like a doormat—queer. I like it. Besides, the doormat uses the user. It's complicated."

As Huxley grew farther away from the real Nancy, and as the memory of whatever had actually occurred between them faded, two themes remained. The first was the memory of his own humiliation; the second was the frightening power over men possessed by the beautiful independent woman who uses her sexuality without love. In *Point Counter Point* the intelligent, admirable Maria Huxley-like Elinor Quarles describes Lucy's conduct very much as Nancy's friends still remember hers.

"Lucy has another advantage where men like Walter are concerned. She's one of those women who have the temperament of a man. Men can get pleasure out of casual encounters. Most women can't. They've got to be in love, more or less. They've got to be emotionally involved. All but a few of them. Lucy's one of the few. She has the masculine detachment. She can separate her appetite from the rest of her soul."

Increasingly, Nancy was to show herself capable of doing so. More women are capable of such behavior than most men and women allow. Many have always behaved so, but discreetly. Nancy never bothered about discretion. When men indulge themselves sexually, there may be disapproval, but it seldom spills over into contempt or becomes a reason for dismissing them as unbalanced, or reflects badly upon their work, or colors all their activities with a lurid haze. Women still take a greater risk when they break rules; in the 1920s, for all the talk of a new sexual freedom, the rules were still strong.

Nancy did not encounter either of the Huxleys again, after the middle twenties, although she is mentioned in Aldous Huxley's correspondence as a possible publisher for *Lady Chatterley's Lover* in 1929. Nor, apparently, did she talk of him much, though his biographer recalls a lunch party in the south of France in the late fifties or early sixties when Nancy spoke of her regard for Huxley's writing and, in a detached and almost puzzled way, of her surprise at realizing that such a minor romance for her had apparently meant more to him. There is one odd postscript to the affair; John Johnson, the son of a friend of Nancy's who lived in Rome and whom she saw sometimes in the fifties, vividly remembered her remarking one day, inconsequentially, that she was of course the woman in the memorable episode in *Eyeless in Gaza* when a dead dog falls from an airplane onto two lovers sunbathing on a sunny rooftop in the south of France. Apart from this bizarre and elusive fragment, there is no evidence that she ever gave her role as inspirer of Huxley's female characters even the irritated attention she gave to Arlen's writings.

Because Nancy's presence in the fashionable and influential novels of Michael Arlen and Aldous Huxley was strong, and undeniable, she has tended to be cited ever since when any novelist of the period introduces a certain kind of heroine. The notion has persisted, for instance, that Lady Brett Ashley, in Ernest Hemingway's novel *The Sun Also Rises,* was based on Nancy; but there is no evidence for this identification apart from hearsay. Both Brett and Nancy lived in Paris (when Hemingway's novel was published in 1926, Nancy was based there), conducted open love affairs, drank too much, and were willful, well connected, and rich. But Brett's rueful gallantry, her figure ("built with curves like the hull of a racing yacht"), and her idiom ("Hello, you chaps") are not Nancy-like in the least. Moreover Nancy never knew Hemingway at all well and herself believed Brett to be modeled on another expatriate Englishwoman, Duff Twysden.

As time passed, the novelists' version of Nancy became more and more remote from the realities of her life and character. That Michael Arlen and Aldous Huxley had been infatuated with her helped them to capture her unusual beauty and sexual power, but much of her nature is missing. Both, however, perceived the shadows of dissatisfaction and self-destructiveness beneath the bright mask; no heroine based on Nancy was likely to live happily ever after.

Decades later, Nancy, in yet a further fictional disguise, appears in the pages of another important novel. Evelyn Waugh knew Nancy slightly, and was for a time pursued by her mother. In the last volume of the Sword of Honour trilogy, the literary magazine editor Everard Spruce talks about the death, late in 1945, of one of Waugh's memorable anti-heroines, Virginia Troy. Spruce tries to explain to two young secretaries what was special about Virginia, and why, despite her appalling behavior, he had admired her.

"Virginia Troy was the last of twenty years succession of heroines," he said. "The ghosts of romance who walked between the two wars." He reads aloud a passage from *Antic Hay* describing Mrs. Viveash's elegant, floating walk.

"I bet neither of you know who wrote that. You'll say Michael Arlen. . . . Anyway the passage I read, believe it or not, is Aldous Huxley. Mrs Viveash. Hemingway coarsened the image with his Brett, but the type persisted—in books and in life. Virginia was the last of them—the exquisite, the doomed and the damning, with expiring voices—a whole generation younger. We shall never see anyone like her again in literature or in life and I'm very glad to have known her."

1 Nevill Holt, Leicestershire, in
1902. The girl in the doorway is
probably Nancy, age six.

2–3   Far left: Sir Bache Cunard, Bart., in 1881, age
30, in a *Spy* cartoon. Left: Bache Cunard as a boy,
age 10. He is dressed as a Greek soldier. Above: Sir
Bache and Lady Cunard, formerly Miss Maud Alice
Burke, at the time of their marriage in 1895.

4–5 Left: George Moore painted by J. B. Yeats, 1905. Below left: drawing by Max Beerbohm of Nancy taking George Moore for a walk. Below: Sir Thomas Beecham, about 1920. Right Lady Emerald Cunard in the late 1920s.

TELEGRAMS, MEDBOURNE.

NEVILL HOLT,
MARKET HARBORO'.

6–7 Nancy with her
father at Nevill Holt, 1912.
Oval inset: with E. W.
("Bimbo") Tennant, about
1914. Below: Nancy
(right) with two friends,
July 1914.

3–9 Clockwise from top left:
Nancy (left) with Lady Diana
Manners at the races, April 1914;
Nancy's wedding day, Novem-
ber 15, 1916; Sydney Fairbairn
about 1914; Sydney with a
brother officer, about 1915;
Nancy (right) with Lady Diana
Manners and other friends, April
1914; Felicity Tree, Nancy, Lady
Violet Charteris, and Lady Diana
Manners in a musical tableau at
the French Embassy, July 1914.

10–11 Left: Nancy painted by Alvaro Guevara in her mother's drawing room in Grosvenor Square, winter 1919. Below: portrait of Nancy wearing her mother's top hat, by Eugene MacCown, Paris, 1923. Right: Janet Flanner before a fancy dress party, wearing the same top hat, Paris, 1924.

12–13 Drawing of Nancy by
Wyndham Lewis, Venice, 1922.
Photograph by Curtis Moffat,
about 1927.

14–15 Friends of the early twenties.
Top left: Michael Arlen. Left: Aldous Huxley.
Above: Edith and Osbert Sitwell.

16 Below: at Sanary in the south of France, 1921. Left: with George Moore at Sanary.

Travels and Poetry

To turn from the fictional Nancy to the actual Nancy of the early 1920s is to realize how much the novelists had left out. Her life was full of movement and contrast. She was constantly traveling, mainly between London and Paris but also between Berkshire and Normandy, Venice and Biarritz, the resorts of the south of France and the hilltop towns of Tuscany. Nancy led the life of a rich society girl, but what she longed to be was a poet. Poetry was a serious matter for Nancy during those years; between 1921 and 1925 she had a series of poems published in journals, and she brought out three volumes.

Early in 1921, when Nancy was still in Paris recovering from her illness and series of operations, her first book of poems, *Outlaws,* was published in London by Elkin Matthews and Marrot. She subsidized the publication herself (a practice that was more usual and acceptable then than it is now; Elkin Matthews and Marrot had a good reputation and had published Pound's and Eliot's early poems). *Outlaws* includes five poems that had appeared in *Wheels* in 1916.

Nancy's subjects were nature—the River Nene, the changing light of evening—and her own emotional complexities; they reveal her cast of mind at twenty-five as romantic, impassioned and rebellious. There is a sense of strain about the poems; the feelings and perceptions are too strong and confused for the language, which is often curiously stilted, old-fashioned, almost archaic. Many of the poems are written in a monotonous iambic pentameter. In "Voyages North" she longs to escape from people and cities:

> . . . —But if I were free
> I would go on, see all the northern continents
> Stretch out before me under winter sunsets: . . .
> . . . I should cure my heart of longing and impatience
> And all the penalties of thought-out pleasure,
> Those aftermaths of degradation
> That come when silly feasts are done.

In "The Wreath" she talks, melodramatically, about love.

> Love has destroyed my life, and all too long
> Have I been enemy with life, too late
> Unlocked the secrets of existence! there
> Found but the ashes of a fallen city
> Stamped underfoot, the temple of desires
> Run through with fire and perished with defeat . . .
> My loves have been voracious, many coloured,
> Fantastic, sober, all-encompassing,
> Have flown like summer swallows at the sun
> And dipped into a wintry world of water: . . .

"In Answer to a Reproof" is one of the more successful poems; it manages a comparatively clear statement of its writer's agitated, rebellious state of mind and feeling of being different. Read in the context of Nancy's later life, the poem seems prescient; but in 1921 it was self-dramatizing.

> Let my impatience guide you now, I feel
> You have not known that glorious discontent
> That leads me on: the wandering after dreams
> And the long chasing in the labyrinth
> Of fancy, and the reckless flight of moods. . . .
>
> . . . I the perfect stranger,
> Outcast and outlaw from the rules of life,
> True to one law alone, a personal logic

That will not blend with anything, nor bow
Down to the general rules . . .

But the reviews of *Outlaws* were, on the whole, remarkably good; more than good enough to encourage a young poet. The *Times Literary Supplement* wrote: "Nancy Cunard has an unquestionable gift of language, even of eloquence, and some of the pieces are strongly and skilfully fashioned. . . . There is enough good work in this book to make us anxious to hear Miss Cunard again." The *Nation* was only slightly less laudatory: "Miss Cunard's poems are of unequal quality, due rather to a wavering technique than any poverty of central fires. . . . Pride, disillusion, irritability, vanity of quest, frustration, the unprofitableness of experience mingled with an intellectual pride and dignity are almost the whole story of these entirely genuine and strangely individual, if imperfect poems." The *New Statesman's* young reviewer, Edgell Rickword, who ten years later was to be very close to Nancy, bracketed her book with new poems by Robert Graves, Maurice Baring, and Charlotte Mew; "one can feel the pulse of an original mind beating through a rather uncongenial medium."

George Moore reviewed the book for the *Observer* on February 27, 1921, in a long piece that managed to combine, as Nancy wrote years later, "great praise and hard criticism." His verdict was that *Outlaws* was a book "in which there is much more genius than there is in the mass of her contemporaries, and much less talent. By genius we mean a special way of feeling and seeing that separates a man or woman from the crowd, and by talent we mean handicraft, tact, judgement. Genius cannot be acquired, we have it or we have not; but talent can be."

He urged Nancy to work on her technique because "the beauty of the book is marred by much negligent writing"; he questioned especially her syntax and punctuation. However, the passion behind the poetry reminded him of Héloïse, Saint Teresa, and Emily Brontë. What Nancy had to do, he felt, was to learn control and to be prepared to correct and rework her poetic outpourings. "This is well enough in a first book, but ultimate genius is not in explosions but in restraints."

Nancy was pleased and grateful. Moore wrote her an encouraging letter and received a "most enthusiastic" reply. But a fortnight later, he still had not heard from Lady Cunard: "I hope you liked the article I wrote about Nancy's book," he wrote to her. "Everybody I met during the week spoke to me about it, writers, publishers, and friends. Mary Hunter thought that I mingled praise with admonition most skilfully." It seems that Lady Cunard had reservations. Moore was soon writing to her again, a little reproachfully: "I am glad you liked the review I wrote about Nancy's book, but am puzzled, for you say 'some parts of your review.' You surely do not think it should have been all praise? The faults I mentioned were mentioned for I wished the review to read like a genuine expression of opinion."

Lady Cunard took a keen interest in the promotion of her daughter's poetry. The distinguished editors she invited to lunch or dinner were likely to receive strong hints that it would please their hostess if Nancy's poems appeared in their journals. During the spring of 1921, when Nancy was traveling in France and Italy, Lady Cunard acted as her agent, first with H. W. Massingham, editor of the *Nation,* and then with J. L. Garvin, editor of the *Observer.* Each paper published two of Nancy's new poems. On May 30 Garvin wrote to Lady Cunard: "Will I publish both? Rather: I had no idea your daughter wrote so well"—apparently he did not read the reviews in his own newspaper—"and you know I am fastidious about poetry." Even the social columns started to notice Nancy's writing; one item from France during the summer informed its readers that the fashionable Mrs. Fairbairn "writes poetry and is certainly emulating her well-known mother, Lady Cunard, in her liking for the intelligentsia."

During the summer of 1921 Nancy must have sent one of her new poems to Ezra Pound, whom she had first met over tea with her mother in 1915. Pound in 1921 was living in Paris with his wife Dorothy and, among other literary activities, acting as a talent scout for the American literary magazine, the *Dial*. Pound wrote Nancy a long and detailed letter of criticism and advice about poetry; Nancy stuck it into her poetry scrapbook.

Lovely Nancy:
I will take the poem to the Dial this evening, but, my dear, why, why the devil do you write in that obsolete dialect and with the cadences of the late Alfred Tennyson. What is good in the poem is that you have not tried to lie or to exaggerate, and as in other poems of yours that I have seen, you do hunt about for a visual accurate adjective. It is not Georgian, at least that is a gain. I mean Georgian as someone defined 'em "Ils détachent des sentiments pour les accommoder à leur vocabulaire."

You haven't asked for criticism only I don't know who else is to give it to you, nobody in England knows anything, except Eliot, and he is too weary and too polite to distribute it. Old Hueffer knows, and has written more common-sense about getting rid of the dead [hand] of poetic dialect than anyone else has; only nobody reads him. And it is damned hard to get the order of words in a poem as simple and natural as that of speech. Iambic pentameter is a snare because it constantly lets one in for dead phrases like "in this midnight hour"; and rhyme is no good unless you use it without letting it disturb the order of words, or inducing words that add nothing to the meaning. Does *"estray"* exist save as a legal term, adjective for lost cattle? Twice "all," *all* friendly, *all* gay. . . . One must get the palate clean; must get the speech of poetry even more vivid than that of prose; one adjective per noun usually enough; though there are times when you can use ten (at least I don't know whether any poet has ever done that *tour de force* but . . .) . . .

Damn it all, midnight is midnight, it is not "this midnight hour," also you twist the tenses for the sake of rhyme. And lots, lots of words that do not add anything to the presentation, but tell the reader nothing he wouldn't know if you had left them out. . . .

Art is long. Paris is sweltering hot and unfit for human habitation. I wish you would come back and deliver me from the ferocious mercies of wandering American females. I am almost certain the Dial will throw out this poem, but if you wd. go through your stuff and cut out the needless words and the phrases that have been used already, and the hwill or whatever the Welsh call it, the motion of pentameter dragging with it the Victorian or Elizabethan "poetic" word order, I think we might get something through.

Vale et me ama

Ezra

Most of this excellent advice must have wounded Nancy, though she remembered it always as an example of Pound's kindness and generosity to young writers and claimed that he had taught her useful lessons. However, there is little evidence that she took it to heart in her subsequent writing. Nancy, for all her approval of modernism and the avant-garde and her long arguments with George Moore about free verse and the necessity of abandoning poetic conventions, had been too deeply imbued with the Edwardian notion of poetic language and the romantic, old-fashioned image of the poet and his calling ever to let it go. She did not have a natural, unforced poetic talent. She tried too hard. As for "too weary, too polite" Eliot, it was during the winter of 1921 that Ezra Pound worked over Eliot's first draft of The Waste Land and persuaded him to cut out a long section that ridiculed a society girl who writes poetry. The girl is named Fresca and sounds suspiciously like Nancy. (See Appendix 1, page 443.)

Nancy was happiest when she could combine writing poetry with living in the country and entertaining her friends. She spent the summer of 1921 at a rented house in Saint-Martin-Eglise, four miles from Dieppe. She had relays of guests, including her cousin Edward Cunard, Tommy Earp, Michael Arlen, Marie Beerbohm, and Iris and Curtis Moffat. George Moore stayed for five or six days at a nearby hotel, and Nancy remembered the pleasure he took in the lush Norman countryside, with its willows and poplars and purple loosestrife, the fields of yellow mustard, and "the way the rooks flew one evening, the peculiar run of the stoat." Moore was

shocked to discover when he arrived that Nancy was alone
with a young man (she maintained that far from being a lover
of hers, the young man was attached to one of her women
friends whose arrival had been delayed). They had long talks
about her writing, and Moore tried to persuade her to attempt
a narrative poem; he even provided her with the plot, a section discarded from his recently published *Héloïse and Abélard*.
It concerned a "Lady Geraldine (or any other name that
strikes your fancy), living in a castle . . . brought by the romance of the forest to dream of adventures that might befall
her." Nancy was touched, but found the theme altogether too
pre-Raphaelite for her taste: "none of this, with all due defer-
ence, was for me."

The scrapbook Nancy kept during the early 1920s evokes
the astonishing whirl of places and people in which she lived.
The year 1922 is especially hectic. Until February she was in a
rented villa at Sanary in the south of France, with guests
including Curtis and Iris Moffat, and their little son, Ivan.
(Curtis Moffat took some delightful photographs of Nancy
with the small boy, in which, despite her usual lack of interest
in children, she looks relaxed and affectionate.) Once again
George Moore was among those present. In March she
moved on to Monte Carlo, where Lady Cunard was staying;
a report in the social columns of *Sketch* described how "Lady
Cunard's daughter Mrs. Fairbairn—who is almost more like
Lady Cunard than Lady Cunard herself!—is often to be seen
tempting fortune at roulette. One afternoon she wore a
mauve tulle scarf tied across her eyebrows, with floating ends,
under a big grey felt hat, which looked oh, so Spanish!" By
April she was back at Fontainebleau, near Paris; in the summer, she took a house at Eddington, near Hungerford in
Berkshire, where St. John Hutchinson, T. W. Earp, Nina
Hamnett, Marjorie Trefusis, Diana and Duff Cooper, and Aldous Huxley among others visited her and had their photographs taken sitting on the grass or visiting a local fairground.
When Nancy herself appears in these snapshots, she usually
looks very thin, very lively and holds a cigarette in her hand.

In the late summer she moved on to Deauville; in September, she went to Spain. By October she had taken a house in Venice; another society reporter informed readers that she was seeing something of her friend Lady Diana Cooper; "but as a rule Nancy affects the society of Futurist Artists and Highbrows." Among the friends she saw or had to stay with in Venice were the Sitwell brothers, William Walton, two new American friends she had made in Paris, the writer and publisher Robert McAlmon, the painter Eugene MacCown, and Wyndham Lewis, who was photographed sitting at Nancy's side smoking a pipe and glowering from beneath a huge black hat. Nancy and Lewis had a brief affair in Venice; but she would later recall that she soon became tired of his boastfulness about his success with women and his habit of making jealous scenes. A few years later, Lewis, according to his widow, included Nancy in his satirical novel *The Roaring Queen* as the teen-age Baby Bucktrout, bent on seducing the gardener at her mother's country home; but in Venice he made a lovely drawing of her standing at the window of her *palazzo* and sold it to the *Sketch* as number 2 in a series of "Wyndham Lewis Portraits of Society People."

In December, she was back in the south of France; then briefly in London before returning to Paris in January 1923. Anyone who loved Nancy at this time had to catch her on the wing; as she took off for Paris, George Moore sent her a plaintive rondel entitled "For Nancy Who Is About to Leave Us."

> Summer has passed away
> And loveliness is dead;
> And all the books are read,
> What shall I do today?
>
> The autumn dight in grey
> Brings winter to her bed
> Summer has passed away
> And loveliness is dead.

Only the robin's lay
Is heard around the stead
And from its eaves are fled
The birds that came in May.
Summer has passed away.

The Paris of the early 1920s was bursting with talent and originality. The expatriates—mostly Americans, mostly aspiring writers or artists—who made Paris their center were attracted by the bohemian tradition, which made experiment in the arts appropriate rather than eccentric, and by the exchange rate, which made living cheap and good. At the same time a new generation of young French intellectuals was developing an approach to art and society that challenged all existing ideas.

Nancy was strongly drawn to both groups; indeed she, along with a handful of other foreign women (such as Sylvia Beach, Peggy Guggenheim, or Caresse Crosby), played an important part in linking them together with patronage and friendship. Among the Americans she made friends especially with Robert McAlmon, Walter Lowenfels, Eugene Mac-Cown, and Kay Boyle. When, thirty years later, she picked out 1923 as the year when she began to be her real self, it is likely that she had two things chiefly in mind. During that year she began to settle down in Paris, instead of simply including Paris as a frequent stopping place in her gyrations around Europe; and it was around that time that she began several friendships that were to have a deep and lasting effect on her. She became ally, lover, and patron to a number of her new friends, most of whom had very little money. Nancy had plenty, along with her other striking attributes of looks, style and intelligence, and those who moved in her circle at that time all remember one thing clearly: Nancy always paid, and appeared to enjoy doing so. She believed fiercely in her protégés' talents (sometimes, though not always, without much reason) and supported them morally and materially in any way she could.

Probably the most crucial new friend she made at this time was Tristan Tzara, the young Rumanian writer and iconoclast who had invented Dada, an irreverent, deliberately random approach to art and writing and life in Zurich in the early years of the war. Tzara was a small, dark, energetic character whom Nancy took to at once; they became close friends, drank and laughed together uproariously, went to parties in bizarre costumes. Man Ray photographed them together before the Bal Beaumont in 1924, Tzara on his knees kissing Nancy's hand, she wearing a silver trouser suit, a mask, and her father's old top hat. It was largely through Tzara that Nancy became linked with the newest, most provocative avant-garde movement in Paris, which was soon to evolve out of Dada into Surrealism. Tzara wrote a strange Dada play for Nancy and dedicated it to her, *Mouchoir de Nuages;* he also introduced her to another expatriate Rumanian, Brancusi, who was soon to make a wooden sculpture inspired by Nancy, *Jeune Fille Sophistiquée*.

But Nancy's links with her background remained strong. When she was in London, she would always join some of her mother's lunch or dinner parties; Lady Cunard had recently moved to an even grander house in Carlton House Terrace. Nancy preferred to stay in rooms above the Eiffel Tower. "The comfort was nil, the room cheap, the convenience considerable," Nancy recalled. "Food, drink, and hours perfect." In Paris, where she would stay in small left bank hotels or rented flats in Montmartre or Montparnasse, she would also see her mother when Lady Cunard descended on the Ritz or another grand hotel on her way to the fashionable resorts. Puzzled though she was by Nancy's raffish new friends and peculiar interest in Dada and ultramodern painting and writing, Lady Cunard was quick to recognize talent when it suited her. She commissioned the clever young American photographer Man Ray to take pictures of herself and her daughter in 1923, soon after he had become a friend of Nancy's. Raymond Mortimer, who was beginning to make a name for himself as a critic, remembers "delightful" dinners in London and Paris with Nancy, Lady Cunard, and Sir Thomas Beecham.

Above all the aged George Moore, as well as writing steadily to Nancy about her poetry, and giving her tender, sensible (and unheeded) advice about the need to live a quiet, more disciplined life if she wanted to attract the Muse, saw her frequently in Paris. They were both aware that she was finding in the Paris of the 1920s the same kind of release and inspiration he had found there in the 1870s. Unlike the prosaic Sir Bache, the old lion could easily be made part of Nancy's life. She enjoyed seating him among her new friends, as she did one special evening in the winter of 1923:

"It was Christmas Eve or Christmas night that I set him at the top of a long, narrow table of twelve at the dinner I gave for him in the room upstairs at the Rotonde. . . . I hoped he would not mind, nor did he mind in the least, that everyone else save Brancusi was rather young." She placed Moore between Marie Beerbohm and Dolly Wilde, Oscar Wilde's niece. Tzara and Brancusi were there, Eugene MacCown, Iris Tree (now separated from Curtis Moffat), and Jan Sliwinski, a Polish musician.

More friends appeared after dinner: Pierre de Massot, a writer; Mary Reynolds, the American who lived with Marcel Duchamp; the painter Nina Hamnett. Two women in particular pleased Moore that evening. "Yvonne Georges, the singer and diseuse, with her Eton Crop and immense, expressive eyes, and Clotilde Vail, whose long golden hair could be flung to the ground. Both had dressed themselves to perfection for him. One looked like a Manet in black and white with something vaguely pink that nestled or floated; the other in blue and green with a touch of yellow was a Renoir come to life."

An extraordinary episode took place between George

Moore and Nancy in Paris around this time that she later described with great gentleness and delicacy. Moore was an old man reminded of his romantic youth in Paris by the beautiful, wayward Nancy, for whom he felt a love that was partly paternal, partly not. When they were alone together, they would often talk about her loves, and his. "Tell me about your lovers," he would say. Then he began to ask her to let him see her naked. " 'I wish you would let me see you na-aked. . . . I am sure you have a lovely body, now why won't you let me see it?' . . . I told him there was a long scar on one side of me, he would hate the sight of that." But Moore persisted; the scar was nothing; he was an old man; what was the harm? Nancy, although not shocked, was puzzled. "At no time between us had there been any passages—the word he sometimes applied to amorous tentatives—unless that delaying kiss, now on the cheek, now on the lips, un vrai baiser plantureux, could be called such?"

Then, one night in Paris, after a leisurely dinner at Foyot's where Moore had taken rooms, he asked her again:

> "I do wish you would let me see you naked . . . I am an old man . . . Oh! At least let me see your naked back!"
>
> Now equally suddenly, something within me said "Do this!" and without more ado, facing away from him, I took off all my clothes, standing motionless a few feet from where he sat. How lightly, how easily it came about. My clothes left me, lying in a graceful summer pool on the floor, as if they had slipped away of themselves. The night was warm and the mood serene. Without hesitation, my long, naked back and legs were at last in front of him and the silence was complete. It would be full-on he was looking at them and I did not turn my head. Of what could he be thinking? At length came a slow, murmuring sigh: "Oh what a beautiful back you have, Nancy, it is as long as a weasel's. What a beautiful back."

When Moore's next book, *Ulick and Soracha,* came out in 1926, Nancy found her back had been given to the Irish peasant woman, Brigit, married to the old, dying harper, Tadgh.

"So when you read of the back that is like a weasel's, with a dip in the middle, that back is mine as he saw it, with never a word or a gesture, but only a long, slow sigh to end the silence in the room."

In the spring of 1923, on another trip to Italy, Nancy met a man, again, like George Moore, a well-known writer many years older than herself, for whom she formed a lasting affection that had some of the same ingredients as her feeling for Moore: the respect of the pupil for a literary master and a certain complicity in matters of sexual adventure. In Florence she found Osbert and Sacheverell Sitwell, friends since her debutante days; they decided that she must be introduced to their friend Norman Douglas. Since the publication of *South Wind,* which had so impressed Nancy in 1919, Douglas had become famous, and slightly scandalous in just the way that would attract Nancy. He had had to leave England in 1917 after a homosexual scandal involving a young boy. She was intrigued by the way in which the Sitwells, half-teasingly, gave Douglas "the big build-up. . . . The aureole of legend around [him] was high in colour and, above all, mysterious. . . . They kept saying, maddeningly, 'I should be careful if I were you . . .' What could that possibly mean? A sudden, covert pill in my wine? A giddy moonlit drive round the town under the rug in an old cab?"

After a long wait over dinner in a *trattoria,* Douglas finally appeared. Nancy observed "a perfectly normal, if dignified and courteous presence: tallish, broad-shouldered, well-set, a man of fifty or so, I thought—with a fine head, very clear cut features, sharp tip to long nose, piercing blue eyes of aquatic flint under thick curving eyebrows. . . . A rather florid or high complexion, . . . very forthright and straightforward in manner. . . . Not in the least formidable. . . . We had a good, long look at one another."

Nancy and Norman Douglas seemed to have taken to each other at once, despite the fact that she revealed during their first conversation that when in Florence she liked to look at paintings by Signorelli, Benozzo Gozzoli, and Piero della

Francesca, prime examples of the Renaissance period, which Douglas had elected to despise as weak and over-aesthetic.

They met again in Italy the following year; this time Nancy brought Tristan Tzara and Eugene MacCown to meet him. As she remembered, Douglas and Tzara got on well, though she could have wished there had been more discussion of what Dada was all about. "I should have liked to hear you [Douglas] on the score of Dada philosophy, for there were many things in its attacks on academic pomps that would have appealed to you." She remembered thinking at the time that the meeting would have made a good subject for a cartoon by Beerbohm, and invented a caption: "Prandial first encounter between author of famous novel incorporating all known and several invented sins—*South Wind*—and founder of greatest modern iconoclastic movement—*Dada*."

Douglas's great friend, the Florentine bookseller Pino Orioli, was there too—and, predictably, a young Italian boy who apparently told Orioli he thought Nancy would look like an asparagus with her clothes off because she was so tall and thin.

The warm friendship between Nancy and Douglas never wavered, despite his alarm at her restlessness, sometimes excessive drinking, and chaotic personal life. Mutual friends like Harold Acton remember him as a steadying influence who was never afraid to tell her when she was going too far. Douglas, who loved food, deplored her lack of appetite; he once said she ate like a dyspeptic butterfly.

Meanwhile, in London, another book of Nancy's poems was about to appear; *Sublunary* was published by Hodder and Stoughton in June 1923. The characteristics of *Outlaws* were still strongly present: introspection and self-analysis, defiant statements of independence from convention, and a passionate, romantic grasping after complex, metaphysical poetic statements. The style is more varied, but the poetry still seems strained and wordy. She included a handful of poems in French, and the book was illustrated by Wyndham Lewis's Venice drawing.

Sublunary contained several poems about Nancy's childhood. In "These Rocked the Cradle" she imagined malign fates standing around her when she was born, including "crooked courage, backbiting and self-defiant" and claimed "a mist of uncertainty/Was my fond nurse." The only one of "this life's alarmers" whom she did not claim as a guiding spirit was "Jealousy."

Another poem is simpler and somewhat more successful. She wrote it about the only one of her governesses whom she remembered with affection.

> She was a rebel governess,
> Who came from Toulon in the south,
> Red cherries tumbling on her hat,
> Loud laughter breaking at her mouth.
>
> Came to the Midlands there to teach
> A girl of seven sullen-hearted—
> Her voice was full of life's adventure,
> Her eye too gay, so she departed. . . .

She was also moved to write poems about a walk through the "feathery fields,/Of ancient mustards golden to the sun" near Cahors, in the Dordogne (which she first visited around this time after hearing about its beauties from Ezra Pound) and about a painted old woman she saw eating alone in a restaurant at Bandol, in the south of France. She also included a long, nostalgic poem, "To the Eiffel Tower Restaurant." She recalled

> Those old nights of drinking,
> Furtive adventures, solitary thinking . . .

and she could not help wondering whether the Tower was still the same. The poem ends:

> I think the Tower shall go up to heaven
> One night in a flame of fire, about eleven.

> I always saw our carnal-spiritual home
> Blazing upon the sky symbolically . . .
> If we go to heaven in a troop
> The Tower must be our ladder,
> Vertically,
> Climbing the ether with its swaying group.
>   . . . Stulik shall lead the pack
> Until its great disintegration, when
> God sets us deftly in a new Zodiac.

The reviews of *Sublunary* were less encouraging than those of *Outlaws,* but by no means bad. The *Times Literary Supplement* called the book "thoroughly acceptable" but noticed "a tendency to be thin and wordy." The *Daily Telegraph* praised the poems' "haunting lyricism," but the *Manchester Guardian* decided the book "shows promise rather than achievement." Among the least kind was a review in the *Spectator* by Amabel Williams Ellis, whose brother, John Strachey, was to become a close friend of Nancy's. She discerned "A permeating sense of effort not to be young lady-ish."

Back in Paris in the autumn of 1923 Nancy made two more important new friends in the young American writers Janet Flanner and Solita Solano. Janet Flanner was a journalist from Indianapolis, whom Eugene MacCown christened the Great Stone Face because of her striking looks. She had been in Paris since 1921, wanted to be a novelist, but was to be deflected into becoming one of the finest American reporters in Europe after she began writing for the young *New Yorker* in 1925. Solita Solano was small, dark and pretty and had written about the theater for a Boston newspaper before arriving in Paris in the early twenties. She too was writing novels. Both women had steadier natures than Nancy. ("To be in the presence of Nancy," according to Solita Solano, "was more like coming to grips with a force of nature than being out for an evening of gossip and dancing after a hard day's work.")

They were both about Nancy's age; like her, they had both experienced early, unsuccessful marriages. Their lives were to be founded on friendship and companionship between women, and through them and their circle Nancy came to value female solidarity, affection and mutual support in a way that was new to her. Her relationships with several women friends often contained a touch of romantic intensity; but her life remained full of attachments to men. Nancy's restlessness and impulsiveness often worried her friends; Janet Flanner has spoken of feeling protective toward her, of feeling that she needed to be shielded from her own nature. Nancy had a great talent for friendship and great loyalty; only once or twice in her life did she decide that someone she had originally liked could no longer be a friend of hers, and in those cases, no matter whether the breach was justified or not, she did not relent. She always felt a special link with Janet Flanner and Solita Solano and regarded their threesome as something permanent and solid, often until the end of her life signing letters to them "⅓," or with a small drawing of a three-legged stool, or three small owls, as did they to her.

Solita Solano has described how they met, in a Montparnasse café on a rainy evening, at the prompting of Eugene MacCown, who shared a Middle West background with Janet Flanner and felt the women would be sure to "get along."

> Nancy arrived late, but only one hour, which was quite early for her to be late.
> How could I have said, but I did, "You are late" to that golden head set with sapphires.
> "But of course, darling," she said kindly.
> We "got along" indeed. The three became a fixed triangle, we survived all the spring quarrels and the sea changes of forty-two years of modern female fidelity.

The three women went around together in Paris, sometimes going to parties wearing the clothes sent over to Nancy by her mother, usually the latest Vionnet or Poiret models; and Janet Flanner sometimes borrowed Sir Bache's top hat. Or they would make trips into the French countryside, staying at small inns. Once, walking through the fields as night fell, Janet Flanner asked Nancy about her mother. Nancy said she would give the unpleasing topic as much time as it took for the glow-worm nearest to them in the dusk to lose its light. Both Janet Flanner and Solita Solano remembered how passionately Nancy swore that she would never forgive them if they succumbed to her mother's charm. She would prefer them never to meet Lady Cunard.

Stabilized for the moment by these new friendships, Nancy found a flat of her own in Paris and moved into it early in 1924. It was a ground floor flat in the rue le Regrattier, on the Île Saint-Louis, at the southern corner of the island overlooking the river toward the left bank and with a splendid view of Notre Dame. This was the first of Nancy's settled homes in France; she brought over books and furniture from England and engaged a Breton maid, Anna, who also cooked for her. The sitting room, small but beautifully proportioned, with two windows opening onto the view of the river, had smoky red walls above black wainscoting, a plum-colored velvet sofa, and walls hung with new paintings by some of the artists she had recently discovered. She had acquired two Chiricos, two Tanguys, and "a large Picabia gouache of a man with four pairs of eyes, a body spotted all over with vermilion dots, and one arm sheathed in black." She also bought several of Eugene MacCown's paintings, which she greatly liked, although some of her friends though her enthusiasm for his talent misplaced. However he was to paint one of the most striking portraits of her, wearing Sir Bache's top hat. She bought it from him and kept it until the end of her life. She greatly preferred it to the portrait done during the same period by Oskar Kokoschka.

Thirty years later Nancy jotted down a list of the people she remembered coming to her flat in the rue le Regrattier. George Moore was one, of course, and Arthur Symons, who once brought along Havelock Ellis; and childhood friends such as Iris Tree, who was living nearby, and Marie Beerbohm. She recalled a crowd of American expatriates—as well as Eugene MacCown, and Robert McAlmon, there were Laurence Vail and his sister Clotilde, Man Ray, Peggy Guggenheim, the brilliant young woman photographer Berenice Abbott, the poet William Carlos Williams and his wife, and Walter Berry, the bibliophile, friend of Proust and Edith Wharton. Not all the French visitors were of the younger generation; there was Marie Laurencin, Léon-Paul Fargue, André Derain, and Moise Kisling. But then followed a long list of names of the French avant-garde: René Crevel, Jean Cocteau, Raymond Radiguet, Louis Aragon, André Breton, Drieu la Rochelle, Philippe Soupault. "How very many more," she wrote.

For all her pleasure in having her own establishment in Paris at last, Nancy was still on the move for much of the year. In March 1924 she was in the south of France, at Sanary and Monte Carlo, seeing her cousin Victor, William Carlos Williams and his wife, and Robert McAlmon. But she was increasingly interested in the avant-garde scene in Paris, especially intrigued by the new influx of black entertainers and musicians to Paris, and kept a headline from a Paris paper proclaiming "Paris, Coeur de la Race Noire." On one of her visits to London she was invited by *Vogue* to write an occasional letter from Paris, which she began to do, mentioning her exciting new friends and their activities, praising Dada, Surrealism, and Josephine Baker.

That summer, Nancy again went to the country for a month, this time to Berneval near Dieppe. She told Janet Flanner she was intending to work very hard on a translation into French of Marlowe's *Faust,* which Tzara planned to put on the stage. He visited her at Berneval, as did a young English poet, critic, and publisher, John Rodker, who became close to Nancy for a time. They went on a walking tour of Provence in August. Rodker was a friend of Ezra Pound's and had published his poetry as well as T. S. Eliot's; the following summer, 1925, Nancy and Rodker went to Italy together, and visited the Pounds at Rapallo as well as Norman Douglas in Florence.

She was still writing poetry; and in April 1925 the Hogarth Press, run by Leonard and Virginia Woolf, brought out her long poem *Parallax,* with covers designed by Eugene MacCown.

Parallax is probably Nancy's best poetry. It recounts the thoughts and wanderings, imaginary and real, of a young poet, from London to Provence, Paris, and Italy; he broods on love, age, friendship, and aspiration, exploring his relationship with the past and the inspiration of great poetry and painting. The poem has powerful, sometimes obtrusive, links with T.S. Eliot's *The Waste Land,* which had obviously had a profound impact on Nancy when it was published in 1922. Some of the reviews concentrated on this link with devastating effect; the *New Statesman* reviewer wrote a detailed comparison of *Parallax* with *The Waste Land,* not to Nancy's advantage. The *Daily News* called it "a rather delirious echo of Mr T. S. Eliot's Waste Land." The *Manchester Guardian* found it "almost a study in obscurity."

But again, on the whole, the reviewers were impressed. The *Times Literary Supplement* said *Parallax* "seems to be the creation of a resilient mind; it has a complexity and grasp of reality which is so frequently lacking from women's poetry." The highest praise of all came from Nancy's friend Raymond Mortimer. He found it "one of the most moving poems of our time," full of "a desolate sort of beauty which I think is peculiarly poignant to my contemporaries." From his knowledge of Nancy, as well as from his reading of the poem, Mortimer gave a perceptive analysis of the state of mind of the writer: "one who perseveres through a life whose point he continually seeks in vain, too intelligent either to be content with one or to accept the facile explanations that soothe others."

Nancy was particularly pleased with a review by a woman, then unknown to her, who soon became a close friend. Louise Morgan, writing in the *Outlook* in July 1925. praised the poem's "curiously disturbing emotional effect." "The peculiar characteristic of *Parallax,*" she wrote, "is an almost sensational repression; one feels in the reading as if one were treading a clear swept, trimly bordered garden path around the crater of a volcano."

Parallax contains lines conveying strongly how Nancy had come to see herself:

> Think now how friends grow old—
> Their diverse brains, hearts, faces, modify; . . .
> Am I the same?
> Or a vagrant, of other breed, gone further, lost—
> I am most surely at the beginning yet.
> If so, contemporaries, what have you done?

The summer of 1925 saw Nancy back in the south of France, at le Lavandou, with René Crevel, Eugene Mac-Cown, Janet Flanner and Solita Solano. She went on another walking tour, this time in the Dordogne, with John Rodker. By late August or September she was again in Venice; John Rodker was still with her, but she made a new friendship there that was to be for a while something more, with John Strachey, who was in Venice with his friend Oswald Mosley and Mosley's first wife, Cynthia. Both Mosley and Strachey were at this time still members of the Labour party; Strachey had stood unsuccessfully as a Labour candidate for Parliament at a by-election in 1924. He and Mosley were working together on a book, *Revolution by Reason*. Strachey was seriously involved with a Frenchwoman, but became, according to his biographer, powerfully attracted to Nancy and "intoxicated by the free world in which [she] lived."

In the late autumn of 1925 Nancy went to London, where, she told Janet Flanner in a letter, she had dinner with Louise Morgan, who she discovered was married to the *Outlook's* editor, an Austrian journalist, Otto Theis. She persuaded Raymond Mortimer to read and review the novel that Solita Solano had just written. Then she had a disagreeable encounter at a party: "went to an appalling party, where a perfect swine, an ex-guardsman, . . . tried to find out once and for all whether or no I was the Green Hat! Can you beat it? As for the Hat, it is indescribable." Michael Arlen's novel had appeared in 1924, and he was at the peak of his success. The references in Nancy's letters of the time make it plain that although she saw him occasionally in London, there was some tension between them. He questioned some of her new activities and friendships, and she felt her life had changed in ways that he could not possibly understand.

Although Nancy had not intended to stay long in England, when she discovered that her father was very ill, she postponed her departure. She went to Sir Bache's bedside at the Haycock, and was with him when he died, on November 3, 1925. "It has all been rather terrible," she wrote to Sybil Hart-Davis the next day. "All very curious to see someone die." She stayed on for several weeks while Sir Bache's affairs were sorted out and the contents of the Haycock sold. Sir Bache had left instructions "that my funeral may be of the most simple kind and that black horses be not employed. I would prefer to go to my grave in a farm waggon rather than a hearse."

Apart from a few small bequests of his sporting prints and books, workshop tools, guns and other sporting equipment to his male relatives, Sir Bache left everything to Nancy. He did not mention Lady Cunard in his will. Nancy eventually received £14,418 13s. 2d., a silver vase presented to her great-grandfather Samuel Cunard by the citizens of Boston, and a life-size silver figure of a fox, presented to Sir Bache by his hunting friends in 1888. Leonard Woolf, who had known Nancy slightly since about 1920 and had seen something of her over the publication of *Parallax,* remembered seeing Nancy with this unlikely bequest.

"One afternoon she drifted into our flat in Tavistock Square carrying in her arms a large fox made of silver. . . . She had just fetched it from the bank, and according to her, it was the only thing which her father had left her. She was amused by and laughed at her absurd silver fox but one felt that life had hurt her somewhat." Leonard Woolf always remembered a touching quality in Nancy. "I had from the moment I saw her a great affection for her and she had, I think, an affection for me. One's affection was tinged with apprehension, or anxiety, for she had an air of vulnerability, deep down of sadness. Not that she was in the least sad on the surface of life; she was essentially gay, but often I felt behind or beneath the gaiety this vulnerability."

Nancy took a small house in Sussex during her time in England; she had visits there from John Rodker and Raymond Mortimer, who, she told Janet Flanner, "departed murmuring 'healthy walks and healthy talks.' " She also had a visit from René Crevel, for whom she was working on another translation into French, this time from Waley's version of the Japanese classic, *The Tale of Genji*. She wrote often and affectionately to Janet Flanner, saying "I would rather hear anything from you than everything from any other teller" and urging her to come over to stay; "Comfort is here—cat and dog—cat for lap and dog for walk—a yard and a half of books—plenty of wine—sleep without dreams and baths without shudders—do come." Janet Flanner spent two weeks with Nancy in February.

Nancy was still in England on her thirtieth birthday, March 10, 1926. She celebrated it "through several bottles" at the Eiffel Tower, where she stayed for three days, but was getting over flu and feeling low. "I have been desperately unhappy for quite a while (that is for you two)," she wrote to Janet Flanner, "and you did so much to mellow it here." The next day, she left for Southampton, "to look for African and Oceanic things—because that is the most recent and now a very large interest in my life—ivory, gods, masks, fetishes." Nancy was beginning to make her famous collection of African ivory bracelets, which she took to wearing all up her slender arms. This new style was soon noticed by the columnists: "Ivory shackles: one thing Nancy Cunard did while in London was to create a new fashion in ivory bracelets. Each time I saw her she was wearing three or four huge ivory bracelets, each of them extremely thick and two or three inches wide."

When Nancy returned to France in the spring of 1926, she must have felt more than ever detached from her former existence. Sir Bache was dead, she was increasingly at odds with her mother, and another tenuous link with her past had recently been severed. In mid-1925, she had finally obtained a divorce from Sydney Fairbairn, who had returned to England and wanted to marry again.

Now, back in Paris, she started another love affair. It was to last longer and have a more permanent effect on Nancy than any of her attachments since the death of her wartime lover.

Louis Aragon

In France, as in England, there was in the postwar years a powerful mood of revulsion among the younger generation against the values and institutions that had led to such disaster. There was a feeling of rebellion against authority and convention, against parents, the church, schools, and universities, the army, and all established cultural and social rules. But whereas among English intellectuals this mood was vague and disorganized and gradually dissipated itself in mild forms of social protest and one or two "daring" or "cynical" novels, in France, with a history of experiment in art and a revolutionary tradition, something more specific soon began to take shape. The Modernist movement in writing and painting had begun well before the war, and there was nothing new in the antagonism between young intellectuals and bourgeois conventions; but after 1918 the differences sharpened.

By 1926 Louis Aragon was twenty-nine, a year younger than Nancy. He came from a petit bourgeois background; his mother kept a boarding house in a modest part of Paris. After a Catholic education, he spent two years as a medical orderly at the front. There he met another medical student, André Breton, and after the war, in Paris, the two men rapidly became leaders of the group of young intellectuals most determined to create something positive and new. At first, Aragon and Breton, with Philippe Soupault and Paul Éluard, used the Dada magazine, *Littérature,* founded in 1919, as a rallying point and outlet. Perhaps because its random energy and iconoclasm suited the immediate postwar mood, Dada, with its founder Tristan Tzara, had a brief period of wild success. The point of Dada was its pointlessness, which irritated and intrigued the public and stimulated the younger Parisian artists and intellectuals. The Dadaists published apparently nonsensical writings, showed bizarre paintings and staged peculiar happenings. They aimed to provoke, and they succeeded; several times the police were called to their meetings. But Dada was too chaotic and nihilistic to last.

In 1922 Breton, Aragon and Éluard abandoned Dada; in 1924 they decided to form a group of their own, which they called Surrealist. The term had been coined by Guillaume Apollinaire, the prewar poet. At first the Dadaists and the fledgling Surrealists remained close; they shared many of the same ideas, particularly a belief in the significance of dreams, random selection of images, and juxtaposition of ideas. They were also convinced that the origins of creative impulse lay in the subconscious. But the Surrealists wanted to make constructive statements about society and to spread the revolution outside the purely artistic sphere, which to the pure Dadaist was heresy.

As the Dadaists declined, the Surrealists flourished. In 1924 they founded a new review, *La Révolution Surréaliste,* which proclaimed across the cover that "a new declaration of the rights of man must be made." Aragon soon became, alongside Breton, the leader of the Surrealist movement.

In those early years Surrealism was something exciting and extraordinary. The notion of political upheaval was dormant, or rather expressed itself indirectly in outrageous statements or demonstrations; but in writing, and in painting, the energy and originality of the young Surrealists was truly revolutionary. By 1925 or 1926, they were at their peak. All Paris was fascinated by their activities. It is hardly surprising that Nancy was drawn to such a group, nor that she became particularly interested in one of its leaders.

In 1926 Aragon must have been outstandingly attractive. Even his detractors concede his great charm as well as his intelligence, and he has always shown unusual power over people, personally as well as intellectually. He was tall and dark, with striking blue eyes, beautiful manners, and a rather cold, old-fashioned courtesy concealing a passionate, romantic nature kept well under control. He was exceptionally successful with women; his friends used to complain that Aragon could go into a crowded bar or café and walk out with any woman he chose, whether she was there on her own or not. He was always well dressed, almost a dandy and—unlike some of the other Surrealists, notably Breton—enjoyed parties and fashionable society. He had great energy and worked immensely hard at whatever he decided to do. In many ways he must have been a most suitable companion for Nancy.

Those who remember seeing them together at the beginning of their two years of close companionship recall a strikingly good-looking, stylish couple who seemed happily absorbed in each other. John Banting, a close friend of Nancy's who was to become England's sole self-proclaimed Surrealist painter, saw them once at a party in London dancing together, Nancy looking particularly dazzling in an "icy emerald green velvet dress." They traveled together through central and southwest France, where Rupert Hart-Davis met them sitting beside the road eating a huge dandelion salad and drinking red wine. Aragon was often at the rue le Regrattier, where Nancy introduced him to George Moore, who found him remarkably good-looking and articulate and seemed to approve of the friendship. (Aragon was eventually to put a glimpse of Nancy and her flat into a novel, Blanche ou l'Oubli.) Nancy became a familiar figure in the bars and cafés patronized by the Surrealists, in particular the Café Cyrano in the Place Blanche, where the group met daily at noon and again in the evening. Georges Sadoul, a younger recruit, remembers meeting her there for the first time in late 1925 or early 1926 with Aragon, Breton, Soupault, Éluard, Max Ernst, and René Crevel.

"Nancy's allure was striking, and lasting," he wrote. "One noticed first her eyes, which were very blue and quite strange, her fine, bony face, her lion-like mane of fine blonde hair; then one was amazed to see how her thin arms were covered, from wrists to shoulder, with African ivory bracelets."

The ivory bracelets had become her trademark. She and Aragon shared an interest in primitive art, which still seemed crude and ugly to most people, though Picasso had been struck by the power and beauty of African masks and carvings soon after the turn of the century. They would visit the docks in the East End of London, and bars where French sailors could be found in seacoast towns, searching for pieces to add to Nancy's growing collection. John Banting remembered Nancy at another party in the mid-twenties, "in a pale shell pink taffeta with a plunging back-line and both arms elbow deep in beautiful African bracelets of ivory. When I danced with her I gently made the bracelets click and clack in accompaniment to the music."

It is only possible to describe Nancy's relationship with Aragon, at the beginning, in glimpses. She never wrote about it directly, and he declines to discuss it, saying that anything he could now say after so long would be "either inadequate, or indiscreet." At first, it seems, they were both very much in love; but while Aragon's nature was to be constant and exclusive in love, Nancy's was not. This caused him great and increasing pain. Also, she told one or two friends at the time and later, she found him sexually too demanding. Nancy's sexual pattern was clear enough by this time; one lover was never enough for her for very long, either physically or emotionally. She seems, however, to have been compulsive rather than passionate about sex; certainly most of her happiest and her most enduring relationships were those in which sex played a small or insignificant part.

But for a while all went well. In 1926 they went together on a long trip to Spain, where their open sharing of hotel rooms caused a minor scandal. Their liaison was picked up by the press at this time, and a story even appeared in the *Daily Express* that they were planning to be married soon. Both immediately made public denials. The same year they were together in Italy, where Nancy took Aragon to meet Norman Douglas over a meal in Florence; it is striking how Nancy seems to have used both George Moore and Norman Douglas as touchstones, almost as father figures, in her relationships with younger men. She remembered how they were both made uneasy while in Italy by the fascist regime; Nancy had a raincoat that turned from rust to blood red when wet by the rain, and the young fascists in the streets of Florence or Venice seemed to her to be hostile, taking the scarlet coat to be a political gesture.

Apart from personal difficulties, there were other reasons why having Nancy as his recognized mistress cannot have been easy for Aragon. Women played a small part in the Surrealist scheme of things. For all their desire to live unconventionally and to shock the bourgeoisie, the Surrealists had highly conventional, even traditional, ideas about women. No woman writer or painter emerged to join their activities or sign their manifestos. They found it thrilling to visit brothels and befriend prostitutes, but at the same time there was a strong romantic, almost puritanical streak in their sexual attitudes. The ideal was an exclusive, reciprocated love with the perfect woman. Foreign women were fashionable in the group, perhaps because they tended to be more independent and available than middle- or upper-class Frenchwomen; but Nancy was all too obviously someone, a person in her own right, with more money and freedom of movement than seemed safe or appropriate. Breton in particular disapproved of Nancy and feared her influence on Aragon. She represented the rich, fashionable world that he despised. The Surrealists went through a stage of applying stringent rules about what sort of artistic and social activities were allowed. When at Picasso's suggestion Max Ernst and Miró undertook to design the decor and scenery for Diaghilev's *Romeo and Juliet,* Aragon and Breton attempted to exclude them from the group for their collaboration with "the international aristocracy."

Increasingly, Nancy's money was a problem. None of the Surrealists was rich, indeed most of them were desperately poor. Nancy was free with her money to Aragon and his friends, but the power this gave her must have often been awkward for Aragon, especially when their romance began— inevitably—to be stormy.

Apart from her emotional impact on Aragon, which was considerable, Nancy made little contribution to Surrealist ideas; but it is remarkable how neatly several of her traits were reinforced by their beliefs, and as a result strengthened.

Her difficulties with her mother were familiar to most of the young men in the Surrealist group. Their own personal histories are dotted with tales of how they fought with their parents to be allowed to live as they pleased, renouncing conventional education or careers; how they were not only frequently cut off without a penny, but occasionally pursued by irate fathers who were not beyond calling in the police to track them down and frighten them into mending their ways. There was a strong conspiratorial streak in many of them, even a touch of paranoia, and they tended to elevate and dignify such problems by viewing them as part of the revolution in art and society, toward which Surrealism was supposed to be leading. All this must have been very appealing to Nancy. It was true that she could not honestly present Lady Cunard as a bourgeois, conventional parent, much as she may have longed to. Indeed, one of Nancy's problems with her mother was precisely that in her way Lady Cunard was herself unconventional, even provocative. But Lady Cunard's links with the established world of politics and the arts were well known. The Surrealists' urge to defy and provoke that world, to make outrageous if trivial gestures like urinating in holywater fonts, and decorating lavatory chains with crucifixes, and their pleasure in making speeches and public statements ridiculing and insulting older writers such as Gide or Anatole France, or encouraging cadets in the army to rebel against their training, must have stimulated Nancy's increasing desire to strike out against her mother and her mother's world.

Paradoxically, it was partly Nancy's grand background that

most appealed to some of the Surrealists. Several survivors stress how she exemplified the capacity to live unconventionally which to them typified an established English aristocratic tradition. Some of them saw Nancy as a modern female Byron, if not in talent then in style. To her this was heady stuff.

Even the fact that she was still subsidized financially by her despised elders fitted a pattern. Nancy's family simply had more money; but she was as dependent as any provincial official's son who joined the Surrealists yet still had to live off grudging checks from home.

Above all, it was undoubtedly through Aragon that Nancy was drawn toward left-wing politics. The Surrealists in the mid-twenties were obsessed with the problem of whether or not their ideas of revolution jibed with communist doctrine. Some joined the Communist party and others did not; and by 1930 the original group split irrevocably over the issue. At the beginning of 1927 Aragon himself became a communist (and remains one to this day). Nancy must have heard endless arguments and quarrels about his decision. She had never been particularly interested in politics; she herself never joined the party, although many people assumed she had. Doctrinal differences bored her and seemed puzzling and irrelevant; Janet Flanner has described her as "a poetic anarchist," which is as good a label as any. But though fundamentally apolitical, Nancy was a great believer in taking sides, and from the late twenties onward, the communist side was for Nancy the right side to be on.

Like many of her contemporaries, she came to have a romantic idea of communism as the party of natural justice and respect for ordinary people. This notion, supported by her natural rebelliousness, was strengthened by a growing hatred among most of her friends and in Nancy herself for the fascist movements in Italy and Germany. In any case, to associate with communists, to have a Communist party member as a lover, and to espouse communist ideas was a wonderful tease for her mother.

A House in the Country

With the money her father left her, Nancy decided to give up the flat in the rue le Regrattier and buy a house in the French countryside. During 1927 she found an old peasant farmhouse in the small village of La Chapelle-Réanville, in Normandy, near Vernon, sixty miles from Paris.

The village has changed little in fifty years. It lies on a gentle slope, surrounded by rich fields and orchards. Nancy's house, which she called Le Puits Carré after the old stone well in the front courtyard, stands slightly outside the village up a small hill. It is a long, low, two-story building at right angles to the track leading up to it, with roofs and rooms on different levels, and two or three separate outbuildings scattered around a long, tangled garden. Two great lime trees stand in front by the well. Nancy loved the simplicity of the house and never tried to make it luxurious, though she bought it in bad condition and had to do some rebuilding as well as decorating. Aragon helped her plan the rooms and move in. The house was cool in summer but freezing cold in winter, and the arrangement of rooms was curious, since they opened into each other on both floors, rather than having corridors. Nancy used to deplore its inconveniences, but she made it charming and original and loved it; it was to be her home for the ten most dramatic years of her life.

Georges Sadoul has described what Nancy made of the house:

At one end of the long low house was her bedroon, and at the other end a large sitting room, with the valuable old furniture inherited from her father, and a large window whose glass framed a peasant landscape worthy of Corot. In her bedroom she had the old yellow chalk stone walls uncovered. At the foot of a staircase leading to the first floor were placed, like curious bannisters, shelves with horizontal bars threaded with her five or six hundred, perhaps even a thousand African ivory bracelets; some were as wide as manacles, others narrower, carved with human figures or wild animals. Next to her bedroom was a dining room, painted green, with low chests round the walls on which were placed paintings signed by Chirico, Malkine, Picasso, Yves Tanguy, and a good many African idols.

Nancy loved to have her friends to Le Puits Carré. From the spring of 1928 on there was a stream of visitors: Janet Flanner and Solita Solano; Aragon, Sadoul, Crevel, and other Surrealists; friends from England, such as Harold Acton and John Banting. Banting in particular saw a new side of Nancy when she was at home in the country.

> Naturally I loved every part of it [the house], for each detail reflected her inventiveness—both visual and practical. Her wonder and delight in every detail of the countryside now reminds me of Colette's. The surprisingly short seasons for fantastic beetles was observed and insects and the changing pageantry of moths—a new species every evening—one with short white fur all over its head, wings and legs; another with folded wings like a splinter of silver, and one with a yellow body and transparent green wings. After twenty varieties we gave up counting. They came into the reading lamp and had to be saved from being smothered inside the sheets.

In the early days at Réanville Nancy had two or three servants; later, according to Banting, she enjoyed looking after the house herself. "I did all the cooking," he wrote,

> on a woodstove which, carefully banked up with coke, stayed glowing for three days on end. She once confessed that she had

always hated eating, but I am among those who with the aid of the fresh country produce of France, and country air, succeeded in arousing quite a hearty appetite. The "square well" (so useful for cooling white wine) was shaded by two large lime trees whose branches swept down nearly to the grass, forming a magnificent shady dining room (in June scented with the golden tasseled blooms). At night an electric lamp on a long flex from the house was hung among the branches. But in cold weather the warm kitchen with its Benin heads was our refuge. Nancy swept, polished and dusted with zest and conscientiousness. She was as fastidiously neat as any of the creatures of the woods she loved and with as much unforced natural ease. No fuss, no bother. Everything was in place and shone there with its own personality respected.

By the early summer of 1928 Nancy had decided to put the outbuildings of Le Puits Carré to use. She was determined to start her own small private publishing house. She wanted to learn how to print by hand and to publish contemporary poetry.

Nancy was lucky to find a rare old hand press for sale at the right time. An acquaintance of hers, the American journalist and publisher William Bird, decided in the spring of 1928 to sell his Three Mountains Press, which he had been running in Paris since 1921. He had produced work by Ford Madox Ford (who ran the *Transatlantic Review* from the same house as Bird's press), William Carlos Williams, Hemingway, and Pound; so Nancy felt that the huge early nineteenth-century Belgian Mathieu machine that she bought from him for three hundred pounds had "a distinguished, even an illustrious lineage and connections." Bird threw in some wooden furnishings, some Caslon Old Face type, and a good supply of superior Vergé de Rives paper. he also came down to Réanville himself, in April 1928, to supervise the setting up of the hand press, and introduced Nancy to a professional printer, a Frenchman called Lévy, who agreed to help her.

Nancy had the small stable building a few yards from the main house converted to hold the press. A balcony was built, "with shelves for supplies and paper and the drying of the printed sheets." She was tremendously pleased with the whole arrangement. "We had good daylight and electric light, and, later, a stove, and it was so near the house, some twenty-five yards away, that I was sometimes tempted, in those early days, to rise from bed and go straight to work. Looking back on the printery I think nothing could have been so well devised for my purpose."

Lévy was bewildered and not too pleased when he arrived at Réanville to find that he was expected to teach Nancy and Aragon, who were there together much of the early summer of 1928, to print. They were full of enthusiasm and extremely strong-minded, not to say willful, about learning as fast as possible and making all kinds of experiments with Nancy's new toy. To Lévy's annoyance they proved quick learners. Nancy loved the feel of the composing stick and the technicalities of printers' language, choosing which size of type to use, and learning to read the letters in reverse. Lévy was amazed at their proficiency, but to Nancy it was simple.

> His surprise was great at our learning to handle type so fast. Yet it seemed to me that anyone who likes doing this at all must acquire the feel of it the first or certainly the second time he brings the *composteur* or printing stick together with the letters; a few hours are sufficient to get the feel of it all. Aragon and I were both fairly quick at composition from the start. Learning the correct sequence or rather non-sequence, alphabetically, of the compartments where each letter is kept in its scores and hundreds, is another matter and takes somewhat longer. We were soon decent apprentices. With neither occurred any catastrophic collapses of lines or paragraphs when tipping out the *composteur;* our pages could be tied up almost as well as if set by a professional. Distributing the type after printing four pages or so was pleasant and not the bore it is considered to be by printers, and everything about the craft seemed to me to be most interesting.

Lévy did his best to put Nancy in her place by telling her that, in France, apprentices had to wait for seven years before they were allowed to print. Nancy was astonished. "And what is all that stretch filled with?" When he told her about sweeping the floor, picking up the fallen type, and running errands, she was dismissive. "Thank goodness there's none of that here, Monsieur Lévy. We are going to forge ahead. My intention is to learn from you everything I possibly can as quickly as may be, so as to be able to work without you, do you see? I like this beginning very much."

To Aragon's amusement, she tried to explain further that the Hours Press was to be experimental, and that innovations in printing would suit the character of the work she hoped they would print. Lévy was not convinced. "Now and again Aragon's dark eyes would flash or laugh at me behind M Lévy's hefty shoulder. Why waste talk on the man who would never understand or agree? he seemed to be saying."

Almost at once Nancy and Aragon had a printing job to do. Norman Douglas sent Nancy a six-page report he had written for the British Foreign Office in 1895 on the pumice stone industry of the Lipari Islands. Nancy set to work at once, but found it a "pesky little piece" because it had to be set in small type, and "a little grim . . . by reason of its dry, conventional style and content." Later, she wrote feelingly, "for someone starting to learn typesetting, this was a horribly complicated work to begin with." But they got eighty copies done within two weeks, and sent them to Douglas as a present.

Nancy never regarded the Douglas piece as the true beginning of the Hours Press publications. Despite her wish to publish new writing, she was touched and pleased when George Moore told her, "I want to start your press off with a good bang." She realized too that it would not do the press any harm to bring out something by a famous writer. With Aragon back in Paris, Nancy and Lévy set to work on a short story by Moore, *Peronnik the Fool,* which he had originally written as part of *Héloïse and Abélard* but had left out because of its length. But she was nervous, too, because Moore was known to be particular about the design and layout of his books, especially those published in small limited editions.

Moore suggested that *Peronnik* might sell better if Nancy wrote a preface for it, describing her memories of him at Nevill Holt. "I wish you would turn those past times over in your mind," he wrote to her,

> spend an evening or two with the subject, and perchance it may flash into your mind in literary form. The story is a very living one and will delight everybody as much as it delights you when I remind you of . . . I stop without having said all, leaving the selection of the subject matter to you.
>
> Of course a preface of the kind I suggest would cause that cheerless soul, T. S. Eliot, to frown, but personal literature, as I have often impressed upon you, is the only literature for the age it is written and the age that follows. It isn't easy, however, and it has to be cultivated.

It was a good idea, but Nancy was not taken by it. "I wrote to GM: 'the learning of printing has engulfed me entirely; you cannot imagine how every hour of the day goes into it, but such is the case, dearest GM.' " It was to be nearly thirty years before she took up his suggestion, in writing her memories of him as a book of her own.

Soon after learning to print, Aragon was struck by an idea for the new press. He would translate Lewis Carroll's poem *The Hunting of the Snark* into French. Nancy wondered whether his English, good though it was, was up to the task, and also whether the poem was not too extraordinary to be translatable; but Aragon was determined. He felt that he had a special understanding of the poem because Carroll's nonsense verse and Surrealism had much in common, and he produced a remarkably successful French translation, *La Chasse au Snark,* in four or five days. He then could not wait to see it in print, so he and Nancy set a few lines. Lévy, who could never bring himself to ask Aragon exactly what Surrealism was, was utterly baffled by *Snark,* though Nancy and Aragon tried to explain. "C'est un animal fabuleux," they said.

Next, Aragon started experimenting with designs for a cover. He stayed up all night and emerged with an exceptionally delicate, original design in which the title is made up of curling arabesque shapes, formed by punctuation marks or symbols. Nancy was full of admiration. "Aragon had been at typesetting a mere two or three weeks and had turned out several samples of ornamental composition that would have honoured any of the seven-year printers Lévy had told us of."

One of these experiments has survived in Nancy's Hours Press scrapbook, where there is an entry entitled "Aragon's Composition, 1928." Beneath the heading is a piece of paper with A TOI NANCY L'AMOUR on it in big black lacy capitals, made up of small printing symbols. Aragon also printed twenty-five copies of a two-line poem, "Voyageur," built around an obscene pun. Nancy translated it as:

> From Port to Port, for ever onward faring,
> Ever more sad becomes the traveller.

adding "the word in French is not port but a feminine word connected with love. . . . There was no need to show this item to M. Lévy."

Aragon took an interest in pornography, as did most of the Surrealists, given their passion for breaking taboos and exploring the subconscious. Nancy, too, was intrigued by pornography though she could demonstrate a rather surprising puritanical distaste for it; she certainly preferred the Rabelaisian to the subtly erotic, perhaps finding grossness less disturbing. She disliked *Lady Chatterley's Lover* and rejected the suggestion that the Hours Press should publish it. Among her papers is a sheaf of pages in Aragon's handwriting, containing part of his one venture into pornography, *Le Con d'Irène*, which had a considerable underground reputation before being republished as *Irène* in the 1960s. One of Nancy's other Surrealist friends remembers that she never cared for it very much; however, several pages apparently relate to Aragon's love for her.

Nancy was immensely impressed by Aragon's capacity for work. She wrote later that she had never known anyone with his powers of concentration. "He once wrote in front of me a long analytical essay, Philosophie des Paratonerres, which he began one evening before dinner and finished some thirty-six hours later, with hardly any time off for sleep or meals. The subject of this ten-thousand-word criticism was philosophy, stretching from Heraclitus to Spengler, through Marx, Engels and Dühring. Another example was his *Traité du Style,* a book of medium length, which he planned and wrote to the end in the single month of September 1927 at Varangéville."

The summer of 1928 was very hot, Aragon was back in Paris and Nancy found herself working on *Peronnik* alone while Lévy had a few days off, struggling with the typesetting, spacing, pulling, and folding in her petticoat in a temperature of 95 degrees. To Lévy's delight on his return, she found printing much trickier than composing; the paper had to be damped because the heat made it too stiff, the ink evaporated, and the Mathieu seemed to be pressing unevenly. She found it slow and exhausting work and began to realize that printing by hand was not all that easy or quick after all; but she realized too that she really had become a printer. She also discovered something that was to help make the Hours Press books unusually pleasing to look at. "I began to learn that letters are one thing, and a mass of type something else to be thought of in relation to the space to be printed and the unprinted space surrounding it. . . . Every bit as important in the total aspect is the non-printed as well as the printed surface." When she sent some sample pages to George Moore, he wrote back approvingly, but underlined the importance of looking at the page as a whole: "When I saw so much gutter in the first specimen that you sent me I felt it to be my duty to beg you to take note that in all the 17th and 18th century books a beautiful title page was always the printer's first consideration."

After about a month's work on *Peronnik,* Lévy went away for his summer holidays and Nancy too decided to break off and go abroad. Lévy agreed to return in the autumn. The Hours Press had hardly begun, as far as the public was concerned, but Nancy never forgot the pride and satisfaction of learning to print. She had in fact learned more than that; she had discovered, at the age of thirty-two, that she had the capacity for sustained hard work and that there was immense satisfaction to be had from seeing a job through from start to finish.

Meanwhile, the relationship between Nancy and Aragon was near the breaking point. Another young Surrealist, ten years or so Aragon's junior, André Thirion, met them both around this time; Aragon's desperation was evident. Nancy he found

> aristocratic and British, like a character from a novel, with the assured demeanour of women accustomed to being entertained, and entertaining. She dressed very well, with a touch of eccentricity which she accentuated little by little until eventually she went too far. She spoke polished French, with no accent, but sometimes using amusing or picturesque Anglicised turns of phrase, in a melodious, siren's voice . . . like many high-born Anglo-Saxon women, Nancy drank and became drunk often. Then she would become unpleasant, slapping her companion's face with the ivory or metal which clasped her from wrist to elbow. Sometimes she too bore traces of one of these violent scenes, which she disguised with thick purple veils attached to one of the small extravagant hats then in fashion. She was also a traveller by nature, crossing the seas on an impulse, giving her friends bizarre addresses, suddenly sending impenetrable telegrams, written while drunk, arranging a rendezvous in Bermuda or Naples as other people would issue invitations for a weekend in the country. . . .

Nancy, who knew how to be charming, tender, loving, full of attentiveness, was a difficult and destructive companion. She loved men above everything; when she wanted someone, he had to satisfy her desire then and there; she attacked; it is difficult to imagine the tortures her inconstancy and her sudden hungers inflicted on her lovers.

Venice and
Henry Crowder

In the late summer of 1928 Nancy went off on another of her trips to Venice. She had no reason to suppose that this particular visit to the city she had known since she was sixteen would change her life. The pattern of such Venetian interludes was established; Nancy would take a *palazzo,* or part of one, sometimes with friends, sometimes with one of her cousins. She would probably arrive with a lover, invite other friends to join her, and plunge into the round of carnivals, nightclubs, and masked balls. Eventually the parties would be over for that year, the summer visitors would leave, and Nancy would have, perhaps, a new lover for a short season. Nancy herself caught the mood when remembering her early friendship with Norman Douglas, who one day asked her about that summer in Venice.

I described all the people I thought could interest you—the joy of some, the bane of others; the petty intrigues and funny scandals; balls, fancy dress galas and festivities—the whole hectic spin of Venice in August and September during the twenties, all the more exotic on account of its cosmopolitanism. . . . Well, it had all been spectacular for several weeks—that blazing Lido strewn with society stars in glittering jewels and make-up—that brilliance of Grand Canal Barge-Parties—those spontaneous dawn revels after dancing in some of the rather sinister new night-bars. A time came when everyone thought everyone else crazy.

For the 1928 Venice season Nancy had Louis Aragon with her. He was in a weak position. He had no money and was feeling humiliated by his poverty as well as by Nancy's coolness toward him. She still wanted him in attendance, but she resented his claims on her and had no sympathy for his financial predicament. Aragon has discussed his situation that summer in Venice in a long interview he gave in 1968 to a French journalist. He did not identify Nancy by name, but there is no doubt that he was speaking of her.

> . . . there was a woman in my life then, who was very beautiful, with whom I had been living for several years and with whom, in fact, I was not made to live. Or perhaps was she not made to live with me? . . . This life gave rise to all sorts of complications which had nothing to do with the basic relationship between the two of us. Social elements arose between us which dislocated our relationship. This woman, whom I loved, her life was based on assumptions very different from mine, and I could not carry on this life as a couple. It was difficult for me in material terms to establish myself on her level, and how could I accept that she do it for me? We had arrived at a point where the disparity in the style of our lives, on top of personal problems, presented me with all the usual questions about how one carries on one's life. And I found myself in Venice, where I had gone on certain very precise conditions, counting on the means which alone could insure my independence.

The "means" were obvious enough: he was in the process of selling a painting by Braque, and he had been promised a good price for it.

He was able to get hold of some of the money before leaving Paris; the rest was supposed to follow him to Venice. The transfer was endlessly delayed. "I was in a false position, perfectly intolerable, which made the situation between us yet more intolerable."

Among the other friends Nancy invited to Venice that year were Janet Flanner and Solita Solano. They both witnessed, with mingled horror and amusement, the scenes that took place continually between Nancy and Aragon. He would yell at her that he could not stand the situation a moment longer, that he was leaving for Paris immediately. She would shout at him to go ahead. The *palazzo* resounded with their quarrels at all hours of the day and night. "Aragon was always packing and unpacking his suitcases," Janet Flanner recalled. Solita Solano remembered worse scenes. At least once she heard Aragon threaten to kill himself, and Nancy telling him to go ahead, the sooner the better, though she doubted if he would have the courage since he always came crawling back to her in the end.

She was very nearly wrong. It is known that he attempted suicide around this time. Nancy was directly responsible. One day, Aragon stormed out and did not come back. Gradually, the party became uneasy. Eventually, someone began to search the hotels and, by a miracle, he was found in time. He had taken an overdose of drugs. "I was rescued with great difficulty from this drama but in the end, I was rescued," he later wrote.

According to Aragon, he tried to buy more drugs and start all over again, but the pharmacist would not sell him the stuff. When he got back "to that place that I could not call my home," he found the check he had been waiting for. He left at once for Paris.

This was not quite the end of Aragon's affair with Nancy, but it was the beginning of the end. He moved in with André Thirion and Georges Sadoul, who were sharing a large flat in the rue du Château. They knew what had happened; Thirion describes Aragon as "literally broken." He had a huge, life-size photograph of Nancy by Man Ray stuck up on the wall, and he would pace up and down, drinking, gazing at it, and talking about her. He put something of what he was feeling into a poem about the end of a love affair, "Poème à crier dans les Ruines," which was included in a collection he published the next year, *La Grande Gaité*.

No one who remembers the episode recalls Nancy being deeply moved. She wrote about it almost casually much later, when it was all safely in the past. "It had been the hell of a time in many ways—gay and mad, fantastic and ominous, and horribly dramatic too, for there was nearly a sharp physical tragedy . . . a great friend of mine had nearly committed suicide; it was only avoided at the last moment and all of that had been ghastly. . . . And then," she continued, "with the rains, had come the great withdrawal of the great tide of people. And one night—well, this was something entirely new to me." And Nancy, more than ever, was in the mood for something new.

One evening in Venice, toward the end of the season, Nancy and her cousin Edward Cunard went out to dinner and to dance at the Hotel Luna. A group of black American jazz musicians, Eddie South and his Alabamians, were playing there that night. One of them was a pianist called Henry Crowder. Nancy and Edward were struck by their playing and felt like company. When the set was over, they asked the group over to their table for a drink.

This was the beginning of the most crucial relationship in Nancy's life. In Henry Crowder she found more than a new lover with a different-colored skin; she found a cause, a symbol, a weapon, a victim. Hitherto, for all her erratic behavior, she had remained someone whose conduct and interests were containable within the loose boundaries of upper-class bohemia. Through Crowder she became something else: a woman who chose, deliberately, to cross the boundaries of convention, class, and race in pursuit of a cause. The process was to be painful for her and for quite a few others, not least Crowder himself. It was also to be confused, at times tasteless, and occasionally absurd. But in 1928 Nancy blundered into, and for the next few years floundered around in, one of the most intractable and serious of human problems: the sexual, social, and political attractions and antagonisms of whites and blacks.

Henry Crowder, who was to transform Nancy's life and have his own life turned upside down in the process, was an unlikely candidate for such a role. The success of black musicians and entertainers during the 1920s had made a handful of black stars fashionable, even socially acceptable. Crowder was not a star, but he was caught up in this tide and found himself picked out by a woman who, it turned out, was looking for more than just an interesting, exotic addition to a string of lovers. The more one learns of their life together and what it meant to him, the clearer it becomes that he often wondered what had hit him.

"I feel I owe it to my race," he wrote in the preface to his account of his life, "to let it be known what was in my mind during my struggles, and especially during the years one of the strangest relationships that has ever taken place between a black man and a white woman was being unfolded. . . . It is my hope that the experiences which I have gone through may be of some value to Colored men who become enamored with white women."

There can seldom have been a couple with more dramatically contrasting backgrounds. Crowder's life, even before he met Nancy, could serve as a textbook example of how the jazz boom in the 1920s changed the lives of innumerable black Americans. He had grown up in the 1890s as the youngest of the large family of a poor Georgia workingman. His father was a devout Baptist who, with the help of his half-Indian wife, struggled hard to educate his children and bring them up respectable and God-fearing. He worked at various times as a tanner and carpenter and barely kept his head above water; the family made several abrupt moves, ending in Atlanta. Crowder's mother became a cleaning woman and took in washing to make ends meet.

Henry Crowder learned his music singing in church and playing the piano for the YMCA. His first experience of the world outside the South was when he was chosen to be a member of a school quartet that toured holiday resorts and camps in the North. On this trip Crowder had his first chance to mix on equal terms with whites and his first dance with a white girl. After this, by his own account, Crowder was determined to escape from the South and try his luck up North.

After a brief spell at Atlanta University, and working as a postman, Crowder had an unhappy love affair and decided to leave town. He made his way to Washington, D.C., where he worked as a dishwasher and handyman before finding a job as a piano player in a brothel. Falling in love with a respectable young girl from Atlanta, he managed to improve his position, taking a job as singer and pianist with a dance orchestra in order to give her a decent life.

Gradually, he moved up in the world. He became manager of his orchestra, then of several others, until he was handling a good part of the jazz orchestra business in the city. Then he put some money into a tailoring business that prospered and was able to buy a handsome house in a good area. When the First World War broke out, he did not, as a married man, have to join up right away. In 1916 his only child, Henry Crowder, Jr., was born. Briefly, he was driver to a general in Washington; when the general lost his temper with him one day, he walked out. After the war Crowder found himself once again out of work and short of money. He had a married sister in Chicago, who wrote to him of its opportunities. He decided to try his luck there.

Although he had trouble at first in finding a steady job, he sold his house in Washington and brought his wife to Chicago, where they rented an apartment. But the marriage was beginning to show signs of strain. Eventually, he found work as the piano player with a jazz quartet called the Alabamians, run by a well-known violinist, Eddie South. "And there," says Crowder, "began the trail that led to Europe." Eddie South and his Alabamians were a success in Chicago; so much so that a well-known white singer made them the background for her act, which brought them recording contracts. Next they moved to New York; they were playing in Greenwich Village one night when a white patron asked them if they would like to go to Europe.

The plan was that their patron would open a cabaret in Paris especially to launch his girl, a singer, and Eddie South and the Alabamians would be sent over to be part of the show, all expenses paid and with a year's contract. Crowder did not hesitate. He accepted the chance to go to Europe and sent his wife back to Washington. He felt that the marriage was over.

He embarked for Europe in 1928 with a light heart. He was completely broke, but he felt his big chance had come. Among the resolutions he made as the voyage began was not to get involved with white women. When he heard his friends joking about the girls they hoped to meet in Paris, he disclaimed any such plans for himself. "You can have all the fun you want to," he said to them, "but I am going to Europe to study, work and save. I care nothing for white women: they mean nothing to me."

When they arrived in Paris, the musicians quickly became anxious about their future. There was no sign of their benefactor; it soon became apparent that the grandiose plans for opening a cabaret were in ruins. The backer paid their bills, but then returned to America, leaving them to fend for themselves.

They were lucky. First they got a short engagement at the Empire Music Hall, which led to other offers. Then they were invited to go to play in a hotel in Venice for about two months and decided to accept. "It was just about twilight on a sweltering mid-summer day in 1928 that the four of us got out of an international train in Venice," Crowder wrote. "The reality of it was something far beyond my wildest imaginations." They moved into a modest hotel and found the café-restaurant where they were to play, the Luna, "next to the Royal Palace near St. Marks Cathedral." They began work the next night. Within a week Nancy was among their regular audience. Crowder recalled:

> One evening, on about the fourth or fifth night we worked, we were all startled to see a most peculiar and striking woman enter the ballroom accompanied by a tall man. I say we were startled because Negro musicians always carry on a running fire comment on all women who come into a night club,

cabaret or restaurant where they are working. When this particular woman appeared, looking so thin, so white and so fragile, all sorts of exclamations came from different members of the band and quite a lot of laughter. . . . The woman continued coming to the dance night after night. She always seemed to enjoy the music but I don't remember any of us paying any particular attention to her.

One evening as he was leaving the restaurant, Crowder saw that Mike, the handsome banjo player, was sitting with the white couple. "I had to pass the table where Mike was sitting with his white friends. As I passed, I heard a feminine voice say, 'Won't you sit down and have a drink?' " He accepted, and

I then found myself being introduced to Nancy Cunard and her cousin Edward Cunard. . . . It was she who was to open up new avenues of thought for me and because of her I was to change my ideas of life and opinions about many things. As I sat talking to her I could not help but notice the intense though impressive eagerness of her attitude. She was no ordinary person. Everything about her even down to small mannerisms denoted high breeding and graciousness.

She was not exactly what I would call a beautiful woman but she did make a very striking appearance that compelled attention. I thoroughly enjoyed that first conversation with her.

As for Nancy, she loved the music the Alabamians played and was intrigued by their good looks, relaxed manners, and their color. Soon after she made the first move toward meeting the quartet, she probably decided that an adventure with one or another of them would be a possibility.

In 1928 Crowder was in his late thirties or early forties—eight or ten years older than Nancy. He was tall, as tall as Nancy or taller, well built, with slightly receding hair and regular, neat features. His high cheekbones and faintly oriental eyes may have come from his Indian blood. His skin was a coppery brown. It had been a long struggle for him to escape poverty, the South, and the shadier side of the entertainment world. A bit of luck and the tide of fashion had brought him to the Hotel Luna that summer; he was determined not to lose any chances, and above all not slip back into seedy obscurity if he could help it.

According to Crowder, after their first meeting it was Nancy, not he, who made the first move. First, she appeared one afternoon while he was practicing the piano at the hotel, asking where the proprietor could be found. Then,

> A day or two later all four members of the band were sitting at dinner when the waiter came and said a lady wanted to speak to the pianist on the telephone. Imagine our surprise and mine most of all for I was not only the most conservative man in the crowd but also the oldest.
>
> All of the other boys had definitely announced that they were on the look out for a chance to have an affair with some woman of wealth and position. I had always derided their ambitions so we were all naturally startled that I should be the first to get this much-desired opportunity. We all felt that a telephone call from a white woman after such a short time in Venice could not possibly mean anything else. The boys all exchanged knowing glances as I left the table.

Nancy pressed Crowder to leave his friends and dine with her. "It was hell. There were the three men behind me who had heard me speak my views on the subject any number of times. There was a soft, persuasive voice in the receiver at my ear dangling an interesting invitation before me. I hesitated: I accepted."

The Alabamians teased Crowder ferociously when he returned to the table to say he was leaving. He was rescued by a gondola sent by Nancy to fetch him. He found her alone, and dinner was served immediately, as he had to get back to the Luna to play that evening. Crowder was impressed by Nancy's beautiful apartment and by her sophisticated intelligence. After dinner she suggested he might like to see some of her collection of African jewelry. "We moved into the bedroom which was adjacent to the dining room. She then showed me some African bracelets, beads and one or two objects of gold. They were the first of their kind I had ever seen but in some peculiar manner they elicited my warmest admiration. In all, she showed me quite a number of things, some of which she was wearing."

As they looked at the bracelets and beads, they found themselves close together. Still Crowder did not feel confident enough to follow up Nancy's lead. But as he was leaving, "what I thought I saw in her face made me throw caution to the winds." He tried to kiss her but she turned her head away. Then, as he was about to go, she quickly kissed him on the lips.

Crowder said good-bye and the gondola took him back to work. He kept quiet when his friends pressed him for details; his fingers moved mechanically over the keyboard while he asked himself "what it all meant and where it might lead."

Soon after that evening, Crowder discovered "who Nancy Cunard really was." He had resolved to work hard and further his career; he had also resolved not to get entangled with a white woman. Now a white woman, who turned out to be rich and influential, was showing a decided interest in him.

Probably Crowder, whatever his doubts, didn't really have a chance. Nancy was used to getting what she wanted. She left Venice for a few days to visit Florence and Rome, and while she was away, she kept up a steady correspondence with Crowder. A handful of letters from Crowder to Nancy have survived; a few of them date from Venice at the very beginning of their relationship. They read like love letters: he calls her "the sweetest woman I have ever known," regrets that "my command of words is entirely too inadequate to permit my ever telling you what a divine person you are." But also they show that Crowder was fully aware from the very first that he and Nancy were starting something out of the ordinary. One letter opens, "It seems that I am bridging centuries in writing this to you."

He told her how a group of English people came into the Luna, sat at "their" table and stared at him, and asked him to sing a solo. "I sang 'I can't help loving that gal of mine.' I thought of you all evening." She wrote him long letters that he found "so interesting" and which seem to have given him the impression that she did not find life easy. Crowder wrote back: "Nancy I do believe I understand and although I know that I love you as I have never loved anyone, there is the element of understanding and sympathy. . . . Whatever the outcome of this romance of ours, you may know now that mine is a love that though deep, strong and passionate is withal highly protective of you, and intensely sympathetic."

Nancy impressed him by describing her work at the Hours Press. "You say you are one of the toilers of the world, and that you must get back to your printing. . . . How I love you for wanting and trying to [do] something of a tangible nature."

When she came back to Venice, Crowder gave in.

"I knew that the feeling of mutual pleasure was real. . . . I kept telling myself that I was doing the right thing; that the choice I had made was for the better. But I am afraid real reason had little to do with the decision. I was infatuated beyond all reason."

After this, Nancy began to see a lot of the band. She especially liked the drummer's wife, a beautiful black American woman who had come over with them and who caused a sensation in Venice. Nancy used to join the group after they had finished work for the night, and she would stay up late drinking and watching them play cards. She gave them all Venetian glass rings. Crowder's was jade lined with gold.

But according to Crowder, he and Nancy were not yet lovers. Since such delay was not like Nancy, one can only suppose that Crowder was still feeling cautious. Then Nancy decided to give a masked ball. She asked the group to come on after they finished at the Luna to play for her guests. Crowder remembered in particular Oliver Messel "because he had his eyelashes done up in silver" and a curious man who had lost a box of cocaine and tried to inveigle Crowder into the bathroom with him. "I escaped the ordeal, however, by attaching myself to Nancy. The party ended at daybreak in a downpour of rain. Although I felt rather sad for some reason as I stood at the window watching the rain, everyone else seemed in the highest spirits as they left. I stayed behind. . . . We had breakfast together later in the day. It was my first experience of that kind."

To his slight surprise Crowder found himself explaining the American Constitution to Nancy over their first breakfast. He was baffled by her, but there seems no doubt that at this early stage he was genuinely infatuated with her. "Somehow I felt this woman had something that I had never discovered in any other person. I greatly admired her intelligence, experience and certain independence of thought. Later, I learned of other characteristics but at that moment I thought of her as a wonderful creature and allowed myself to be held by an invisible power she seemed to possess."

Life must have seemed good, even if puzzling, as the summer wore on. He was working hard—people like Elsa Maxwell were soon asking the group to play at their parties—and the romance with Nancy seemed established. But before long, he began to notice things about her that struck him as odd and disquieting. One night a fight began in the nightclub where they were playing. Nancy resisted all efforts to get her to leave; "she wanted to watch the last blow struck." Then he began to suspect that he was not Nancy's only lover. There was a handsome waiter she had taken a fancy to, and there was also a young Italian count in attendance. With her compulsion for keeping her sexual options open and her dread of being taken for the property of any man, Nancy was unable to resist playing Crowder and the rest off against one another. One night there was a scene in a restaurant when Nancy went off with the count.

Crowder was alarmed as well as angry, and disgusted by Nancy's conduct. He told himself he was taking a risk in becoming the rival of a powerful man in a foreign country. He resolved to break off the affair; but he found himself unable to do so. In thinking about it afterward, Crowder decided that that night in Venice was crucial. Even though it was not enough in itself to end his relationship with Nancy it was enough to introduce an element of cynicism, even of calculation on his part. "After that brawl I did know though that any love I might have had for Nancy had been killed. I saw myself as a pawn upon her chessboard of life. I realized I was no longer the king I had imagined myself to be but still I was in the game and I thought in a strategical position. And even though I was only a player in her game I felt I had been cast for an important part."

Nancy was unable to avoid the trap that society and her own nature had set. Both she and Crowder knew she could do a great deal for him. She wanted to help him, but in her own way, on her terms. Perhaps it was just as well that she did not know how clearly he saw the situation. She told him how much she wanted to help him and further his career. Crowder could not resist such an opportunity.

> The proposals she had made led me to believe that my progress would be greater if I saw the end of what had begun. Maybe it was a spirit of adventure, but something would not let me stop there—I wanted to see where it would all lead. But I was determined from that night on to do so in a detached and coolly calculating way. Even if I was going to be used to satisfy some other person's pleasure I felt I was going to enjoy it also. I might lose in the end but the path she followed promised innumerable new things to a black man who had only seen life from a colored man's viewpoint.

When the engagement at the Luna ended early in October, the group began to make plans for returning to Paris. Nancy was staying on for a while. Crowder decide to stay on too.

The end of that summer in Venice was not propitious. Before leaving, Crowder's musician friends had filled his ears with warnings. Victor Cunard had also made cautionary noises to Nancy about lingering in fascist Italy alone with her black lover, and about assuming that they could travel together freely and openly. Crowder's hotel proprietor seemed hostile. He and Nancy began to feel that they were being watched. They decided to return to Paris.

As the train approached Paris, Nancy became more and more nervous. She finally told Crowder what had happened in Venice between her and Aragon; she was afraid that Aragon might have discovered when she was returning to Paris and be at the station to make a scene. He was not, but Nancy hurried Crowder off to a small hotel, and made a point of telling him all the places where Aragon might be in Paris, so that they could avoid him. This uncharacteristic nervousness did not last long; and in fact, as Nancy was soon to discover, there was about to be another powerful woman in Aragon's life. A few weeks after his return from Venice he had met a small, determined, red-haired Russian girl named Elsa Triolet. She fell deeply in love with Aragon and became determined to capture him. Once their romance was under way, it dominated his life as thoroughly as his allegiance to the Communist party.

Yet even now, according to André Thirion, Aragon was for a while unable to resist Nancy, in spite of all that had happened. "He had not put a stop to his relationship with Nancy entirely; for she, with a tenderness and a snakelike power, would fascinate her victims for a long time, and prevented them taking back all their liberty. She like to go on seeing her old lovers. In fact, she took life in all it complexity and could not understand why she should force herself not to be in love with Aragon any more, just because she wanted to sleep with Henry Crowder."

Aragon would see her in Paris or down at Réanville; according to Thirion, he would come back from these encounters "in pieces." Even after Elsa Triolet forbade Nancy's name to be mentioned in her presence, Aragon could not keep away. Thirion and Sadoul used to act as go-betweens. But slowly Elsa Triolet's power over Aragon grew and Nancy's diminished. Elsa Triolet was single-minded; Nancy had other interests and other men—Crowder in particular.

When Crowder made contact again with the quartet, he found them relieved to see him and curious about his relationship with Nancy. He also found that the news of Nancy's new affair had already spread around Paris, especially black Paris. He found himself for the first time notorious, and envied. He admits he rather enjoyed it. He also enjoyed meeting Nancy's friends, several of whom he knew already from Venice. Both her cousins, who had met Crowder in Venice, were friendly to him; indeed all Nancy's Paris friends, whatever they privately thought, were intrigued by her latest romance and happy to spend time with the couple.

However, to one observer at least, it still seemed in the winter of 1928–29 that Nancy must be mad not to commit herself once and for all to Aragon, who still loved her so desperately, instead of convincing herself that she was now in love with what seemed to him the unlikely figure of Henry Crowder. This observer was Richard Aldington, an English poet and aspiring novelist who, having been through the war and having come to the end of a complicated marriage to the American poet Hilda Doolittle, had moved to Paris. He had been a friend of Ezra Pound, Wyndham Lewis, and T. S. Eliot since before the war; thus he and Nancy had friends and interests in common. Yet they did not meet until the autumn of 1928, in Rome, just after Nancy met Henry Crowder. Nancy would later describe how one morning after a party given by Ezra Pound she was awakened by Aldington, who came into her room and announced: "I've come instead of Ezra." Nancy would describe, wickedly, how dirty his trousers were and how generally slovenly he looked, and how he held his hand over his balls and "pounced," though she declined his favors. "Oh, no no! Not this!" After which, she went on to say, they had a nice talk and a drive in the country.

Whatever the truth in this tale, Nancy and Aldington became friends who talked poetry and publishing, probably had a passing affair (although with his reddish hair and pink cheeks Aldington struck Nancy as "the typical Englishman and not the type I find particularly comely"), and by the autumn and winter of 1928 saw each other often in Paris. But by this time Nancy was caught up in her new romance with Crowder, and Aldington had just fallen in love with the woman he was to live with for ten years, Bridget Patmore. His letters to Bridget give an especially vivid picture of Nancy at this critical time in her life.

Nancy features in these letters often for several reasons, Aldington was fascinated by her and by the situation she had created for herself. He was anxious to reassure Bridget, whom he was trying to persuade to join him in Paris, that he was not in love with Nancy; but he was also using his relationship with Nancy as a smokescreen to conceal his romance with Bridget, who did not want it known. He was also desperately anxious to get his work recognized (this was before his first big success with his war novel *Death of a Hero*) and interested in Nancy's plans for the Hours Press; his friendship with her was thus not entirely disinterested.

Aldington had a strong streak of the puritan in him; and while he admired Nancy's extraordinary qualities, he was frequently repelled by her drinking and aggressive sexuality. He protests slightly too often, after a late night out with Nancy around the cafés and nightclubs, how much he disapproves of such a way of life, and there is smugness in the way he deplores Nancy's sexual conduct; but there is no mistaking the fascination with which he observed her gyrations nor the fears he had for her future.

Richard Aldington and Bridget Patmore had spent part of the summer of 1928 staying with D. H. Lawrence and his wife Frieda on an island off the south coast of France. By the early autumn, news had leaked out that Aldington was seriously involved with someone new; and he decided to encourage the rumor that his new love was Nancy. He wrote to Bridget from Paris: "I shall rather *affiché* myself with Nancy, go to Barney's [Natalie Barney] and cafés with her, and write to Lorenzo [D. H. Lawrence] from her house when I am next there. Won't that bother him." The plan worked, at least with Pound: "Ezra's letter was most amusing. He is convinced that Nancy is the cause, and says

> 'Behold, what perils do environ
> The man what meddles with a siren. . . .' "

And again: "Amusing letter from Ezra. He does think it is Nancy. Have written letter denying it in such a way that he will think it true. He will write to everybody."

Aldington seems to have heard nothing of what had happened in Venice; but he soon caught up when Nancy and Crowder reached Paris.

> . . . at 10:30, just as I was finishing a page, and thinking of bed, comes a tap at the door, and enter Nancy, literally clothed in cloth of gold (wouldn't Lorenzo rub in the talisman). She insisted that I get into evening clothes and to to Montmartre. I didn't particularly want to go. . . . However out we went, sat in a café and talked for an hour and agreed to be good friends and not lovers. . . . Well, that important point settled, went off to Montmartre and went to a most amusing nigger cabaret. (Between ourselves, I deduce that Nancy has now passed to the *culte des nègres,* and is no longer interested in poor white

trash.) The dancing room was decorated in Style Moderne
with fanciful patterns in blue and silver of no particular shape
or meaning; there was an alcove with a large picture of a
Mississippi steamboat seen in oblique perspective from the
front; the walls had a number of black panels rather like school
blackboards, with very clever sketches of negroes in white
outline. There were wall seats of pinkish velvet, and tables
with red and white check tablecloths. The nigger orchestra
was good, but I didn't think it very exciting; but I was introduced to "Henry," the nigger pianist and he turned out to be
one of Jelly Roll Morton's Red Hot Peppers. Such a thrill.
There were some turns—a nigger songstress whom Nancy
thought marvellous and I thought rather bad; a nigger lady,
clothed only in a red and silver cache sexe and silver breast
containers, who dances with remarkable undulations of her
lumbar regions; and a negro man who cut double shuffles with
unusual celerity.

We met Aragon, Dolly Wilde, Victor and Edward (? Cu-
narders) and Nancy danced with Victor and Dolly with Edward while I watched and talked to Henry and Aragon. I like
Aragon very much; he has a very beautiful and sensitive face,
and a charming manner. But he is jealous as a million devils,
and made a frightful scene with Nancy about 3 a.m. apropos a
girl whom he said Nancy had taken away from him, and also
apropos of "Henry." Nancy was furious, and they went out
and had a row in the street, and then came back and rowed
over supper like husband and wife.

At last, Aldington relates, Nancy jumped up and took Aragon off in a taxi, saying she was going to the country then
and there; but whispered to the others to stay, rejoined them
half an hour later, and "discussed the unfortunate Louis until
4:30. I tried to persuade her to make it up. But she wouldn't,
and I left her to Henry at 4:30 and returned home."

When Aldington discussed his own romantic problems with
Nancy, her reply was characteristic: "Never mind, darling,
you'll solve those complications by getting into others." This
remark, casual though it certainly was, offers a clue to
Nancy's own behavior. Rather than attempting to sort out

difficulties, physical or emotional, in any serious love affair, Nancy would plunge into another. There was arrogance and cruelty in her conduct, but there was also desperation and fear.

Aldington played the same role on other evenings. Nancy would summon him, or pass by his hotel and demand his company until Crowder, who by now was playing at the Plantation, had finished work for the night. Usually he went, sometimes with a good grace, at other times, if his letters to Bridget are to be believed, reluctantly. He wanted to tell Nancy how deeply he was in love, and eventually, overcoming Bridget's scruples, he did and found her sympathetic and helpful. She was always a loyal friend to lovers, and she admired and like Bridget, whom she knew slightly. Aldington was touched when she said, "Bridget's a *divine* woman," and he passed the remark on. In return, he saw her through some violent storms of emotion over her new romance.

Aldington's attitude to Nancy and Crowder was ambivalent. He was well enough disposed toward Crowder as a person; but his view of the relationship was influenced by snobbery, both racial and social. Above all, he became increasingly skeptical about the depth and reality of Nancy's feelings. Her behavior under emotional strain horrified him.

"Last night I met Nancy at a foul little bar near the Opera at midnight. . . . Nancy *of course* was dead drunk, but I managed to get her to the 'Plantation' (Henry's place). . . . How Nancy does it, I don't know. But I like Henry very much. I think Nancy is right to love him—he has a mysterious, 'all right,' d'aplomb quality which I like. He isn't beautiful, like Louis (whom Nancy tortures in an abominable way), but he has the poise, the sense of life of the blacks, which we whites are losing."

In fact, Aldington wrote so often and so much about Nancy that Bridget Patmore must have wondered whether there was as little between them as he maintained. Aldington tried to explain.

Last night I saw Nancy, with Louis and Marcel Jouhandeau (the nicest man I've met here). It was rather awful and squalid. There had been a row there with Henry (this time) and Nancy was dead drunk, talking of suicide or taking drugs. I must say I rather admired the tenderness of those men. After all it wasn't very pleasant for Louis and J to have their amie dead drunk and in despair over a black, but they were both perfect to her. She drank more gin at the D'Harcourt, and got so incoherent I couldn't understand her in French or English. So J and I talked about Gérard de Nerval and le problème de la folie and left Louis to deal with the situation.

Aldington was greatly impressed by Aragon's patience.

I must also say that I think Nancy is crazy not to stick with Louis. He loves her in the most complete and touching way, the look in his eyes and his whole expression—so soft, so gentle when he looks at her, whereas he is so ferocious and truculent (like Ezra in our youth) with the rest of the world. She is a goose not to take the man who loves her, and whom she really loves. Henry is a sort of caprice, and the despair is only because someone else, another woman, liked Henry. In other words, Nancy wants every kind of freedom and liberty, even to hurt like hell, but won't grant it. . . .

Do you think this pharasaical? Do you think it pharasaical to add that I think her a "warning"? . . . Good God, I am glad I never got involved with her. . . .

Understand about Nancy once and for ever. . . . I do not love her at all. But I like a certain manly "decency" about her, and I'm desperately sorry for her. I've sometimes thought in the past that my own life was dreary and messed up, but, my god, when I look at hers—She lacks not only elementary common sense, but the capacity to love with any purpose, continuity, tenderness. Maybe I'm hard on her because I like Louis so much, and want to push her into his arms. So much for her. But don't you think that there is anything to bother about there.

At times Aldington saw the atmosphere and way of life of the international group in Paris as the key to Nancy's behavior.

"These 'quarter' types leave me a bit staggered and feeling rather 1880. They seem to have killed all beauty, all poetry, all sensibility, all feelings, all love, with drink, cynicism and unlimited promiscuity. You ask what it is that Nancy misses—well, it's just that. Only there is a fineness in her which rebels against this squalid soddenness; her only hope is her misery." At other times he felt it was all a question of her own difficult nature, and as the weeks passed, he became more critical.

As 1929 approached, he was busy planning an important New Year's Eve party for himself, Bridget and her elder son, Derek, at the Plantation, where Crowder was still playing. "I was on the phone to Nancy last night, and told her I was bringing 'friends' to the Plantation, and she said—'What fun—how dear of you, Aldington.' You see, darling, she really feels *awfully* the condemnation of her affair with a 'black' and I'm sorry for her. Be nice to her."

But a few months later, his tone had changed. By this time, Nancy was obsessed with the idea of making a trip to Africa with Crowder, who, as his own account makes abundantly plain, had reservations about any such project.

"Nancy now wants to go back to Africa with Henry. I give up. I've tried to 'help' (Lord help me) and fix things up between her and Louis, but it's hopeless. Nancy thinks she loves Henry—but she doesn't love—he's a stronger sexual drug, that's all. She sent me some of her poems—rather beautiful, but very pathetic. At the rate she's going she'll be dead in five years. So much for Nancy."

Gradually, Nancy's hold over Louis Aragon was broken. She always regarded him as one of her most special friends, and they continued to meet from time to time, though less often as the years went by. His impact on her was certainly less dramatic, in emotional terms, than hers on him; but her time with Aragon and her link, through him, with the Surrealists had a deep effect on her life. Her wish to live outside conventional society was reinforced, and her belief in artists and intellectuals as a catalyst in society grew stronger. So did her sense of having the right, almost the duty, to shock.

As for Aragon, it can hardly be a coincidence that after his confused years with Nancy he found strength and security within a happy, exclusive marriage, which in time became elevated by conscious choice to the ultimate public demonstration of the ideal love that Nancy had been so dramatically unsuited to represent. Aragon and Elsa Triolet lived, worked, traveled, and wrote together. The solidarity of their relationship flourished within the stern context of the Communist party. They maintained loyalty and silence at times when others cracked and spoke out. Aragon's life became more and more disciplined, and his work flourished. Nancy's life became even more erratic; for her too, her work and her life became one, but through confusion and chance rather than through certainties, whether emotional or political.

Nancy wanted to return to Réanville and take up the Hours Press in earnest, but first she needed to make a trip to London. Before she left, she suggested to Crowder that since he needed somewhere to live, he should find an apartment and that she should pay half the rent. "This struck me as extraordinary," wrote Crowder. "Since our first meeting I had never asked for help of any kind and had certainly never broached the subject of money gifts. I did not need or really want an apartment but agreed to her proposal, thinking it would not do to argue about a few hundred francs at that stage of our friendship." This disingenuous explanation rings only partly true. As Nancy must have quickly realized, and as his own account of their relationship confirms, Crowder was vulnerable where money was concerned. His judgment, or his conscience, or his dignity, would tell him that he should not depend on her, but he always ended up taking what she offered. He says, almost indignantly, "At no time during our relationship was personal financial gain any part of my thought," and this was probably true. The trouble was, as he himself admits, that he had taken up with Nancy because he thought she could help him get on, and this in itself—the interesting people, the parties, the travel—meant spending her money.

Nancy returned from London full of plans for the Hours Press. The report for Norman Douglas—the production of which earlier in the year had taught her and Aragon the printer's trade—was the only publication that had actually appeared so far. Now, she had Douglas's *One Day* to work on (he had given it to her in Florence) and she wanted to get Moore's *Peronnik the Fool* into print before Christmas. Richard Aldington was eager to give her his work. She decided to leave Paris for La Chapelle-Réanville and concentrate on the press.

But while Crowder was playing at the Plantation, Nancy continued to spend a good deal of time in Paris, particularly in the evenings and at weekends. She contrived, despite the late hours they both kept and the hectic life she was leading, to show him life in Paris. Some aspects of it were a revelation to Crowder, who despite his experience with the brothels of Washington seems to have been, if not innocent, at least conventional in his attitudes to sex. His attitude to lesbians led, according to Crowder, to their first quarrel.

"She told me flatly that she liked lesbians; had enjoyed their company before and hoped to do so again. My answer was that I wanted nothing to do with lesbians or anyone who had anything to do with them. 'In that case,' Nancy replied, 'we had better separate right here.' " They did; but not for long. Crowder's prejudice was overcome. "Since that time I have met, dined and danced with many lesbians and have had reason to radically change my opinion of them. . . . I think I can now number several lesbians among the best friends I have known in Europe."

Nancy and Crowder were each introducing the other to new worlds. Through her, he was now meeting the rich, fashionable, and intellectual and finding out what it was like to live among such people on a more or less equal footing. Meanwhile, through Crowder, Nancy was able to penetrate the seductive, raffish world of the blacks in Paris, where she met musicians, actors, boxers, and dancers. In Paris both of them found they could explore these new territories with intoxicating freedom. Sex, inevitably, played a part in these explorations. Nancy's curiosity about blacks and her drive to know them was, especially to begin with, partly sexual. Just as from the first she was quite prepared to take other white lovers while she pursued her affair with Crowder, so not very long after their return together to Paris she was to start sleeping with other blacks.

At first, Crowder found this especially painful, even though he had realized that physical fidelity was not to be expected from Nancy. He noticed that she remained interested in Mike, the handsome banjo player who had introduced them in Venice, and he felt humiliated when, after a while, he was forced to recognize that Nancy was having a passionate affair with another black musician, Dan. Aldington observed this development with much disapproval. Crowder never made scenes or attempted to remonstrate with her over her affairs. He had already accepted that side of her nature, and he knew there was no point.

And Crowder's own role among Nancy's circle was not entirely innocent. Since a number of her men friends were homosexual or bisexual, and since the sexual appeal of blacks was as novel and exciting to homosexuals as to heterosexuals, Crowder and his friends were soon popular in homosexual circles. Crowder professes to have felt outrage and bewilderment when any of Nancy's homosexual friends made advances to him, but several people remember him being, if not acquiescent, anyway relaxed about it at the time. One of them recalls a party given for Henry Crowder by an elderly rich homosexual, at which the host presented the guest of honor with champagne in a glass shaped like a phallus.

But Crowder was popular among Nancy's friends for other reasons, too. Although in no way a brilliant or exceptional man, he was good-natured and good company, with a lot of common sense and a quiet, ironic humor that often acted as a useful brake on Nancy's wilder impulses. He did a good deal of looking after Nancy, which was much needed, particularly when she had been drinking, and often got an armful of ivory bracelets across the face by way of thanks. Janet Flanner remembers meeting him one day with a fine set of bruises, and asking him what had happened. "Just braceletwork, Miss Janet," he said calmly. He was patient, in a mildly embarrassed way, with Nancy's often expressed wish that he had a blacker skin, or that he behave in a more primitive, exotic manner. "Be more *African*, be more *African*," Harold Acton remembers Nancy saying to Crowder one evening. "But I *ain't* African. I'm *American*," Crowder replied mildly.

He was also quietly resistant to one of Nancy's plans which she pursued more and more persistently. She longed for them to travel together to black Africa. Crowder didn't much care for the idea of visiting a British colony as the companion of a well-connected white woman who enjoyed making scenes, nor did their friends when the plan came up, as it frequently did. Someone had the idea that perhaps if a third person, white, went with them, it would be better. Nancy tried hard to persuade Norman Douglas to join in the scheme, and he toyed with the idea, but more for the fun of doing so than for any serious reason. She also tried to enlist her journalist friend Otto Theis, but he decided it would not be sensible either.

Before long, as the winter arrived, Nancy wanted to settle in at La Chapelle-Réanville, and she wanted Crowder with her. Apart from liking his company, she needed his help. She started to persuade him to stop working and to join her in Normandy, where he could play and compose as much as he liked, and help her with the running of the press. Later on, she made it sound as if the move was largely for his own good. "Henry, always a thoughtful, serious minded man (although on occasion in rhapsodically rollicking mood), was sick to death of night hours, of all the drinks sent to him at his piano, of the fatigue attendant on the adulation of Montmartre and those interminable 'crapgames' at dawn he and the other musicians would be playing in the Flea Pit, too weary to go home and sleep. I got him away from all that and we hired a piano for Réanville."

He felt he could not allow a woman to keep him. It was a

nasty shooting incident in Montmartre, he says, that changed his mind. Mike, the banjo player, was drinking heavily, and one night after finishing work, in a truculent mood, he got into a fight with another musician about the rival bands and the merits of black musicians. They both had guns, and the quarrel ended in the small hours with bullets spraying the street outside the fashionable Bricktop's nightclub. Several innocent bystanders were hurt, Mike ended up in jail, and Nancy and Victor Cunard had to come to his rescue with clothes, food, cigarettes, and a lawyer (found with Aragon's help). The band broke up, Crowder was out of work, it was winter; he decided to go to Réanville. But he tried to ensure that he would not simply be living off Nancy. They agreed that he should be paid a weekly salary and arranged a routine of work for him.

For a time, Nancy and Crowder were happy to be alone together in the country. Crowder liked the house itself very much, though it was bitterly cold and he could not quite see the point of the arrangement of rooms Nancy and Aragon had devised. He thought the eccentric plan reflected the oddness of Nancy's character. They went for long walks, explored the countryside, and read, and Crowder played the piano. There were two servants (a chauffeur and his wife), the cook, plenty of drink, and it looked as if Nancy was really trying to make Crowder happy with his decision. "I knew if those first weeks we spent together in the country were any criterion of what was to follow I would never regret having set all of my other ideas on the shelf. At that moment the future again looked bright for the way she talked I felt I might yet accomplish big things and complete a life which my race could point to with pride."

During these early weeks together at Le Puits Carré Nancy and Crowder had a conversation that both of them remembered forever as a turning point. "One night during a regular after-dinner conversation the question of Negroes and conditions affecting them in America came up. I was amazed at Nancy's ignorance about such matters," says Crowder.

But she was interested and eager to learn. I told her of Negro writers; told her where she could get books on and by Negroes. Gradually she began to build up her library with Negro books. She took a yearly subscription to *The Crisis* a left-wing Negro magazine published in New York. American Negro newspapers also made their appearance.

I was glad and pleased that she showed an interest in my race and thought from the way she talked she really wanted to do something for the Negro cause. I did not have the slightest idea at the time, however, that such a chance topic of conversation would lead to the amazing chain of events which were destined to follow.

For the moment, however, Nancy was principally concerned with getting the Hours Press off to a proper start. For the next two years, the press and Crowder were the two pivots on which her life revolved.

The Hours Press (I)

The late twenties and early thirties were the heyday of the small publishing venture. Several of Nancy's friends and acquaintances in London and Paris had been running their own small publishing and printing operations for years. In London the most substantial and successful was the Hogarth Press, founded in 1919 by Leonard and Virginia Woolf, who had published Nancy's *Parallax* in 1925. John Rodker, whom she knew well, had also been running his own publishing firm since 1919. She was acquainted with David Garnett, who joined the Meynells in the Nonesuch Press in 1923, and with Jack Lindsay, who started the Fanfrolico Press in 1926. She knew of Laura Riding and Robert Graves, who set up the Seizin Press in London in 1927. These enterprises shared aims with which Nancy was strongly sympathetic: to publish good writing that was not necessarily commercial and to produce handsomely printed, well-designed books.

In Paris, Nancy's world had always overlapped with the world of the little magazines and presses run by expatriates—most of them Americans, several of them women—which during the twenties managed to produce an astonishing flow of new talent. She was one of the original subscribers to Sylvia Beach's lending library at her bookshop in the rue de l'Odéon, and had bought *Ulysses* when it came out under Sylvia Beach's imprint in 1922. She was friendly for a while with Robert McAlmon, the American writer who had been married to Bryher, the poet and daughter of Sir John Eller-

man, one of the richest men in England. McAlmon founded
Contact Editions in Paris in 1922, where he was the first to
publish Ernest Hemingway. She had visited Norman Douglas
and Pino Orioli while they were publishing and selling Douglas's work at the Lungarno Press in Florence. And she had
known Ezra Pound for over ten years; during the early
twenties in Paris Pound was the center of most avant-garde
writing and publishing, as foreign editor of Margaret Anderson's *Little Review* and of the *Dial,* as one of the most original
and prolific writers himself, and as one of the most consistent
suppliers of material, either his own or his friends', to the
small magazines and publishers.

Nancy had two aims in mind when she started the Hours
Press. She wanted to publish contemporary poetry, and she
wanted to learn how to print by hand—"not so much," as she
later wrote, "from the purely aesthetic point of view as from
the sense of independent creativeness it might give one." Although Nancy never said so, it is possible that she had begun
to doubt whether she had the talent to sustain her career as a
poet. She kept on writing and publishing occasional poems,
but she needed to try a more practical outlet for her energies.
Her approach to her press was only partly amateur; she was
determined to do most of the work herself, but from the first
she intended it to be run in a businesslike manner and, if
possible, to make a profit. Unlike several of her contemporaries who used their publishing ventures to get their work
into print, Nancy never seems even to have considered using
the Hours for her own writing.

Some of her friends found it hard to envisage her in this
new role; after all, she had shown little sign of application or
organization so far. John Rodker, she would remember, "was
positively bewildered," though "encouraging, if rather surprised at me." The Woolfs wrote to warn her that printing by
hand was dirty work. "I cannot think they wanted to dissuade
me, yet I can still hear their cry: 'Your hands will always be
covered with ink.' . . . This seemed no deterrent. And it was
with curiosity I looked at my black and greasy hands after the

first go with the inking table." In fact, it was to be the physical, practical side of the business that Nancy enjoyed most. She loved handling the type, choosing the paper, designing the pages, and running them off.

> The smell of printer's ink pleased me greatly, as did the beautiful freshness of the glistening pigment. There is no other black or red like it. After a rinse in petrol and a good scrub with soap and hot water, my fingers again became perfectly presentable; the right thumb, however, began to acquire a slight ingrain of grey, due to the leaden composition. I soon learned that greasy black hands do not matter when one is at the proofing stage, but an immaculate touch is most important in handling the fair sheet when one has reached the pulling stage.

During the early summer of 1928 Nancy had decided how the financial side of the Hours Press would work. After the production costs of each piece had been deducted, the authors would receive one-third of the profits, except for such famous and established writers as George Moore or Norman Douglas, who would get half. "In a large, black ledger I noted on one page the cost of every successive book, such as printers' time, light, heat, paper, binding, postage, and a small percentage of the expenses of circulars and their postage—and that was all. On the opposite page were entered orders, addresses and payments. There is a great deal to be said for doing things oneself, by one's own system."

She had also sent out a circular to likely individual buyers listing the first eight books she planned to publish over the next eight months. She lined up bookshops in London (the Warren Gallery), New York (the Holiday Bookshop), Paris (Edward Titus), and Florence (Pino Orioli). On Norman Douglas's advice, she offered bookshops a relatively small discount of 10 percent, but the response she received was "gratifyingly prompt." She resented the amount of money required to advertise her books, though she occasionally did spend it. She was skillful in securing free publicity by approaching journalists on such papers as the Paris *Herald Tribune* or *Sketch* (London). The first circular, sent out in the summer of 1928, listed *Peronnik the Fool* by George Moore, *Saint George at Silene* by Alvaro Guevara, *The Hunting of the Snark* by Lewis Carroll (translated by Aragon as *La Chasse au Snark*), *The Eaten Heart* by Richard Aldington, the *Probable Music of Beowulf* by Ezra Pound, *One Day* by Norman Douglas, *A Canto* by Ezra Pound, and *A Plaquette of Poems* by Iris Tree.

Nancy did not look very far outside her circle of acquaintances for material; this was to remain true for virtually all her productions. All her first authors were friends. Actually she did not publish Ezra Pound's *Cantos* until 1930 (and he never finished the advertised essay on music), and Iris Tree's poems did not materialize; but the rest appeared as advertised, with the addition of a short book of three essays by Arthur Symons, *Mes Souvenirs*. Symons was a friend of George Moore, a poet and critic of the older generation, whom Nancy had known since the war in London, when they would discuss Verlaine (whom Symons had introduced to London) and Mallarmé (whose work he would urge Nancy to translate).

At first, after Nancy returned to Réanville in November, she and Lévy were working alone. Nancy described the return as "dire." The house was freezing cold, and the stove in the printery gave off fumes that made them sleepy; there were no more long, light evenings and there were frequent power cuts. Lévy lodged in the village, and Nancy soon found she did not care for living and working alone except for him and two "gawky French servants." She struggled on with *Peronnik,* and received a kind letter from George Moore regretting that he could not pay her and the press a visit "and walk round your little domain with you." She was relieved that he could not; "the thought of G.M. at Réanville in such conditions and temperatures, made me shudder. What would he have found? Icy draughts in the nice but uncomfortable house. No steaming cups of tea in a warm room over literary conversation, for work in the printery would see to that. No leisurely walks through wooded glades such as we had known in past summers. No smiles of attainment in me, more likely a worried frown."

In her later account of the Hours Press, Nancy omitted all personal details that were not relevant to the press and its authors; but, as Crowder's and Richard Aldington's accounts make all too plain, she was leading a hectic life in Paris as well as trying to run the press and keep to her schedule of publications. She was delighted when Crowder accepted her offer of work, though not surprisingly in her later account she was reticent about the terms on which he came to Réanville and the precise part he was playing in her life. What stands out is her immense relief at having a reliable able-bodied man about the place. "By now the amount of clerking, as we called the billing and circularising, account-keeping and correspondence, was taking away much of my time in the printery. Henry, I thought, could assist me with this work, as well as in the printery. My hopes were soon realised, for Henry quickly learned to manipulate the press lever, and it was the three of us who finished the last pages of *Peronnik* at an accelerated rhythm."

Crowder, indeed, was "invaluable." He loved the house, and painted the whole of the outside and the fences. Nancy would often lose her temper at its inconveniences and talk of selling it, but Crowder would calm her down. He took over the packing and wrapping, where his early experience in the U.S. Postal Service came in useful. "It was he," Nancy wrote, "who taught me the right length of string to compute per package and the size of wrapping paper to prepare for one or more books." He addressed hundreds of envelopes, occasionally confused by the correct modes of addressing titled English customers. He and Lévy did not get on well, and Crowder kept out of Lévy's way as much as he could. He also mentions some tension between himself and George, the chauffeur, whose attitude to Nancy seemed overfamiliar until Crowder realized that at some stage they had been to bed together. Finally George was sacked, and Crowder took over driving the car on postal and other errands to Vernon and Paris.

Crowder remembers several guests at Réanville that winter, including Richard Aldington and Bridget Patmore, and Aragon, whom he describes as "a well bred French boy, very handsome," who "spoke excellent English and in all struck me as being very intelligent." Nancy assured Crowder that it was all over between Aragon and herself, adding, untruthfully, that "in her case the new love always definitely replaced the old." Crowder observed Nancy's annoyance as Elsa Triolet's hold on Aragon tightened until eventually he stopped coming to Réanville.

Peronnik was out just before Christmas 1928, as Nancy had intended. The binding was done in Paris to Nancy's specifications, as were most of the other Hours Press books, and although she did not think the bindery had followed her instructions closely enough, she was very pleased with Moore's praises and especially with his remark to her mother that the paper was the finest he had ever seen. The two hundred copies were sold out by publication day, and the reviews were good.

The next piece of work was Alvaro Guevara's four-page poem, *Saint George at Silene,* which he had given Nancy ten years earlier. Nancy and Guevara had seen something of each other since he had returned from Chile in 1925, bringing her as a tribute two huge primitive stone heads, and since he was no longer desperately in love with her, they had become friends. He was fascinated by the Surrealists and interested to see Aragon going through the same misery Nancy had made him suffer. He came down to Réanville while Nancy was working on *Saint George*—a poem based upon the Saint George legend, which Nancy described as a "tender and violent narrative in verse"—and designed the covers himself, with words formed out of tiny, weeping red leaves. Nancy did the stitching and binding. The poem was kindly reviewed by Ezra Pound in the *Dial*.

While they were working on Guevara's poem, Richard Aldington suddenly asked Nancy to produce one hundred copies of a satirical anti-Christmas message, *Hark the Herald*. Nancy did it at once and sent it to him as a present.

For all his reservations about Nancy, Aldington continued to see her and Crowder in Paris and at Réanville. He urged her to expand the Hours Press, to print more copies of each work, and to double the size of the list. Nancy herself set his narrative poem based on a troubador legend, *The Eaten Heart*.

She and Crowder were involved in a car accident while driving the sheets of *The Eaten Heart* to Évreux to be bound. To Crowder's alarm and Nancy's fury the case dragged on, and they both felt that the French courts were being unfair to them because they were foreigners. They left France for England in the summer of 1929 with the case still unresolved.

This was Henry Crowder's first visit to England. He had heard from his black musician friends that London was not as relaxed as Paris about blacks mixing with whites; but he had spent so much time with Nancy's white friends in the preceding months that he had gained confidence. He had also come to know Nancy better. "I learned of her moods, her insatiable desire to always be doing something, of the quick-fire decisions she would make, of her will to finish what she had started regardless of the circumstances."

When they arrived in London, they had trouble finding a room for Crowder. Nancy had reserved a room for herself at the Eiffel Tower, but it was Derby week and Stulik had no more room. They set off by taxi to find somewhere else for him to stay but met with a series of refusals. Eventually, at the taxi driver's suggestion, they managed to get him into a hotel in Bloomsbury. Crowder found the humiliation worse because it was unexpected in London. Nancy was enraged.

Apart from this, things went smoothly. Crowder went sightseeing, and Nancy was constantly busy. She saw a great deal of her mother (according to Crowder, they met practically every day), but he observed that "she disliked doing this seemingly most natural thing very much and did it like a person taking a nasty dose of medicine."

Crowder met many of Nancy's friends, including the Theises and a handsome red-haired woman, also involved in publishing, called Wyn Henderson, whom he liked very much; they went out somewhere every night and met no sign of prejudice, although Crowder noticed that they met no other blacks at all.

Since Nancy and Crowder stayed in London over a month and went about together quite openly, it seems odd that they did not bump into Lady Cunard, and even odder to suppose that the many friends of Nancy who were also friends of her mother did not give Lady Cunard the news of the daughter's latest lover. It is inconceivable that Nancy asked people to keep her new romance a secret; but she clearly went to some trouble, on this and later visits, to keep Crowder and her mother apart. On one occasion when Tony Gandarillas, a rich Chilean who was a close friend of Lady Cunard as well as of Nancy, invited Nancy and Crowder to lunch, Nancy happened to mention the appointment to her mother. Crowder describes what happened:

> Nancy and Tony were laughingly discussing Her Ladyship when someone asked me jokingly if I would like to meet Lady Cunard. I replied with a very positive no. At that very moment an automobile drew up at the door and Tony, looking through the window, recognised it as belonging to Her Ladyship.
>
> "My God, Nancy," he cried. "Here is your mother. What shall we do?"
>
> Utter confusion reigned for a moment. I quickly saved the situation by telling Tony that I would not permit Her Ladyship to see me and immediately went upstairs.
>
> Lady Cunard came in, remained for a few moments and left, taking Nancy with her. I descended from my refuge and the meal resumed.

After half an hour or so Nancy reappeared, furious with her mother for spying on her, but "the lunch terminated in a very lighthearted and good-humored manner."

After Nancy and Crowder left England, they went back briefly to Réanville, where they discovered that in his absence Crowder had been summoned to court over the car accident and because of his nonappearance had been sentenced to a month in prison and a stiff fine. They managed to prove that they had never received the summons, and the case was set again for the autumn. They went on to Paris, where they met a man calling himself Prince Tovalou, described by Crowder as "a black pretender to the throne of some African kingdom," who much impressed Nancy, although Crowder was suspicious. Prince Tovalou also claimed to be a lawyer, so Nancy decided he was just the man to handle Crowder's accident case. They then left for what Crowder describes as a "hectic" summer, traveling all over southwest France and the Pyrenees, stopping in Bordeaux, Biarritz, Saint-Jean-de-Luz, visiting caves and châteaux in the Dordogne.

When they arrived back in Normandy, they discovered that Prince Tovalou had not only done nothing about the court case but had failed to turn up at court for the second hearing. Crowder was fined, the insurance company bore the costs, and Crowder wrote the prince a letter telling him he was a disgrace to the black race.

Faced with another winter at Réanville, Nancy decided to move the Hours Press to Paris. The practical difficulties in the country were too daunting. Plans for the next series of publications were ambitious; Crowder felt that Nancy had taken on more than she could handle. "Personally, I thought Nancy was trying to do too much and could see she was tiring of the whole business. I could feel that she wanted more freedom than the press allowed." He did not think much of the idea of moving the press to Paris; he does not explain why, but perhaps he feared the effects of a return to Paris on their relationship, which was beginning to show signs of serious strain.

As they traveled about together during the summer, Crowder had found his dependence on Nancy for money galling, especially as she would only give him cash in small amounts so that he was continually having to ask her for more. She seemed to have forgotten that it had been her idea that he should give up his job in order to help her. He was her employee as well as her lover—not an easy situation; and Nancy found it increasingly hard to be consistent in her attitude to Crowder and money. She was rich and he had no money at all; therefore when they traveled at her suggestion and direction, she would naturally pay. When he was working regularly for the press, he would be paid; but why pay him for traveling at her expense? And for all her advanced behavior, there was always an old-fashioned streak in Nancy, which came out in curious ways; one of them was perhaps an instinctive scorn for a man who could not pay his way, even though she deliberately made such men her friends and lovers.

One day at lunch with an American friend of Nancy's, Walter Shaw, and his friend Jean Guérin, a painter, Nancy started picking on Henry. "She had been showing little signs of being rather tired of me and we had exchanged some rather acrid words about my not doing anything. She accused me of being lazy, saying that I ought to get to work playing somewhere. . . . 'Why don't you get something to do?' was the essence of some of her remarks and 'You know you should go to work.'

" 'By heaven, I will,' I replied, and left."

Crowder soon found himself a job playing the piano and singing at Le Bateau Ivre, a nightclub near the Odéon, and took a room at a nearby hotel. Before long Nancy was staying there too, but although the breach between them was not lasting, it coincided with the removal of the press to Paris and meant that Crowder had less to do with the daily running of the business.

The end of 1929 found Nancy, going on thirty-four, in some ways more solidly based than she had ever been. She had found an occupation, the press, that had led to real achievement and promised to lead to more. And Henry Crowder had turned out to be something more than just another lover. And yet there were storm warnings; the press was a burden as well as a satisfaction; her relationship with Crowder was already fraught with problems.

Some clues about Nancy's state of mind and view of herself at this time in her life appeared in her answers to a questionnaire sent out by the *Little Review* to a number of artists and writers living in Paris and published in the early summer of 1929. Nancy's answers reveal some common sense and a degree of self-knowledge clouded by her distaste for direct self-revelation and her tendency to theorize in the abstract about emotions and ideals. What she most wanted to be, she claimed, was "impervious, egocentric, concentrated, secret, unquestionable, and yet all things to all men." What she feared most was "lack of change, repetition of and similarity to the past." For the happiest moment in her life so far, she chose "one childhood day on sands . . . or perhaps any one of certain visual moments in Italy." The unhappiest: "one death, and, each time, any important prolonged deterioration." Her weakest characteristic she considered, "sense of inability"; her strongest, "sense of latent endurance (when not annulled by weakest characteristic)." Among the things she most liked, she listed wine, "new turns in the reactions of emotion set going by a new person," music, dancing, new places, "faces in the street," and "entire freedom of words." What she disliked most was war and "governmental tyrannies and intolerance to individual moeurs."

As with her poetry, what emerges most clearly from Nancy's answers to the *Little Review* is her fear of being tied down in any way. No wonder Crowder, after living with her for a year, was unsure about the future. It was beginning to look as if no relationship, nor any occupation, was likely to hold Nancy for very long.

It was one of Nancy's Surrealist friends, Georges Sadoul, who found her the perfect base in Paris for the press. She rented a small shop with rooms behind it at 15, rue Guénégaud, one of the narrow gray side streets leading away from the river on the left bank, off the rue de Seine; the profits of the press's first year paid the rent, which pleased her newly discovered sense of economy. Sadoul and André Thirion helped her with the move, and Sadoul became her assistant. Nancy was delighted with the new arrangement. "In Paris the press began to function again at once, at irregular but productive hours with Sadoul as a rather elastic secretary and general factotum. . . . We both knew that strictly regular hours are no *sine qua non* if one is rather bohemian by temperament."

Nancy was still in close touch with the Surrealists through Sadoul and Thirion, both of whom used to carry messages between her and Aragon before Elsa Triolet completed her exclusion of Nancy from his life. At one stage she and Thirion had a brief romance, which started when Nancy called on him unexpectedly late one night when he was in bed getting over a bout of venereal disease and so unable to make love. She arrived very drunk but composed, took off her dress, and settled down to sleep beside him in her black petticoat. They never had a serious affair, partly because Thirion was in love with a woman who had returned to her husband in Hungary. Nancy became deeply involved in helping him plan how to get her back, giving him money, lending him her suitcases covered with international stickers, urging him to go to Hungary to fetch her, and promising to use all her influence in diplomatic circles if necessary. His expedition was successful, and he was always grateful to Nancy for her support.

One typical Surrealist intrigue a little later on led Nancy to meet a young man who was to play a large part in her life. Raymond Michelet was an eighteen-year-old student from a stuffy provincial family; his father was a policeman who disapproved strongly of his son's wish to join the Surrealists in Paris. Sadoul and Thirion hid Michelet for a while with them, but after two attempts at arrest and several visits by the irate father, they decided to send him to Nancy's house at Réanville to hide. Nancy was intrigued by the nervous, rebellious Michelet and, as Michelet himself recalls, was at first bemused and then touched by his shyness and by the fear of sex that his repressive upbringing had left him. She decided, despite Crowder, to undertake his sexual education. Not surprisingly, he fell in love with her.

Nancy was proud of the look of her Paris establishment. Behind the glass panels of the front door she arranged a printed African cloth and decorated the shop with paintings by Miró, Malkine and Tanguy as well as pieces from her growing collection of primitive art: "painted shields, fetish figures and sculptures from Africa, New Guinea and the South Seas." Black and white chessboard linoleum covered the floor; Sir Bache's buhl desk served as the office table, and "good lighting shone on the rich assembly of bright African beading here and there and the multi-coloured splendour of Brazilian tribal headdresses in parrot feathers. The little place could be brought to a blaze." The two presses were in the back room, operated by an easygoing young printer who had replaced the uncongenial M. Lévy. In the shop window she placed Hours Press books, including Aragon's Snark, Surrealist paintings, and a wooden African mask.

The press was around the corner from the Galerie Surréaliste in the rue Jacques Callot, the center of operations and social life for the Surrealist group, and the avant-garde generally. The Hours Press also quickly became a good place to drop in, and Nancy used to have to lock the doors sometimes in order to get the work done. She preferred meeting people at a nearby bar or restaurant. Even so, some of her friends who called at the press were surprised that any work was achieved at all. Harold Acton was one old friend who dropped in regularly during the Paris days of the press.

> . . . the shop had an hysterical atmosphere; the printing press seemed to work in paroxysms, and everything else seemed ready to lose control. In that sloping street like one of Meryon's darkest etchings, fetishes from Easter Island and the Congo held rendezvous among freshly printed poems. "What are we doing here?" they asked. "Let's run away." They refused to stay put. They disturbed conversation with their antics and distracted one's thoughts. . . . One expected them to march out of the door and up the street, shouting slogans in a truculent procession.

Acton found Nancy more frenetic than ever. "The clock did not exist for her: in town she dashed in and out of taxis clutching an attaché-case crammed with letters, manifestoes, estimates, circulars and her latest African bangle, and she was always several hours late for any appointment. A snack now and then but seldom a regular meal; she look famished and quenched her hunger with harsh white wine and gusty talk."

Perhaps Nancy's most illustrious caller at the rue Guené-gaud was James Joyce. She had not met him before, despite her mother's early efforts on his behalf and the fact that several of her friends in Paris—Ezra Pound, Robert McAlmon, Wyndham Lewis—saw him often. She was in bed one day at the Hotel Crystal (where she regularly stayed in 1930 and 1931), hardly able to speak because of an abscess in her throat. "The knock on the door revealed a tall, austere figure whose hands went faltering after some piece of furniture, for he was already nearly blind.

" 'I am James Joyce,' he announced 'and I have come to talk to you about something it seems to me it is your duty to accomplish.' " He wanted Nancy to use her influence with her mother to get Sir Thomas Beecham to hear an Irish singer, Sullivan, and have him hired to sing opera in London. "I presume Joyce thought this quite simple," wrote Nancy. "What he probably did not know was that my relations with her were not of the friendliest; at any rate I had no influence with her whatsoever—as I now tried to make clear." Nancy told Joyce that she would tell her mother what he wanted, but that she could not do more. He seemed annoyed and continued to insist that Sullivan must be found a position and that Nancy must use her influence with her mother. He paid no attention when Nancy tried to remind him that he knew her mother himself and might find her receptive, and pointed out that Lady Cunard was in Paris at that moment. He seemed convinced that Nancy could do what he asked if she wanted. As she steered him toward the door, Nancy felt she was in a false position. "As for Lady Cunard, would she even listen? . . . She did not listen much." Nancy told her mother that Joyce had been to see her and why, and her mother replied that it was a matter for Beecham and he was extremely busy.

About two weeks later Joyce appeared again, this time at the rue Guénégaud. Nancy and the friends who were there ran forward to welcome him and pressed him to have dinner or at least a drink with them. But he only wanted to repeat his request to Nancy about Sullivan. The implication was that Nancy had not tried hard enough—and "then he dropped a hint that, if things went well on the score of Sullivan, a little piece of writing might perhaps come to me for publication at the Hours Press." Nancy and Joyce met once or twice more; once she inadvertently kept him waiting for her at Fouquet's, and on another occasion she sent Wyn Henderson to have dinner with him in her place. Nothing came of the hint that he might give the Hours Press some writing.

Early in 1930 Nancy sent out a circular announcing her second series of books. There were three sections: poetry, prose, and music; poetry was by far the most substantial.

The music section in fact consisted simply of the entry "Henry Crowder: Six Piano Pieces with Poems by Richard Aldington, Walter Lowenfels and Nancy Cunard." Nancy was convinced that Crowder was a creative musician; she and their friends liked to listen to him playing and improvising, and she was determined that he should write some music that would bring him the recognition she felt sure he deserved. Crowder himself was charateristically cautious, even reluctant. Under "prose" were listed *A War Story* by Richard Aldington and *Four Unposted Letters to Catherine* by Laura Riding, the American poet and associate of Robert Graves. The poetry section listed Walter Lowenfels, Robert Graves, Laura Riding, Bob Brown, Harold Acton, Roy Campbell, and Brian Howard. The space down the middle of the card was filled with the announcement "Ezra Pound: Collected Cantos in One Volume."

Nancy had ambitious plans for the poetry series. She wanted the books to appear in the same format, with covers designed by contemporary artists. She found Yves Tanguy for Lowenfels' book and Len Lye, the Australian artist and graphic designer, for Laura Riding's and Robert Graves's, and she persuaded Man Ray to undertake the covers for Crowder's songs. Elliott Seabrooke did the cover for Acton's poems, and John Banting for Brian Howard's. All this took some arranging, and Nancy began to find that she was getting bogged down in administration, which she did not enjoy.

> I had less and less time for typesetting, for authors were being met and talked to, publicity organised, and the bills and accounts increased and had to be dealt with. Success was good, yet it actually vexed me at times since I would so much rather have been the artisan, typesetter and printer, proofreader, never-ending letter writer, rather than the "Director," responsible for keeping accounts in the approved French manner, with a chiffre d'affaires and all the rest of commercial bureaucracy. We even had to have a monthly accountant. This man would have pleased some authors as a model of pettifogging, but he was a great trial to me.

Nancy had a brush with the French law when she had a mysterious visitor one day asking for "special books." She started to show him what she had and could not understand why he seemed irritated and then abruptly left. The young French printer explained to her that as she had recently been keeping two books of pornographic drawings and writings for some Surrealist friends, the police must have sent a man around to see whether she was in the dirty book business. Nancy was indignant, but also found the episode wonderfully funny, remembering how she had pressed *La Chasse au Snark* on the unlikely customer.

Nancy was working hard, but her emotional life was if anything more chaotic than ever. Crowder's misgivings about the move back to Paris were soon borne out. Nancy's conduct became wilder and more erratic, partly because with Crowder at work until the early hours of the morning—after which he only felt like going home to bed—she needed other companionship for the evening. She would sometimes spend the first part of the evening with Aldington, who continued to observe her gyrations closely and with mounting alarm, or Walter Lowenfels and his wife, Lilian, the handsome American couple she had come to like very much, or with Eugene MacCown (for whom the Hours Press printed a special catalogue for an exhibition of paintings, consisting of alternative titles supplied by a series of friends and acquaintances). With MacCown in particular Nancy would get very drunk and behave very wildly, often to Crowder's disapproval.

Crowder also found out that Nancy was still seeing a great deal of the black musician, Dan, who played the piano at Le Grand Écart. The black world of Montmartre was buzzing with rumors about them, and Crowder soon found out that the affair looked serious. He found this new development hard to take. "I was not in love with Nancy and I was not jealous but I had a great deal of pride and to have people laughing at me and considering me a fool was not pleasant."

Eventually the affair with Dan burned itself out, but not before Crowder had threatened to go back to America and gone to Réanville to collect his things. Nancy followed him there and persuaded him not to leave.

By the early summer, despite everything, the Hours Press had produced the MacCown catalogue, Walter Lowenfels's long poem *Apollinaire, Ten Poems More* by Robert Graves (which sold out immediately and made Graves eighty pounds), and Laura Riding's *Twenty Poems Less* and her prose piece *Four Unposted Letters to Catherine*. Plans were well in hand for the first single volume edition of Pound's cantos (which had previously been published in two separate sections by Bill Bird and John Rodker). Nancy's press was too small to do the production, so Pound himself directed the project, which was farmed out to a larger Paris printer. It was eventually published in 1930 under the Hours Press imprint.

Nancy was aware that, despite her intention of publishing new work, she had not yet actually discovered any writers. She and Richard Aldington decided to offer a prize, hoping it would flush out new talent and bring the press some useful publicity. They sent an announcement to the literary reviews in Paris and London: "Nancy Cunard, Hours Press, in collaboration with Richard Aldington, offers £10 for the best poem up to 100 lines, in English or American on TIME (for or against). Entries up to June 15, 1930."

Nancy and Aldington took the entries, over a hundred, down to Réanville one weekend, where they read them aloud to each other. Disappointed by their quality, and with only three or four days to go, they thought they would have to divide the prize among two or three entrants. Then, back in Paris, Nancy found a final entry pushed under the door of the Hours Press during the night of June 15: "Across the cover of a small folder was written 'Whoroscope'; beneath was the name Samuel Beckett. His name meant nothing to either Aldington or myself. The poem, on the other hand, meant a very great deal, even on the first, feverish read-through."

Nancy and Aldington knew at once that this was the prize-winning poem, and they sent for Beckett to tell him so. Apparently he had not even heard about the prize until the last afternoon, when his Irish friend and mentor Tom Mc-Greevy—also a friend of Aldington—had dropped in to the École Normale Supérieure, where Beckett had a teaching job, and told him about it. He started to write the poem on the life and ideas of Descartes (with whom he was obsessed at the time), went out for dinner, came back and finished it and took it straight to the Hours Press.

Beckett was pleased with the prize, both as recognition—he had barely been published yet—and for the money. He was very poor. He spent the prize the same night on dinner for McGreevy, Aldington and Bridget Patmore at the Cochon au Lait.

In 1930 Beckett was twenty-four. He had been living in Paris since October 1928 after taking a degree in modern languages at Trinity College, Dublin, and teaching for a time. By the time he met Nancy he had become part of Joyce's circle in Paris, helping Joyce with reading, research, and typing. Apart from academic papers on philosophy and an essay on Joyce's *Finnegans Wake,* he had had a short story and a poem published in *transition,* the avant-garde magazine edited by Eugène Jolas.

Although "Whoroscope" is not often admired by students of Beckett's work, by publishing it Nancy advanced the career of one of the few aspiring writers in Paris at that time whose later development proved them to have genius. It is a complex poem, packed with tortuous thoughts and consciously lurid imagery, and Nancy and Aldington were right to recognize something special in it and in its author. They suggested that it needed explanatory notes, in the style of Eliot's *Waste Land,* which Beckett quickly added. Nancy printed three hundred copies, with one hundred signed for five shillings and the rest for one shilling. She gave the six-page booklet a dull scarlet cover with black lettering and a banner across the cover showing it as the prize-winning poem, and she put it in the window of the shop in the rue Guenégaud.

Nancy and Beckett became friends. She thought he had a look of an Aztec eagle, and "a feeling of the spareness of the desert about him." Nancy always had great respect for intellectual quality, and recognized it in Beckett; she liked his Irishness (she described him in a letter to a friend as "a lovely Irish young man"), his linguistic brilliance, his modesty and "self-containedness." Beckett was taken with Nancy as well; he appreciated her striking looks (without thinking her exactly beautiful), her remarkable energy, and her good mind. He thought she had some talent as a writer, and particularly liked parts of *Parallax;* he also found her an excellent talker, and they would meet for a drink at the Café d'Harcourt on the long summer evenings, or drive with Crowder to Montmartre in an open car to listen to music or have dinner *à trois.* He liked Crowder and enjoyed hearing him play.

Nancy believed in Beckett's work and wanted to help him. Once, to Crowder's slight resentment, she suddenly gave him one hundred pounds. Beckett inevitably heard, from Aldington and McGreevy (who did not care for Nancy), of her wilder side, but he simply found her a good and generous friend, which suited them both. Possibly she was slightly in awe of him. He was occasionally drawn into one of her endless nights out, which he found exhausting and pointless; Harold Acton recalls one occasion at a nightclub when Beckett, looking gloomy and ill at ease, finally burst out: "What, in God's name, am I *doing* here?"

By August 1930 Nancy was longing to get away from Paris. She decided to hand over the management of the press to Wyn Henderson and go off to southwest France with Crowder. The idea was that they should find somewhere peaceful where he could write the music for the poems they had been given by Aldington, Lowenfels, Acton and their new friend Beckett. Before leaving, Nancy supervised the production of Roy Campbell's book of poems, but it was decided that John Rodker's *Collected Poems* would have to be printed in London. Wyn Henderson and her young printer assistant, John Sibthorpe, were to look after the publication of a new short story by Richard Aldington and the volumes of poems by Harold Acton, Brian Howard, and Bob Brown.

Although Henry Crowder was becoming increasingly uneasy at his position in Nancy's life, he agreed to go off on a holiday again with her. In a small dark blue car Nancy had given him, they drove south almost as far as Spain, but they could not find anywhere they wanted to settle. Nancy insisted they should turn back north and look in the Dordogne; eventually they decided to stop at Creysse, a tiny village near the river.

For Nancy, this month on the Dordogne with Crowder was idyllic. They rented two primitive rooms for about one pound for the month; they drew water from a fountain, bathed in the river and cooked by candlelight. The villagers were amazed by them—by Crowder's color, by Nancy's English accent and Parisian clothes, by their wish to hire a piano (which arrived drawn by two oxen). Crowder worked on his compositions while Nancy went down to the river or into the fields to read or write.

> The nights were velvet dark and hot, with an old village woman forever washing loads of linen in a great ancient copper outside, the sparks pricking nightlong out of the wood beneath it, and Henry's hands going over his compositions as long as we thought permissible. Nearly everthing was written here in the course of four weeks, so that we went back to Paris with the Opus almost finished. Creysse, said Henry, had been an inspiration.

Crowder's account is less rapturous. Nancy was frequently bad-tempered, their living conditions he considered primitive, and he did not care for the food in the village restaurant. But they laid in a good supply of drink, and he found the village peaceful.

> With the aid of many Pernods I completed the composition of a book of songs I was writing and we spent a very pleasant time in the place. Yet, as the summer progressed, I realized more and more that Nancy and I would never get along together. The constant clash in temperaments, the frequent harsh

words we exchanged over mere nothings presaged trouble in the future and too my memory was pregnant with thoughts of what had happened in the past.

When they left Creysse, Nancy and Crowder drove on toward the Riviera, stopping in Marseilles and Toulon. As autumn was closing in, they stopped again, at a small town near the Italian border. According to Crowder, it was there that Nancy decided to embark on an anthology of Negro history, politics, and art. He did not quite know how to take this new notion. "She had mentioned doing such a work before but I had never taken her announcements very seriously. I had never encouraged her greatly, for knowing her as I did, I hardly thought her the right person to produce such a work and obtain the best results." However, Crowder did his best to steer her in what he thought the right direction, by giving her the names of serious black leaders in America with whom she should get in touch.

After they returned to Paris, Crowder's songs were the last Hours Press publication for that year. Nancy took great pains with the cover. She got Man Ray to do a photomontage in black and white, showing Crowder's dark head and neck encircled by her own slim white arms wearing her fine African ivory bracelets. Walter Lowenfels's song was a rallying cry about Sacco and Vanzetti; Beckett's poem, "From the Only Poet to a Shining Whore," was subtitled "For Henry Crowder to Sing," and Nancy contributed "my own small effort at a rather sophisticated 'Blues,' which Henry sang with all the nostalgia the words imply":

> Back again between the odds and ends,
> Back again between the odds and ends,
> What once was gay's now sad,
> What was unknown's now friends.
>
> Each capital's not more than one café
> Wherein you lose, wherein you lose

Yourself in what you have and have had
Why worry choose, why worry choose?

The Waiter waits, he will wait all night
And when you're tight he will set you right
Back in tomorrow, or even yesterday.
Time plays the piper, but what do we pay?

Oh Boeuf sur le Toit, you had one song,
But when I look in the mirrors it all goes wrong—
Memory Blues, and only back today
I'm a miserable travelling man.

Nancy decided to leave Wyn Henderson in charge of the
Press while she started to work out her anthology. The remaining publications included Aldington's story *Last Straws*,
Acton's and Howard's books of poems, Bob Brown's *Words*,
and an essay by Havelock Ellis, *The Revaluation of Obscenity*,
which was Wyn Henderson's idea entirely, although Nancy
fully approved. She planned another short publication by
George Moore, but this project was to be affected by a major
crisis in Nancy's life that in the autumn of 1930 was not far
off.

With the Hours Press Nancy produced beautiful books,
well up to if not above the standard set by other little presses
of her time; she had a natural eye for good design and good
printing. She made one major literary discovery in Beckett,
even though it was to be twenty years before he was recognized; and she published one of the great works of twentieth-
century poetry: Pound's first thirty *Cantos*. There were certainly some eccentricities in her lists, but nothing that she
published now seems entirely worthless or dull.

Eventually she sold the Minerva press to a rising Paris publisher, Guy Levis Mano, but she kept the old Belgian Mathieu
at Réanville after the rue Guenégaud was given up. She was to
find good use for it again in time.

The Breach with Lady Cunard

On December 23, 1930, as Nancy was about to leave Paris for another visit to London with Crowder, she received an agitated telegram. "Seriously advise you not to leave Paris for London until you receive my letter tomorrow," it read, "impossible to explain in telegram but matter very important. Thomas Beecham."

This telegram marks the beginning of the end of Nancy's relationship with her mother. Lady Cunard had just discovered, to her horror and dismay, that her daughter had a Negro lover. It was astonishing that she had not been confronted by the fact earlier, since Nancy and Crowder had been living together openly for the preceding two years. They were in England together more than once between 1929 and late 1930, but Crowder's account is confused on the timing of their visits; and he never mentions an expedition, still remembered there, to Nevill Holt, where the headmaster of the school showed them around, allowed Crowder to play the piano in the great hall, and allowed Nancy to show him her old schoolroom (by then a dormitory, where an ailing schoolboy was greatly startled when Crowder's black face came around the door).

It seems likely, in fact, that Crowder was with Nancy when she spend several weeks in London in the early summer of 1930. Curiously, what was to be one of Nancy's final appearances in her mother's social life, a big dinner party at Lady Cunard's house in Grosvenor Square, was recorded by two of the more famous guests, Harold Nicolson and Evelyn Waugh.

Waugh, then twenty-six and enjoying the great fashionable success of his second novel, *Vile Bodies,* had recently been taken up by Lady Cunard. (He met Lady Diana Cooper, who became a lifelong friend and inspiration for Mrs. Stitch, at one of Lady Cunard's parties.) In his diary he notes that on June 13, 1930, he met "Nancy Cunard and her negress and an astonishing, fat Mrs Henderson" at a cocktail party given by Harold and William Acton at their large house in Lancaster Gate. "Negress" was presumably a slip (or a private joke) for "Negro"; certainly Crowder did go with Nancy to call on the Actons at Lancaster Gate, as Sir Harold has recalled. So has another visitor there, Lady Mosley, the former Diana Mitford, then the Hon. Mrs. Bryan Guinness and a favorite of Lady Cunard's. Lady Mosley describes Nancy as "rather beautiful" but "snakelike." And as for Crowder: "Her black friend, a simple soul, had been taught by Nancy that he must admire everything African. He equated African with large size: 'Is this *African?*' I once heard him ask, pointing to one of William Acton's enormous rococo Italian tables."

Lady Cunard's dinner party on July 21 was overshadowed by a plane crash that day in which the marquess of Dufferin and Ava was killed, along with five others. Waugh had spent several hours commiserating with Lady Dufferin. "I went later to dinner at Lady Cunard's," he wrote.

A very large party. Some of the young women did not see fit to turn up so that I found myself with an empty chair on one side and Gavin Henderson on the other. Opposite but too far to speak to, Oswald Mosley, Princess Bibesco, Imogen Grenfell, Lord Ivor Churchill. A badly arranged table. Lady Lavery between the Sitwell brothers. The dinner was very good. After dinner we sat and drank and Lady Cunard made efforts to get us upstairs. The party seemed to be half for George Moore and half for Nancy Cunard. . . . Lady C very restless throughout the evening, obviously dissatisfied with me as a lion.

The same occasion was described by Harold Nicolson as "a ghastly dinner supposed to be literary. . . . I do not enjoy it and a gloom hangs over the whole party. George Moore talks rubbish about all great writers having lovely names, instancing Shelley, Marlowe, Landor. I ask him what about Keats? 'Keats,' he answers, 'was not a great writer.' What a silly old man."

Possibly Nancy's presence contributed to the awkwardness of the occasion. Although Crowder was not among the guests, several of the guests knew of their relationship, and at least one of them—Wyn Henderson—knew him well.

But although this particular party may have been a flop, Lady Cunard's social dominance and brilliance at this time was unrivaled. Another diarist, Chips Channon, himself no mean social arbiter, regarded her as one of the pillars of London society; her charm, wit, erudition and talents as a hostess are praised over and over again in memoirs by authors as different as Oswald Mosley and Beverly Nichols. Not quite everyone fell for her, though; Virginia Woolf thought her a "ridiculous little parakeet-faced woman." Physically, she struck almost everyone who knew her as birdlike, both because of her small, sharp, brightly painted face and canary gold dyed hair, and the hopping, pecking quality of her conversation. She had two principal techniques as a hostess. She arrived late at her own parties, thus leaving the guests to get over any initial awkwardness by themselves, and she directed conversation by means of abrupt changes of topic and bold direct questioning of the most important people present.

One of her special favorites among the beautiful women she regularly invited was Lady Mosley. It is tempting to see both Lady Mosley and Lady Diana Cooper, also a favorite guest and friend, as surrogate daughters, filling the gap that Nancy had deliberately created. Lady Cooper was much the same age as Nancy, Lady Mosely a bit younger: they were fair, beautiful and highly intelligent like her, but unlike her, they led lives that Lady Cunard could understand. They took social life seriously; their politics were comprehensible; and their personal lives were models of duty and tranquillity by comparison with Nancy's.

Lady Mosely (who, according to Sir Oswald, was nicknamed "Golden Corn" by Lady Cunard and designated by her to take over the leadership of London society in due course) saw something else in her friend besides social skill and wit. "Emerald★ was always in love," she writes. "She kept the capacity—as rare in old age as it is common in youth—for concentrating her affection, esteem and illusions upon an individual." Partly to make up for difficulties with Sir Thomas Beecham, Lady Cunard cultivated a series of platonic but romantic relationships with "languid" young men. One particular favorite was the art fancier and dealer Sir Robert Abdy, who though twenty-four years younger than Lady Cunard became her close friend and confidant. It was Lady Cunard's need to give and receive affection, according to Lady Mosely, "together with her vivid intelligence and wide reading, that lifted her into an altogether higher category from the general run of snobbish worldly hostesses of whom one has known so many. This is not to suggest that worldliness and snobbishness had no part in her; they had, but there was more to her besides." As for the other famous hostess with whom Lady Cunard was and is so often compared, Lady Colefax, "there was no comparison between them. . . . Emerald made her guests perform to the best of their ability, so that the atmosphere was exhilarating and charged. She fanned the spark of intelligence, fun, interest and amusement into the flame of conversation in a way that was rare in London."

★It was in the autumn of 1926 that Lady Cunard decided on a sudden whim to discard Maud as her Christian name and call herself Emerald instead. She managed to impose this change on most of her friends, but George Moore took the news badly. He thought a letter to him signed "Maud Emerald (a new name)" must mean she had married, and spent some miserable hours looking through telephone directories for a possible husband surnamed Emerald. He then sent her an agitated telegram: "Who is Emerald are you married" and was vastly relieved when finally he received the explanation. Moore, however, continued to call her Maud, as did a few other recalcitrant old friends, including Margot Asquith.

But all this charm and brilliance seemed more and more remote and superficial to Nancy, quite apart from the strain of taking part in her mother's occasions with Crowder somewhere in the wings. In fact, Lady Cunard probably had some idea of what was going on between her daughter and Henry Crowder, but she had hitherto managed to avoid facing the unpalatable facts. Then something happened that meant she could not pretend ignorance any longer and provoked the furious reaction that led Sir Thomas Beecham to warn Nancy.

One day in December Lady Cunard gave a lunch party in Grosvenor Square to which her old friend and social rival, Margot Asquith, was invited. As Nancy put it:

"At a large lunch party in Her Ladyship's house things are set rocking by one of those bombs that throughout her 'career' Margot Asquith, Lady Oxford, has been wont to hurl. No one could fail to wish he had been at the lunch to see the effect of Lady Oxford's entry: 'Hello Maud, what is it now?—drink, drugs or niggers?' " After this public taunt (which was soon all over London, to the amusement of Lady Cunard's friends and the delight of her enemies), she could not restrain herself any longer. She fell into one of the passions of hysterical rage to which she and her daughter were both prone, and Beecham's wire must have been a reaction to her frantic threats of drastic action at the prospect of Nancy and Crowder arriving in London. It was said that she threatened to set the Home Office and the police onto Nancy and her Negro and to have him arrested and deported.

Beecham's letter went astray; it did not reach Nancy until her return to Paris at the end of January and has since vanished. In any case she did not hesitate after receiving his telegram; she and Crowder left for London the same day.

Beecham's letter claimed, according to Nancy, that "it would, at that juncture, be a grave mistake to come to England with a gentleman of the American-African extraction whose career, he believed, it was my desire to advance, as while friendships between races were viewed with tolerance on the continent, by some, it was a very different pair of

shoes in England, especially as viewed by the Popular Press."
The letter was evidently pompous rather than threatening.
But it is clear from Nancy's subsequent account of this stay in
London, which lasted less than a month, and from Henry
Crowder's account too, that their mood was very different
from the days when they and their friends had found it amus-
ing to dodge Her Ladyship.

Nancy was tense and overwrought. Part of her was genuinely outraged at the prejudice behind her mother's attitude;
part of her was spoiling for a fight with Lady Cunard and all
that she stood for; part of her was undoubtedly apprehensive
of what her mother might do. Crowder, who was born and
bred to racial injustice and who knew about worse forms of it
than social embarrassment, disapproved of Nancy's deepening
loathing for her mother. Prejudice, he agreed, was always
deplorable; but you should never turn against your own
mother, whatever the reason. This was not a view likely to
find much favor with Nancy.

Nancy began to feel hunted. After all, her mother knew
"everybody," and with a word to her powerful political
friends perhaps Crowder could really be in trouble. Then,
soon after their arrival at the Eiffel Tower, where they had
again reserved rooms, alarming things started to happen.
Some detectives came by, as did the police, and, the telephone
rang incessantly. "The patron (so he said) received a mysterious message that he himself would be imprisoned 'undt de
other vil be kilt.' Madame wept 'Not even a black man, why,
he's only brown.' " After a few days of this, they decided to
relieve the anxious Stuliks by moving to another hotel. Nothing more happened, and, as Nancy put it, "the Popular Press
was unmoved."

Nancy, though, was concerned enough to visit her lawyer
to ask whether there was any possibility that Crowder could
be in danger. "He, as I expected, informed me that no bar
exists against the entry into England of any person of whatever nationality who is not guilty of offence against the
State."

Meanwhile Nancy was involved in another intrigue. One of her reasons for visiting London was that she had decided to arrange a private showing of *L'Âge d'Or,* the film by Luis Buñuel and Salvador Dali that had caused an uproar in Paris during the preceding months. When Lady Cunard heard rumors of this project, she became even more furious about her daughter's conduct. The film is a Surrealist fantasy that in a series of powerful images attacks hypocrisy in the state and church, and orthodox morality. Priests were shown consorting with prostitutes, and Christ shown leaving a brothel. It was financed by the vicomte de Noailles and first shown privately in the summer of 1930; in late November the Surrealists organized public screenings at a Paris cinema. Inflamed by the right-wing press, some members of the League of Patriots and the Anti-Jewish League broke up a screening by throwing smoke bombs, attacking the audience, smashing seats, and destroying an accompanying exhibition of paintings by Dali, Max Ernst, Man Ray, and Yves Tanguy. On December 12 the French authorities banned the film, and the police seized every copy they could find. One of the copies that survived was smuggled over to London by Aragon and others and eventually reached Nancy. According to Crowder (who disapproved of the film, which he described as "extremely sexy and very anti-religious"), from the time the row broke in Paris Nancy had been obsessed with the idea of showing it in London.

She arranged a screening for January at a Wardour Street cinema and sent invitations not only to all her friends but also to everyone whom she considered ought to be on the side of the avant-garde and against censorship. She also printed a synopsis of the film, an account of the campaign waged against it in Paris, and a statement about its serious intentions and artistic importance signed by, among others, Aragon, Breton, Crevel, Dali, Éluard, Sadoul, Thirion, and Tzara. This literature was distributed at the cinema before the screening by several friends, including Crowder, who thought some of the guests peculiar and observed that the audience as a whole did not seem very taken with the film. But his mood may have been affected by the presence of Bob Scanlon, a black boxer with whom Nancy had become suspiciously close in Paris (though she insisted he was only giving her boxing lessons), and by an openly lesbian admirer of hers, who joined the group that Nancy took to a nightclub after the show. According to Crowder, Nancy soon disappeared in pursuit of Scanlon, leaving money with her woman friend (rather than with him, which he found humiliating) to cover the bill.

Nancy's screening, perhaps because it was private, caused little stir in London, and despite her mother's warnings (Lady Cunard was afraid Nancy might be prosecuted for showing a blasphemous and obscene film, as she certainly could have been) no move was made by the authorities. Before the end of January Nancy and Crowder were back in Paris; but Nancy was still preoccupied with what was happening in London. Around this time she had a letter from her bank, telling her that her mother's financial position and taxation problems forced her mother to reduce her allowance. Nancy had always bitterly resented any attempt by her mother to use the financial lever against her. Now she had proof, she felt, and not without reason, that because of her relationship with Crowder she was to be punished financially.

Almost as soon as she was back in Paris, Nancy sat down to write to George Moore. It is a curious and touching letter that could just possibly be read as an appeal to her mother through him. It is certainly a plea for his understanding, if not his approval, and is evidence both of her affection for him and of her need to have him as an ally in a matter concerning love and personal freedom. She wrote on Hours Press writing paper, from the rue Guénégaud, on January 24, 1931. She kept a copy of the letter.

> Dearest GM,
> I did not see you in London, though the desire to do so was particularly in mind. Have you guessed the reason?
> It is high time that certain *facts* should be recognised and

appreciated, certain facts in general which are convictions in me. I speak of the thing known as the colour question; viz the inferiority of the African race in particular to the white races. Till now these convictions have not been challenged in me; they are now being so. Hence this letter to you only, as I should like to know how YOU feel about it personally and, for that matter, impersonally.

Here is the point—you will remember that we had a little talk some months ago about red, black and yellow men, and that you said you thought you could "not do better" (in the sense of "go further") than "a yellow man," and that you had never known a black man, though no doubt they could be charming. I did not tell you that I have known and closely loved a black man for over two years. You will have heard by now that I do. . . .

At this point, in mid-paragraph, she switches into French for the rest of the letter. "Paraît que Mme ma mère en à une crise . . ." She explains that she does not feel able to argue with her mother about a decision that had already been taken, that concerns everything she has always believed to be just and the right of every human being to freedom and love.

She goes on to say that she had perhaps been wrong not to call on him in London, but had feared that there would not have been time to explain the situation fully and that any misunderstanding or quarrel between them would have upset her. So she has decided to write.

Finally, she urges him to realize that people of color are mostly admirable, that depsite oppression and mistreatment they have managed to educate themselves ("as the awful saying goes"), and that

in brief, they are loved and admired quite openly, frankly, by people like us who can speak, thank god, without lying.

This last paragraph is not propaganda nor explanation. It is simply a fact.

If you want to write to me, would you do so here, at the Press?

Love, N.

It is hard not to feel sympathy for George Moore, an old man of seventy-nine caught between two women he loved. According to Nancy he never replied to her letter.

Early in February Nancy and Crowder left for Obergurgl, to visit her friend Brian Howard. Howard had been in Austria about a month and was deep in what his biographer describes as "a stormy and characteristically unrequited love affair with a young man." Brian Howard and Nancy were in some ways alike: talented, dissatisfied, at odds with their families, and capable of passionate commitment to people and causes that struck their more conventional friends as unsuitable. They attracted each other and were maddened by each other, but there was a lasting affection and bond between them.

It is striking how many of Nancy's closest friendships all through her life were with homosexual men. It was not only that she needed some relationships in which sex played no part; indeed, Nancy is said to have succeeded in proving the pleasure (or at least the possibility) of heterosexual relations to more than one otherwise confirmed homosexual friend. (Her attitude can be summed up by a remark she once made when encountering doubts at such an enterprise on board a cross-Channel steamer: "Oh, *do* let's try.") Certainly, with such friends as Brian Howard or John Banting, sex was part of the friendship at some stage, but never the key to it; also, Nancy was linked to her homosexual friends by something more subtle. She shared with them a feeling of being different, of living outside the herd, partly by choice, partly as the inevitable result of sexual habits. Conventional English family life was not for them; any homosexual wanting to live a reasonably open life had to live abroad, as Nancy also chose to do, and she shared with her homosexual friends a deep dislike of the dreary and intolerant side of English life, the narrowness of its culture and the smugness of its attitudes.

The journey started badly; Nancy disappeared the night before they left Paris and arrived to catch the train in such a curious condition that Crowder, who specifically denies that during their time together she used drugs, concluded that she must have been drugged. Crowder gives a resigned account of how she spent most of the journey, including part of the night, with an Englishman who turned out to be a journalist living in Vienna and made plans to visit him there on the return journey. At Obergurgl Nancy discovered that in the confusion of their departure some of their luggage had been left in Paris. She turned on Crowder in rage. "I was indifferent to everything by that time. . . . From the very beginning the trip had been a headache for me. Many times that day I wished I had stuck to my intention of returning to America."

It was bitterly cold and Brian Howard met them with sleighs to transport them up to the village. It was getting late, and Crowder wanted them to stay the night at a hotel and continue next day. He was overruled. Nancy suffered badly from cold and soon became desperate. She later told Crowder that she thought she was freezing to death and contemplated suicide.

Howard had been apprehensive before Nancy and Crowder arrived, although he hoped that perhaps they could distract him from the pain of his unhappy love affair. But, as he wrote to a friend:

Our "set" here is already considered absolutely dotty, and when Nancy and Henry come I simply cannot conceive what will happen. I have given up all attempt to look hearty. I consider, quite rightly, that my excellent skiing compensates for it, and so I simply sit about in clouds of Queer de Russie, with all my handkerchiefs knotted round my neck, the tears streaming down my face, writing impassioned letters, like any character in a Rossetti poem. One alarming thing has occurred. The only place for Nancy and Henry that I can find for their first week is in the house of the *local priest*. I suppose they will simply insult him. I have visions of Obergurgl ending in such a storm of craziness as never was before. The priest is tremendously severe, and I can hear him praying all day and all night from *my* bedroom, so considering their room will be next to his I simply cannot imagine what will happen.

He described their arrival in his journal:

> 2nd February:
> Well Nancy and Henry arrived, rather like a hero and heroine
> of a highbrow revue . . . Nancy with a lump of gold at her
> throat (me with one in mine), a little brown hat, with her
> white pencil face poking out of a black veil. Long stick legs in
> large furry "bottines," Henry in one of those terrible Hom-
> burgs that are rimmed in tape and turn up all around, and Sir
> Bache's coat. Great rivers of sable over his shoulders. So off
> we set, Nancy full of the London row and her Ladyship's
> detectives. . . . We were looked at, and treated, like rich, royal
> lunatics. It was the most fantastic progress.

Once they were installed and had recovered from the
journey—though Nancy was far from well, and Crowder
had a cold—Howard and Nancy had long talks about their
respective predicaments. Howard found Nancy sympathetic,
as she always was about romantic problems. She told him
about the *L'Age d'Or* row and at length about the breach with
her mother. Brian was a good skier and Crowder did well for
a beginner, but Nancy gave up after one attempt. She had too
much time for brooding and for drink. Howard found her
condition alarming, though he admired her as much as ever.
"She talked so much, seemed unable to stop," he wrote in his
journal.

> The whispery, disjointed voice goes on and on. A kind of
> sober drunkenness. Drinking is now fatal to her, particularly
> cognac. She has the most marvellous face. The best woman
> face of our time. That extraordinary, wavering, perched walk.
> Thinness—other people are thinner of course—reaches a sort
> of thing-in-itself for her. She is the only woman I know who
> can be *really* impassioned about ideas almost continuously. She
> is anything but "right," of course. And her bickering with
> impassive, infinitely patient, stupid Henry is very rasping to
> me. She is in an extremely nervous condition now, of course.

Nancy began urging Howard to write a pamphlet for her, an attack on conventional attitudes to religion, royalty, homosexuality, color. He was tempted to comply. But before long he began to realize that although he felt pretty desperate himself, Nancy was in a much worse state. Also, her feelings for him began to scare him. She seemed to be hinting that they might go off together as lovers. In a rather disjointed, semi-hysterical entry in his journal he describes how she came to his room one day and lay on the bed and pulled him down beside her to "comfort" him. "Not sexily, but with sex near enough. She is definitely in love-ish, put it like that. It simply makes me freeze." He realized that she really was ill, partly physically, partly emotionally. "Drink, plus never drawing the line." He was torn between affection and admiration of her "as an object" and fear of her as a sexual predator.

Crowder soon realized that Howard was having difficulties with his boyfriend and that Nancy was interested in Howard, which would lead to complications. One night the whole group went to a dance. Howard's friend had another admirer, who started pursuing him with some success. Howard made a jealous scene and Nancy joined in on his side. Crowder went back to the hotel. Later, he heard Howard and Nancy talking intensely next door, with Nancy, as he thought, trying to persuade Howard to spend the night in her room. Suddenly, he saw Howard slip through his (Crowder's) bedroom and out through the window into the snow. Next Nancy appeared, screaming at Crowder for being such a fool as to let Howard escape because he had been threatening to kill himself, and if he did, it would be Crowder's fault.

"My reaction to this outburst was an absolute blank," writes Crowder wearily. "I turned over and proceeded to go to sleep to the accompaniment of her sobs next door. Nothing came of the supposed suicide attempt but the situation became more tense and conditions were disagreeable on every side."

One night Nancy became drunk and aggressive over their plans to return to Paris via Vienna. When Howard refused to go with them, she went to her room, picked up a shoe and systematically broke every small pane of glass in her window. The next day, when the astonished manager questioned her, Nancy simply said that she would pay for the damage.

After about two weeks, Nancy and Crowder left for Vienna, where Nancy seemed to recover her equilibrium. They stayed with the English journalist they had met on the train, and Nancy once again played her game of humiliating her established lover by taking another man under his nose. Crowder was resigned but "disgusted," and he determined to return to America as soon as possible after their return to Paris.

Brian Howard, meanwhile, put down his impressions of Nancy and Crowder in letters to his mother. He found himself defending Nancy and stressing how much he admired her.

There is one thing I want you, seriously, to realise. And that is that I adore and admire Nancy and I always will. She has the kind of integrity, spiritual purity and devotion to ideas that is unique. Nothing can deter her or make her dishonest. She is a marvellous woman, and if she were younger and less ill and attracted me, I'd marry her, I almost believe. But really her advent here, and Henry, was simply volcanic. She is ill, which I didn't realise." He ascribes her illness to her mother's having her "hounded" by the police; her worries over Raymond Michelet, also on the run, hiding in her house in France; a nose and chest infection aggravated by the cold; the discomfort of the hotel annex; and too much alcohol. "There were fights, with poor dear coal-black Henry being so good and patient." Howard used a telling phrase to sum up the visit. "It may have been Michael Arlen on the surface—to read of—but it was King Lear underneath all right."

Nancy, eventually, was to write about the visit as if it had been perfectly normal, but she confessed to John Banting soon afterward that it had been a nightmare. She added that she had felt sorry for Howard.

About a month later (by which time Nancy had moved down to Cagnes, in the south of France), Harold Acton, who was basically on Nancy's side but whose natural urbanity enabled him to keep a cool head, wrote to her with some details that greatly disturbed her. A friend had seen Moore soon after he received Nancy's letter, and found him "in a feverish state, shocked (as she worded it) for the first time in his life, and so pained that he had already summoned his lawyer to change some arrangement by which he intended to leave, or bequeath, you his Manets. . . . He spoke of you, to her, as always, as the light of his life, passionately, paternally."

Nancy was outraged at the story about the will and, one suspects, hurt. She challenged Moore with the news. On February 27 he wrote back. The letter was brief:

> Dearest Nancy,
> I have made no change in my will.
> Always affectionately yours,
> George Moore.

For the next few months Nancy continued to hear stories of her mother's threats and anger. It seemed that Lady Cunard was still trying not to believe what she now knew about Nancy and Crowder; she would express dismay and incomprehension to Nancy's friends who defended the couple by explaining that among their generation blacks were liked, accepted, even fashionable. On one occasion she was reported to Nancy as having remarked that "she could not be 'chic' if she lived in Paris because all the 'chic' Parisians live nowadays with negroes." She met Robert Byron and tackled him. "You belong to a generation that consorts with colour, what is it like?" Sir Robert Abdy felt that the thought of her daughter having a sexual relationship with a black man repelled her.

In May Acton wrote to tell Nancy that he had recently dined with her mother in London. "There is a distinct cloud between us." She had asked about Henry Crowder. "I replied that I knew and liked him. She then asked me not to speak of this to anyone. Her voice was troubled. . . . She also said that she had not spoken of it to anyone but Wyndham Lewis. . . . I cannot help being fond of Her Ladyship and am regretful that the curtain has fallen. . . . It is a difference of generation and the rigidity of mondaine prejudice: Her L has always been, for me, the magnificent exception."

Another friend who tried to smooth things over was Wyn Henderson, who remembered having lunch, at Nancy's request, with Lady Cunard and finding her anxious rather than angry. "Tell me . . . is he really black?" asked Lady Cunard. When told that he indeed was, Lady Cunard wiped a tear from the corner of her eye with a tiny lace handkerchief. To console her, Wyn tried to explain what a nice, civilized, intelligent person Crowder was. But Lady Cunard could only think about his appearance and degree of visible negritude. "Is his hair very—?" she asked, twirling her finger above her head. Wyn Henderson could only answer yes again, in her own words "a lovely little black astrakhan cap."

Both Nancy and her mother were hearing rumors that were not helpful in an already tense situation. Nancy continued to fear that her mother would cut her off completely or take steps to restrict her and Crowder's freedom of movement. Lady Cunard heard not only about Crowder, but about Nancy's other black lovers. Acton wrote in the summer of 1931 that he had found Lady Cunard anxious about Nancy's health and full of exaggerated stories about orgies, maniacs, and underworld characters.

In her subsequent accounts Nancy gives no credit to Sir Thomas Beecham for his role in the drama. But a fragment of a letter has survived among her papers which shows that he tried to calm Lady Cunard and to keep up a helpful connection with Nancy. Unfortunately, by the summer, things had almost certainly moved too far for any mending to be done. Beecham's letter was obviously well meant, but it only provided Nancy with more fuel for her indignation.

He wrote from London on June 11:

My dearest Nancy,
Something has happened about which I feel I should write to you at once. . . .

I had a long interview with Her Ladyship on Tuesday evening.

It happened this way. She rang me up on the telephone, to ask about the change of your banking account, and brought in all sorts of extraneous things such as the Film in January, "Henry," etc. etc. She appeared to be in high dudgeon. I said that I always found it difficult to discuss such affairs over the telephone and offered to call upon her. I saw her by appointment on Tuesday evening and was with her for more than an hour.

She said that she had cut you out of her will, except to make a small provision for you, adding that under her mother's will she had a complete power of disposition, and that she intended to cut off your allowance altogether.

I said I was very sorry indeed to hear that things were so bad, and that I felt that she would not have the heart to cut off her daughter altogether. Thereupon she appeared to soften somewhat, but launched into an enormous list of grievances she felt against you—that you have never cared for her, that you associated with undesirable people, and lived a scandalous life which reflected upon her, that you had introduced into England a blasphemous and immoral film for which you and your accessories were liable to be imprisoned and had only just escaped it (I hastened to inform her that in that respect I was one of your accomplices), that you squandered money given to you by her on worthless friends and dependents etc., etc. But I gather that your friendship with "Henry" is really her greatest grievance of all.

The letter breaks off. No evidence exists of any later contact between Nancy and Beecham. As the years went by, she referred to him with increasing bitterness.

As for Lady Cunard's threat to disinherit Nancy and stop her allowance, there are no records available to prove exactly what followed. What evidence there is indicates that though she may have reduced Nancy's income, she continued to supply her with more than enough to live on. There was certainly no dramatic change in Nancy's way of life. Although Lady Cunard's fortune was very large, she spent it lavishly, not only on herself and her entertaining but also in supporting the opera, ballet and theater she loved. Her American invest-ments were hit by the stock market crash of 1929 and the depression that followed. Her defenders insist that she would have had to reduce Nancy's income around this time anyway; Nancy's supporters regard this as too much of a coincidence. Many of Nancy's friends remain convinced that she was alto-gether cut off, or alternatively that she allowed the money supplied by her mother to accumulate untouched in the bank. Both possibilities are unlikely. Nancy never earned any seri-ous money, and although during the 1930s she increasingly showed a preference for cheap travel, modest hotels and clothes bought from market stalls, she clearly had enough money to live as she wanted, which included traveling and subsidizing the interests she chose. Apart from the relatively small sum she inherited from her father (most of which, she always said, went into the house at Réanville) her mother was her only source of income; and, when she died, the bulk of her capital was in American shares left to her by her mother, whose will benefited Nancy equally with two others.

However, Nancy never forgave her mother—first, for her attitude to Crowder, second, for her use of her money as a weapon. The threats, which as Sir Thomas Beecham's letter proves were certainly made, were to Nancy bad enough, whatever actually followed. One friend has recalled that Nancy's allowance was in fact reduced around this time by about one-quarter. The fact that her whole life was based on her parents' wealth was increasingly awkward for Nancy; she concealed the awkwardness with anger.

Although it was Nancy's relationship with Henry Crowder which precipitated the breach with her mother, the tension and distance between them had been growing steadily for at least ten years. Exactly when they met for the last time is unclear, but was probably during the winter of 1930–31; Nancy remembered an ugly, angry scene. Whether it was recognized at the time as a final encounter is impossible to tell; but Nancy was to make sure, within the year, that reconcilia-tion would be long in coming, if it came at all.

The Black Cause

The story of Nancy, Henry Crowder, and the black cause is riddled with paradox. The idealism and generosity of her intentions toward his race is often in striking contrast to the way she behaved toward him. The irony of her relationship with Crowder going badly at the same time as she was most strongly demonstrating her allegiance to his race would not have occurred to Nancy; she was not sensitive in such ways. But she was not self-deceiving either. When Nancy treated Crowder abominably, as she frequently did, it was not because he was black.

The breach with her mother reinforced Nancy's determination to do something to demonstrate the dignity and genius of the black race and to expose the injustice of prejudice. Meanwhile, after they got back from Austria, Crowder had decided he had had enough. He was tired of the chaos and humiliation involved in being Nancy's lover and companion; he wanted to go back to America and to see his wife again. This time Nancy gave in. She bought him a return ticket, however, and made him promise to return.

As he sailed back across the Atlantic, Crowder was not sure whether he would return or not. He reproached himself for not having done as well as he had hoped in Europe; the bright future he had glimpsed for himself as a result of his association with Nancy still seemed far away. He had greatly enjoyed the freedom he had found in Europe, but getting back to Harlem was a relief. He went to Washington to see his wife, and found her full of questions about his well-publicized life with the rich white woman and not too pleased with the answers. After this, he wrote, they reached a friendly understanding that each would live as he or she saw fit. He also found it a relief to be away from Nancy.

Meanwhile, Nancy had decided that she had to get away from Paris and Réanville if she wanted to make progress with her plans for the anthology on race. She left Wyn Henderson in charge of the Hours Press, and by early April she had moved south and taken a house near Cagnes. She took Raymond Michelet with her.

Michelet was sixteen years younger than Nancy. His youth and innocence, and the fact that he was on the run from a conventional and repressive father, had immediately appealed to Nancy when he was sent to her house in Normandy by Aragon and Sadoul the previous winter. He was to live most of the next two years with Nancy and to become her chief assistant and collaborator. During the early summer of 1931, they became lovers. Nancy fell sufficiently in love with him to reveal all the tender and romantic side of her nature. Indeed, Michelet, remembering that summer, has testified how enchanting a lover Nancy could be.

He still remembers with gratitude and affection how, when Nancy discovered that the taboos instilled in him by his parents had given him a disabling fear of sex, she briskly set about curing him. He was not so young and inexperienced, however, that he did not soon realize, while they were living at Cagnes, how problematic was Nancy's own enjoyment of sex and how in some ways she remained deeply inhibited. She had found Aragon too demanding sexually, and she remained oddly conventional in her approach to lovemaking. In Michelet's view—and he is the only one of Nancy's lovers now willing to discuss this aspect of her nature—Nancy's operation in 1920–21 had physically impaired her sexual responses; hence her constant search for new lovers and her fear of being found inadequate in any prolonged relationship. He thinks now that Nancy did believe that black men were more exciting and better-endowed lovers than most white men and chose them as lovers hoping to find a satisfaction that eluded her. Michelet has given a remarkable evocation of her nature as he remembered it from his youth and understood it in his later middle age.

Nancy lived three or four parallel lives, which sometimes connected, sometimes contradicted each other, sometimes stayed independent of each other. From one hour to the next, she could change completely, become another person. That was why her personality could be so fascinating, and also exhausting for those of her companions who really shared her life.

For it was not just a question of changing moods. Nancy did have terrifying rages, often unfair and excessive, for she pushed every feeling to its extreme. But there was something more . . . Nancy forged ahead, fleeing from something, never stopping to consider, never turning back, burning everything behind her, things she had loved, people she might have loved . . . What was she escaping from? I lived more than two years with her, and I do not know. I had a sense of it, and it was sometimes frightening. But a boy of nineteen does not live at the same pace as a woman of thirty-five, even if he is violently in love, and she whom he believes he knows remains an enigma to him.

Once she told me she needed a day absolutely alone. She emerged from it not relaxed or rested but more violent than ever. Moreover, she could not bear prolonged solitude. She was afraid of it. Even to be alone with one person was only tolerable to her in rare moments when she felt in perfect equilibrium with external things, with the landscapes and rocks around her. At such perfect moments, she showed herself to be romantic in a way no one would have suspected in a woman apparently so precise, so hard. Then she would show a streak of desperate lyricism which she would reject a few hours later, as if she regretted having shown herself naked. Solitude terrified her: when one companion left her side, she had to have another human warmth beside her at once. Thus it happened that she would pick up along the way the first person who came to hand, even if of all her friends he was the least likely to share her life, until she sent him away—and in what a manner, with what arrogance!—a few days later, or even the next day.

Nancy pursued her sexual needs as she pursued her emotional needs. She had many black lovers, nearly all musicians, some of whom she loved passionately, but whom she left, or who left her, scorched by the flame she kept burning within herself. . . .

Nancy could weep with emotion, at thirty-five, like a young woman taken by surprise by unexpected and suddenly burgeoning love. Nancy could be as hard as an independent woman used to playing with men. She could be simply a woman in love, all passion, and the next day, unable to choose between two men she loved, she could try to construct a totally unrealistic life in which she lunched with one of them, spent the afternoon with the other, dined with the first, and spent the night with the second. In each situation she went to the limit, whether it was simple, whether it was complicated, whether it was logical or absurd, whether it was dangerous or not. She had to extract from each moment all there was to have. Nancy burned like a flame.

Michelet's account of Nancy provides vital clues to the sexual side of her nature. Her sexuality was so dramatic, it was such a powerful influence on her behavior, and it so baffled, intrigued, and increasingly unnerved her lovers and friends that for all the difficulties inherent in any effort to explain it, an attempt must be made to do so.

By the time Nancy was in her early thirties, she had acquired the reputation of a nymphomaniac. She had not only had a succession of lovers, but had conducted several sexual relationships at the same time. She was capable of engineering sudden sexual encounters with strangers almost under the nose of the lover at her side. Nowadays, students of sexual behavior incline to doubt whether there is any such condition as "nymphomania"; the variations, physical and psychological, in the makeup of highly promiscuous women (or men) are thought to be so wide as to make any generalized conclusions meaningless. However, if there is such a condition, two origins have been suggested for it: one physical, and extremely rare, in which the person concerned has an urgent need to experience orgasm frequently and is as incapable of avoiding occasions for sex as an alcoholic is of abstaining from drink; and the other psychological, in which a personality disturbance leads to a compulsive need for sex, not for physical release but for a variety of emotional reasons, including the search for affection and security, fear of solitude, or the exercise of power.

Nancy does not fit any of these patterns neatly. Michelet says she found orgasm difficult but not impossible. Other men and women who were close to Nancy have said that, in their view, she was not someone of real sexual warmth and that she was probably technically frigid most of the time. What seems clear is that, despite her many lovers, her appetite for sex and her interest in all sorts of sexual habits, she remained, as far as she herself was concerned, inhibited and self-conscious about variations in sexual behavior. Michelet has said that oral sex seemed abhorrent to Nancy, that she perhaps found it humiliating or disgusting. She may have felt threatened by the prospect of any intense, lasting relationship involving physical or emotional dependence on another person. And yet, even after at least ten years of promiscuity, Nancy was still capable, with Michelet, of behaving like a woman in love—showing tenderness, passion, and emotion.

Michelet offers two clues as to why Nancy was as she was. There was the effect of her hysterectomy ten years earlier—which she told him she had chosen to have in order to live as freely as she wished—and there was her fear of being alone. At this time in her life, and for many years to come, Nancy was never without a lover for very long. Then there was her constant wish to control her own life, to be able to move at a moment's notice in pursuit of what seemed to her right or necessary at that moment.

There are some other clues. It is striking how many people writing about Nancy, whether in memoirs or in fiction, describe her sexuality in almost mystical terms—as if she were a martyr or an ascetic who undertook sex as a kind of ordeal or torture, finding a voluptuous pleasure in degrading herself. To those who looked deeper, a kind of purity, almost self-sacrifice, seemed to lie behind her wild behavior. Certainly Nancy never came to despise love or sex, although increasingly her behavior gave the censorious or fastidious plenty of opportunity to despise her.

For a time, then, Nancy and Michelet were happy together; but there were as always plenty of people around to provide distraction and complications. Michelet remembers the musician, George Antheil, the painters Hilaire Hiler, Raoul Ubac, and René Crevel, staying nearby with Paul Éluard and Georges Auric. Nancy asked Georges Sadoul to come and stay with them; he had recently been in Moscow with Aragon and Elsa Triolet and was preoccupied by the growing split within the Surrealist group over allegiance to the Communist party. Sadoul would lunch every day with Nancy and Michelet on the terrace of a little restaurant near the Château Grimaldi, looking out over the splendid view toward Vence and the mountains of Provence. They would talk about race prejudice, with Nancy lecturing the two Frenchmen on the iniquities of persecution and lynching in the United States and efforts of various black organizations and leaders to get racial justice. They also discussed the dramatic news from Spain, where in 1931 the monarchy had been thrown out, and a popular liberation movement was in progress.

It must have been around this time that Nancy first heard of the Scottsboro Boys case, which although in no way exceptional as an example of southern American justice, was to become the first such case to receive worldwide publicity and stir the conscience of white sympathizers internationally. On March 25, 1931, nine black youths, aged from thirteen to twenty, were arrested in Scottsboro, Alabama, on the charge of raping two white girls who had been found riding the rails with them in a boxcar on the Chattanooga-to-Memphis freight train. Two weeks later, eight of the youths, all but the youngest, were sentenced to the electric chair, after a travesty of a trial with a lynch mob gathering outside the courtroom.

In America the established moderate black rights organization, the National Association for the Advancement of Colored People, took up the defense of the Scottsboro Boys, as they came to be called; but it was the International Labor Defense, the legal arm of the American Communist party, which soon forged ahead of the NAACP in the effort not only to take over the defense, but to create as much publicity as possible in America and elsewhere for the Scottsboro Boys and the plight of American blacks in general.

To Nancy the Scottsboro Boys came to stand for everything she had been moved by when she first heard Henry Crowder describe American racism. She was not at all interested in the arguments that developed over whether the communists were putting the party's interests above the interests of the nine accused; to her, as to many other observers, whoever was trying the hardest to explode the farrago of distorted evidence and prejudiced testimony that the prosecution was using against the Boys deserved total support.

Meanwhile, she was still eager for news from London about her mother. Her correspondence shows that some of the time she was apparently able to preserve an amused detachment.

Nancy suspected, perhaps unfairly, Lady Cunard's influence behind a quarrel she had with George Moore during the spring of 1931. She had planned to publish a short piece by Moore, *The Talking Pine,* based on a conversation she had had with him on one of their last meetings. She thought he had agreed that the piece should appear and that he would sign the copies. But when she sent them to him, he wrote to say that he had changed his mind, that the piece was too slight and that he did not approve of selling his signature. Nancy was furious at what she regarded as a broken promise; but Moore would not budge and *The Talking Pine* was never published. Moore was eighty by this time, and not well; and in 1933, he died. In his will, he left many of his most treasured possessions to Lady Cunard. Nancy always remembered him with deep affection.

The end of the Hours Press was not happy. Richard Aldington was unaccountably angry when he discovered that Wyn Henderson rather than Nancy was in charge of his latest book, *Last Straws,* although it made a profit and Nancy felt he had no cause to complain. Soon afterward, she found that Wyn Henderson had run out of money and that more was needed to pay off the final bills. Nancy felt the press had been mismanaged and that she had been let down; none of Wyn Henderson's careful explanations and accounts convinced her. She was also suspicious about Wyn Henderson's contact with Lady Cunard, although she herself had suggested that her friend might try to talk to her mother. To Wyn's amazement and indignation, Nancy quarreled violently with her and broke off their close friendship.

By the middle of May 1931 Henry Crowder was back in France. He still thought he could do better for himself in Europe than in America. He found that Nancy had left money for his fare from Paris down to Toulon, where she wanted to meet him. "The question again arose whether I wanted to continue the affair. What had I gained and where had it gotten me were some of the thoughts that ran through my mind. I had gone to America and come back too at her expense. I felt I owed her something more than a thank you and a goodbye when I returned. She wanted me to meet her in Toulon. I went."

There followed a period of strain, peculiar even in Nancy's life, as she attempted to divide her life between Michelet and Crowder. Crowder was less bemused by Nancy's behavior than was Michelet. Nancy told him not to come to her house since Michelet might not understand, so they met at his hotel. He noticed that, apart from Michelet, Nancy seemed very interested in Eric Walrond, the West Indian novelist, who was staying nearby. After a few uneasy days Crowder asked Nancy about her plans for the summer. She told him she intended to go to the mountains with Michelet and suggested he go on into Italy, find a house and a piano and practice his music. Crowder was not prepared to accept this solution.

After a series of unhappy arguments Crowder left for Paris,

intending to go on to London. But within a few days he decided that as soon as he could, he would go back to America, this time for good.

He wrote to Nancy to tell her this. But Nancy had just decided on another dramatic move. She too wanted to go to America, to follow up her plans for the anthology. She was going to America; Crowder wanted to go; they would go together. Michelet, bewildered at this turn of events, does not seem to have counted in her plans at this stage. What Nancy wanted to do, she did. As for Crowder, he was appalled at the whole idea.

"I had been surprised at many things Nancy had done but never had I even guessed she would want to do such a foolhardy thing. Imagine, a Negro man sailing into New York in the company of a wealthy white woman. I couldn't. To make matters worse Nancy was the kind who would want to go everywhere and see everything."

Once again, just as Crowder had decided that his relationship with Nancy had no future and that he must make his own way, she persuaded him that it was not so. He had thought that it was Michelet she loved and wanted to be with; but Michelet was to be left behind. Neither Nancy nor Crowder comes out of this episode well. Nancy would never have admitted it to herself but her strongest weapons in inducing Crowder to fall in with her wishes were the same weapons she hated and despised her mother for using against her: social prestige, and money. For Crowder, the prospect of renouncing all the plans for his future that he and Nancy had envisaged was again too demanding. Then there was the question of money; he was not quite proud or confident enough to reject Nancy's financial support. He seems to have felt by this time that after nearly three years of putting up with Nancy's vagaries he was entitled not to find himself back where he started, adrift in Europe with no prospects. So, against his better judgment, he agreed to accompany her to New York.

Years later, Nancy summed up her two visits to the United

States: "1931: no trouble, but great disgust. 1932: much trouble, little disgust and great interest." Compared to the furor her presence was to provoke the following year, the visit of summer 1931 was uneventful. But it nevertheless made a powerful impression on Nancy: to revisit her mother's country (where she had last stayed as a small girl in the utmost luxury) with a black companion, living in the middle of Harlem—it was a satisfyingly dramatic experience.

The journey across the Atlantic was not happy. Nancy was a bad sailor and kept to her cabin. She missed Michelet and sent him wireless messages almost daily. Crowder fretted about what would happen when they reached New York. He was determined, when they arrived, to take Nancy straight to Harlem. He was afraid that she would want to test race prejudice as they had in London by trying to find rooms in "white" New York. Fortunately she wanted to stay in Harlem anyway. Nancy was appalled by the heat and also by the bedbugs that infested their first hotel, but they soon moved to a better one. She wanted to explore the whole city. There were rows when Crowder showed his normal caution—cowardice, Nancy would say—about attempting to get into such places as a smart Fifth Avenue ice cream parlor where he knew he would not be served. She persuaded Crowder that they should go downtown to see the play about southern blacks by Marc Connelly, *Green Pastures,* which was playing successfully to mixed audiences. When she wanted to stroll up Broadway after the show, Crowder refused.

Nancy was looking for trouble; Crowder wanted to avoid it. All Nancy's instincts led her toward confronting prejudice in order to prove something to herself and the rest of the world. She was always courageous to the point of foolhardiness, and all her fighting instincts were aroused by incidents like one when a car containing white men slowed down by her and Crowder and a voice yelled: "Can't you get yourself a white man?" Crowder had his work cut out avoiding scenes.

By the time Nancy got to Harlem, it had begun to lose some of the glamor of its heyday. During the 1920s, as well as being the capital of the black entertainment world, the place where the postwar craze for black music, dancing and vitality found its focus, Harlem had become the center of a movement among young black artists and writers determined to shake off the old racial stereotypes, celebrate their blackness and their race's links with Africa. Alain Locke, the black academic and writer, was the originator and leader of what came to be called the Harlem Renaissance, and produced an anthology, *The New Negro,* in 1925, to demonstrate it. White patrons, of whom Carl van Vechten was the most important, helped writers like Langston Hughes, Sterling Brown, and Claude McKay find publishers.

But by the early 1930s the Harlem Renaissance had begun to falter. Both personally and artistically, black artists and writers found dependence on white standards and patronage increasingly difficult. It became obvious, too, that the popularity of Harlem nightclubs and the publication of a handful of novels and poems had done nothing to alter the position of American blacks outside fashionable Negrophile New York. With the depression bearing down especially hard on the black working class, black intellectuals, like their white counterparts, began to feel a need for political commitment. The Scottsboro Boys case was crucial; the Communist party's stand appealed to many of the New Negroes. Some of this complexity Nancy appreciated; much of it escaped her. But for the moment, anything connected with black art or black activism was grist to her mill.

Nancy put down some of her first impressions of Harlem in a long article she later wrote for her anthology.

"When I first saw it, at Seventh Avenue, I thought of the Mile End Road—same long vista, same kind of little low houses with, at first sight, many indeterminate things out on the pavement in front of them, same amount of blowing dust, papers, litter." She noticed "ghetto-like slums around 5th, bourgeois streets, residential areas, a few aristocratic avenues or sections thereof, white-owned stores and cafeterias, small general shops and the innumerable 'skin-whitening' and 'anti-

Kink' beauty parlours." She saw the new Rockefeller apartments built for black workers, the YMCA and YWCA—"institutes for 'Uplift' "—and the Harlem public library with its famous collection of books on black subjects and even a few pieces of African art. She puzzled fiercely over why, as Crowder had told her after his visit earlier in the year, most American blacks seemed to care so little about their African past. "The American Negroes—this is a generalization with hardly any exceptions—are utterly uninterested in, callous to what Africa is and to what it was."

At night, she went to the Lafayette Theatre, where most of the black actors and dancers then in vogue had first appeared, and to the famous Savoy Ballroom. "No one who has not seen the actual dancing of Harlem in Harlem can have any idea of its superb quality. From year to year it gets richer, more complicated, more exact. And I don't mean the unique Snake Hips and the marvellous Bo-Jangles, I mean the boys and girls out of the street.'

Very quickly, to her credit, Nancy saw through the fashion for Harlem to the more complex feelings beneath. "Notice how many of the whites are unreal in America: they are *dim*. But the Negro is very real; he is *there*. And the ofays know it. That's why they come to Harlem—out of curiosity and jealousy and dont-know-why. This desire to get close to the other race has often nothing honest about it." Some of the smartest Harlem nightspots no longer admitted black customers; in the places patronized by both races, the whites, Nancy observed, often felt insecure. Many of the whites who visited Harlem, in Nancy's view, "treat Harlem in the same way that English toffs used to talk about 'going slumming' . . . it doesn't affect their conception of the Negroes' social status." Nancy felt nothing in common with such people; she believed that another kind of relationship was possible. "There are, however, thousands of artists, writers, musicians, intellectuals, etc., who have good friends in the dark race, and a good knowledge of Harlem life, 'the freedom of Harlem', so to speak."

Gradually, during her visits to Harlem, Nancy came to detest the travesty of blackness, as she saw it, purveyed by writers like Carl Van Vechten, author of *Nigger Heaven,* who had given Harlem the image of "nothing more whatsoever than a round of hooch-filled night clubs after a round of snow-filled boudoirs." She saw it different. "Harlem is romantic in its own right. And it is *hard* and strong; its noise, heat, cold, cries and colors are so. And the nostalgia is violent too; the eternal radio seeping through everything day and night, indoors and out, becomes somehow the personification of restlessness, desire, brooding." She admired, unselfconsciously, the young blacks she saw in the streets and parks, "the strength of a race, its beauty." And she always remembered the children. "One of the first things I was impressed by, the best thing that remains of Harlem, was the magnificent strength and lustiness of the Negro children. As I walked from end to end of it, down the length of 7th Avenue, the schools were just out. The children rushed by in rough leather jackets . . . shouting and free."

In New York Nancy met several people who were to contribute to her anthology and one or two who became good friends. Crowder remembered introducing her to the staff of the NAACP magazine *Crisis,* whose editor was the great Negro leader and journalist, W. E. B. Du Bois. She also met and talked with Walter White and William Pickens. She quickly made friends with Langston Hughes, the poet, and saw something of Countée Cullen, who was back in New York from Paris, and took their advice on which black poets might be persuaded to contribute. She and Crowder spent some time with William Carlos Williams and his wife, and visited them in Rutherford, New Jersey. The Williamses acted as poste restante for Nancy during her stay.

But despite these useful contacts, the trip continued to have an awkward flavor. Crowder remained nervous: "Me, of all people, a great big black man, running around New York with a white woman! I must have been crazy." And Nancy continued to miss Michelet. They both drank too much.

At the end of a month, they had both had enough. After one last drunken party, they staggered on board a German steamer and headed back to Cherbourg. Crowder had no doubt that the expedition had been a mistake. "That stay in New York was one of the most unpleasant incidents in my life . . . and I am sure the visit was just as miserable for Nancy as it was for me."

They agreed to separate, for the time being, when they reached Europe. Nancy was going to meet Michelet in France; Crowder was going to London to look into the possibility of studying music under the successful black singer John Payne. But they also decided that they would make a trip to Germany together before long.

When Crowder reached London, he quickly felt a familiar indecision and helplessness. The singing lessons did not come to anything. Within two weeks he was back in France. Although Nancy had been happily reunited with Michelet, she still wanted to go to Germany with Crowder.

As Michelet remembered it, Nancy's purpose was to visit the ethnological museums of Germany in search of material on black art and culture. Crowder's account does not mention museums, but describes how they motored slowly through small Bavarian villages, where his color caused a sensation. In Munich they found Brian Howard, with whom they visited the homosexual nightclubs. When Howard and a friend went up to the mountains, Nancy and Crowder joined them. A certain amount of drinking and undressing went on, rather to Crowder's alarm.

After a quick visit to Berlin and Hamburg, they returned to France. Crowder suggested to Nancy that he should study music and French in Paris. She agreed, and paid the fees in advance. Then it emerged that Nancy thought she could continue to divide her life between Crowder and Michelet. Michelet would stay at Réanville and help her with the anthology; Crowder would stay in Paris studying; and Nancy would move between them.

Again Crowder rebelled. "I told Nancy I was going to

leave her and return to America. We talked about it many hours and as Nancy was planning to visit America herself we arranged to meet early in the spring in New York. She insisted that I take the auto."

So in the early autumn of 1931 Henry Crowder made his third transatlantic voyage that year at Nancy's expense. He saw tears in Nancy's eyes as they parted; she told him they would visit the West Indies together next year, but "although I believed she was absolutely in earnest about this trip, I had absolutely no intention of going with her. I was through, and I intended for my subsequent conduct to prove this parting would be the final one."

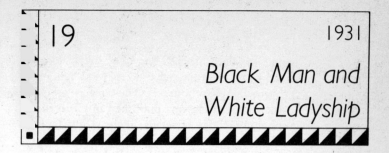

Though she was reunited with Raymond Michelet, whose one wish at this time was to be with Nancy and help her with the race anthology, and though the Hours Press was finally closed and Crowder was across the Atlantic, Nancy still could not quite settle down to her new project. For all her capacity to appear lightheartedly scornful about the breach with her mother, she was still simmering. She felt compelled to put what had happened on record; she also wanted to punish her mother for her ignorance and unkindness.

The idea of a pamphlet, which she had discussed with Brian Howard in Obergurgl in February, had stayed in her mind. It was as if she could not commit herself fully to her real work against race prejudice, the anthology, until she had struck a public blow against her mother and all she stood for. Also, Nancy needed to link herself directly with the cause she now felt was the most important thing in her life. She had a strong, even exaggerated, sense of her own significance; but there was nothing affected about her wish to demonstrate her feeling of solidarity with the victims of prejudice.

In the aftermath of her visit to America and her meetings with the *Crisis* editors, Nancy dashed off a short article for them called "Does Anyone *Know* Any Negroes?" The title was a remark her mother had made to her in 1930, before she fully realized that Crowder was Nancy's lover. The piece is Nancy's summary of her experiences of race prejudice since she had met Crowder in Venice in 1928, but the heart of it is her account of her mother's attitude. As an introduction, Nancy printed, in quotes, a series of remarks made by her mother. "Does anyone *know* any Negroes? I never heard of that. You mean in Paris then? No, but who receives them. . . . What sort of Negroes, what do they *do*? You mean to say they go into people's houses?" The tone is mocking rather than hostile. The article was published in *Crisis* in the issue of September 1931; if, as seems likely, Lady Cunard heard about it, she must have been still more hurt and angry. But Nancy had not finished; indeed, she had hardly begun.

During the autumn of 1931 Nancy spent some weeks in Toulon with Michelet. Shortly before Christmas she wrote and had privately printed a pamphlet, eleven pages long, entitled *Black Man and White Ladyship: An Anniversary*. There can seldom if ever have been a more savage public attack by a daughter against her mother.

The pamphlet was divided into two sections: The first, headed "Her Ladyship," opened with Nancy describing the ingredients of the situation.

> I have a Negro friend, a very close friend (and a great many other Negro friends in France, England and America). Nothing extraordinary in that. I have also a mother—whom we will at once call—Her Ladyship. We are extremely different but I had remained on fairly good (fairly distant) terms with her for a number of years. The English Channel and a good deal of determination on my part made this possible. I sedulously avoid her social circle both in France and in England. . . .

After telling the Margot Asquith story and describing what happened when she and Crowder arrived in London, Nancy launched into a more specific tirade against her mother.

> But, your Ladyship, you cannot kill or deport a person from England for being a Negro and mixing with white people. You may take a ticket to the cracker southern states of U.S.A. and assist at some of the choicer lynchings which are often announced in advance. You may add your purified-of-that-

horrible-American-twang voice to the Yankee outburst. . . .
No, with you it is the other old trouble, class.

Negroes, besides being black (that is, from jet to as white as
yourself but not so pink), have not yet "penetrated into London Society's consciousness." You exclaim: they are not "received" (You would be surprised to know just how much they
are "received"). They are not found in the Royal Red Book.
Some big hostess give a lead and the trick is done.

For as yet only the hefty shadow of the Negro falls across
the white assembly of High Society and spreads itself, it would
seem, quite particularly and agonisingly over you.

For three pages, Nancy attacked her mother at every vulnerable point. She began: "It is now necessary to see Her
Ladyship in her own fort, to perceive her a little more visually." She described her as "petite and desirable as per all
attributes of the nattier court lady" and in a fierce temper over
a description of herself in Cecil Beaton's recently published
Book of Beauty. She mocked her conservatism. "What is the
matter with people these days? Bolshevism is going on too,
England is breaking up." She presented her as bewildered by
and hostile to all forms of change and vulnerable to mocking
criticism. "Her Ladyship may be as hard and buoyant as a
dreadnought but one touch of ridicule goes straight to her
heart. And she is so alone—between little lunches of sixteen, a
few callers at tea and two or three invitations per night."

Her Ladyship, according to Nancy, was frequently swin-
dled by art dealers and jewelers because she was unable to
detect fakes, and she was not above cultivating rich people
who would buy and sell paintings and furniture from and to
each other. Her extravagance over clothes was exposed by a
useful quote from the *Daily Express*. "I have not the faintest
idea how much I spend on clothes every year. It may run into
thousands. I have never bothered to think about it."

Nancy attacked her mother's snobbery. "If a thing is *done,*
she will, with a few negligible exceptions, do it. And the last
person she has talked to is generally right, providing he is
someone. The British Museum seems to guarantee that African

art is art? Some dealers too are taking it up, so the thick old Congo ivories that she thinks are slave bangles are perhaps not so hideous after all. Though still very strange; one little diamond would be better." Her mother, Nancy continued, "likes to give—and to control. It is unbearable for her not to be able to give someone something. But suppose they don't want it—what does this *mean*?"

She went on to portray her mother as inhibited and hypocritical. "Some days she will even shy at the word 'lover.' " Although she had homosexual friends, wrote Nancy, she affected ignorance of and distaste for homosexuality. Communism was another taboo topic. "Her Ladyship is the most conscientious of ostriches and when she comes up again she hopes the *un*-pleasant thing has disappeared." Her quickness of mind was mere picking of brains; she pretended to despise gossip while fomenting it; she would drop people she suddenly heard were thought undesirable. Lady Cunard's famous generosity, hospitality and wit were derided by her daughter as empty and meaningless. "Is it an amusing atmosphere? It is a stultifying hypocrisy. Yet, away from it it has no importance; it is, yes it is unreal. There is no contact, the memory of it are so many lantern slides. They move and shift together in a crazy blur of dix-huitieme, gold plate and boiserie, topped with the great capital C, conversation, rounded off with snobbery and gossip."

In the second section, "The Black Man," Nancy wrote an impassioned summary of the history of the slave trade, lynching (with special reference to the Scottsboro Boys) and the inconsistencies of a white America that exploited and brutalized the blacks yet allowed them to nurse its children and fight its wars. Using a conversation she had once with a white Virginian friend (her old dancing partner Beale Davis), she derided the show of affection that southerners put on while basically believing "the damn niggers had to be kept in their place."

She appealed to her readers to try to put themselves in the blacks' place. Finally she proclaimed her passionate belief in the stupidity of racisim and the gifts and potential of black people.

> I believe that no fallacy about the Negroes is too gross for the Anglo Saxon to fall into. You are told they are coarse, lascivi-ous, lazy, ignorant, undisciplined, unthrifty, undependable, drunkards, jealous, envious, violent, that their lips, noses and hair are ugly, that they have a physical odour—in the name of earth itself what people, individually, can disclaim any of these? The knave and the fool will out, the dirty will stink.

But the times were changing, she wrote, and people would have to wake up to the new condition of the Negro. "The days of Rastus and Sambo are long gone and will not re-turn . . . the pore old down trodden canticle singing nigger daddy who used to be let out to clown for the whites has turned into the very much up-to-date, well educated, keen, determined man of action."

As for the notion that the African black was primitive, she would have none of that either. "It is certainly true he has not got himself mixed up with machinery and science to fly the Atlantic, turn out engines, run up skyscrapers and con-trive holocausts. . . . Who tells you you are better off for being 'civilised' when you live in the shadow of the next war or revolution, in constant terror of being ruined or killed?"

The last lines of the pamphlet read: "There are many truths. How come, white man, is the rest of the world to be re-formed in your dreary and decadent image?"

Nancy sent out hundreds of copies of the pamphlet as a sort of Christmas card to all her friends and acquaintances in France, England and America. She also sent it where she knew it would cause most pain, to Lady Cunard's friends and relations. Allegedly she sent one to another dancing partner, the Prince of Wales.

Brian Howard, who was in Toulon while Nancy was pro-ducing the pamphlet, wrote to his own mother:

You've no idea what it's like. Her mother behaved with utmost folly and narrow-mindedness and has, of course, brought
it on herself. I should regret to write such of you, I may say.
But I quite understand Nancy. Her mother has been "asking
for it" from Nancy, by behaving *vilely* to her and her friends,
for years. . . . I think it is going to create an explosion such as
has never been known, and will very likely be her end "socially." (It is going to everyone and is being printed here—I
am helping.) Take heart, because I'm not mentioned in any
way, indirect or direct.

Nancy's broadside brought her little sympathy, much less
approbation. It was her hatred of her mother rather than her
hatred of racism that struck people most forcibly. The general
feeling even among her close friends was that Nancy had gone
too far. Even the most loyal of them, such as Harold Acton,
Janet Flanner, and Solita Solano, felt some sympathy for Her
Ladyship, who apparently behaved with great dignity. "One
can always forgive anyone who is ill," was all she said. Those
who did appreciate Nancy's point of view and felt her mother
had much to answer for also regarded the pamphlet as evidence of Nancy's lack of sense and balance. The rest simply
found it outrageous. One letter that has survived must be
typical of many. It came from a doctor, described in a note
from Nancy as "a so-called 'family friend' to Her L and self."
It refers to Nancy having sent the pamphlet "to all the friends,
ex-friends or acquaintances of your mother," and said: "It is
difficult to describe the feelings of disgust which the reading
of your pamphlet against your own MOTHER has caused to
me."

As for the man behind the pamphlet, the man whom it was
all about, he regarded it as a most dubious honor. "I never
really agreed with Nancy in her attitude towards her mother," wrote Crowder.

I often asked her not to discuss Her Ladyship in my presence.
Once Nancy wrote a very nasty letter to her mother about the
allowance incident and read it to me before posting it. I re-

member she gave me the letter to mail but I destroyed it instead. Nancy never knew.

Subsequently Nancy wrote the "Black Man and Her Ladyship" [*sic*] pamphlet which she had printed and distributed herself. I thought it a most idiotic thing to do. I received a copy while in America. Why she ever wrote that atrocious piece is more than I know.

Not one of Nancy's friends, then or later, had any words of commendation for *Black Man and White Ladyship*. Those who admitted she had a valid point or two to make about prejudice and snobbery felt she probably damaged her cause, and certainly damaged her own reputation for seriousness, by basing her attack on so much personal experience and vindictiveness. The pamphlet became evidence, for those who looked for it, of an unbecoming hysterical outburst, and contributed to the growing feeling that Nancy's convictions and campaigns were signs of instability. Read forty-five years later, it shows courage, insight, and acute observation, and it deserves consideration as a serious statement. In attacking her mother in public, Nancy was breaking one of the most powerful of all taboos. It was one thing to be known to be on bad terms with your mother, but quite another to commit literary matricide and expect to be applauded.

In one way the pamphlet achieved what Nancy wished. It made reconciliation with her mother out of the question; she had gone too far to climb down. Not only did she never see her mother again, but she never communicated with her in any way either, nor did she express any interest in her. Lady Cunard, on the other hand, occasionally spoke of Nancy, but she too failed to make positive overtures even when she became old and ill.

Though the appearance of *Black Man and White Ladyship* gave Nancy a feeling of triumph and relief and her mother embarrassment and pain, it became clear as time went on that in the eyes of the world Nancy had done herself more damage than her target. For years Nancy had been able to shock the world she grew up in without being rejected by it. But by the early 1930s, as a direct result of her relationship with Henry Crowder and the breach with her mother, she was in danger of being written off as someone whose bohemian eccentricity had turned into dangerous, distasteful unacceptability. This may have been what Nancy wanted, but the strain on her was nevertheless considerable, and the damage done to her reputation for seriousness has persisted to this day.

Some idea of the violent disapproval Nancy incurred among people who had once been her friends can be obtained from a story by Richard Aldington in a collection called *Soft Answers,* published by Heinemann in 1932. As a public attack by a writer on a close friend and patron, it must be almost as unprecedented as Nancy's pamphlet against her mother. Making every allowance for creative license, and always remembering that Aldington was to become famous for his vindictiveness in exposing the faults of his friends in print, his portrait of Nancy in "Now Lies She There" is outstandingly vicious.

Aldington had not forgiven Nancy for the transfer of his work to Wyn Henderson during the last months of the Hours Press, and he had been shocked by her behavior since 1928; but the timing and tone of the story must be related to Nancy's activities during 1930 and 1931. It is an effective story, and what makes it so is the mixture of attraction and disapproval felt by the narrator for his heroine, and the insights born of close knowledge on which that reaction is based.

The story concerns a woman, Constance, rich, beautiful and talented, whose faults of character lead her to a nasty fate. The narrator, Bob, is a friend rather than a lover, who makes one or two irritated attempts to intervene in Constance's life, and speculates on what lies behind her downfall.

All Constance's emotional dramas, according to Bob, had meant little. "They were a kind of emotional magic-lantern show, an attempt to enliven a very unconvincing life-performance with dramatic images. With no defined aim in

life, no standard of conduct, no points of reference, no genuine culture, no sense of individual or collective responsibility,
Constance desired to cut a figure in the world." Nancy-
Constance's mistake lay in trying to shine among writers and
artists, to be one of them, without really having the talent.
Bob then launches into the heart of the matter, a bitter
attack on Constance as a predator on men.

> She specialised in being the temporary wife of a series of *faux
> grands hommes,* almost anyone who was remarkable for false
> pretentions which brought him humiliation. She liked unread
> poets, painters who never sold a canvas, musicians who had to
> play in restaurants, boxers who were always knocked out,
> remittance men, jockeys who had been warned off the course,
> drawing room anarchists who got into trouble with the police,
> unofficial representatives of oppressed national minorities,
> fraudulent solicitors and unfrocked priests. . . . She loved
> cads, because she could destroy them utterly. But they must
> not be common gigolos—any woman with five thousand a
> year could destroy them. Her prey must have had the hope of
> better things, must have slid down the ladder and be trying
> madly to struggle up again. . . . Then, under the pretext of
> espousing their cause, she settled on them like a lecherous
> octopus, and flicked the husk of a man to contempt and de-
> spair. Not a female Don Juan—one would applaud that legiti-
> mate revanche of the sex—but a kind of erotic boa constrictor.
> She swallowed men whole. You could almost see their feet
> sticking out of her mouth.

There is an hysterical relish behind the writing of this passage, which in the context of Aldington's friendship with
Nancy is astonishing. Perhaps, after all, she had rejected him
sexually; perhaps she really had let him down over publication
of a book. His revenge was to turn every aspect of her character and behavior into a nightmare caricature, not allowing
her any taste, brains or passion, not allowing her lovers or
protégés any success or distinction, not granting her any generosity of mind or body. He painted a vicious portrait of a

rich, useless erratic girl in rebellion against her family and class for want of anything better to do or be.

In the climax at the end of the story, Constance goes slumming in a low bar in London's East End with her current boyfriend, a handsome lower-class nonentity named Eddie, and Eddie's former girl friend, whom Constance takes pains to mock and humiliate. There is a fight, the lights go out, and in the dark the infuriated ex-girl friend breaks a bottle and slashes Constance across the face. The story ends with Constance, disfigured and half blind, living, veiled, as the mistress of an Arab in North Africa.

Aldington-Bob sums up this cautionary tale by musing on how appropriate such an end seemed to him. "I remembered how Constance had often seemed to me a symbolical figure, an embodiment of the postwar plutocracy and its jazz Dance of Death. Well, the plaster visage had fallen off the Death's Head in her case. . . . My feeling was one of serenity and hope, as if a sickness were ending, and health was in sight." There is no record of how Nancy felt about "Now Lies She There." It is not even established that she read the story, though, given her interest in the writings of her friends, it seems unlikely that she did not; and given the nature of gossip in any circle, it is even more unlikely that no hint of Aldington's deliberate, savage caricature reached her. Certainly their friendship was over by the mid-1930s. For the rest of her life she regarded him with dislike.

For all its exaggeration and unpleasantness, Aldington's story contains some shrewd insights. It goes much too far in depicting the fruits of Nancy's Paris years and loves as totally pointless, squalid, and unproductive. Even as Aldington was writing and publishing his crude attack, Nancy was well into her new project, the anthology on race. And though cruelty and absurdity were elements in its creation, it was to stand as a considerable achievement and evidence of a moral commitment that, however clumsy or confused, does her credit.

From the end of 1931 until the spring of 1934, Nancy's life
was dominated by her determination to produce an anthology
on black politics and culture. The way she went about it was
simple enough in principle but led in practice to huge complexity and confusion. Without any notion of structure, still
less of themes apart from the fundamental one, she simply
started approaching possible contributors with a request for
material. Occasionally she suggested a subject; mostly, she
gave her possible contributors carte blanche. As she herself
realized in later years, she had no idea when she started how
the book would end up. "My making of it was, I suppose,
much of it, going out into the blind." And as Raymond
Michelet has put it, "*Negro* was not at any time a reasoned
enterprise. And neither was it a reasonable one . . . there was
never any original plan. There was never any question of
constructing a thesis in an academic manner, or of searching
all known archives or cataloguing possible sources. . . . It was
above all a work of passion, and impassioned." What Nancy
remembered most clearly ever afterward was how she felt
about the cause. "The indignation, the fury, the disgust, the
contempt, the longing to fight."

The circular that Nancy had produced in April 1931 shows
that, from the start, her idea of the book was idiosyncratic,
wide-ranging, and ambitious.

The new book on COLOR here described comprises what
is Negro and descended from Negro. It will be published as
soon as enough material has been collected.

It will be entirely *Documentary,* exclusive of romance or fiction.

There will be at least 4 separate sections:

1 The contemporary Negro in America, S. America, West Indies, Europe (writers, painters, musicians and other artists and personalities). With photographs.

2 Musical section. Last century and modern American Negro compositions (Spirituals, Jazz, Blues, etc.)—Reproduced. As much African tribal music as obtainable—Reproduced. This section is in charge of the composer George Antheil.

3 African. Ethnographical. Reproductions of African Art. Ivory Carvings, etc. Explorers data. Recent African photographs.

4 Political and sociological (the colonial system, Liberia, etc.) by French, English and American writers—the French translated beside the original text. Accounts of lynchings, persecution and race prejudice.

The book also to contain—Poems by Negroes, Poems addressed to them.

A list of Museums containing African Art.

Reproductions of Colored Advertisements.

Many English and American authors will write articles, essays and give new documentary facts on Africa and the question of Color in U.S.A. and in Europe.

I want to receive contributions from Negroes for inclusion in any of these 4 sections or in the intermediary parts of the book.

I want outspoken criticism, comment and comparison from the Negro on the present day civilisations of Europe, America, South America, the West Indies, African Colonies, etc.—where conditions are best for Colored people—individual documents, letters, photographs, from those that have travelled and can judge the attitude of diverse countries and races.

This is the first time such a book has been compiled in this manner. It is primarily for the Colored people and is dedicated to one of them.

I wish by their aid to make it as inclusive as possible.

As this remarkably confident, even naïve, statement indicates, Nancy was undeterred by her ignorance of many of the subjects mentioned or by the prospect of sorting and arranging the material she was so enthusiastically calling in. As usual, she counted on her friends for help and contributions. Several of the blacks she had come to know in London, New York and Paris had their life stories to tell; what did it matter if they were not all very literary? Old friends such as Ezra Pound, Norman Douglas, and Harold Acton she assumed were in sympathy with her on racism; surely they would send her something? The French Surrealists, who had led the way in discovering African art, would no doubt want to figure in the book. Meanwhile, as she read through books and magazines and newspapers, especially the left-wing American Negro press, new names and ideas struck her all the time. She wrote to academics, journalists, politicians, poets and anthropologists. Money was not one of her considerations, whether possible profit or likely cost. She assumed that contributors would not want payment; this was to lead to trouble later.

Virtually all of the immense correspondence connected with the making of *Negro* has disappeared. The fragments that remain show that Nancy received much encouragement initially from some of the people she wrote to out of the blue. One particularly interesting series of letters has survived, from the black writer Claude McKay. McKay grew up in Jamaica but moved to New York in the 1920s and became one of the new voices of Harlem. He wrote poetry and essays and worked on the left-wing magazine *Liberator*. In 1928 he published *Home to Harlem,* the first novel by a black American to become a best seller. By the end of 1931 he was living in North Africa, and from there he wrote to Nancy.

> I feel very excited about your book, of course, because I think from your attitude and angle of approach, if I surmise rightly, you will produce a fresh and artistically stimulating contribution. We poor negroes, it seems to me, are literally smothered under the reams of stale, hackneyed, repetitious stuff done by our friends, our moral champions and ourselves that never strikes people piercingly anywhere. We most of us live in fear of the fact of ourselves. And can hardly afford to

render even the artistic truth of our own lives as we know and feel it; but it is unimaginable that you could be handicapped or allow yourself to be by the social-racial reactions that hamper us sometimes unconsciously even. And so I hope the stuff you are going to put out will be a revelation and inspiration to us.

This was exactly how Nancy saw her role; she must have been immensely encouraged to hear such words from a leading young black writer.

By the end of April 1932 Nancy was ready for her second visit to America. She wanted to follow up the contacts she had made the previous year and to make new ones; she also needed to chase down some of the contributors whose material she was expecting. She had in mind making a trip to the southern states, and she was certainly assuming that she would see Henry Crowder and that he would accompany her on a visit to the West Indies.

There does not seem to have been any question of Michelet going with her on this trip. She went first to London, where she was joined by John Banting, who shared her feelings about blacks and race prejudice. They decided to go to America together. They checked into the Grampion Hotel in Harlem and began to explore, to meet their friends and visit shows and nightclubs.

Within a few days a major furor blew up. On May 2 a story appeared in the New York *Daily Mirror,* one of the Hearst papers, saying that Nancy Cunard, the London heiress to the shipping line, had arrived in New York in pursuit of Paul Robeson, the well-known black actor and singer, and was staying in the same hotel as he in Harlem. Other papers and the newsreels picked up the story. The Grampion Hotel was besieged by reporters, but Nancy had left town for a couple of nights. As soon as she saw the story, she sent a furious telegram to the *Mirror:*

Racket my dear sir, pure racket, heiress and Robeson stuff. Immediately correct these. Call Monday one o'clock give you true statement. Nancy Cunard. Publish this.

The denial was not published, although a simultaneous denial by Robeson was. But the press conference called by Nancy for the following day took place and received full coverage. John Banting, who was with her—as was one of their black friends, the novelist Taylor Gordon—found his initial nervousness turning into admiration as Nancy took charge of the conference and handled the press with great verve and aplomb. Her blood was up; she was determined to scotch the Robeson rumor (which was untrue and must have started as a distorted version of her relationship with Crowder) and to turn the occasion to her own advantage by obtaining publicity for the anthology and for the Scottsboro Boys. She arrived with a typed statement, which she handed out to the reporters. It began:

> Press Gentlemen,
> How do you get this way? I am astounded at your story of myself and Paul Robeson. You must correct this immediately. I met him once, in Paris, in 1926 at the Boeuf sur le Toit cabaret, and have never seen him since. He has said so himself, in the Evening Graphic May 2nd, good for him. Indeed he needs no patron; he is one of your greatest singers—everyone knows that.

In the same jaunty, positive tone, she went on to point out that her family was financially disassociated from the Cunard Line, adding, "I travel tourist third, on a German line, and my name is NOT 'the Hon. Nancy,' it is Nancy Cunard." She told them about the breach with her mother over a friend who was "a gentleman of colour. . . . I never see her or her lot." She directed them to a book about the Cunard Line that showed that one of her American forebears had signed an antislavery protest in Pennsylvania in 1680. As for the purpose of her visit to America: "I am working here on the huge anthology I am making on the Negro race. As for Harlem . . . you wouldn't expect me to be any place else would you, for this work? A student must be as close to his subject as possible. And I have many friends here." Another denial about any relationship with Robeson, a remark about feeling a link with the press because of her press in Paris, which she now wanted to sell; then she sailed into her peroration.

> And now after your interest in my private affairs (I hope I have sufficiently satisfied this) I want something in return. I want money for the defense of the 9 Negro framed-up boys held under death sentence in prison since a year, the Scottsboro, Alabama case. I ask for money to be sent immediately to me for the Scottsboro Defence. *Why are you Americans so uneasy of the Negro race?* This question is the epitome of the whole colour question as it strikes a plain English person such as myself. Who'll write me the best answer to this? I'll print it in my book on Colour.

Nancy answered the questions that followed with good humor, but she would not give the name of the man who had caused her breach with her mother. Banting described the extraordinary occasion: "I was half sick with horror but I need not have been, for she stood up to the barrage smilingly in her bright armour of belief and her quick wit."

Her courage and charm had some effect. The *Daily Mirror* the next day ran a long story headlined "Miss Cunard Asks Aid for 9 Doomed Negroes—Scottsboro Case Draws Girl's Help." The reporter described how Nancy "smilingly refused yesterday to name the Negro whom she presented to London as her close personal friend. 'Call him John Doe,' suggested Miss Cunard." She was quoted at length. " 'The more mystery there is the better I'll like it,' frankly stated the English society girl. . . . 'This is all what you Americans call ripping ballyhoo for the volume. I am delighted that the stir I seem to have created may result in some widespread publicity for the opinions about my friends, the Negroes, I am so anxious to spread.' " The *Mirror* printed a picture of Robeson, while saying, "Nancy sincerely deplored the fact that her present arrival in America has resulted in mention of the name of Paul Robeson, the Negro singer and actor." The *Mirror* also sent some reporters to investigate Nancy's residence at the Grampion Hotel.

> Yesterday Miss Cunard visited Boston. . . . Her absence from the Hotel Grampion gave rise to rumor that she had fled from the publicity. The Grampion staff, exclusively colored, went into mourning, the lone white guest of the hotel having become something of a patron saint to these colored workers. Her return at nightfall gave rise to rejoicings and yesterday during the meeting with the press in the hotel's assembly parlor, the staff lingered on the outskirts of the newspapermen throng and burst into discreet laughter and cheers whenever Miss Nancy made one of her points in favor of "justice" for the black man.

But predictably, although the press let the Robeson angle fade away, they did not let the Nancy Cunard story die. To Nancy's fury, the *Mirror* obtained a copy of *Black Man and White Ladyship* and ran long extracts from it without her permission. Her article "Does Anyone Know Any Negroes?" from the *Crisis* (which identified Henry Crowder by name) was also pirated. Reporters persisted in asking the hotel staff for details of Nancy's hours and visitors. A photograph taken of Nancy outside the hotel flanked by Banting and Taylor Gordon was widely reproduced with the white man cropped out and the black man left in. And before long an enterprising reporter tracked down Henry Crowder.

Nothing had gone well for Crowder since his return to America. After his first excitement had faded of driving down to Washington in the smart little car Nancy had let him keep as a good-bye present, he found the car a liability. "Being a black man and driving such a flashy car with French number plates caused me to be constantly stopped and questioned by the police." He was determined to start again as a musician; but after finding a partner, joining the Musicians' Union and sending out printed announcements to "wealthy and high social circles of Washington," he still found no work coming in. He thought he knew the reason.

"My association with Nancy Cunard has received wide newspaper publicity in America, and many of the socially elite in Washington knew Lady Cunard personally. So upon finding that I was the self-same colored man who had figured in these reports they naturally would have none of me." Among blacks, too, he found he was regarded with mixed feelings.

> Fantastic tales had been told concerning my relations with Nancy while in Europe . . . my appearance in public always caused a murmur of whisperings.
> "That's Henry Crowder. Who is he? Don't you know? He's the fellow that the rich white woman who owns the Cunard line is crazy about." Of course, all gross exaggerations. And from the men: "Boy, you sho' is lucky," etc. . . . if only they had known.

Evidently it was not proving easy for Crowder to settle down after his life with Nancy, whether the problem was hostility from some blacks, envy from others, white disapproval, or his own sense of grievance. Nancy had written to him before she left Europe, announcing her arrival in New York and reminding him of their plan to visit the West Indies. This news did not arrive at the best moment. Crowder wrote to Nancy advising her not to come. This was not at all what Nancy had wanted to hear.

> Her reply was one of the sharpest reprimands I have ever received from her. She told me that she did not need my advice about coming to America; that she would do as she liked about the matter. She insisted on calling me a traitor and a rotter and said as far as she was concerned I could go to blazes. My reply to that was in a few words. I wrote: "My, what a temper you must have been in when you wrote that letter" and signed my name.

While Nancy was tangling with the New York press, Crowder stayed put in Washington, hoping that the fuss would die down. He did not feel too sorry for her, knowing how she loved a fight.

The first reporter to tackle Crowder was a young white man who produced a telegram from a big New York newspaper instructing him to "find Henry Crowder and get a story of his relation with Nancy Cunard." Crowder told him "that I had known her in a very impersonal way." The young reporter thanked him and left.

Crowder's account of how he managed to dodge publicity at this time—he certainly featured hardly at all in the press coverage of the next few weeks—does not altogether fit with his complaint that he was ostracized by smart Washington because of his notorious association with Nancy Cunard. What is true also is that whether out of loyalty, nervousness, or good nature, Crowder refrained from telling any journalist anything about Nancy that could damage her or make her look ridiculous. But this time he stuck to his resolution. Twice, Nancy cabled him to come to New York and sent him the fare. He spent the money and stayed in Washington. After this she made two trips to Washington to see him, but he managed to avoid her.

The publicity Nancy received, and her request for statements from Americans on their attitude to race prejudice, inevitably provoked a flood of letters—five hundred, she later said—and though many of them applauded her stand, a number of them were from the Ku Klux Klan. There were threats of violence and of abduction, demands for ransom, insults, and obscenities.

Though some of her friends tried to keep the more extreme letters from her, Nancy, characteristically, was fascinated and amused rather than appalled by them. She told John Banting that all debutantes or stage stars who got their names in the papers were used to that kind of thing. She decided to put a selection of the more printable hate letters into the anthology to illustrate the virulence of race hatred. A few more remained in her papers; they make pathetic as well as frightening reading.

Mrs. Nancy Cunard take this as a solemn warning, your number is up. You're going for a ride very shortly. You are a disgrace to the white race. . . . Either give up sleeping with a nigger or take the consequences. This is final.

We shall call for you just as soon as the necessary plans have been completed for your reception. The secretary of the second caucasian society of America.

Some were unpleasantly obscene:

Miss Cunard you are making a lousy hoor of yourself associating with niggers can't you get a white man to satisfy you I have always heard that a negro has a large prick so I suppose you like large ones is that why you are taking the part of these 9 niggers.

One, signed KKK, called her "insane or downright degenerate you dirty betraying lowdown piece of mucus. . . . I hope that when you try to free the lousy niggers down in Alabama the white people will lynch you."

Though Nancy herself took such communications in her stride, her friends thought it prudent to get away from New York for a while. Later, she was to remember this withdrawal with resentment, as an act of cowardice, but at the time it was necessary. Her movements and meetings with friends were being watched. She had to move out of the Grampion because the constant callers and phone calls annoyed her and upset the proprietor. She moved into an apartment belonging to a Jamaican who ran the hotel restaurant, but she was pursued there too.

Even Nancy must have realized that the kind of publicity she was attracting could cast a lurid light not only on her but on her black friends, who were more vulnerable than she was. So when a sympathetic white friend, Lawrence Gellert, suggested that she should move to a peaceful farm belonging to friends of his in Dutchess County, in upstate New York, she agreed.

She stayed there about a month, working on her material and writing endless letters. Gellert remembered afterward how deplorable her cooking was, and how her idea of making coffee was to fling coffee and water alternately into the same pot for days on end; he also remembered how she loved the beauty and quiet of the countryside and how hard she worked. The reporters did not find her, even though one day when she and Gellert visited the local store, they found the shopkeeper reading a newspaper with the headline "Nancy Cunard Disappears from Harlem."

Toward the end of May Nancy decided that she had been in retreat long enough. She and Gellert made a quick visit to Boston, where several of her possible contributors were to be found. One of these, the black journalist Eugene Gordon, has left a long account of his meeting with her.

Gordon had been a reporter and feature writer on the Boston *Post* for thirteen years. He had contributed articles to *New Masses, Opportunity, Journal of Negro Life,* and *Nation,* some of which Nancy had read. She had written to him asking for a piece on the Negro's relation to the United States radical movement; he had written it but not sent it off. She had also sent him a copy of *Black Man and White Ladyship,* which he had not read.

On his way home from work one evening he stopped off at a cinema where he caught the end of a newsreel showing "Lady Nancy Cunard" going into a "Harlem negro hotel." She was "supposedly" in America to gather material for an anthology. She was referred to as the heroine of Michael Arlen's *The Green Hat* and Huxley's *Point Counter Point.*

Gordon was intrigued enough to call in at the library after the cinema and take out *Point Counter Point.* When he got home he looked through his copy of *The Green Hat.* The phone rang. "A woman asked cautiously but politely: 'Eugene Gordon?' Having been reassured, she called: 'Hullo, Eugene.' I didn't know the voice. Before I could word a suitably polite apology she said: 'I'm Nancy Cunard. You promised . . .' 'Oh' I hardly believed my ears. 'The "Shipping Heiress" of today's headlines?' Her slow, husky laugh ended abruptly."

As Gordon began explaining that he would send her the promised article in the mail, Nancy broke in. She was in Boston and would take a cab over to his apartment immediately.

Feeling slightly nervous at the thought of the Boston press, Gordon tidied *Point Counter Point* and *The Green Hat* out of the way. To his amazement, as he looked down the stairs, he saw that Nancy Cunard was wearing a green hat that evening. As for the rest of her appearance:

"She was thin faced . . . I remember most clearly the bold, direct, probing of her impersonal green eyes." She was wearing a dark dress and a black leather jacket; she produced a flask out of her bag and offered it around.

Nancy sat down at once to read Gordon's article. "Her left cheek inclined against the left palm, cheek smudged, downcast eyes framed in a half circle of the tight-fitting green hat's downcast brim, she read with concentration and speed. . . . Presently she looked up, smiling as to herself, saying, casually, 'Very good,' then, emphatically '*Very* good.' She took the sheets, folded them and put them into the handbag."

After that, they talked for a while.

> She was disinclined to talk about the press harassment; but talked with intensity about going to the Negro workers natural habitat. Incredibly, I listened, restraining an impassioned protest. Let her begin considering the Negro's interest if she didn't consider her own! Her going into the Deep South as she had gone into Harlem, I wanted to say, would end tragically for Negroes and for her. I believed she was talking for its effect on me and that she had no intention of going South. . . .
>
> She said something about *Negro* (as the anthology had come to be called) as a better title than *Color* and, incongruously, across the back of my mind flitted the half formed idea that if the anthology, whatever she named it, was to be filled with stuff as hastily written and as carelessly read and accepted by its editor as mine had been I'd have scant respect for it and less for its editor.

Nancy avoided the press in Boston, but for the rest of her time in America she was under constant observation. At the end of May the *American* produced a huge story, filling a whole page; the tone is typical of the publicity Nancy was receiving. The headline read: "Lady Cunard's Search for Color in New York's Negro Quarter." "Disinherited by her Mother for her Unconventional Conduct, the Heiress of the Famous British Steamship Fortune Takes Up Residence in the Harlem Black Belt." Alongside pictures of Nancy and Taylor Gordon, the paper used pictures of Nancy's mother and Nevill Holt. There was also a Covarrubias drawing of frolicking Negroes at a party, and a photograph of Nancy sitting at a table with some blacks, captioned: "Lady Nancy Cunard Enjoying Herself Among Her Colored Friends in Her Apartment in Upper New York."

After retelling at length the story of Nancy's break with her family, most of it lifted from *Black Man and White Ladyship* and the *Crisis* article, the *American* turned to Nancy's recent activities in Harlem.

> In studying the public and intimate home life of the American colored family, Nancy was taken to restaurants, dance halls, cabarets and rent parties. . . . As life does not become very active in Harlem's Negro section until nightfall, most of Nancy's visits about the district were at night. With a group of friends picked up more or less indiscriminately, she traveled from speakeasy to nightclub and dance hall. She enjoyed dancing and in many places negroes were her partners.

But the real sting came at the end.

> One of the most curious developments of the whole affair is the feeling of resentment among many of the colored people that this white woman should have taken up residence in their midst. Complaints about her were made by the other dwellers in the apartment house where she stayed and the proprietor intimated that the sooner she terminated her stay the better pleased he would be.

There is no evidence that this was true; but it could have been. Nancy was never bothered by what other people thought about her, and it probably never crossed her mind to wonder whether her presence in Harlem might not be welcome. She was sure of her cause, and of its virtue, and it was not in her nature to question her own motives. And so when, on the eve of her departure for the West Indies early in July, another storm blew up in the press, her indignation was totally genuine.

What seems to have happened was that Nancy met a black Bostonian named A. A. Colebrooke, and decided that he would be a suitable companion for her trip to Cuba and Jamaica. Presumably she had realized by this time that Crowder would not change his mind, and wanted someone to go in his place. The Boston *Post* discovered that Nancy and Colebrooke were traveling together and printed a story saying that Colebrooke was wanted by the police and was supposed to have deserted a white wife and six children. Other papers, including black papers, took up the story. The *Afro-American,* a black Baltimore paper, claiming that Colebrooke was wanted by the Boston police about a stolen car, put a rather different emphasis on the story.

> Mrs. Colebrooke has told inquirers that her husband has gone to Havana on business. The condition of the family has improved since Colebrooke, a man of education and a former Elk exalted ruler, secured employment with Miss Cunard. He has paid off the mortgage on his home and made arrangements to send his wife an adequate weekly sum while he is serving Miss Cunard.
>
> The fact of Colebrooke's employment and of his care for his family is suppressed by the white newspapers because of the desire to use him to humiliate the white Englishwoman.

It must be admitted that Nancy frequently asked for trouble while she was in America, and sometimes, as on this occasion, she got it. It is perhaps surprising that there was not more open hostility to her from the blacks themselves, though one black observer later described how Nancy first struck him in the summer of 1932:

I remember her as a rail-thin woman with an unfortunate faculty for producing reams of scandalous publicity. Just another white woman sated with the decadence of Anglo-Saxon society, rebelling against its restrictive code, seeking new fields to explore, searching for color, she was not to be taken seriously. I must confess that I shared with Harlem the quite general impression most effectively expressed by a slight upward twist of the lip and a vague shrug of the shoulders.

To Nancy, whether or not she was having an affair with Colebrooke was nobody's business but hers, and any comment on such matters was evidence of prurience and prejudice. Her indignation was spontaneous and unfeigned at what she described as "all kinds of lurid lies and insinuation and hints that my interest in the black race was merely sexual." From the first, she acknowledged that it was her relationship with Crowder that led to her interest in black people and the black cause. Beyond this she saw no reason to analyze or explain. She did what she liked, sexually or otherwise, as she had done for years.

She seems to have been wholly unaware that she herself was regarded as being as much a part of the problem as the solution by a number of the blacks she met. Several of them found something unnerving and suspicious about this reckless white woman with her ambitious project who made no secret of her personal liking for black companions and who found such a thrill in proclaiming herself their champion. To some she had a long way to go before she could be regarded as a trustworthy ally; meanwhile, she was likely to be more trouble than she was worth.

Among the doubters was William Patterson, then a young lawyer who had joined the Communist party, spent two years in Russia in the late 1920s and returned to become a party organizer in Harlem and Pittsburgh. He was a member of the International Labor Defense, the party's legal arm that fought the Scottsboro case. To him and to his wife, Louise Thompson, Nancy's seriousness and usefulness were reduced by her penchant for "white man's niggers"—blacks like Taylor Gordon, who preferred fashionable society to political commitment—and by the lingering effects of her upper-class background. Louise Thompson was particularly critical—perhaps because she herself had been through a traumatic time as one of the black protégées of a rich, elderly, white Park Avenue matron, whose generosity to talented young blacks was based upon a need to keep them simple, joyful, and dependent.

Looking back, still as convinced Marxists, the Pattersons view Nancy as a woman with a genuine, strong humanitarian interest in the injustices being done to blacks, who discovered, through the Scottsboro case, that race prejudice was part of a wider political and economic repression and who thereby learned surprisingly quickly that the class struggle was the fundamental problem. While they disapproved of her flamboyant, unpredictable nature and her uncontrolled sexuality, they felt some sympathy for the difficulties encountered by anyone trying, for moral reasons, to break out of her class and do what she felt to be right. But Nancy's contribution was bound to be limited because it was based on emotion, not on a reasoned political commitment. They regarded her as irreparably damaged by her background and what it had done to her character.

Nancy spent about three weeks in the West Indies, first in Cuba and then in Jamaica. She was not in Cuba for long, but she met the Cuban revolutionary poet Nicolás Guillen and arranged for a contribution for *Negro* from him and for articles on the history of the island. In Jamaica she explored more of the island herself, talking to the people, staying in cheap hotels, and she was fascinated by her first experience of life in a black country under colonial rule. It seemed ridiculous to her that the whites ruled Jamaica, and she was angered by the bland assurances of the colonial administrators that they were doing what was best for the local people.

Nancy met Marcus Garvey while she was in Jamaica. She was the guest of honor at a reception given by the Universal Negro Improvement Association, which Garvey had organized. She approved of his idea that blacks should aim to go back to Africa but found his political ideas too reactionary for her taste. There can be no doubt that during this second trip to America the blacks and whites who most impressed Nancy on all racial questions were the communists and their sympathizers. Nancy was never much interested in the details of communist political thinking and still less in problems of tactics and timing, but she was naturally in sympathy with the line taken by the communists and others on the far left that racism was an unnatural by-product of capitalist exploitation. The white workers, the line went, were not racist by instinct; they were as much victims as were the blacks. The union of black and white working-class people would sweep away racism and bring about social revolution.

Above all, Nancy was captivated and impressed by the ordinary people of Jamaica.

> I am walking along those blue winding macadam roads after rain, when the steam rises through the indescribably lovely trees, through the whole outpouring of these tender and dark green tropics that were so fluid after the dry and tawny Cuba. The black women come out of their houses laughing. "Take us to Eng-land with you" (in a rich sing-song), "we want to go a-way from here" (scanning it, unforgettably). To England, "mother-country" of so many plundered black peoples, to the brutality of colour bar and all the talk about the "not wanting the damned niggers"? They know nothing about these things. "Oh we would like to see Eng-land so much." These are the loyalest subjects of Great Britain. I pass on, wondering how much longer the roguery, insolence and domination of the whites must last.

By the middle of August Nancy was back in France, without having seen Crowder. She rejoined Michelet; he was still in love with her, he was eager to help her with the anthology and there was a mass of work to be done. They went to the Dordogne together, staying for a while in the old monastery at Carennac, exploring other villages, living simply. Nancy was immersed in writing, translating and adapting the material that by this time was pouring in. Michelet remembers the excitement but also the disorganization and random nature of it all. "To tell the truth, we didn't know quite where we were heading. The direction of it all was determined by whatever Nancy or I could discover on the subject . . . in fact the book was pushing out in all directions." He knew German much better than English, so he coped with the German material. Nancy was chiefly preoccupied with the English contributions, especially those from America, so Michelet found himself dealing with Europe generally and in collecting and organizing much of the African material. He started work on a huge research job on the impact of white colonialism on African countries. He had no experience at all in that field, but he had enough academic training to be a good researcher.

He and Nancy were not discouraged by the lack of structure of the book as it took shape. They were clear in their own minds about what they were doing: "It was a question of erecting a monument [to black culture]—of denouncing fallacious arguments about the benefits of civilization so generously brought to the blacks—and of saying to the blacks themselves that they would have to find a compromise between the ancient, almost moribund civilizations that could be regenerated and the European style of life." They felt sure such an approach was badly needed. He and Nancy had been appalled at the low standard of an exhibition of colonial art held in Paris in 1931, where ancient African art was virtually ignored in favor of hideous machine-made modern objects. In France in particular, academic thinking was dominated by the views of a leading anthropologist, Lucien Lévy-Bruhl, who held that the primitive mentality was such that there was a huge gulf between the intellectual capacity of Africans and Europeans.

When the autumn came, they went back to Paris, and then to Réanville for the winter to get the book finished. Nancy had been trying to sell the house there, and she had moved much of the furniture into storage in the rue Guénégaud; but she had not found a buyer. So they camped there for three months, "working a bit later every night, so that gradually, going to bed at dawn, we would start the day again as the early nights of winter were closing in."

During this time, they spent two weeks in Brussels at the Tervueren Museum, where the painter and photographer Raoul Ubac took pictures of the African sculptures and carvings, and Michelet made sketches. But mostly they worked at Réanville, Nancy writing her own contributions to the book and arranging for the translations from French. One or two she did herself; her cousins Edward and Victor Cunard did others; but most were done by Samuel Beckett, who by this time was back in Ireland, unhappy in another academic post, having had little luck getting his writing published, and very short of money. He was glad of the work, though the content of the articles he worked on did not mean a great deal to him; but he was impressed by Nancy's devotion to so good a cause.

There were endless minor crises and interruptions. Some promised contributions did not arrive at all; Nancy wrote the long articles on Harlem and Jamaica herself because expected material never arrived. To her amazement and indignation, such old friends as Norman Douglas and Ezra Pound sent in rather inadequate pieces. Then she began to find that several of her contributors expected payment; she thought she had made it plain that the whole book was to be a labor of love, on their part as well as hers. The trouble was, many of them felt that for a rich white woman not to offer the usual fees was patronizing, even in its way racist. Also, they needed money. Claude McKay was furious and threatened to withdraw; and Sterling Brown, the black poet whom Nancy greatly admired, took a firm line (according to a friend of his at that time):

> She had asked permission to use a poem of his and he wrote back asking how much she planned to pay him. She in her turn expressed disappointment that he had raised the issue of money since, she said, she was publishing the book at her own expense, in the interests of his race and without thought of

financial profit. "But," said Sterling, "I just wrote back: 'Miz Cunard, I 'preciates your good intentions but you'se a rich white lady and I'se jes' a po' black boy tryin' to git along as bes' I can, so I sho' would 'preciate it if yo'd pay me jes' a little sumpthin' fo' dat lil ole poem o' mine.' "

Nancy paid.

Michelet has one curious and revealing story of an article that never got written. Nancy had suggested that Michelet write an article on the African ivory bracelets she loved so much. Michelet did some research and came back to her with a piece that included discussion of the erotic significance of the ivories. He gave as an example the fact that when the bracelets were worn regularly and the ivory became warm from contact with the wearer's body, they gave off a smell very close to the smell of semen. This was too much for Nancy, and, as Michelet refused to omit the passage, the article was never used.

By the early spring of 1933 Nancy felt that the time had come to move to London, where the book would be printed and published. Michelet did not go with her; and this separation marks the end of their close two-year relationship. As he recalls, he was as much in love with Nancy as ever and felt she was deeply attached to him; but she would not agree to settling down permanently with him, and he felt he could not continue to live at her direction.

Nancy arrived in London in the spring of 1933, bringing with her the huge bulk of manuscript and pictures she had amassed over the previous two years. She hoped to have it on sale before the end of the year; she realized that it would present problems to any commercial publishers and had set money aside toward the costs. But she had underestimated the dimensions of the problems and the time it would take her to overcome them. It was to be a year before *Negro* finally appeared, a year of more than usual confusion and upheaval for Nancy and those involved with her.

17   Photograph by Cecil Beaton, 1930.

18–19 Left: photograph by Cecil Beaton, London, 1930. Above and below: photographs by Curtis Moffat in the late 1920s. With Louis Aragon, above.

20–21 (Overleaf) Left: portrait by John Banting, 1930s. Right: photograph by Cecil Beaton, London, 1930s.

22–23 Left: Henry Crowder in the late 1920s. Right: Nancy with her Hours Press books, 15 rue Guenégaud, Paris, spring 1930.

24–25 Nancy (far right) with
Henry Crowder and a friend, late
1920s. Inset: cover for *Henry-Music*
(published by the Hours Press in
Paris, 1930), designed by Man Ray,
showing Crowder with Nancy's
arms along his shoulders and some
of her African ivory bracelets.

HENRY MUSIC by HENRY CROWDER

POEMS BY
RICHARD ALDINGTON
HAROLD ACTON
NANCY CUNARD
WALTER LOWENFELS
SAMUEL BECKETT

26–27 Nancy and Henry working together at the Hours Press, Paris, spring 1930. Left: a list of new works from the Hours Press, summer 1930, designed by Nancy. Below left: Len Lye's photomontage cover for *Four Unposted Letters to Catherine* by Laura Riding (1930).

HOURS PRESS
HOURS PRESS
HOURS PRESS

15 Rue Guénégaud
PARIS 6e
Tel. Littré 50-03

New works by living authors. Signed, numbered and limited editions privately printed.

POETRY	E	PROSE
Walter Lowenfels Apollinaire. An Elegy 150 signed copies £ 1.10.	Z R A	*Richard Aldington* A W a r S t o r y 300 signed copies £ 2.
Robert Graves Ten Poems More 200 signed copies £ 1.10.	P O	*Laura Riding* Four Unposted Letters to Catherine. 200 signed copies £ 2.
Laura Riding Twenty Poems Less 200 signed copies £ 1.10.	U N D	MUSIC
Bob Brown Words. Cover by Man Ray 150 signed copies £ 1.10.	• C	*Henry Crowder* Six Piano Pieces with poems by Richard Aldington Walter Lowenfels and Nancy Cunard.
Harold Acton This Chaos. 150 signed copies £ 1.10.	O L L	
Roy Campbell P o e m s	E C	*Covers by* Frank Dobson, Eugene Mac Cown, Man Ray, Yves Tanguy, Hilaire Hiler, Elliott Seabrooke.
Brian Howard First Poems	T E D	

CANTOS
in One Volume
200 Copies £ 2.

POETRY

Right: John Banting's cover for Brian Howard's first book, *First Poems* (1931). Below right: cover by Elliott Seabrooke for Harold Acton's book of poems *This Chaos* (1931).

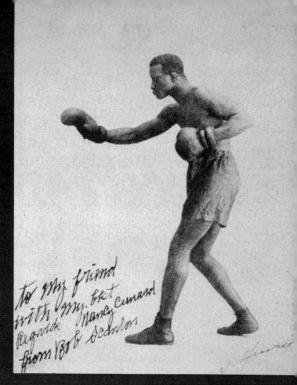

To my friend
with my best
regards Nancy Cunard
from Bob Scanlon

28–29 Photographs from
Negro. Clockwise from top
left: Nancy in Austria in
1931, with (from left)
Brian Howard, Henry
Crowder, and two other
friends; George Padmore;
Bob Scanlon; Chris Jones
and Kwesi Oku holding a
John Banting poster before
a May Day march, Lon-
don, 1933; Marcus Garvey,
whom Nancy met in Ja-
maica in 1932; Lady Emer-
ald Cunard with an Indian
rajah (this picture, reproduced from a newspaper
clipping, appeared with
Nancy's angry question,
"How is it that Indian Rajahs are not discriminated
against?").

Taken by John Banting
in Barcelona, while we were
there together, in Oct or Nov 1937.
Sent me, Dec 1956, with the
words:

"I do so love this picture of you in
the brief, sharp sun of Barcelona (1937)
even though you look tired. If I look
closely into the shadow-filled eyes
I can see such wells of kindliness
and patience and unmistakable
love and steadfastness (And you
look pretty cute too by the way.)
To me all the other photographs appear
to leave off you are faultless looks
beside it — and partly your own
fault too because you always
attend "obsequiously for the photogra-
ther, and in this quick one you
were utterly relaxed — a bit tired
and wanting to get on to the
place we were going to."

30–31 Left: Nancy in Barc
lona, autumn 1937, photo-
graph by John Banting. Thi
was Banting's favorite pictu
of her; she copied his comments about it onto the back
of the photograph, below.
Facing page, below left: wit
her cousin Edward Cunard
the south of France, mid-
1930s. Top right: Tristan
Tzara at Réanville in June
1935, photograph by Nancy
Below right: at Giverny, Ju
1948. Top left: in Capri, Oc
tober 1949, on the occasion
her last meeting with Norman Douglas.

32 With Clyde Robinson in Majorca, 1959.

Once Nancy had established herself in London—to begin with she stayed in a modest Bloomsbury hotel—she started seriously looking for a publisher for the anthology. Nancy was a publisher's nightmare. Her experiences at the Hours Press had left her feeling that she had just as much knowledge of the technicalities of printing and production as any of the publishers she approached; also, she was determined to have the book exactly as she wanted it, and any criticism of its scale, shape, or content was not well received. She had asked her journalist friend Otto Theis to sound out publishers for her in advance. She told him that she would want complete control over the content of the book; that any publisher would have to guarantee "much advance advertising in England and America"; that the book must be sold at the lowest price; that although she did not expect to make money out of it, she would take a 10 percent royalty, and that she wanted to be consulted at every stage of the publication process. She explained that the publisher could expect "quite an amount of advance publicity in England and America; large interest and buying probability from all Negro institutions; immediate correction of all proofs by the editor; the guarantee that no book like this has ever appeared before in the world, because of its character and representativeness," which, she admitted, "may be a deterrent."

As usual, she first approached her old friends. Rupert Hart-Davis, the little boy who had played cricket with Nancy's true love in 1919, was now a rising young editor with Jonathan Cape. Nancy had kept in sporadic touch with him, writing him affectionately after his mother, her great friend Sybil, had died in 1927 and occasionally asking him to look after one or another of her French friends when they visited England. He has recalled what happened when Nancy turned up at the Cape offices at Bedford Square. "I treasure the memory of the interview at which she showed Jonathan Cape an enormous dummy of her anthology *Negro*. He spent some time painstakingly explaining how the book's bulk could be reduced and its format improved. 'But you don't understand, Mr. Cape,' she squeaked at him, 'this *is* the format.' " Cape and Gollancz, among others, turned the book down, but Nancy continued her search. She had a promise from an American publisher, Donald Friede, to bring the book out in New York if it found a publisher in England. At one point she complained that trying to place *Negro* was "like selling oriental rugs to manure merchants."

At last, through another, more recent friend, she found the solution. She had met Edgell Rickword, a talented poet and critic of strong left-wing views, a year or two earlier through the Scottsboro case. They met again in London in 1933; he was now working for Wishart & Co., the small radical publishing company. He was a contributor to *Negro* himself, and he became strongly attached to Nancy. In 1933 Rickword was thirty-five, two years younger than Nancy. He had fought in the trenches and after the war had gone briefly to Oxford. He soon became a leading young critic, one of the first to appreciate T. S. Eliot's early poetry, and an expert on modern French writing. He wrote a remarkable study of Rimbaud in 1924 and reviewed regularly for the *New Statesman* and the *Times Literary Supplement* in the 1920s. (He had reviewed Nancy's *Outlaws* for the *New Statesman* in 1921.) From 1925 to 1927 he edited the *Calendar of Modern Letters*, a critical periodical with high standards that became a model for F. R. Leavis and *Scrutiny*. At the time he and Nancy became close, he was translating French poetry and writing reviews as well as working for Wishart. He was close to the Communist party in 1933, though he did not become a member until 1934.

Through Rickword, Wishart & Co. agreed to publish *Negro* at Nancy's expense. With Rickword to help her, Nancy plunged into the long, elaborate process of designing the book, getting blocks made, correcting, and proofreading. At the same time she was still accepting contributions. She could not bear to leave anything out until the last possible moment. Rickword remembers her passion for work and apparently inexhaustible energy; she would think nothing of staying up all night and expected him to do the same.

At this time Nancy was again very active on behalf of the Scottsboro Boys. The case had been appealed to the U.S. Supreme Court, and money was badly needed. Nancy became honorary treasurer of the British Scottsboro Defence Committee, which organized demonstrations, benefit evenings, films and petitions. Nancy gave money herself, bullied her friends for cash and signatures, and marched in the demonstrations, waving banners designed by John Banting and at least once getting into a fight with the police. "I've been very occupied with all that," she wrote to a friend in America about her efforts.

No-one taking any notice of it at all till I arrived and the re-trial began. Now we have constant speeches and we've had May Day and Labour Day and some others, and delegations to US embassy and the like. And lists of noted writers in papers who've signed my protests and all that. Parties for, anything for to raise funds. . . . Oh the photographs of the Scottsboro Boys in the Labor Defender of NY. I'm not really thinking of anything else but them all the time.

According to some notes she kept, between March and May 1933, Nancy collected about fifty pounds "by various appeals, donations, sale of cards at dances, meetings, etc." She also sent small sums herself individually to the Boys' families.

One letter, dated 1933, has survived from Mrs. Ida Norris, mother of Clarence Norris, from Molena, Georgia.

> Dear Comrade Nancy Cunard, I thank you so much you just wont know how much I thank you for the money. . . . Well the last letter I got from my boy he said they was all getting along all wright . . .

At one stage, Nancy had a brush with the Communist party of Great Britain, who tried to get her to turn over any money she collected to them. Nancy refused and continued to communicate directly with William Patterson of the ILD in New York.

As part of the campaign Nancy organized a series of interracial dances in the East End of London. At one of these there was an ugly incident. A friend of hers, the painter Arthur Lett-Haines, brought two acquaintances along with him after dinner. Lett-Haines found an attractive black girl and went off to dance with her; the other two men got drunk and started making insulting remarks about blacks. A fight started; Nancy's cousin Victor had to intervene, and the police were called.

Nancy engaged in various running battles with the press while she was in London. She was still simmering about stories that had appeared in English papers after her trip to New York the summer before, and she was contemplating legal action. A story published by the *Empire News* (Manchester) shows the tone and approach she was objecting to. It was headlined "Auntie Nancy's Cabin—Down Among the Black Gentlemen of Harlem." After describing how Sir Thomas Beecham had said Nancy ought to be tarred and feathered ("A Strong Beecham Pill"), it said,

> But, bless you, Miss Nancy Cunard, daughter of the famous London hostess Lady Cunard, and descendant of the founder of the great shipping line, doesn't let a bitter pill like that spoil her complacency. . . . I don't want to dishearten the young

lady. Not that she's so young as this implies, for she's had time to interest herself in a lot of other questions like Surrealism (I wish I knew what that was, really I do), Negro Sculpture, Interior Decorating, Poetry, Printing and Publishing *and* Communism.

The writer derided Nancy's efforts on behalf of the Scottsboro Boys as interference in something that was not her business ("Cheek, I call it") and asked how the English would like it if Paul Robeson came over to sort out an unresolved murder in England. Finally,

> But there, nothing I can say will influence our bright Nancy.
> "I intend" she says "to devote the rest of my life to work on behalf of the coloured race."
> Sez she.
> I give her less than twelve months in which to change the colour of her opinions.

Nancy initiated libel proceedings against several newspapers: Allied Newspapers Ltd., the *Empire News,* the *Sunday Chronicle* and the *Daily Dispatch.* In the end she settled out of court and was awarded £1,500. This money went toward the financing of *Negro,* which inevitably cost far more than the £350 that she had originally set aside.

Sometime in the spring of 1933 Henry Crowder returned to London from Washington. By his own account, everything had gone from bad to worse for him in the months since Nancy had left the United States. His health had been poor, he had no money, he was out of work and was drinking heavily. When Nancy heard of his plight, she sent him money and they started to correspond again. She urged him to join her in London, but he hesitated. It was the familiar pattern. Nancy wanted Crowder with her, he wanted to be financially independent; but between them them they were unable, or unwilling, to work out how he could be with her without being dependent on her. This time, Nancy had a new, ambitious scheme.

"In ensuing correspondence," Crowder wrote, "Nancy proposed that I take charge of a bureau in London for Negroes that would be sort of a welfare center. Included was to be a bookshop, information bureau, a register of hotels and boarding houses where Negroes coming to London might stay, reading room etc. This was to be worked in connection with the Negro Welfare League of London but I was to be in charge."

Crowder was persuaded; but his tone suggests he was not exactly enthusiastic. He had little choice, or so it seemed to him.

"With that definite promise I thought it better for me to return. All arrangements were completed as regards salary, etc. and I accepted. I considered it a God-send to me in my then sorry condition so with my steamship fare pre-paid I once again left New York for Europe."

Nancy met him at Victoria Station—"Nancy, the woman I had once tried to kiss and had been kissed for my trouble. She looked older, she looked more tired but she was the same."

Nancy rushed Crowder straight off to a party being given by one of her new black friends, an African, Douglas Papafiou. She told Crowder it was a party to celebrate his arrival. Crowder was about to discover that Nancy's life in London in 1933 was very different from her life in Paris in 1932—let alone 1928, when he had first lived with her. Then, she had still spent a good deal of time with smart, rich, stylish people. Crowder enjoyed all that; he wanted to be part of that world, and he always disapproved of Nancy's liking for nobodies, black or white. Now, in London, he was to find that Nancy through *Negro* and Scottsboro, was spending much of her time with people he thought undesirable. Crowder was not attracted by communism, and he did not much care for the African and West Indian blacks who were Nancy's new friends. He was perhaps jealous of their influence with Nancy; certainly he felt very different from them. The party was not a good beginning to this new stage in their relationship. "Even though I was there because a white woman had been kind to me when I needed help, I could not but feel superior to many who attended that party."

If in one way Nancy's life in London surprised Crowder, other aspects of it were all too familiar. When they got back to the large studio flat in W.C.2, where she was staying, she told him she had to go over to France for a few days to see Raymond Michelet. According to Crowder, this was because Michelet had come into some money and was thinking of getting married. Nancy went; she came back after a few days saying that the relationship was now over. She seemed bitter and upset.

Before she left, she told Crowder he could stay in the flat, and she left a bundle of clothes for someone who might be calling for them. They turned out to belong to Edgell Rickword. "It appeared that he had been living at the studio but upon my arrival was compelled to, at least temporarily, vacate." Wrote Crowder, "This amused me very much. I could not help thinking 'just one of the boys.' "

Crowder liked Rickword; but he didn't change his mind about Nancy's other new friends and associates. The West Indian communist organizer Chris Jones was a friend of Nancy's at this time, and there were frequent meetings of black radicals at her flat. Nancy admired Jones's skill as an orator and political organizer and told Crowder that someone should subsidize him so that he could have a political career. Crowder was not impressed. When it became clear that the projected Negro Welfare Centre was not going to come to anything, Crowder found himself back in the old trap. Not surprisingly, his relationship with Nancy was deteriorating. Nancy realized that Crowder was not really interested in her projects, including *Negro,* and that he disliked her black friends. He would not even join her in demonstrations or go to Scottsboro protest meetings. Moreover, he refused to become, as he put it, "one of her lovers in the intimate sense of the word." She went away to the country for a while to work on *Negro;* but before she left, she told Crowder that she was thinking of moving into a new flat with Rickword. He did not object but said he would not live in the same building himself.

Nancy gave Crowder a small living allowance. He could not find a job, he said, because of difficulties over work permits. "Many were the nights during those times that I wished I had remained in America and rotted rather than be in such circumstances." However, he took the money and rented himself a place to live near Regent's Park; Nancy rarely went there.

Nancy took an attic flat in Percy Street for herself and Rickword, not far from her old haunt, the Eiffel Tower. Crowder helped her with the move and the decorating, but he and Nancy then lived virtually separate lives. He found a black English girl friend and spent most of his time with her. Nancy knew of this relationship and liked the girl. Crowder thought Nancy seemed happy with Rickword. He commented rather sourly on the pace Nancy set as *Negro* neared completion.

> Nancy's life in London during this period was one terrific rush. She was up to her ears in work on the anthology. She fussed and fumed; cursed and damned . . . in this work Rickword did yeoman service. He helped her immensely. He was very kind and obliging. I often looked at him working away with sincere pity. I knew from experience that regardless of how hard he worked that his time to be dumped would come eventually. Whether he realized this, I had no way of knowing but I did feel sorry for him for I felt he was being played for a dupe.

In fact, Rickword was caught up in Nancy's project because he believed in it; while Crowder, the inspirer and originator of the work, had less and less interest or confidence in it.

Nancy celebrated Christmas 1933 at a party with her black friends; Rickword was away, and Crowder accompanied her reluctantly. By this time *Negro* was at last about to be published. Nancy kept up her perfectionism about every detail of its appearance to the very end. She insisted on paper of a particular texture and color, which had to be specially made, and a special cloth for the cover that had to be dyed to exactly the right shade.

Publication was scheduled for February 15. But now, with *Negro* out of her hands, Nancy began to get restless. This was the period of great distress and unrest among Britain's million unemployed; stirred by the drama of the hunger marches and politically stimulated by her new contacts in London in the last year, Nancy wanted to play her part. To Crowder's amazement, she decided to join in.

One afternoon he went to her flat and found her wearing a bizarre collection of garments—a man's overcoat, an aviator's helmet and several scarves—which, she told him, were partly for warmth and partly for disguise. She informed him in mysterious tones that she was off to join the marchers and that he was to tell no one. "Off she went with a small movie camera in her hand. 'Well, well,' said I to myself, 'what the dickens will she do next?' "

Shortly afterward, a young hunger marcher turned up to stay at Nancy's flat; when Edgell Rickword, finding Nancy too exhausting a companion, moved out, the new young man stayed on for a while.

Negro finally appeared on February 15, 1934. The day before, Nancy inscribed a copy and sent it off to Raymond Michelet in France:

> Dear Raymond, comrade and collaborator in chief—here is our book, your copy—is it significant that revolutions are breaking out in the days of its production—and that in this country the hunger marchers are marching on London—I am joining them, at this time
>
> With my love
> February 14th 1934.   Nancy

Negro is an enormous book. It contains 855 pages, measures twelve inches by ten and a half inches, and is nearly two inches thick; it weighs nearly eight pounds. The cover is dark brown hessian with the title printed diagonally across it in large red capitals, and again vertically down the spine. There are roughly 250 contributions by some 150 authors, two-thirds of them "coloured." Over half the book deals with America; there are 60 pages on Europe, and 315 on Africa. The entries vary dramatically in length and style. A few are as long as 20 pages and closely argued; some are simple statements of half a page. There are many full-page illustrations and dozens of smaller pictures inserted in the text; there are 20 pages of music and 12 of poetry. It is a huge mine of a book, both impressive and unmanageable. It is as hard to digest as it is awkward to handle. As she had intended from the start, Nancy dedicated *Negro* to "Henry Crowder, my first Negro friend"; and she also acknowledged, less prominently, "special help" from Raymond Michelet and Edgell Rickword.

In a two-page introduction Nancy sets out the book's purpose. "It was necessary to make this book—and I think in this manner, an Anthology of some one hundred and fifty voices of both races—for the recording of the struggles and achievements, the persecutions and the revolts against them of the Negro peoples." She leaves no doubt where her political sympathies lie. "There are certain sections of the Negro bourgeoisie which hold that justice will come to them from some eventual liberality in the white man. But the more vital of the Negro race have realised that it is Communism alone which throws down the barriers of race as finally as it wipes out class distinctions. The Communist world-order is the solution of the race problem for the Negro." In particular, she claims, Soviet Russia, encompassing some 130 different racial groups, has once and for all solved the "problem" of races, and wiped out the false concept of "inferiority." "Today in Russia alone is the Negro a free man, a hundred percent equal."

It is quite clear that Nancy intended *Negro* to support the Communist party's claim to be the champion of the black race worldwide. Much of the material reflected this belief; but where it did not, she let the opposition stand, with the occasional dissenting editorial remark. The scope and variety of the anthology make it something much more than a political tract and show that even when Nancy wanted to toe the party line, she could not manage it.

The book opens with a full-page portrait of a cloth-capped black worker, captioned "An American Beast of Burden." On the facing page is Langston Hughes's poem, "I, Too":

> I, too sing America.
> I am the darker brother.
> They send me to eat in the kitchen
> When company comes;
> But I laugh,
> And eat well,
> And grow strong . . .

After this simple and effective opening, the anthology plunges into the American section, a mixture of history, reporting, personal and political statements. There are articles on the early history of the blacks in America, slavery, Nat Turner's revolt, black leaders such as Frederick Douglass and Booker T. Washington, and "Three Great Negro Women"—Phillis Wheatley, Sojourner Truth, and Harriet Tubman. The black woman anthropologist Zora Neale Hurston wrote on black folklore and speech patterns. After her own long article on Harlem Nancy put in a list of Negro slang words, with her own forthright translations.

> Boody: light-hearted term for what Mommer [*sic*] does her lovin' with.
> Cracker: a pestilential white, lousy with race prejudice, generally a Southerner who can't keep it to himself, but makes trouble.

It is frequently hard to follow Nancy's editorial system of selection and juxtaposition. There are several purely personal accounts of race prejudice, including Taylor Gordon's and Henry Crowder's; then suddenly Nancy includes an oddly patronizing piece by William Carlos Williams on how attractive he found the black maids in the household when he was growing up. This is followed by a cogent plea from Arthur Schomburg, the librarian of the Harlem library, for "the establishment of a chair of Negro history." Now and again she interjects a sharp footnote correcting her contributor, as in an article entitled, "Some Aspects of the Negro Interpreted in Contemporary American and European Literature," by a black academic, John Frederick Matheus. He refers admiringly to the NAACP leader and editor of the *Crisis,* Dr. W. E. B. Du Bois. Nancy's footnote reads: "The editor cannot do otherwise than state here the profoundest and uttermost disagreement with Professor Matheus' qualification of both Dr. Du Bois as a militant leader and *The Crisis* as intellectually of any importance whatsoever." Forty pages on, Nancy prefaces an article by Du Bois himself with a fervent attack on him, entitled "A Reactionary Negro Organization," in which she pours scorn on the bourgeois liberal attitude of the NAACP and Dr. Du Bois, and calls it "treachery." (This hostility to Du Bois and the NAACP arose directly from the struggle between the NAACP and the Communist party over the handling of the Scottsboro Boys defense. At the time Nancy published *Negro,* the communists were fighting to keep control of the case; not until 1935, the following year, was a joint defense committee set up.)

Some of the most impressive material is strictly factual. There is an effective account of the inadequacy of public education for blacks in the South by James Ivy, and a devastating ten-page compilation of stories of lynching and persecution taken from American newspapers. There is a powerful account of a visit to chain gangs in Georgia, by John Spivak, a white communist writer who had recently published a firsthand report, *Georgia Nigger.* Nancy wrote her own long, impassioned, detailed account of the Scottsboro case, in which she made the point that though Scottsboro might be thought to be a unique outrage, it was in fact typical of innumerable incidents in the South. Her piece is followed by the text of a speech supporting the Scottsboro Boys by Theodore Dreiser.

There are several articles on blacks and communism by black and white communist writers, and the last part of the American section is undiluted Communist party rhetoric. Nancy printed a map of the Black Belt, the strip of southern states that the party was claiming should be handed over to the blacks as a separate territory, a speech from the 1932 Communist Party Convention that nominated a Negro, James W. Ford, as vice-presidential candidate, and a speech by Ford himself.

The next section, "Negro Stars," opens abruptly with a full-page picture of Duke Ellington and his orchestra and a long article on jazz by a French writer, Robert Goffin, translated by Samuel Beckett. The style is ornate and romantic, an abrupt change from the dry dogmas of the would-be Negro vice president. "Oh you musicians of my life, prophets of my youth, splendid Negroes informed with fire, how shall I ever express my love for your saxophones writhing like orchids, your blazing trombones with their hairpin vents, your voices fragrant with all the breezes of home remembered and the breath of the bayous, your rhythm as inexorable as tom-toms beating in an African nostalgia." Visually, this section is one of the most effective. Nancy restrained her tendency to put small pictures in the middle of the text and had marvelous full-page illustrations of Louis Armstrong, Cab Calloway, Bill ("Bojangles") Robinson, and the beautiful Blackbirds star, Florence Mills. Most of the section simply aims to remind readers of the quantity and quality of black talent, though one analytical piece by a black critic, Ralph Matthews, points out sharply that "the big names among Negro performers are only those who have appealed to the whimsicalities of the white race and conformed to their idea of what a Negro should be."

John Banting contributed a description of the superb dancing to be seen in Harlem, and another white friend of Nancy's, Kenneth Macpherson, wrote a plea for a more serious black cinema. John Payne, the elderly black singer who gave singing lessons in London, contributed his own story, as did two of Nancy's boxer friends, Bob Scanlon and Jack Taylor, alongside large photographs of themselves in shorts and gloves.

The music section starts with one of the most striking pieces in the book; "The Negro on the Spiral" by George Antheil, the white American composer, in which he argued that Negro music had not merely influenced European music—much less been absorbed by it—but had taken it over. "Since Wagner," he wrote, "music has had two gigantic blood transfusions; first the Slavic, and in recent times the Negroid." He wrote several particularly effective lines on the African influence over European culture in the 1920s:

> The great war had come and gone, we had been robbed and ransacked of everything; and we were on the march again. Therefore we welcomed this sunburnt and primitive feeling, we laid out blankets in the sun and it killed all of our civilized microbes. The Negro came naturally into this blazing light, and has remained there. The black man (the exact opposite color of ourselves) has appeared to us suddenly like a true phenomenon. Like a photograph of ourselves he is the sole negative from which a positive may be drawn.

Nancy included several pages of music and songs, spirituals, blues, and a long piece by her friend Lawrence Gellert on "Negro Songs of Protest." She reprinted Walter Lowenfels's song for Sacco and Vanzetti and Crowder's music, from *Henry-Music*. She included three pictures of Crowder in the collection of photographs of black musicians—one alone, two with Eddie South and the Alabamians. Determined to throw the net as wide as possible, she printed examples, with music, of Creole folk songs, Jamaican musical instruments, digging songs, a Brazilian chant originating in Africa, tribal songs from East Africa, three Zulu songs, and songs from the Congo set down by Antheil.

The poetry section is one of the shortest in the anthology, a mere dozen pages, each with several poems in small print. Several of the best poems came from collections already pub-

lished in America—Sterling Brown's *Southern Road,* published
by Harcourt Brace in 1932, and Countée Cullen's anthology
Caroling Dusk, published by Harper in 1927. Several of the
poems she chose have become classics, such as Sterling
Brown's "Memphis Blues" and "Children of the Mississippi," powerful reworkings of black folk themes, or Countée
Cullen's deceptively simple ballad, "Incident":

> Once riding in old Baltimore
> Heart-filled, head-filled with glee,
> I saw a baltimorean
> Keep looking straight at me.
>
> Now I was eight and very small
> And he was no whit bigger,
> And so I smiled, but he poked out
> His tongue, and called me "Nigger."
>
> I saw the whole of Baltimore
> From May until December:
> Of all the things that happened there
> That's all that I remember.

She printed five of Langston Hughes's early, angry poems
(of the kind which were to cause him trouble with Senator Joe
McCarthy thirty years later, because of their communist leaning), including "Always the Same" and "Goodbye Christ."

> Goodbye
> Christ Jesus Lord God Jehova,
> Beat it on away from here now.
> Make way for a new guy with no religion at all.
> A real guy named—
> Marx Communist Lenin Peasant Stalin Worker ME.

Langston Hughes also translated poems from the West Indies
by Nicolás Guillen, Regino Pedroso, and Jacques Roumain.
Then follows a selection of poems on black themes by
white poets, including a long poem by Nancy herself, "White

Sheriff," a venomous, jerky monologue by a racist southern sheriff, and poems by Alfred Kreymborg, Louis Zukofsky, and William Plomer.

The West Indies and South America section includes Nancy's long article on Jamaica, a piece on labor conditions in Jamaica by A. A. Colebrooke, her companion on the journey, and reports from other West Indian islands, Uruguay, and Brazil.

The fifty or so pages on Europe are an especially curious mixture. Edgell Rickword contributed a scholarly investigation of the eighteenth-century slave trade from original documents; Anthony Butts and Nancy wrote about their experience of the color bar in England; Harold Acton produced a piece about Pushkin, whose mother had colored blood; the Surrealist group sent in a manifesto denouncing racism and colonialism (the signatures included Breton, Crevel, Thirion, and Sadoul—but not Aragon, who by this time had broken with the group and transferred his allegiance to the Communist party). Sadoul also wrote an article comparing unfavorably the treatment of black characters in French strip cartoons with those produced in the Soviet Union.

Nancy's piece on her experience of the color bar in London was based on her visits to London with Crowder and included another sharp dig at her mother. She printed a photograph of Lady Cunard in an evening gown, standing with a tall dark-skinned Indian in a magnificent jeweled turban and silken tunic. Alongside, Nancy wrote:

How is it that Indian Rajahs are not discriminated against? And how does it happen that society women, and even America-born frantically prejudiced society women, pose for photographs in their company when they pretend to faint at the mere thought of a Negro? The answer is so simple . . . Rajahs have money, and are 'important people,' chiefs, etc. Also, India is 'dangerous' to England. That is the mentality of these society folk in their utter snobbishness and ignorance. It is, once again, economic. Like the entire question of race prejudice.

The last piece in the European section is especially striking; René Crevel wrote an essay on white treatment of blacks, especially women, called "The Negress in the Brothel," in which he discerned the double exploitation involved: "Man in the middle, obedient to God, obeyed of women—chaplet of subordinations."

The last section in the book, "Africa," is about two hundred pages long. Again, it is an eccentric mixture of ancient and modern history, ethnography, folklore, politics and personal experience. Michelet compiled a studious account of ancient African civilizations, and a detailed map of tribal areas. George Padmore wrote approvingly about the new Ethiopia under Haile Selassie. Ezra Pound sent in an obscure note about the neglect of African subjects by lazy academics. There are several pages of gnomic Ewe proverbs and riddles, examples of Hausa writing, and an article by Wyn Henderson's mother, Ada Lester, on "Clicking in the Zulu Tongue." Norman Douglas contributed a letter explaining why he could not write a proper article after his visit to East Africa, followed by a slightly patronizing parody (by himself) of what he might have written. There are some short extracts from William Plomer's *African Notebook*.

The core of the African section is a series of photographs and drawings of African sculpture—masks, effigies, fetishes, and votive objects. Most of them came from European museums or private collections; some were owned by Nancy herself. She put in two pages of pictures of her ivory bracelets.

The last section consists of several articles on the evils of colonialism and includes pieces by two young African nationalists Nancy had met in London—Ben Azikiwe, who wrote about Liberia, and Jomo Kenyatta, writing on Kenyan aspirations. Both men later became leaders in their countries. Padmore contributed an extract from a book denouncing the pass laws in South Africa and British racism in Africa generally.

The anthology ends with Raymond Michelet's long compilation of facts and figures about colonial exploitation in Africa, "The White Man Is Killing Africa."

A thousand copies of *Negro* were printed, costing two guineas each. Nancy sent free copies to all the contributors, with a characteristic letter.

Dear Collaborator,
I am glad to be able to send you your copy of the Anthology you helped to make.

As you see, it is a very large volume and has, consequently, been very expensive to produce.

It is therefore my hope that each collaborator will endeavour to secure an order for the sale of one copy. . . . And, if possible, out of justice to our subject, to arouse interest in the press and reviews.

Yours for the freeing of the innocent
Scottsboro Boys and the true emancipation
of Negro peoples.

She also sent copies to the press and to libraries in England and America with an interest in black subjects. All this was expensive, especially since the book was too heavy to qualify for special postage rates and had to go full rate.

Two days after publication, the *New York Times* carried a news story headlined "Cunard Anthology on Negro Is Issued." The story mentioned the book's dedication to Henry Crowder, Nancy's "two-year" stay in Harlem, and her conclusion that communism was the solution to the race problem.

But as the weeks went by, Nancy was increasingly disappointed and angry at the lack of serious reviews, particularly in the left-wing and communist press in America, which she had expected to be highly receptive and sympathetic. The London *Daily Worker* gave *Negro* a good review, and the *New Statesman* was friendly; but the coverage she had confidently expected in the United States was scanty.

Part of the trouble was that *Negro*'s huge size and omnibus nature made it hard to read and difficult to summarize and judge. Politically, Nancy had fallen between stools; the strident communist opinions in the book alienated liberal commentators, while the many other points of view the book contained annoyed the dedicated communists.

But if the public response to the book was disappointing, Nancy received many private letters from her contributors and sympathizers that pleased her. She pasted some of them into an album. One of the first is a letter from Henry Crowder which, despite his fundamental reservations, is generous and encouraging.

Langston Hughes wrote: "Your book is marvellous." William Pickens of the NAACP called it "excellent" and "tremendous" and "of very permanent value." Alain Locke, the distinguished black writer and teacher, went further. "I congratulate you—almost enviously, on the finest anthology in every sense of the word, ever compiled on the Negro. . . . I shall try to spread the influence of the book everywhere possible." Arthur Schomburg reviewed the book very favorably for the Associated Negro Press, a large news agency serving black papers, and wrote Nancy a personal letter as well.

> My dear little lady . . . you have made good . . . I want to say
> I never doubted your word nor questioned [your] integrity.
> By By, roseleaf . . . Arturo.

Taylor Gordon told her she had silenced many of her critics. A formal letter from the editor of the New York *Daily Worker* said carefully: "It appears to be an excellent collection of material on the Negro question."

Some of her distinguished white contributors also wrote. Theodore Dreiser called it a handsome piece of work and offered help in getting it published in the United States. William Carlos Williams called it impressive and promised to review it somewhere, while one of the most complimentary letters of all came from Mike Gold, a leading white American communist intellectual. He said he would review it for the *Daily Worker* and the *New Masses* and went on:

> But the anthology is really serious and fine, and damn it all
> as good as a thing as we've had. . . . I feared, honestly, a
> dilettante venture. Not that I didn't believe you a really fine

woman trying to get orientated to a new world of feeling and ideas. But the remnants of an old culture and life cling, and sometimes it takes many years to shake them off. But you have come through splendidly in this book.

However, the review promised by Gold was never written, and Nancy was furiously upset when the *Afro-American,* instead of a proper review, simply printed an attack by James W. Ford on a *Negro* article by black Marxist activist George Padmore, who by then had fallen out irrevocably with the party. What caused the quarrel, and what impact it had on Nancy is described in the following chapter. But as far as *Negro* was concerned, Nancy was learning that in race, as in other matters, the party line was sometimes hard to follow, and that for the well-disciplined communist it was not enough that her heart was in the right place.

In Boston Eugene Gordon could hardly wait for the end of his working day and a chance to take his copy of *Negro* out of its wrapping. He too was more impressed than he had expected to be. Years later he remembered hearing several criticisms of *Negro* at the time: One was that the book was too wide in scope and too varied in content to be given "scholarly treatment" because each section would have to be reviewed by an expert in that particular field; more surprisingly, another was that Nancy had ignored black women and youth. Gordon felt that "such false reports originated with the accusation that Miss Cunard's primary interest in Harlem was Negro men." He came to think that Nancy had been too hard on Dr. Du Bois and the NAACP, but at the time she was only following the party line. But above all, he too felt that she had demonstrated her seriousness beyond question.

The bulk and expense of *Negro,* and the sporadic reviews meant that it did not sell well; and the communist label and the lurid gossip surrounding Nancy's interest in blacks were damaging. Within a few months the book was banned on grounds of communist subversion in the British West Indies (the Trinidad governor described it as "seditious") and in several African colonies. It is not known what Lady Cunard's reaction was to Nancy's achievement, or whether she ever knew that her picture with a colored man was in the pages of the anthology.

Several hundred copies were still in Wishart's stock when the war came and were destroyed in the blitz. After the war the book was virtually unobtainable and fetched increasingly high prices in the rare books market. (A good copy was quoted in 1976 at $1,500.) But to the end of her life *Negro* linked Nancy to the inexorable drive of black aspiration, nationalism, and revolt, and young blacks who found it in libraries would write to her or call on her to thank her or ask her advice.

Five years after she died, a shortened version of *Negro* was published in New York. The response among reviewers in 1970 of an anthology published in 1934 was generally good; *Negro* was recognized as an extraordinary document, flawed perhaps, but ahead of its time, bursting with ideas whose time had only come in the intervening years or have yet to come. Perhaps what strikes a modern reader most powerfully is that it is still impossible to regard *Negro* simply as a piece of history or a collection of voices from the past; too many of the ideas and questions it contained remain painfully unresolved. *Negro* was Nancy's greatest achievement; she was proud of it to the end of her life, and she was right to be so.

A Visit to Moscow

Soon after *Negro* came out, Nancy went back to France. Crowder stayed in London and managed to find a job. For the next few months they were not in touch at all.

The immense effort of producing her anthology must have left Nancy with a sense of anticlimax. The book was published; she had achieved what she had set out to do; what was she to do next? Her relationship with Crowder, the man who had first aroused her interest in the black cause, was virtually over. Nancy herself had changed during the past five or six years; she was now thirty-eight years old, and she had irrevocably broken with her mother and, apart from her continuing affection for the handful of friends they had in common, from her mother's world. She had emotionally and publicly allied herself with the far left in politics. Communism attracted her, as it did many others in the early 1930s, because it offered a coherent explanation of economic disasters, social inequalities and oppressive political regimes, and because it provided a rallying point for the fight against fascism, which was beginning to loom on the horizon. Since 1930 Nancy had been turning steadily away from poetry and the arts toward politics and journalism; she felt this a more appropriate direction for the times.

But for the time being, she settled again at Réanville, making occasional trips to Paris. John Banting came over to stay with her. She was juggling with ideas for various projects arising out of *Negro*. One was another anthology, this time simply of black poets; another was a script for a film about the slave trade. Neither of these projects came to anything. She was also trying to find American and French publishers for *Negro,* without success, and trying to persuade left-wing publishers in America or England to reprint Raymond Michelet's long anticolonialist piece from *Negro* as a pamphlet.

In the early summer of 1934 Nancy and Banting were joined at Réanville by George Padmore, the black communist activist. Nancy had first met Padmore in Paris in the autumn of 1932, soon after her return from her second visit to the United States; they had already corresponded over *Negro.* Padmore was six years younger than Nancy, and when she first knew him, he was one of the Communist party's leading policymakers and spokesmen on racial and colonial matters. He was born in Trinidad, but he went to the United States to study first medicine and then law and joined the party there in 1927. In 1930 he went to Moscow, where he soon found himself in a position of some power; he worked with James Ford, the leading black American communist, to organize the First International Negro Workers Congress, held in Hamburg in 1930, and he edited *Negro Worker,* a monthly magazine dealing with international black politics, which was one of Nancy's main guidelines and sources for her anthology. In 1933, after Hitler came to power in Germany, Padmore was imprisoned and then deported to Britain, where Nancy met him again during the final stages of editing *Negro.* But by this time, Padmore's position in the Communist party had begun to change. Hitler's takeover in Germany led to a series of readjustments in the party's attitude to the Western democracies, and one of these was that anticolonial agitation should be played down in order to improve the chances of Western sympathy for Russia as a bulwark against fascism. Padmore was not prepared to put the interest of the party worldwide ahead of the needs and rights of colonized peoples. As a result he was expelled from the party in June 1934, and soon after he was attacked in the communist press for "petty bourgeois nationalist deviation."

Although Nancy should have been prepared for what happened after Ford's *Afro-American* attack on Padmore's article in *Negro,* she was puzzled and angry. At first she thought it must all be a misunderstanding; then she believed that once Padmore was faced with specific charges, he would be able to refute them and all would be well. Nancy remembered him as being very distressed by the situation, and she was too. "NOTHING has so much upset me as this 'case,' in the whole of my life. . . . On the one hand Padmore, one of the few people I reverenced for his integrity and very being . . . on the other hand that this should come from members of the ideology (Communism) that I admired also entirely and wholly. It was inacceptable—and yet it had happened."

Nancy was impressed by the way that Padmore nevertheless kept on with his work. He was writing a book, *How Britain Rules Africa;* he finished it that summer at Réanville, and Nancy typed it out for him. They talked about conditions and politics in the West Indies, and she asked him why either the example or the guidance of Moscow should be pertinent in a part of the world where conditions themselves so plainly demanded revolutionary change. " 'So why always Russia?' I would say to George. 'Great as is my admiration for the U.S.S.R. and sympathy, surely the very facts and the lives of the Antillean population are enough reason in themselves to cry out to be changed?' . . . To which he would reply that it is 'always Russia' because it is the first country where Socialism has triumphed; it is the great example, the great encouragement. And of course this is true." Padmore also talked to Nancy and Banting of the time he had spent in Russia; he described "the interest and natural sympathy Russians felt at the sight of a Negro . . ."

Although Padmore's breach with the Communist party shook Nancy, it did not cause her to reconsider her allegiance, which in any case was always emotional and general rather than specific and political. It was widely rumored, at the time *Negro* came out and later, that Nancy was a communist. If this is taken to mean that on matters of interest to her she often followed Communist party thinking, that she had many communist friends and contacts, and that she felt great admiration for the Soviet Union, then indeed she was. However, not only did she never join the Communist party, it is unlikely (as one party member who knew her well in those days has said) that the party would have accepted her.

It must have been as obvious then as it is in retrospect that the mere thought of Nancy taking part in organized meetings or being subject to intellectual or organizational discipline was absurd. Nancy grew to detest bourgeois conventions and upper-class social attitudes, and she was capable of complete dedication and fanatical hard work, but she is a classic example of someone who chooses to play a part in dramatic causes far removed from the dull grind of everyday politics. She had a romantic notion of exploited blacks and workers as people she could help; she could never for an instant have submerged her own identity in a political organization.

She was genuinely puzzled by Padmore's problems because argument about ideas was foreign to her nature. Her own loyalties, once formed, were undeviating, because she was blind to everything except what she perceived as right and wrong. In the 1930s communism was the obvious guiding light. To believe anything else would have seemed to Nancy stupid, or wicked. Anything that threatened this view she either rejected totally or regarded as an unfortunate misunderstanding. Her instinct, as with Padmore, was to carry on and trust that it would all work out in the end. She admired Padmore's loyalty greatly; although he could not agree with the party, he never attacked it.

Nancy was beginning to want to go on her travels again; and she wanted, most of all, to go to Moscow. She had been in touch with Crowder during the summer of 1934 and, according to him, had tried to persuade him to leave his job in London and return to Paris; but he declined. Then she wrote asking him to go on another journey with her, to Haiti or to Russia. Again, he refused. It was only when she wrote again, telling him she was ill and begging him to meet her at Boulogne and sending him the fare, that he gave in. "Regardless of all the ups and downs we had gone through I could not turn down her request if she was ill. We spent the weekend together." When Nancy recovered, she again raised the question of travel. At first, Crowder was adamant. But then, "she hinted at settling a small sum of money on me. I told her that would certainly make me face the future with equanimity." By his own account, Crowder was prapared to risk another episode with Nancy if there was a chance of receiving some financial security as a result.

After a couple of nights in a cheap hotel in Montmartre, they went down to Réanville. Crowder was depressed at the condition of the house; it was dirty and neglected, inside and out. It was winter; Nancy decided to go South. They rented rooms in Mougins, near Cannes.

Nancy was still unwell and was being treated by a doctor in Cannes; the weather was bad; their rooms were bleak and cold. They had constant arguments about money; Crowder tried and failed to find a job playing locally. Eventually he persuaded her that in order to find work, he had to be in Paris. They went back to Paris and took rooms in a small cheap hotel.

They decided that perhaps the best arrangement would be for Nancy to live down at Réanville, while Crowder stayed in Paris. He spent several days helping her clean up the house and garden; but after he returned to Paris and found a flat (at Nancy's expense), Nancy decided that she could not live at Réanville alone. She wrote to Anna, her old Breton maid, to see if she would return; in the meantime she tried to persuade another black friend, Fred, who worked as a cook at a Montmartre nightclub, to come to Réanville as man of all work. The plan collapsed over Fred's demands for money.

Nancy hired a local cook, persuaded a young French couple to stay with her for a time, and made regular visits to Paris on weekends; but her relationship with Crowder was getting worse and worse. Money was a constant aggravation. Crowder asked Nancy for a daily sum to pay for his own meals, since she complained so bitterly over the bills when they ate together. One morning, after a furious quarrel, Crowder told her he was leaving for good. "Oh, you're just like all the rest," said Nancy. "The old girl is broke now. Got no money. You're like all the other rats, leaving a sinking ship."

As Crowder has told it, Nancy was quite unreasonable; she berated him for not finding work, but when he did pick up an engagement, she objected because his plans upset hers. One night after they had spent the evening together, she suddenly said, "We don't like each other any more, so we might as well call it quits." It was four-thirty in the morning, raining hard and Crowder was leaving Paris that day for a job. Nancy announced she was going then and there; he pointed out that that was hardly necessary as he would be gone in a few hours. They quarreled bitterly. Crowder told her to go to hell, and she left. She returned just as he was leaving.

When Crowder got back to Paris a few days later, he found she had left him a note "telling me that she was through. She had informed the concierge that she was not responsible for the flat and that any arrangements I made would be my own." She had also left him two hundred francs and informed him that she had made arrangements for him to receive the same sum every week for six weeks until June 1, 1935.

Once again, Crowder felt stranded. He had no money and no work, and he blamed Nancy. They met twice more in the next few months. Once they passed each other in the street in Montmartre and spoke briefly, once they went to a party together on the outskirts of Paris. Nancy was crossing to England the next day; she appeared surprised when Crowder was reluctant to join her at her hotel after the party. But this time, Crowder knew the relationship had to end.

They never met again. Crowder stayed in Europe, managing to keep afloat with occasional jobs, until he returned to the United States shortly before the Second World War.

As a postscript to his account of their time together, Crowder attempted to analyze his relationship with Nancy and to draw from it some general conclusions. He wrote that he was suspicious of her from the start; first because she was white (he said he had grown up knowing what could happen to black men who "allowed themselves to be enticed by white women") and then because it was obvious from the earliest stages of their relationship that she was "rather free with her affections." He was attracted by her and admired her intelligence and energy, but he admitted, "I overlooked a great many things after the beginning because my heart was never at stake. I imagined that I might carve a successful future out of the situation. I was elated when she showed interest in the Negro question and hoped for some real results."

In the end he felt that these hopes had come to nothing. Nancy had let him down over and over again. He linked her avidity for new lovers with her need to be always frenetically busy on some new project; first the Hours Press, then the showing of L'Age d'Or, then Negro. To him, all this added up to "instability." He was shocked by the streak of cruelty in her; "I really believe she derived a great deal of personal satisfaction in hearing some man threaten to commit suicide because of her."

Crowder felt that although Nancy could be tenderhearted and generous, "nevertheless she handled the feelings of human beings very carelessly indeed." She could turn on people for no better reason than that she did not like their face or manner. She would lead new friends to expect financial help and then be furious when asked for it. "She has often told me that she had never met a colored man who did not want money. I tried to explain to her that when a white woman became intimate with a colored man he usually expected to get money from her. My words never deterred her, however, in her quest of more Negro friends."

As for Nancy's sexual preferences, Crowder stated that he never exactly knew whether or not she believed that black men had "superior sexual powers to those of white men." What he did know was that in this respect Nancy was "a most extraordinary person. She has no bridle to her desire. She goes from one to the other with evident pleasure. The satisfaction of the senses is evidently the driving force." Earlier in his account, he had implied that sex was not very important to him; when he wondered why Nancy kept on wanting him around her, he did not mention sex at all. Once, she told him that he was her "tree"; that she liked to know that she could always go back to him. Another time she said that he was the only person who never bored her. Then, "Why would she always withdraw her assistance at the very moment I needed it most? It was more than I could ever understand."

It seemed to Crowder that perhaps because of her background Nancy always had to be "the dominant spirit in whatever group she moved." At the same time, he felt that her attitude to race alienated her friends. "Not that I think they were prejudiced against Negroes but they did not feel it necessary to go to the extremes to which Nancy went." Crowder seems to have agreed with them. He gave her credit for the energy and effort that went into producing *Negro*, but for little more. He complained again about the "communistic" flavor of the book, which he believed was all Nancy's doing. "Then too, I do not believe that Nancy had the background that a person who attempts to do a great work for a whole race should possess. The book is shallow and empty. It makes a lot of noise, but like a big drum it has little inside."

Above all, Crowder believed that Nancy's erratic behavior harmed the black cause.

I often told Nancy that being in the limelight of the public placed responsibilities upon her. . . . I argued that her name coupled with all of the notoriety brought about by the book made a heroine of her in the eyes of thousands of Negroes. . . .

She pooh-poohed the idea, and told me everyone has the right to live as they choose. Some day this may become a fact but I am firmly of the opinion that when we reach a position where our personal desires or actions reflect to the detriment of others that the good of the many should become paramount. . . . She seems to have forgotten that instead of raising the lowest of the black race to her level by associating with them she lowers herself to their level. Every extreme has a mean and every mean has an extreme. She knows only extremes.

As for his own considered opinion of prejudice and how to break it down: "Equality in relations between the black and white races is a condition that is most desired but in reaching that goal the method of approach should be decent and rational. That is not the method [Nancy] has adopted. I don't think she will ever understand the real feelings most Negro men possess towards white women." For Crowder, those feelings were compounded of scorn for black men who made fools of themselves over women just because they were white and deep distrust of the chances of genuine, lasting love and trust between the races. Crowder himself did not hate the white race; but ultimately, he wrote, "I am absolutely convinced that the greatest happiness and contentment for black people is to be found among themselves."

There can be no doubt that had Nancy ever read Crowder's account of their relationship and his conclusions, she would have been shattered. It would have been bitterly disappointing to read his real view of *Negro,* and to realize that the relationship that had changed her life and bred such profound convictions in her had led the man concerned back to suspicion and skepticism. Nancy's view of race was that it did not exist as a problem between people. Any recognition of difference was prejudice. Crowder's experience as a black man led him to think otherwise; and the history of the black movement has shown how important and serious an instinct that was.

Crowder fully realized that he himself had fallen into the trap he described. He does not present himself in a particularly admirable light, which makes his criticisms of Nancy ring true. She herself seems never to have said or written anything about Crowder after their liaison ended that was other than nostalgic and affectionate. She always regarded him as the most important person in her life. "Henry made me," she told a later American friend. He would have been startled and amused to hear it.

In August 1935 Nancy went alone to Moscow. It had taken her some time to get a visa—so long that she began to wonder if perhaps her connection with George Padmore might have made her suspect with the Russians. She wrote to Aragon, who was in Moscow at the time with Elsa Triolet, and asked him to help; within a few days she was called to the Soviet consulate in Paris and "given an individual non-Intourist visa, very courteously." She went alone, by boat, from London to Leningrad and thence by train to Moscow.

She stayed in Russia about a month. She wrote nothing for publication, and very little privately, about her time there, and she never had much to say about it either. It was a time when foreign party members or sympathizers were frequent visitors to Moscow, but Nancy had no official standing or specific project to pursue, and she was not part of any group being given advice or an instructive tour. It is likely that she did not quite know what to do and that her hosts did not know quite what to do with her.

Aragon may well have kept a circumspect distance for personal and political reasons. Nancy found only a few of her black friends and contacts in Moscow. One was William Patterson, the American lawyer whom Nancy had met through the Scottsboro case. Typically, Nancy took up the party's treatment of Padmore with him: "I could not refrain from talking to him at once, and with some energy, about the ill treatment shown Padmore. I said it was impossible he could be guilty of such charges." Patterson just shook his head at her, smilingly, and said, "Oh, Nancy . . ."

There were strong indications of Russian interest in *Negro,* despite the Padmore connection. As a result of the efforts of Patterson and another black American, Homer Smith, Nancy conferred with a state publishing house. "The Russians were enthusiastic about *Negro* and asked me to let it be translated in whole, also if I thought I could make another anthology, on Colonies alone, and thirdly, if I would consider collecting and bringing, to the Soviet Union, to tour the whole country, a large loan collection of African sculpture. To all these three things I said 'yes' immediately, and was very pleased indeed."

She also found one of *Negro*'s contributors, Eugene Gordon, working for the Moscow *Daily News*. He recalled that she was warmly welcomed by the journalists and that over a glass of tea in the canteen she tackled him over the apparent lack of support for *Negro* among American party workers and left-wing publications. He told her that he thought she had been unfair in an article on the black press. By saying that the Negro newspapers were the black man's worst enemy in the United States she was implying that they were more at fault than the white oppressors. He thought he heard her murmur, "Touché."

Nancy wrote afterward that she discovered while she was in Moscow that it had indeed been her reply to Ford's criticism of Padmore that had held up her visa. She added: "Whoever it was who arranged matters I never knew, but was very grateful to him, or them, for my short, sympathetic visit." After she returned to France, she corresponded with Russian officials about the *Negro* projects, but none of them came to anything. It would have been astounding if they had; although Nancy's stay in Moscow seems to have been remarkable uneventful, for her, her hosts must have realized how dramatically unsuitable she would have been for any sponsored activities.

Soon after Nancy got back to Réanville, in the early autumn of 1935, the Abyssinian crisis came to a head. It had been brewing since 1934, when Mussolini decided to reestablish the Roman Empire in Africa by conquest. At the League of Nations headquarters in Geneva Britain took the lead in asserting the doctrine of collective security and, when Mussolini invaded Abyssinia in October, in demanding sanctions against the aggressor. Nancy, naturally, was passionately on the side of Haile Selassie, whom she and many others saw as a progressive leader of a proud African nation at the mercy of fascist imperial greed. Nancy longed to do something constructive; she got her chance when the Associated Negro Press, a press agency based in Chicago, specializing in copy for black papers, appointed her one of their correspondents. She left for Geneva immediately.

Nancy took her job as a journalist seriously. In Geneva she worked extremely hard, attending the long sessions at the League when Haile Selassie pleaded for stronger sanctions and more support, writing in the evenings, sometimes all night. "Everything but reporting was out of the question for me during those strenuous days." She filed reams of copy, making no attempt at all at objective reporting. As the Abyssinian crisis wore on and it became apparent that the League was unable or unwilling to protect Abyssinia (where Mussolini's armies were pushing toward complete victory), she became increasingly scornful of the whole charade. "Of an evening, when the last words had been written and sent, with what disgust was one filled at the way 'they' carried on—breaking their own clauses and covenants, with supra human cynicism. Such was my baptism in matters of this kind."

During the next eight months Nancy went to Geneva several times. She wrote regular pieces for the ANP and began to plan a short book on the Abyssinian crisis.

Then, a few weeks after the conquest of Abyssinia by Italy and the final debacle at Geneva in June 1936, where Haile Selassie made one last unsuccessful appeal for help, the Spanish civil war began. Within three weeks of Franco's revolt against the republican government, Nancy, on August 10, 1936, was on a train for Barcelona. George Padmore saw her off at the station in Paris.

For the next three years Nancy's life was to be dominated by the struggle in Spain and her determination to do whatever she could to support the republic. She had found her new cause; this time the focus for her energies and emotions was not an individual or a race but a whole country—or her idea of a country. Nancy fell in love with her idea of Spain more completely and permanently than she had fallen in love with Henry Crowder or her idea of the black race. Once again, her passionate allegiance was to lead her to considerable achievement; in the long run it was to bring her much pain but no regret.

From the beginning, the Spanish civil war was of enormous
importance to many people outside Spain itself. The conflict
between the republican government and Franco's rebel armies
stood for more than a collision between socialism and dicta-
torship in one country; it became a trial of strength between
forces that had been emerging in Europe for more than a
decade. There was an immediate and instinctive emotional
response among all progressively minded people in support of
the republic. In 1936 Mussolini had been in power in Italy for
fifteen years, and Hitler had held power in Germany for three;
in Spain, at last, it seemed there was a chance to act against
fascism before it was too late. There was a cause to fight for
and a clear enemy to fight.

All kinds of people, middle-aged trade unionists as well as
young poets, felt compelled to demonstrate support for republican Spain by going there to share the excitement and the
danger, to help in any way they could. There was an idealism
and a romantic fervor in their commitment, which lasted even
after the ugliness and complexity of the war began to be
apparent. Although disillusion set in for some, the Spanish
civil war still arouses feelings of nostalgia for a cause that was
once glorious and unselfish; and while it is easy to see now
that many of those who went to Spain needed to give their
help as much as Spain needed to receive it, at the time such
people, of whom Nancy was one, went to Spain because they
felt they could not morally do anything else.

In her commitment to republican Spain, and in the work she did as a result, Nancy was playing a part much different from her efforts to expose and combat racism. There, she had been a pioneer, even if at times a confused one; she had forged ahead of her contemporaries. With the Spanish cause Nancy joined a movement, one that united thousands of sympathizers from many different countries. Comparatively few of them actually saw fighting, but from the beginning it was apparent how much this war was a war of ideas and propaganda as well as bullets. As the war progressed, the fighting on the ground was sustained from outside Spain—with Germany and Italy helping Franco, Russia helping the republic, and Britain and France maintaining an uneasy facade of nonintervention—and it became crucial for the republicans that their supporters should keep the world informed and hammer home the message that what was happening in Spain mattered desperately. This was the role that Nancy found in Spain and for Spain, and she stands out among the many likeminded people trying to help the republican cause not because of how she felt, but because of what she did.

From her first visit, in the autumn of 1936, until the end in the spring of 1939, and afterward, Nancy saw her main task as that of a reporter. She wrote continuously for the Associated Negro Press, sending off articles every two or three days. She also contributed to Sylvia Pankhurst's paper, *New Times,* and to three publications edited by an Irish journalist, Charles Duff, whom she had known for some years: *Spanish Newsletter, Spain at War,* and *Voice of Spain.*

Nancy worked hard at her journalism; the results were energetic, personal, and impassioned. Although she made no effort at all to be detached and keep her opinions out of her reports, she had the reporter's instinct to find out for herself what was going on and convey as directly as possible what she saw and learned. Given the assumption (admittedly a very large one) that the republican side could do no wrong, Nancy was a useful journalist.

On Nancy's first journey to Spain during the war, in the

summer and autumn of 1936, she made two new friends who impressed her deeply and who were to remain her friends long after the war was over. One was a waiter in the Hotel Majestic, Barcelona, called Angel Goded; the other was the Chilean poet Pablo Neruda, whom she met in Madrid.

In Barcelona in the summer of 1936, it seemed as if the revolution itself had arrived. George Orwell wrote of his arrival there a few months later: '. . . the working class was in the saddle. Practically every building of any size had been seized by the workers and was draped with red flags or with the red and black flag of the anarchists; every wall was scrawled with the hammer and sickle and with the initials of the revolutionary parties; almost every church had been gutted and its images burnt."

Sympathizers from abroad were astounded and impressed by the atmosphere.

> Waiters and shop walkers looked you in the face and treated you as an equal. Servile and even ceremonial forms of speech had temporarily disappeared . . . . In outward appearance it was a town in which the wealthy classes had practically ceased to exist. Except for a small number of women and foreigners there were no "well-dressed" people at all. Practically everyone wore rough working class clothes, or blue overalls, or some variant of the militia uniform. All this was queer and moving. There was much in it that I did not understand, in some ways I did not even like it, but I recognized it immediately as a state of affairs worth fighting for.

For Nancy there were no reservations, then or later. It had always before seemed eccentric or perverse of her to make friends with and share the problems of gondoliers, waiters or taxi drivers. In Barcelona in the summer of 1936 it was not merely acceptable to behave in this way, but expected. As another reporter, Martha Gellhorn, wrote in the same tone: "Barcelona was bright with sun and gay with red banners, and the taxi driver refused money; apparently everything was free. Apparently everyone was everyone else's brother too. Since few people have lived in such an atmosphere even for a minute, I can report that is the loveliest atmosphere going."

Nancy loved the revolutionary atmosphere in Barcelona, sat up late talking with Angel Goded, met his family, sent off emphatic articles to the ANP, and in late September moved on through Valencia to Madrid, where she had an interview that amused and infuriated her with the British acting consul, who tried to persuade her to return home. Nancy decided that his sympathies were clearly not with the republic.

" 'So you haven't decided yet when you will leave?' said the Acting Consul. 'LEAVE!' said I, 'but I've only just arrived two days ago, and there is a great deal I want to learn about here.' "

She found the Chilean consul in Madrid, Pablo Neruda, infinitely more sympathetic. Nancy and Neruda took to each other at once. In 1936 Neruda was thirty-two, eight years younger than Nancy. He was already a well-known poet in Chile and Spain. He had spent seven years as an honorary consul in the Far East before being appointed consul in Spain in 1934. He had strong communist leanings, though he did not join the party until 1947. He was an exceptionally warm, gregarious character, who loved good food, wine, and beautiful women. Neruda was fascinated by Nancy, whom he describes in his memoirs as "quixotic, unalterable, fearless and pathetic"; he respected her courage in breaking with her mother and admired *Black Man and White Ladyship* which he called "as trenchant as Swift, in some passages." He praised "her lovely sky-blue eyes."

Another Chilean writer, Luis Enrique Delano, remembered meeting Nancy in Neruda's house, the Casa de las Flores, in Madrid in the late autumn of 1936. The Casa de las Flores was a center for the many left-wing intellectuals of several nationalities who found their way to Madrid before and during the battle for the city. Neruda was close to the Spanish poets who were inspired by the republican cause, such as García Lorca, Cernuda and Manuel Altolaguirre, and he introduced Nancy to several of them. From Delano's account it is plain that Nancy at forty made much the same impact on a first meeting with the Chilean and Spanish writers and activists as she had made on the Surrealists in Paris when she was not yet thirty. Delano remembered her striking appearance, her energetic determination to experience the war as directly as possible, and her passionate commitment to poetry as an expression of the ideals she shared with the Spanish revolutionary poets.

Encouraged by Neruda, Nancy began to plan how she could help to spread the word about Spain by printing some of the poetry inspired by the war and raising money for the cause by selling it. She decided to use the old Hours Press machine, which was still in the outbuilding at Réanville. She started collecting suitable poems and writing to friends for contributions and advice.

But the last thing Nancy wanted to do was spend all her time in the comparative safety of the cities in republican hands. She traveled as much as she could, getting as close as possible to the fighting. Some detailed notes she kept of visits to the Illescas and Navalcarnero fronts in October 1936 have survived. Illescas was halfway between Toledo and Madrid and fell to the Nationalists on October 17. On October 20, the republicans launched a counterattack. On October 21, on the way to the front, Nancy talked to some Scottish ambulance men and heard they had

about 150 wounded since this attack of yesterday. The attack by the loyalists is continuing at Illescas. This morning a loyal plane was shot at by an enemy (foreign, with three bars showing). The loyalist aviator came down in a parachute, wounded in the arm. No aerial gun at this point to attack enemy plane. The Scotch ambulance has had very much to do.

Proceeded toward Illescas; on left of road, three or four field radio sets; three tanks which show signs of considerable use. Another tank on side road. Just beyond the point which was the line on October 19th a bridge has been blown up (across road) not known whether by us or by enemy. We go on to side lane at this point, on right. Sounds of war, distant, begin. . . . We cut across the ploughed field, towards Illescas; sounds of war (heavy) artillery, considerable; distant machine guns.

That evening, back in Madrid, Nancy watched processions of women and children streaming into the city; about four thousand of them, she estimated. By October 23, the rebel forces had driven back the Illescas counterattack, and Nancy, in Madrid, heard the noise of four air raids not far away, and reports of people killed in the suburbs. "No panic in central streets; cars etc. as usual. Population just looked at sky; continued on its way."

Next day, she and a Spanish friend visited the fronts at Navalcarnero and Torrejón, taking careful note of the numbers of men, vehicles and guns she saw. Most of the vehicles were camouflaged; their driver "has been through some bad experiences; he is somewhat nervy. By this time he has draped our car too with thistles and leaves." They visited a field hospital and talked to the doctor. At Torrejón they went up to the firing line in the commander's car. Nancy coolly noted every detail,

Ours were firing. Machine gun on left of road. Good "sandbag" parapetos to left. Armoured car just on right side of road. A little rise in the ground on the right; natural protection from enemy fire, increased by dug-out trench at its base; they shoot over top. The enemy is at 700 metres; Illescas is at 1600 metres. We run across the road, ducking, then sit talking with those in the trenches on the right for about 20 minutes. Bullets pass. NOISE. In the distance more and bigger noise, muted by distance. León Felipe says "The spirit of those actually in the firing line is better than those towards the back." True.

Nancy seems to have left Madrid before the bombardment of the city by Franco's forces began in earnest, early in November 1936, and before the dramatic arrival in the besieged city of the newly formed International Brigade. Before she returned to France, she made a short visit to North Africa, to

Tangier and French Morocco, where she wrote "much was to be learned about the way the Moors were impressed (mainly) into a war that was no concern of theirs."

Her first visit to the Spain of the civil war left Nancy with two convictions she never lost. First, that the republican side was the side of the people, freedom and revolution, and that to question or criticize it was intolerable. She never seems to have shown the slightest knowledge of or interest in the internal struggles on the government side, with the Moscow-line communists ruthlessly eliminating anarchist or Trotskyist elements; and she was totally uncomprehending and scornful of people such as George Orwell or Arthur Koestler (both of whom she knew slightly), who were determined to tell the truth about this repression no matter how uncomfortable the facts might be for left-wing intellectuals.

Second, she felt all "intellectuals" everywhere were the natural allies of the republican side and that they had a duty to arouse the conscience of the world on its behalf.

Soon after she got back from Spain and North Africa, Nancy started to put into action the plans she had discussed with Neruda and the Spanish poets in Madrid. By the spring of 1937 she was hard at work at Réanville on a series of six leaflets of poems inspired by the war, which she printed herself on the Hours Press machine using the one case of type she had also kept. She called the series "Les Poètes du Monde Défendent le Peuple Espagnol" ("Poets of the World Defend the Spanish People"). Each leaflet had several poems, in English and French as well as Spanish, and were sold in London and Paris to raise money for the cause. Her old friends Tzara and Aragon gave her poems, as did Langston Hughes, Nicolás Guillén and Brian Howard, whose poem was entitled "For Those with Investments in Spain":

> I ask your pardon, half of them cannot read
> Your forbearance if, for a while, they cannot pay,
> Forgive them, it is disgusting to watch them bleed . . .

as well as a good selection of Spanish contributions, from Neruda himself, Rafael Alberti, Gonzales Tunon, Vicente Aleixandre and Lorca. Neruda had been dismissed from his post in Madrid by this time and was living in Paris; he visited Nancy at Réanville to help her produce the leaflets.

Neruda recalls arriving with Nancy at Réanville on a night of swirling snow. He had no experience with typesetting, and was not as quick to learn as Aragon had been. "I started setting type for the first time and I am sure there has never been a worse typesetter. I printed p's upside down and they turned into d's through my typographical clumsiness. A line in which the word 'parpados' (eyelids) appeared twice ended up with two dardapos. For years afterward, Nancy punished me by calling me that. 'My dear Dardapo . . .' she would begin her letters from London."

Brian Howard and John Banting also stayed at Réanville for a while in the spring of 1937; both of them, two of her oldest and closest English friends, shared Nancy's commitment to the republican cause. Hatred of fascism had been a bond between Howard and Nancy for several years; but although Howard talked of going to Spain himself, he never did. He admired Nancy as much as he ever had, writing to his mother from Réanville: "Nancy has been sweet. The pillar that she always is and I respect her increasingly. I think she's the only intimate I have for whom I never sensed the least faint trace of any kind of second-rateness."

Brian Howard had by this time made friends with W. H. Auden, and it was with Howard, in Paris, that Nancy had a brief meeting with Auden that led to the most famous poem in her series: Auden's "Spain," which appeared in the fifth leaflet. Nancy may well have been the first publisher of this poem.* "Spain" is undoubtedly the most famous and influential poem written in English about the Spanish civil war, controversial both at the time and later, when Auden himself renounced it.

*See note.

Auden wrote "Spain" after his return from his one visit there with a medical team in January 1937. He was not yet thirty, but he was already considered the leading English poet of the decade. A recent critic described the poem as "the best of the English war poems from Spain but . . . also the least partisan, the least passionate, the least concerned with actual war, and the least Spanish." To orthodox communist critics at the time, Edgell Rickword among them, "Spain" was too personal, too much concerned with the dilemma the Spanish war presented idealistic, vaguely left-wing young poets such as Auden himself. But Nancy, characteristically, was not bothered by such niceties; she was delighted with the poem, always thought it "extremely beautiful" and was proud to have published it. Her only problem was that the handwritten version Auden sent her (which is till pasted into her one surviving Spanish scrapbook) was hard to read. Nearly thirty years later, she recalled with amazement how he reacted when she wrote to check the text with him. "He replied that it did not matter so much about not being being able to make out about six different words. This upset me greatly. For a POET to feel that! Therefore, doing what I could (loupes and all) it happens that two or three words in my version are different to those in the little red 'Spain' published later by Faber and Faber."

While she was working on the series of poems, Nancy had another idea. She decided to canvass all the English writers and poets she could think of, ask them where they stood on the Spanish question, and publish the results. She felt wholly confident that virtually all of them would support the republic and that such a massive declaration by the most talented and respected writers in the country must be good propaganda and carry weight.

She printed a huge broadsheet, printed in brilliant red and black; it was headed THE QUESTION and vertically down the left-hand side SPAIN. It was addressed to "Writers and Poets of England, Scotland, Ireland and Wales" and continued:

It is clear to many of us throughout the whole world that now, as certainly never before, we are determined, or compelled, to take sides. The equivocal attitude, the Ivory Tower, the paradoxical, the ironic detachment, will no longer do. . . . Today, the struggle is in Spain. Tomorrow it may be in other countries—our own . . .

Are you for, or against, the legal government and the People of Republican Spain? Are you for, or against, Franco and Fascism? For it is impossible any longer to take no side.

Writers and poets, we wish to print your answers, we wish the world to know what you, writers and poets, who are among the most sensitive instruments of a nation, feel.

Nancy collected eleven other signatories and printed their names with hers, in alphabetical order. They were: Louis Aragon, W. H. Auden, José Bergamín, Jean Richard Bloch, Nancy Cunard, Brian Howard, Heinrich Mann, Ivor Montagu, Pablo Neruda, Ramón Sender, Stephen Spender, and Tristan Tzara.

Nancy has not usually been credited with being editor or instigator of this project; but, in fact, it was hers from the beginning. She was "alone in the Normandy country house, without even an old English telephone-book, or any kind of reference. The idea at first was 'just a few authors, perhaps?' but as I went on thinking of them, more and more came to mind. The Questionnaire was quickly written by me and printed in Paris and then sent out, with or without a personal letter or note, as the case might be, and in some cases several (three or so?) were sent to a writer friend, requesting them to be passed on." She was vague about how the additional signatures came to be added: "It was indeed, SOLELY my idea. There was no discussion with any of the signatories as to whether or no it would be a good thing to do—or who would pay—or who would take the kudos, etc. The signatories were all asked BY ME, and by no one else, if they would care to sign. Had every one of them said 'No,' I should have made the little work all the same—and how! You see in those days there did exist ENTHUSIASM for what was felt to be good and right and true."

According to Nancy, the replies came in fairly quickly during the early summer of 1937. Virtually all of the correspondence connected with the project, and the original replies, have been lost; two that survived are a gentle refusal to answer at all from E. M. Forster ("I do not feel that manifestoes by writers carry any weight whatever") and a friendly, but hardly enthusiastic response from one of the signatories, W. H. Auden, to whom Nancy had apparently sent some of her own writings as well as copies of her edition of "Spain."

> Thank you so much for the books and the copies of Spain which looked lovely. . . . I did enjoy *Black Man White Lady-ship* so much.
>
> As to the question, I enclose an answer. I have my doubts as to the value of such pronouncements, but here mine is for what it's worth.

Auden's answer reads:

> I support the Valencia government in Spain because its defeat by the forces of international fascism would be a major disaster for Europe. It would make a European war more probable, and the spread of Fascist ideology and practice . . . would create an atmosphere in which the creative artist and all who care for justice, liberty and culture would find it impossible to work or even exist.

It was one of the 148 answers Nancy eventually collected.. The balance of the replies was exactly what she would have wished: 126 entries supported the Republic, 5 were for Franco, and 16 were neutral. The neutrals included Aldous Huxley, Norman Douglas, T. S. Eliot, Ezra Pound, H. G. Wells, and Vita Sackville-West; the Franco supporters were Edmund Blunden, Arthur Machen, Geoffrey Moss, Eleanor Smith, and Evelyn Waugh. ("If I were a Spaniard," wrote Waugh, "I should be fighting for General Franco. As an

Englishman I am not in the predicament of choosing between two evils.")

Though phrased less emotionally than Brian Howard's ("With all my anger and love, I am for the people of Republican Spain."), Nancy's own answer was among the most impassioned.

> It is as unthinkable for any honest intellectual to be pro-Fascist as it is degenerate to be for Franco, the assassin of the Spanish and Arab people. Spain is not "politics" but life; its immediate future will affect every human who has a sense of what life and its facts mean, who has respect for himself and humanity. Above all others, the writer, the intellectual, must take sides. His place is with the people against Fascism; his duty, to protest against the present degeneration of the democracies.

The shortest answer was from Samuel Beckett; he was back in Ireland, from where he sent her simply the words "Up the Republic!" She wrote to ask him to say more, but he declined.

By July Nancy was in London trying to find a publisher. She offered it to two or three, including Gollancz, who turned it down. Then as a "last resort"—because she had believed that it might make more of an impression on people if it were to be published by "an ordinary commercial firm"—she took it to the *Left Review*, which accepted it immediately. Randall Swingler, one of the editors, was a friend of Nancy's and had contributed a poem to her Spanish series; he was particularly enthusiastic and took charge.

The *Left Review* published the questionnaire as a separate booklet of about ten thousand words in November 1937, priced at sixpence. The only entry they added to Nancy's collection was a late answer from George Bernard Shaw ("Spain must choose for itself: it is not really our business"). They put a pink slip around the cover, which Nancy did not care for: "Your favourite authors take sides—on Fascism, on the Spanish War. This document reveals the minds of leading British authors today. Never before have so many important pronouncements been assembled within a 6d booklet. It is causing a sensation!" As Nancy recalled, it sold well, and she had trouble obtaining copies for herself. But by the time the booklet appeared, she was back in Spain.

It must have seemed doubtful, even at the time, whether a collection of answers to a question phrased as Nancy's was, signed by twelve known left-wingers and produced by the leading left-wing review in London, would have much impact on the unconverted; but Nancy had started something that was to have reverberations for years after the Spanish war was over. The idea that it was useful to collect names of well-known writers and thinkers in support of political causes in other countries has tended to reappear, in the form of letters to periodicals as well as specially published documents.

On her next visit to Spain Nancy was accompanied by John Banting, who joined her in Narbonne, near the border, in October. Norman Douglas, who had been living in Vence for several months since an abrupt departure from Italy after a homosexual scandal, appeared in Narbonne to see Nancy off; despite his refusal to be drawn into the Spanish cause or any other (as he had said in answer to Nancy's questionnaire: "I cannot excite myself over nations and causes and creeds—my contempt for humanity in general is too great. . . . Nobody is going to compel me to take sides. To hell with sides."), her affection for him was undiminished. Nancy was in bed with flu when Banting arrived, and she stayed there while the two men went off to Carcassonne. But a few days later, after some sticky moments at the frontier, she and Banting were in Spain.

Nancy retraced her journey of the year before; she and Banting went to Barcelona first, where they found "icy cold and hunger," then to Valencia, where they met Langston Hughes, whom Banting found a "magnificent and magnetising man." And then, after a ten-hour bus journey, to "freezing, starving Madrid under the December shells." Everything was bleaker, more bitter and more complicated than the year before, but Nancy's responses were unchanged. "Everywhere, but here [Madrid] most of all was that fortitude, that innate faith in its cause of the Spanish people." Banting was impressed all over again by Nancy's resourcefulness, energy and spirit; she seemed to know people everywhere, never to take no for an answer, and never to get tired.

The hotel they stayed at in Madrid was full of foreign correspondents and Red Cross people. Banting remembered it was so cold that they had to put rugs off the floor on top of their bedclothes. There was not much food, and the bombardment was heavy.

Twenty-five years later, in a letter, Nancy described a particularly memorable day she and Banting spent in Madrid in early December 1937.

What a day, what a day! Up at 6:30 A.M. in the dark calm, after uneasy sleep in icy beds, . . . John Banting (my "sort of Irish brother," the painter) and I tumbled downstairs for "breakfast." It was tea (of a kind) and nothing. But why so miserably early? Because the "authorities" (bless them, those!) had thought it might be good discipline for us all to see the restoration of some of the paintings being done in the vaults of the Prado. . . . We set out in a car with a "responsible" interpreter (none of us needing one) arrived at the thoroughly sandbagged Prado, wemt down to its inmost innards, and there, to my appallment, were the corpses, so much smashed, of the plaster horses that had borne the famous knights in armour— bombed into legs and head, individually. That struck me much . . . . And so, in a timeless hush, we came upon such experts in painting as were restoring the for one very lovely Hieronymous Bosch paintings, and others, delicately, using the few candles allotted their frozen, black mittened hands.

We must have been in and under the Prado longer than I think, for when we rose out of its depths there was a little sun, and a tiny fluff of snow coming down. So then John and I walked a good bit—to the office of the International Brigades. We saw Frank Ryan, the Irish "responsible" at that moment. While he was talking to me and ordering many posters to be given us John burst forth (so calmly) with "I want to enlist, *now,* at once." Frank Ryan said, "It's too late. We are to be disbanded. No more I.B.'s. But you can help us so much, in England, if you speak on the air, and write of what you have seen here."

Laden with rolled up posters we went back to our Hotel Victoria for "lunch." And then, well-warmed with the scant food but authentic drink John always seemed able to procure (per day) I said: "Now, darling, is the time for me to show you afoot a bit of Madrid." And so we set out. It was slightly but really snowing by now, with the guns (nor "near" nor "far" I'd judge) going. Down we walked to the Plaza Mayor, and well beyond, all along the lengthy Toledana till we came to the end of it and could go no further because it was the close-front and the sentry stood up to us. Through the Arce de Toledo came both sunset and puffs of battle (1 km or 1½ kms away?). And the sentry had us sit down with him and we all had a cigarette. And then he said: "El Commandante Attlee has just been here, with five other parliamentarians. And so, now, there is much hope because he will have seen for himself how things are with us. He will tell what is true, against the lies, So then, after a while thus, we walked back to the centre of Madrid. And suddenly, we thought of Hemingway. I can't remember if he had sent a message or no, but we knew he was in Madrid. Sure enough he was there—massively—in a warm room in the Hotel Florida. There were about six others—mainly Spanish, I seem to remember. He and I had not seen each other since the twenties. A fine, strong drink was given the both of us—and I remember Hem taking off my boots and warming the cold feet. He was enchanting—such a sympathetic moment—from a non-Spaniard—was never my lot till then, nor yet again.

Banting remembered their meeting with Hemingway rather less warmly; "He was just back from the trenches and resting on a bed. He made some remark about the stimulation of fighting which neither of us liked and commented upon our smoking a horrible mixture of herbs (all one could get) suggesting it might be 'marijuana,' and that we were too late to be put into a play he had just written about the 'war tourists.' We said we were glad to miss that honour. . . . I thought that the mental 'hair on the chest' seemed rather artificial and so did Nancy."

Nancy had never known Hemingway particularly well in Paris, though she remembered "the great, thumping, *so* pleasant mannered youth he was then, in 1923." Looking back, she was surprised and disapproving that he had never absolutely declared his allegiance to the republican cause.

Nancy and Banting returned the way they had come, traveling first to Valencia in an open truck, sitting on the floor, picking up new passengers along the way, sharing wine from skins and singing. They were both sore and aching when they reached Valencia in the middle of an air raid. From there they got to Barcelona and then found a lift to the frontier with a French truck driver carrying oranges. After some complications over their passports they were allowed back into France. "We were there just the allotted three months," Banting wrote, "and lucky not to have been jailed."

Back in Paris and then Réanville, Nancy was obsessed by Spain, and none of her friends was spared her need to talk about Spain and to try to enlist their help. Some were less responsive than others, among them Samuel Beckett, who had returned to Paris in 1937. In the first week of January 1938, Beckett was involved in a bizarre incident that nearly ended his life. He was walking home from the cinema with some friends when a man accosted him and asked him for money. When Beckett tried to push the man aside, he pulled out a knife and stabbed Beckett in the chest, just missing his heart. Among the friends who visited him in the hospital was Nancy. Beckett wrote to a friend on January 12: "Nancy Cunard bounced in the other evening from Spain. I was very glad to see her." According to Beckett's biographer, during Beckett's time in the hospital and while he was recuperating, Nancy saw him frequently, brought him presents, and did her best to cheer him up; but on at least one occasion, when they dined together at the Brassérie Lipp early in February, he found her obsession with Spain rather tiring. "Nancy submerged me in left wing literature. I have never seen so many bad poems altogether as in her Réanville series." At the same dinner Nancy revealed that she had fallen asleep leaning on the stove at Réanville and burned herself. Also, a mouse ran up Beckett's leg ("happily on the outside").

Nancy was seeing Brian Howard, and one evening at the Café de Flore she introduced him to Beckett. The meeting was not a great success. "She said that her having been the first to publish Howard and me should create a bond between us," wrote Beckett. "It did not."

By March 1938, Nancy had a new surprising plan. She and Norman Douglas had recently lunched together in a bistro in Vernon, near Réanville, with his son Archie; Nancy remembered it as a "pleasant, rather sad meal." The shadows were lengthening; in Spain, Franco's forces were moving inexorably forward, and Hitler was devouring Austria without a shot being fired. Nancy and Douglas decided to make a journey to Tunisia together.

It may seem curious both that Nancy should want to make a
journey for pleasure when she was so caught up with the
drama in Spain, and also that she chose Douglas as companion. She wondered why herself. "I mused on how two people
with such totally different interests could get on as we did.
After all, on account of my feelings about the 'colour question' and Colonies, and the Spanish struggle, I must perforce
come into that category you dismissed as 'meddlers'? This
bothered neither of us in the very least, however, and here we
were going off confidently for several weeks." Possibly
Nancy herself wanted a break, and anyway she had her own
reasons for going. "Of Tunisia what I wanted most was to see
something of the way the Arabs live, so as to write a few
articles on general conditions. Was this going to be compat-
ible with what we should be doing? It turned out to be perfectly so."

Early in April Nancy went down to Vence to meet Douglas. To her amusement, she found two old admirers in the
vicinity; Robert Nichols, whom she found "very much
calmed down" and Michael Arlen, who was able to help
Nancy by witnessing her application for a new passport at the
consulate in Nice. Nancy was pleased to find him happily
married, prosperous and eminently respectable.

She and Douglas sailed from Marseilles on April 10. It was
a rough, crowded crossing and they both had a great deal to
drink. Douglas was greatly amused when the rolling of the

ship sent Nancy tumbling across the saloon, but she ended up on her feet with her glass still full. Nancy slept on a pile of luggage in a companionway rather than in a stuffy cabin with three other women.

Nearly thirty years afterward, Nancy wrote a long account of their time in Tunisia in her book about Douglas. It is one of her most revealing and disarming pieces of writing. Her description of the three weeks they spent together visiting the towns, deserts, ruins and oases of Tunisia reveals as much about herself as about her companion and demonstrates with a light and affectionate touch that she was well aware of the curiousness of the expedition and of the differences in the travelers' temperaments that could have made it a disaster.

Norman Douglas had been in Tunisia several times before and had written a book about the country, *Fountains in the Sand*, in 1912. He and Nancy shared an interest in architecture, landscape, and strange characters; but Douglas also wanted good food and wine, and quiet appreciative days driving into the desert to watch the camels drink. Nancy was endlessly interested in the living conditions of the people, local politics (especially the progress of Arab nationalism), the inadequate educational opportunities for Arab children, and whether or not Mussolini might have ambitions in Tunisia. She wanted to talk to the people, to interrupt journeys if they saw something or someone interesting. Douglas liked to get on to their next destination and would start fussing if the arrangements did not go smoothly. Douglas was appalled by the food, Nancy by the lavatories. They could not agree on how to deal with their expenses. He wanted them to pool their money; Nancy would not hear of it. She won. They were both annoyed when they could not hire an open car, and when finally they left Tunis to drive south to Gafsa, Nancy was depressed by the rapidity with which they traveled. "I thought at that moment how much I should have liked to walk some of the way so as to look at everything." She longed to talk to the groups of workmen in the road. "And what were these small children doing, standing opposite each other on each side of the highway, holding up a little knot of something with a hopeful gesture? The fourth or fifth pair revealed this to be a small bunch of wild asparagus. Would any speeding car of the many stop and buy? These emaciated children with their asparagus (and sometimes flowers) became to me later one of the national emblems of Tunisia!"

Nancy was struck by the poverty everywhere. She watched the processions of Bedouin nomads, "gaunt and thin as their camels, driving their meagre sheep along. I could think of nothing finer than such a procession in some old time of ease, in years when the lambs were not 'all dying' but gambolled alongside the healthy ewes, and the men, women and children in windborne draperies strode, or rode on their tall white and brown camels."

She did not care for Gafsa and wondered if the arrogance of the French colonists had something to do with the depressing atmosphere. Above all she detested the cloud of begging small boys that hung around them.

"Norman! For God's sake think of something to drive them away! This is the fifth session of it! We can't even walk in the desert without this maddening troupe! . . . They are driving me crazy!" Eventually, Douglas found the solution; they chose one small boy to be their "guide," and he kept the rest away.

They moved on to the big oasis at Tozeur, which was more tranquil, and where there was a good French hotel and no beggars. Nancy loved the oasis: "One's feet effortless along the light sandy paths, one's eyes lost in enchantment at the feathery wealth of palms and softly waving branches and at the sudden scarlet or yellow in the little gardens, a sensation that nothing sudden or violent could happen 'in here.' One is cupped, hidden, enclosed, encircled and safe from the vastness of 'outside' with its sandtracks merging into infinity."

Nancy delighted in small examples of curious natural phenomena. Douglas showed her how the gardeners married the palms, tying a sprig of the male flower inside the female. They saw palm wine being tapped, and they sampled it. She watched with fascination how the dung beetle rolls its ball down a hole. They found an ideal guide, who took Nancy to visit a nomad family: "Their beautiful manners and their lovely smile!" Neither she nor Douglas had any time for the comments of the Europeans they met who declared that the nomads enjoyed their poverty. Nancy sent a number of anti-colonialist articles to the ANP from Tunisia.

She was amused rather than shocked by an incident in the hotel in Tozeur, when a seventeen-year-old Arab waiter came to her room one day and asked her if she would like to make love with him. " 'I would not!' said I. 'And how come you to ask such a curious question? Don't you think—for one—that I am old enough to be your mother?'

" 'That's no matter,' said he, 'no matter at all! Faire l'amour, ça, c'est toujours bon!'

"And then he bowed himself vaguely out of the room and was soon serving us dinner."

The main adventure of their trip occurred when the car they had hired to drive across the salt flats to the sea broke down in the middle of a flooded area; they were stuck for several hours not sure whether the car would work again or whether the water was rising. Douglas produced a flask of whiskey; and Nancy took photographs of him standing ankle deep with his trousers rolled up.

They stayed at Sfax, a large port on the coast, where Nancy went for a walk on the beach in the early mornings among piles of steaming refuse. To her fascinated horror she saw some Bedouin children scavenging on a huge rubbish heap.

"On the very top was one of the girls. The clear morning light held her immobilised for a moment, poised to perfection against the skyline. And now . . . Oh! My! Look! her gesture said, as with a howl of joy and a swoop betokening 'reward' held up in triumph what she had just come upon: a long, slime covered, snake-like object—a liquefying bean-pod— then threw her head back and, opening her mouth, with a flourish flung the prize within." She told Douglas what she had seen. It evoked a chuckle, along with the staid words:

" 'My dear, there's always been poverty in the world and always will be.' "

During the journey Nancy reflected on her deep feelings for Africa and the desert, which she remembered dreaming about as a child in a curiously prophetic way.

> I wonder now if I ever told you [Douglas] how, when, about six years old, my thoughts began to be drawn towards Africa, and particularly towards the Sahara? Surely I was being taught as much about El Dorado and the North Pole? But there it was: the Deserts. The sand, the dunes, the huge spaces, mirages, heat and parchedness—I seemed able to visualise all of this. Of such were filled several dreams, culminating in the great nightmare in which I wandered, repeatedly, the whole of one agonising night, escaping through a series of tents some-where in the Sahara. Later came extraordinary dreams about black Africa—"The Dark Continent"—with Africans dancing and drumming around me, and I one of them, though still white, knowing, mysteriously enough, how to dance in their own manner.

By early May they were back in France. "It was odious leaving you in Marseilles, and in a particularly abrupt manner, at that, our trains going in different directions and little time to spare. You just waved your stick at me: 'Well, ta-ta, my dear, ta-ta!' "

Soon after Nancy got back to France, she went off again to Geneva, where Alvarez del Vayo, the Spanish republican for-eign minister, was making another demand for the ending of the farce of nonintervention. Nancy wrote impassioned re-ports for the ANP condemning the attitude of the British and French governments, who voted against the Spanish republic. On her way back to Réanville, she met a Spanish woman refugee in Paris whose husband had been killed at Badajoz and whose fourteen-year-old son was trying to join her in France. Nancy took Narcisa home with her. Douglas reappeared and stayed a few days at Réanville, with an American friend; Nar-cisa's son Gervasito managed to find his way there. "I remember those few days as bucolic," Nancy wrote. "The wine let down into the well to cool, everything done in a leisurely fashion and in perfect temperature, the rich Spanish dishes made by Narcisa, our walks and strolls, and as late as midnight—Gervasito's strong young voice ringing out in the hot darkness, spiralling up and down Flamencos and new Republican songs, marching songs and those of the defence of Madrid. I think you [Douglas] were rather fascinated by him."

Nancy left Réanville soon after this visit and went back to Barcelona. Her main impression this time was that "everything could be summed up now by that terrible word 'hunger.' It was, indeed, nigh starvation." She saw people scavenging through smoking ruins for a few beans. She stayed until October, when she left what money she had and all the clothes she could spare with her Spanish friends. (By now, however, Nancy never took much luggage on her travels; in Spain she would simply carry a shoulder bag or a bundle tied up in a large spotted handkerchief, and she carried her typewriter slung over her shoulder.) There is plenty of evidence that on all her trips to Spain during the war Nancy was as generous as she could possibly be; giving away money, clothes, cigarettes whenever she could, buying food if she could find any, and taking it to people she knew were in need. She also operated as a one-person agency for collecting money, clothes and food from her friends in France and London, many of whom remember getting letters from her explaining the situation and asking for help. She did some begging herself; one friend she made through Spain remembers that she once stood holding a sheet open on a street in Paris, asking passers-by for money.

She would also help Spaniards who had had to flee Franco's advance and wanted to escape into France. Several times she simply gave them the money for the train; once or twice she took them back with her. To some of her friends this seemed like folly. Sybille Bedford, the writer, who had known Nancy for some years and shared her affection for Brian Howard (she thought the two had much in common), remembers an occasion, probably in the autumn of 1938, when Nancy appeared at the Café des Deux Magots in Paris with two bewildered Spanish refugees straight off the train with all their possessions in battered cardboard suitcases. Nancy was exhilarated; she introduced her two friends as heroes of the revolution to Sybille Bedford, Brian Howard and Norman Douglas, and they all sat drinking until it was too late to dine anywhere except a stuffy, expensive brasserie nearby. When Sybille Bedford tried to suggest somewhere more modest, Nancy became indignant at the idea that anything but the best would be appropriate for her gallant Spanish guests on their first evening of freedom; an expensive meal was ordered, a lot more drink was consumed and when the bill came, Nancy and Brian Howard had a furious row. Sybille Bedford remembers chiefly feeling sorry for Nancy's bewildered Spaniards and wondering whether to be rescued by Nancy was a wholly desirable fate.

By early the following year. 1939, it was clear to even the most optimistic supporters of the republic that Franco had to win. In Catalonia the nationalist armies started to drive up toward the French border in December, and the stream of refugees became a torrent. There were already a million refugees in Barcelona in addition to the normal population. After Barcelona fell in late January 1939, it seemed as if the whole of Catalonia was on the move. The plight of the refugees was desperate. Nancy was determined to get back to Spain to describe the exodus and to do what she could.

This time she was writing for the *Manchester Guardian,* the most respected of the pro-republican English newspapers, as well as for the ANP. She paid her own expenses. It was in this final stage of the Spanish war that Nancy's courage and tenacity were most striking; no one set off for Spain in January 1939 feeling euphoric or romantic; it was a bitter, ugly situation. Nancy's reports for the *Guardian* were the high spot of her ventures into journalism; she earned her footnotes in the subsequent histories of the war.

She had hoped to get back into Spain itself but only arrived in Perpignan the day Barcelona fell—January 26, 1939. At first, the French government hesitated to open the frontier; they suggested that a neutral zone should be established on the Spanish side to be maintained by foreign relief. When the nationalists refused to consider this, the French decided to allow the civilians and wounded to cross. On January 28, 15,000 people streamed into France. Nancy was watching, in a fury of indignation. Her first report to the *Guardian* that day began: "Today more than ever Franco stands condemned and judged for eternity." For the next two weeks Nancy sent a report every two or three days. As well as reporting she asked for help. On January 30 she sent a cable: "Beseech you open fund immediately in Guardian for possibly as much as half a million starving Spanish refugees pouring in stop situation catastrophic." The *Guardian* did open an appeal early in February and collected money and supplies for the relief of the refugees.

Her figure of half a million was not far off. According to Professor Hugh Thomas, 10,000 wounded, 170,000 women and children and 60,000 male civilians crossed the border between January 28 and February 5, when the French decided they had no choice but to accept the retreating republican army. Between February 5 and February 10 some 220,000 republican soldiers crossed as well.

Conditions were terrible. The weather was grim; after spending a day walking alongside the refugees, Nancy wrote: "Meanwhile on all these miles of human wretchedness headed for the unknown, the rain has poured down for more than a dozen hours." There was little or no accommodation for them: "Pitiful little groups of refugees are still camping out, washing their clothes in the streams. At night there are small camp fires all along the mountain. There are many babies in arms and infants at the breast." The Franco forces were still attacking the retreating republicans. On February 8 Nancy wrote:

When I was sitting on a bench in Perpignan today an old peasant woman came up to ask me for a little money. These were her words: "I left Gerona with my husband the night before last. Eight planes followed us out of the town to the last bridge, machine-gunning us. We got to Figueras. If only you could see it—nothing but ruins, smashed to pieces. I made my husband get into a lorry there; he is ill, so I walked to La Junquera. We had 11,000 pesetas we had saved. We have worked all our lives. They gave us 28 francs for this at the frontier . . ."

This disastrous situation of the exchange is beyond words. Nearly all Spaniards arrive with various sums of money, but cannot, or can hardly, pay for a hotel or a meal.

She watched trucks taking paintings by Goya, Velásquez and El Greco to Geneva for safekeeping: "It is fit to pay tribute to the leaders of a nation in its present agony who care in the way they do for the cultural heritage of their people." She did her best to ascertain and check the exact numbers of the wounded. On February 9, she watched the republican soldiers streaming by.

At Le Perthus, from nine o'clock this morning until 4:30, I have been watching soldiers pass between the two stone posts that are actually the frontier line. They have come by in thousands and thousands, in groups, singly and in numberless lorries. At the posts stand the French soldiers, who immediately search them for arms. The Spanish soldiers give up their arms in an orderly fashion. . . . But all this is only the beginning; we are told: "Tomorrow the rearguard of the army, and afterwards—the army that has fought. On the mountains each side they come, so that the whole landscape seems to be moving. Soldiers on horseback, wounded men, women, children, a whole population, and cars and ambulances."

Later, Nancy described what her days as a reporter during "that cruel February" were like.

Up at seven. On the road in a car by 8:30, or by train, to the frontiers at Le Perthus and Cerbere, and even to Bourg Madame in the snow. Over, on foot, several miles to the first

Spanish village. Scenes of horror along the way. Questioning, noting, talking to hundreds of people in Spanish, memorising things to describe. Often no lunch, from lack of time. Back, come dark, to the unheated, freezing, dingy room in a horrible hotel where, by the worst light imaginable, exhausted and shivering, I would try to make consecutive sense in writing out of the facts and impressions of the day. The three- or four-page airmail despatch then had to go off to the Manchester Guardian. The first real meal and rest came generally about 10 p.m., when, between mouthfuls, one would be discussing events with some of the other journalists. An occasional alternative was afforded by those hour-long waits in the crowded Prefecture, preliminary to obstinate arguings and pleadings with angry officials and the grudging stamping of permits.

Her reports were well received by the *Guardian*, as some letters she kept from the news editor, W. P. Crozier, prove. He wrote to her on February 7: "We are printing at present everything that you are sending . . . . Your articles are admirable and are just about the right length." And she really felt she must have made her point when she had a telegram from Norman Douglas simply saying: "Can I come to Perpignan and help?" But she knew it was not the place for him.

Nancy did not even try to make her stories objective. After Franco's forces reached the Spanish border, at Le Perthus, she wrote: "I do not want to see Le Perthus today, or any day ever again," and though she tried to do her journalistic duty, "it was an effort to make oneself speak to these Falangists . . . the whole bearing of the Spanish facist soldiers is the absolute opposite to that of the republicans; they are taught to be insolent and overbearing."

As a temporary solution to the problem of what to do with the half million refugees, the French government set up a series of camps near the border. Nancy described the first of these, which operated as a clearing house, at Le Boulou, on February 10, 1939.

Some of the camps to which the Spanish refugees are going are not fit to receive human beings. The problem has been too vast to be dealt with as yet.

At the great central camp at Le Boulou are thousands of men, women and children. On one side of the road is an enclosure with wire fencing. On the other the refugees who walked down from Le Perthus yesterday are lying, sitting, standing, doing nothing this cold end of a February afternoon. It is a horrible sight, and all of them, men, women and children are in the utmost depression. This "camp" is a large, flat, bare area, the grass trodden down into a sort of grey compost. They sleep here, in the open. A few have rigged up some vague kind of shelter.

She talked to a woman whose child's head was covered with sores; she listened to people wondering whether they would not be better off back in Spain after all. "Then a woman cries out, 'I shall never get onto a train without knowing where it is going, for I have heard that they mean to send us back to Franco.'. . . . All the men, says a French guard, are going to Argelès; when? No one knows. In all of this families get separated; the men are taken from their families in some cases . . . . As for the wounded—they are lying in the ditch among their crutches; a man limps by in obvious agony."

Argelès, on the coast just above the border, was the largest of seven camps established for the men of the republican army. As Hugh Thomas wrote:

These were simply open spaces of sand dunes near the sea, enclosed by barbed wire, from which the inmates were prevented from leaving by force. Men dug holes for themselves like animals, to find some shelter . . . for ten days there was not water or food supplies, and those wounded who stayed with their comrades were left uncared for . . . . Food was later secured, but there was no sanitation or shelter, and meagre medical services. No doubt the French government hoped, by neglect, to force as many as possible of the refugees to throw themselves on Franco's mercy.

International opinion was shocked and embarrassed by stories of the camps, and indeed by the whole problem of what to do with the refugees. A *New York Times* reporter was asked not to send too many harrowing descriptions; the British and Russian governments refused at first to send official aid or to accept any refugees themselves. To Nancy, among others, it seemed after Franco's victory as if no one could be bothered to do anything for the victims of a war that had largely been sustained from the outside. She was indefatigable, sending reports, writing to newspapers, pestering officials and finally taking matters into her own hands by going to Argelès and personally arranging the release of five men. One of them was Angel Goded, her waiter friend from Barcelona.

Somehow Nancy received a letter from Goded after he found himself in Argelès. It said: "The biggest favor I have ever yet asked in my life. I am counting on you to get me out of here, and I know you will."

Soon after the event, Nancy wrote a long account of how she extracted Goded and four others from Argelès and took them to stay with her at Réanville. (It seems never to have been published. She wrote it using a male pseudonym, Ray Holt, with overtones of her childhood home, Nevill Holt, and she gave the men other names. One of them was César Arconada, the well-known Spanish poet; the others were Goded, an architect, a cartoonist, and a publisher.)

There were endless bureaucratic delays and difficulties involved in getting Spaniards out of the camps, even when French citizens or residents such as Nancy were willing to take responsibility for them. Partly not to offend Franco, and partly to prevent known revolutionaries or communists from congregating in sensitive areas, the authorities would not allow Spanish refugees to settle near the border or in Paris; but in other areas, the prefect of the department could give permission in individual cases. Nancy managed to get the necessary permission to take four or five men to Réanville, and was informed by the officials in Perpignan that she could now obtain their release from Argelès. She was in touch with a

Paris organization working for the release of Spanish intellectuals, who assigned her the four men other than Goded.

At first, it all seemed simple. "The exit business was despatched quickly: we felt intensely sorry for those who remained. . . . We drove to Perpignan. 'You have taken us out of hell,' they said. Can you imagine what the first bath, the first meal at a table, the first bed is like after 32 days in that limbo?" The next day, they took the train for Paris. "By now we were all old friends; we got so near to Paris that we began making up our first menu. . . . And then . . . The Police are here . . .' "

All six of them were arrested and taken to police headquarters in Paris. Nancy was still confident that some error had been made. "Here, I thought, all would be cleared up quickly. We spent ten hours however in that place where, it seemed, the official had far less interest in the validity of my friends' papers than in cross-questioning the one who'd brought them to Paris." Their luggage was searched; Nancy's passport, permits and press credentials scrutinized. Finally she was told that she had committed a serious offense in bringing the Spaniards to Paris, even though it was only on the way to her house in Normandy.

> "But Monsieur," I said, "I am perfectly in my right. I have the official permission of the Prefect of my department to invite these Spanish refugees, friends of mine, to stay in my house . . ." "Well, we're going to let you go," said the Big Man. "As for the Spaniards, *their* case is settled all right, we know how to deal with them," and he added with relish, "You won't see them again." "What are you doing with them—sending them to jail?" "No. They are already on their way back to the concentration camp. Good evening."

Outraged, Nancy said good-bye to her friends, assuring them that she was not giving up. She went straight back to the Intellectuals Committee and took one of the organizers back to the train in time to speak to the Spaniards before they started the long journey back. He promised them that the committee's delegate in Perpignan would sort things out. Two days later, they arrived back in Paris to find Nancy waiting for them. "We leapt into my waiting taxi, sped to the country. The first meal at home was wonderful; it was given us by the owners of my village café."

The five Spaniards stayed with Nancy at Réanville from the middle of March until the early summer. They were all in poor health after their experiences and needed to recuperate; what clothes they had needed to be boiled and steamed to get rid of vermin. Nancy kept some snapshots of Arconada and the others wearing an odd assortment of clothes sent over by some of her English friends: riding breeches and striped blazers. As she recalled, Angel Goded, the ex-waiter, was the one who helped her around the house; the others, 'being intellectuals," were less useful. Not that she minded; her main concern was to make sure that they had somewhere to go after they left France, and the money they needed. Arconada was soon removed to Russia by Ilya Ehrenburg; the others started to make plans to go to Mexico, one of the few countries prepared to accept Spanish refugees.

The end of the Spanish civil war filled Nancy with fury and disgust, but nothing she learned during it or afterward made her feel any disillusionment. She felt the Spanish revolution had been betrayed by anticommunist conspirators inside Spain and by weak democracies and pro-fascists outside. As for the developments in Europe during 1939 that led up to the declaration of war between England and Germany on September 3, there is a striking absence of evidence as to what Nancy was thinking or feeling. She must have been amazed when the Soviet Union signed the Nazi-Soviet Pact in August; and the confusion this event caused in the minds of people who, like Nancy, had for years been looking to Russia to lead the fight against fascism must have contributed to her decision to leave Europe and go, with a young Spanish refugee, a bullfighter, to Chile in January 1940. She had identified so strongly with her Spanish friends that the most obvious solution for them— to go to a friendly Spanish-speaking South American country—seemed like the answer for her as well. What Nancy described later as the "nightmare" of the phony war, before it began in earnest, gave her no sense of purpose; so, "sick at heart and finding no sufficient field for my free-lancing, I decided to leave Europe and go with a Spanish refugee friend to Chile. . . . Maybe I should have stayed in France, been interned, possibly shot, or taken the humiliating but necessary road to Bordeaux."

Whatever her motives were, Nancy left France for Chile—a five-week voyage by ship—in January 1940. Pablo Neruda helped her to get a visa and informed the authorities that he had invited Nancy to stay with him in Santiago. It was to be twenty months before Nancy returned to Europe.

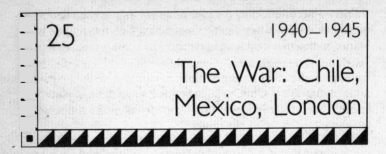

The War: Chile, Mexico, London

For Nancy and her Spanish friends, as for many communist sympathizers and party members, the Second World War failed during its opening months late in 1939 and early in 1940 to arouse any crusading spirit. After the Nazi-Soviet Pact in the summer of 1939 the theme from Moscow had been that a war between Hitler and the European democracies would merely be a war between two capitalist imperialist powers. The Soviet Union, the line went, had had no choice but to sign the pact after all her efforts to forge an alliance with the democracies against Hitler had been rejected. The debacle in Spain had proved that Britain and France did not have the will to resist fascism. Shattered by the crushing of republican Spain, and finding all her efforts at obtaining work as a war correspondent rejected, Nancy sailed for South America in the wake of her refugee friends when the war was only four months old and before either France or England had come under direct attack. All the same, she left with a heavy heart.

She was worried about her house in Normandy, even though her friends in the village had promised to keep an eye on it; and she was wondering how she could find something useful to do. "Am I a refugee?" she wrote to Janet Flanner. "Where can I work at the only thing I like, active journalism?" She wrote a number of articles for the ANP during the thirty-eight-day journey, most of them from recollections and notes, on the League of Nations or Arab affairs, many of them thin. She found she was avid for news of how the war was going.

When Nancy reached Santiago in February 1940, she had a warm welcome from Pablo Neruda, Delia del Carril, and Luis Enrique Delano. According to Neruda, Nancy soon fell out with her companion,

> who left her and the bulls in Santiago to set up a business in sausages and cold cuts. But my dear friend, who was a low-class snob, was not one to give up easily. In Chile she took a poet as her lover, a slovenly vagrant, a Chilean of Basque descent with some talent but no teeth. What's more, Nancy's new lover was a hopeless drunk and gave the aristocratic English woman nightly beatings that forced her to appear in public wearing enormous dark glasses.

Delano later recalled that, although at first they were the only friends she had in Chile, within a week she seemed quite at home and had come to know all the writers, painters, and intellectuals in the city. "Nancy lived among us with extreme naturalness," he wrote, "but then she had an unusual capacity for adaptation. She spoke Spanish, and in a short time she was friendly with everybody, and one would see her at the meetings of the Intellectuals Alliance, at literary occasions, and in the bars where we all used to meet."

Nancy remembered Neruda taking her to a dusty bar called the Café Amaya, where there would be a big plate of mussels open on the counter and "white, sourish and most potent" Chilean wine for five cents a glass. She also remembered swimming in the Pacific off "Pablo's beach," where the undercurrent was dangerous; eating huge crabs at open-air beach restaurants in the March sun; the strange seaweed that the very poor used to eat. Above all, she remembered the "wild children," bands of who lived in scrubland on the outskirts of the city: "People, in the more 'respectable' milieus of Chile, detest this being mentioned."

Nancy was still in Chile when France fell in June 1940. She decided she must get back to Europe. Now that Hitler had taken France and was preparing to invade Britain, she knew where her loyalties lay. It was not easy, however, to find transport to England from South America at that stage of the war; as a first step, and because she was eager to see how her Spanish friends were doing, she took a Japanese boat from Valparaiso to Manzanillo in Mexico. Luis Enrique Delano traveled with her; the voyage once again was slow; it took a month, and there were several stops at ports along the way. Nancy kept up her journalism for the ANP, posting off quick pieces about the places she caught glimpses of —Peru, Panama—and concocting others from war news she read in newspapers, such as the loss of British Somaliland and antifascist revolts in French West Africa. Again she wrote anxiously to Janet Flanner from the boat, but this time she knew what she was anxious about. She wondered what had happened to her French friends, especially Aragon, Breton, and Tzara; and she longed for news of her house in Normandy. "Shall we ever be 3 again? or under the trees at Réanville?"

Nancy always maintained that it was through no fault or decision of hers that it took her so long to make her way back to Europe in 1940. But for all the difficulties of finding a passage across the Atlantic, it is hard to believe that she was really in a hurry to get back. She was certainly unable to resist the opportunities that came her way for visiting new places, seeing old friends, and making new ones.

By the end of August Nancy was in Mexico City. She stayed over two months, and, as in Chile, her life there revolved around her Spanish refugee friends and the cafés, bars, and clubs where they gathered and where she knew she would find artists, writers, and intellectuals with whose ideas and work she could sympathize. Again she kept writing; describing the El Aquarium, a club started by the recent Spanish immigrants, or a day sightseeing at the Aztec pyramids at Teotihuacán on the outskirts of Mexico City, where she characteristically was less interested in pre-Columbian history than in the views of two workmen she met nearby on fascism and the war. Several of the Spaniards she wanted to see were "more or less interned" at a small town on the coast near Veracruz, and she went there to see them.

When she discovered that she was more likely to find a passage on a boat to England from the West Indies, she decided in November to go to Trinidad, where her cousin, Sir Edward Cunard, who had succeeded his father as the fifth baronet, was now private secretary to the governor. It turned out to be difficult to arrange a passage to Europe there too; but in the meantime Nancy found that she was something of a heroine in Trinidad. One newspaper, the *People,* reported her arrival under the headline: "Negro Sympathiser on Short Visit," and pointed out in a editorial that although Miss Cunard's *Negro* anthology was famous, it was banned by the colonial authorities. The Trinidad press was eager to print contributions from Nancy Cunard, and she was happy to oblige: she wrote about Ethiopia, Spain, African art, Mexican painters, and the "absolutely marvellous way" the Mexicans were treating the Spanish refugees.

The people treated her as a distinguished guest. Nancy kept a scrapbook of her stay; one item is the program for a visit she and her cousin, Sir Edward, made to Coryal R.C. School, which is headed "In Honour of Miss Nancy Cunard." Nancy kept several photographs of the occasion, which show her looking immensely elegant in a large white straw hat, surrounded by beaming black children. Several calypsos were written for her:

When talking about outstanding visitors to this Colony,
Who wouldn't be proud and glad to see,
A lady who has an open mind and fair,
We mean Miss Cunard here to enjoy our tropical atmosphere.

Her works as we know are widely read,
Some of the few we laud, and instead
Of blaming her for writing about the Negro,
Authors should have taken the subject up long ago.

One of the most broadminded women of her race
Miss Cunard has defended the Negro with strength and grace,
And today Negroes owe her a debt they could never repay,
For she has taken up their cause in an unusually gallant way.

Another contained a verse she must have particularly enjoyed:

> Black man and white woman, your masterpiece,
> Created a sensation at its release.
> Words are inadequate Miss Cunard dear
> To say how we appreciate you and your career.

By this time Nancy had found a new companion, a young Trinidadian policeman nicknamed Steve. Her scrapbook has a number of photographs of him and of them both together, looking happy and handsome, swimming off sandy beaches, and sitting on the flowered balcony of a small house she rented on the island. With Steve she visited Tobago, Grenada, and Barbados, where they stayed at Sir Edward's house, Glitter Bay, in March 1941. Nancy collected information about working conditions, the economy, and race relations in the British West Indies, and she wrote several pieces for the ANP during her stay.

At last, in July 1941, Nancy started on what she hoped would be the last lap of her journey; she took a Spanish boat that was sailing via Cuba to New York and Bermuda, and from there she hoped to find another boat to take her to England. She must have been even more eager to get back to Europe and join the war effort after Hitler had attacked the Soviet Union in June 1941, thus transforming Russia from an enemy into a gallant ally in the antifascist fight.

After a brief stop in Havana, where she saw something of the poet Nicolás Guillen, she arrived in New York at the end of the month and found herself in trouble. She had learned that it was likely that she might get stuck again in Bermuda; so she wanted to leave the ship in New York and find another sailing to Europe from there. However, she had no American visa and was not allowed ashore. The press picked up the story, and rumors spread that she was a prohibited immigrant, not allowed to set foot on American soil because of her political views and moral undesirability. Nancy was furious and wrote angry letters to the newspapers, the State Department, and the British Consulate, pointing out that she could hardly have been refused a visa since she had never asked for one. She stayed on the boat for several days, during which time her friend the writer Kay Boyle, who herself had just returned from Europe, noticed an item in the papers and went down to the Brooklyn docks to look for her. "Nancy came down the illicit gangplank, laughing softly at the sight of us there. We sat on packing boxes and crates on the covered wharf in the summer heat, drinking beer from cans. . . . Other friends came throughout that afternoon, some journeying from Harlem, bringing more beer with them, and in time, as the gathering grew, a policeman or two joined us, and sat talking with us. . . ."

Nancy then had to spend five days in detention on Ellis Island, the gloomy halfway house in New York harbor for people with passport or visa problems. Characteristically, she did not waste her time; she made friends with a Chinese poet threatened with deportation, helped him get permission to stay in America, and lectured the immigration authorities on the unfairness of their rules and the needless discomfort.

At last, on July 31, Nancy sailed for England. The ship called at Halifax and joined a convoy crossing the Atlantic. On August 15 Nancy looked out of the porthole in her cabin and saw H.M.S. *Dreadnought,* taking Winston Churchill back from his first wartime meeting with Roosevelt; the encounter had "a tonic effect." Nancy found the three-week voyage boring rather than frightening; she read a lot and observed with disapproval the patronizing colonial attitude of the other passengers to the Indian seamen. They docked at Liverpool, and Nancy took a train to London. She arrived on August 22, 1941.

The next three and a half years of the war Nancy lived in London, the only long period in her life after 1920 that she spent there. She had many reservations about living in England, but the time was not unhappy; the conditions of her life were sometimes difficult, but the exigencies of wartime made them something to be expected and shared with other people. Nancy was able to build a life for herself in London that contained the two essentials: the company of people she loved, and work she considered useful. Her personal need for a cause was for the time being swallowed up in the general war effort.

Through Otto and Louise Theis, who met her again on almost her first day back in London, Nancy was able to borrow a flat for a few months in one of the Inns of Court, near Fleet Street. From there she walked around the city, appalled by the extent of the bomb damage inflicted during the blitz, and impressed by the dogged, resilient spirit of the Londoners she met in pubs and cafés. She was amused and pleased by the new attitude toward Russia; she went to a church service where not only were there prayers for Russia but the "Internationale" was played on the organ. She was determined to find work, preferably a regular job linking writing and the war effort. She approached such organizations as the BBC and the Ministry of Information (both of which found room during the war for people just as unusual as Nancy). Meanwhile she made contact with her friends on left-wing publications. Edgell Rickword was editing the communist magazine *Our Time* and promised Nancy a chance to do some reviewing. She went to Communist party meetings to discuss war aims and was particularly interested in the possibilities created by the war for discussion of colonial policy. She found George Padmore in London and starting talking to him and his companion, an Englishwoman named Dorothy Pizer, about how they could work together.

Early in January 1942 Norman Douglas arrived in London after a long stay in Lisbon en route from France. Nancy was delighted to see him again; he was to be one of her regular companions of the war years. He stayed with her for a few days at the Inns of Court, and she did her best to extract an article from him about his experiences in France after the Germans arrived, his impressions of Lisbon, what he thought of England after his twenty-five-year absence and what he thought the outcome of the war would be. She left him a long memo full of serious questions on these topics one day; she returned to find a characteristic answer:

> What strikes me most in England is that you can't get a copy of The Times nowadays. Also that the inhabitants of London are more solemn and preoccupied than they used to be. Who isn't? . . . In southern France I paid no attention to the reaction of the natives in regard to the German occupation. Politics bore me. The food crisis was nearer to my heart. When it became acute, I cleared out. . . . I have no plans, except to try and live in peace henceforward which will be difficult, if this sort of infernal catechising is going to continue.

"What a strange way of taking it all," was Nancy's comment.

One evening, sitting over drinks, Douglas asked Nancy why, for the matter, *she* had felt she must come back to London. This was how she answered him:

"I've told you already, Norman dearest, that this is 'my' war too—insofar as it is (if only partly) against Fascism. . . . Besides, if I can be of use . . ."

"That's very patriotic of you, my dear."

"I'm all for patriotism as *I* see it! To me it means fighting the common enemy in any way, in any country. I would like, preferably, to work in connection with France, within the scope of things here; and I have a very real admiration for England in its dire ordeal."

London that winter was bitterly cold, and the blackout made getting around difficult. Nancy and Norman Douglas would set out, arm in arm on the icy pavements, to see their friends or find a congenial pub. Occasionally there would be a party; Nancy remembered one of John Lehmann's where she met Dylan Thomas, who was drunkenly determined to meet Douglas but was dissuaded by Nancy, who knew he had gone to bed. By this time Douglas had moved to a hotel in Mayfair, and although Nancy continued to see him three or four times a week, she had taken up with an American journalist then working in London with the American army, Morris Gilbert. They were constantly together; Gilbert was a highly professional newspaperman who helped Nancy with her writing, which he felt was "so much of it so good—so much of it needing scrutiny and a blue pencil." Sometimes the three of them—Nancy, Douglas, and Gilbert—would meet for lunch in a pub in Shepherd's Market; they celebrated Nancy's forty-sixth birthday together on March 10, 1942.

Nancy had had no luck yet in finding a job, but she was busy writing. The *New Statesman* published a poem dedicated to Aragon, "France," in January 1942; it was a bitter, effective poem celebrating the resistance spirit, though some readers were shocked by what seemed a glorification of hatred. The war stimulated her to write poetry; she had another poem, "Italy," published by the *New Statesman,* and produced three leaflets of war poems for herself. She also contributed to a volume entitled *Salvo for Russia,* which contained poems, etchings, and engravings to be sold to help the Soviet war effort. She reviewed plays for *Our Time* and continued to send articles on wartime London to the ANP.

Nancy's main project was a pamphlet, with George Padmore, on the question of how the war was affecting, or should affect, the attitude of the Allies, particularly Britain, to race prejudice and the aspirations of the colonies to self-government. The fundamental question seemed simple: if the war was a war of democracy against tyranny, and if the colonies were responding to it by sending their men to fight against Hitler, was it not inevitable and desirable that the rights of black people, especially their right to govern themselves, should be recognized?

The pamphlet, called *The White Man's Duty,* was based on long conversations between the two authors and was written partly as a dialogue. They made their position clear at the beginning: "Are the white people to be the sole beneficiaries [of the war]? The logical feeling exists among coloured peoples: Now Britain is in trouble she needs us but when it is all over we shall be as before." Any demonstration of racial prejudice seemed particularly offensive in the context of a war against a regime loathed for its racist policies toward Jews.

Nancy and Padmore wanted legislation. "We firmly believe that an Act of Parliament making all Colour Bar manifestations an offence . . . would be an efficacious and sensible basis for its eradication." They quoted national leaders on the democratic aims of the Allies and said firmly: "Democracy is not a difficult idea, or theory, or concept, or state of being to understand, and the colonised peoples have a very clear idea of what it means. *It is exactly what they are asking for:* equal opportunities as the white people in all fields of life."

Under Nancy's questioning, Padmore explained what he wanted from the British government. There should be immediate self-government, nationalization of colonial economies, and a federation evolving into "a Socialist Commonwealth." If this process was started during the war, rather than being promised afterward, he argued, the colonies would have something to fight for. The first step had to be political self-government. Nancy asked him whether color prejudice in England had decreased since the beginning of the war; he said it had not. They were both critical of the way in which Britain ruled the colonies; according to Nancy, "the policy of keeping people backward and without education at all is a conscious one." She threw in a vague reference to the superior skill of the Russians in educating their minorities: "I am sure the Russians would tackle all this very well." Padmore was on surer ground when he suggested that large foreign businesses should be replaced in colonial countries by small local industries, which would benefit the people themselves rather than outside interests.

After the usual hunt for a sympathetic publisher, *The White Man's Duty* was published at ninepence by W. H. Allen early in 1943. It had a fierce red and black cover, asking: "What do you know about the Colonial Question? It is one of the greatest issues of our time, and here, in the form of a dialogue between two experts, you get the facts. It is YOUR duty to know them." According to Nancy, the pamphlet was reprinted and sold nearly twenty thousand copies.

In the spring of 1942 Nancy managed to get a job with one of the Free French organizations in London as a radio monitor and translator. It was hard, dull work; she spent six-hour shifts correcting transcriptions in French of enemy propaganda broadcasts. She found it a fairly pointless exercise and was disgusted by the stuff she had to hear and read, which included some of Ezra Pound's fascist rantings from Italy. Douglas thought it an absurd job for her. After three months she resigned but accepted a job as secretary to a French officer who worked in the same building. She worked an eight-hour day reading the English papers and marking items of interest, and filing documents.

Nancy had moved to a room near Piccadilly, not far from where Douglas was living. They often spent the evening together, and once Douglas said to her as they parted, "Eighty-nine steps, my dear, between your place and mine. I count them every time we leave each other like this." Nancy was touched: "How I wished we could ever have managed to live under the same roof. But not once did there seem to be rooms available at the right moment. Back from my office in a not unpleasant trance of fatigue, I would eat my spam and boiled potatoes cooked on that dear little old gas ring, drinking coffee, sitting on the floor by the gas fire—sometimes dreaming, now and then writing a poem." Occasionally they went on expeditions together. In March 1943 they spent a day "looking for spring" in Epping Forest, by bus, without much success; Nancy apologized to Douglas for her gloomy mood. "You can't give what you haven't got," he said. "Nobody can. We're in the grip, my dear, in the grip."

By now Nancy had stopped working for her French employer; she was correcting the proofs of *The White Man's Duty* and also writing a series of articles for the Ministry of Information for distribution abroad, particularly in America. Their purpose was to describe in encouraging terms how blacks in the armed forces, British and American, were welcomed and provided for; Nancy visited places such as the Colonial Centre in Russell Square, a social club that arranged lectures and dances, and the Negro Welfare Centre in Liverpool. She also went often to the West African Students Union, where she loved to talk to the young Africans and occasionally take one of them out for a drink or dinner; she wrote a piece about the WASU for *New Times*. She was on the alert for incidents demonstrating racial prejudice, and she wrote a furious letter to the *News Chronicle* about the case of a colored girl who had been refused entry to the Land Army, the British wartime agricultural labor force. Not only was Nancy busy with her work and her regular outings with Douglas or Morris Gilbert whenever he was free, but she also had plenty of other friends to see in London. Harold Acton passed through and they had a nostalgic dinner in a half-empty Ritz dining room; her cousin Victor, now a distinguished correspondent for the *Times,* was sometimes in London; Herman Schrijver, an old friend from Paris, was staying with Geoffrey Hobson, the art expert, in Chelsea, and Nancy would sometimes dine there. On one of these occasions Hobson's son Anthony was present, and although he was twenty-five years younger than Nancy, they became friends. To a person of Hobson's age, there was already something legendary about Nancy. She had never been exactly ordinary, but now she was beginning to seem distinctly eccentric. She seemed both to accept this and to rise above it. She and Anthony Hobson would meet for lunch in the Savoy Grill or a small Soho restaurant. "Nancy's appearance," Hobson recalls,

bizarrely evocative of the Twenties, with her tall thin figure, waistless dress, bandeau and long string of beads, would make everyone look up as she came into the room. She herself was unconscious of the stir her entrance caused, having learned long before to ignore those she thought boringly conventional. As she crossed the room one saw her for a moment from outside, noticing the superficial eccentricity, only to be captivated immediately by her warmth of greeting, her distinction of poise and manner, her beautifully modulated voice and magnificent wide set blue eyes. She always listened to one's doings with grave and courteous attention. Conversation was punctuated by the rhythmic clash of the rise and fall of her African ivory bracelets . . . . worn seven or eight on each arm.

While Nancy was living in Half Moon Street, she was only a short walk away from her mother, who was settled in a suite at the Dorchester Hotel. Lady Cunard had also found herself on the other side of the Atlantic when the war started; in 1939 she had gone to Mexico, partly to sell some silver mines left her by her mother, partly so as to be able to join Sir Thomas Beecham, who was giving a series of concerts in America. She was staying at the Ritz in New York when war was declared; she was not in good spirits, since her finances were precarious and Sir Thomas was often away on tour. Early in 1940 she received the news, from a stranger over a New York lunch table, that Sir Thomas was going to marry a much younger woman, the pianist Betty Humby. Lady Cunard decided to go back to England; she never lacked courage and did not wish to spend the war away from her friends and the society she loved and had made her own. She crossed the Atlantic in a convoy on a Portuguese boat and flew to London from Lisbon. Her house in Grosvenor Square had been damaged by bombs; she decided to sell most of her furniture and move into a three-room suite at the Dorchester with her maid, Gordon. The defection of Sir Thomas, after thirty years, hit her very hard; but she was soon entertaining again, and during the war years her small dinner parties at the Dorchester were one of the social landmarks of London.

Events since 1931, when their relationship collapsed, had only emphasized the gulf between mother and daughter. In the mid-1930s, while Nancy was preoccupied with *Negro,* Moscow and the Spanish civil war, Lady Cunard's life revolved around her friendship with the prince of Wales and Mrs. Simpson. When in 1935 the prince became Edward VIII, Emerald's finest social hour seemed to have arrived, but the abdication changed all that. However, she soon recovered. The court remained closed to her, but she kept her nerve and continued to entertain. Over the dinner table she, too, had her contacts with the politics of the thirties. Chips Channon, whose admiration for her remained unbounded, noted in his diary that she had rung up the Postmaster General himself to complain that her telephone was out of order; and Harold Nicolson recorded how she "twitted" Anthony Eden over the Abyssinian crisis: "But Anthony, why should Italy not have Abyssinia? She was also heard to ask Ribbentrop (then Germany's ambassador to London) why Hitler was so hard on the Jews.

There never seems to have been any possibility that she and Nancy would end their ten-year estrangement, even though their friends overlapped to some extent and they were living within half a mile of each other. One of Lady Cunard's new friends was John Lehmann, who saw Nancy from time to time during the war and also became a regular dinner guest of her mother, of whom he became quite fond. He found her to have "an aristocratic, but also American, audacity, intelligence, wit, and beneath it all, an almost tragic sense of disillusionment." Behind her worldliness he detected a touching vulnerability. As for her feelings toward Nancy:

> She never referred to her daughter . . . nor did any of her friends, at least in public. If she was aware of how well I had known Nancy in my pre-war Bloomsbury days, she never betrayed it. I was glad of this for as I watched and listened to Emerald, I was constantly struck by the likeness between mother and daughter, in manner and voice and many small traits of behaviour; fascinating memories were evoked from the past of my association with Nancy, memories of absurdly different surroundings and a way of life of which Emerald could never have approved. They presented themselves in grotesque montage against the luxurious hotel suite; but, luckily, unknown to my hostess.

The contrast must indeed have been striking. While Nancy was working with George Padmore, or protesting against the release of her mother's friends, the Mosleys, from prison, or boiling coffee on her gas ring, Emerald was entertaining, Dorchester waiters in attendance, in rooms hung with heavy brocade curtains and cluttered with French furniture and marble-topped tables covered with gold, crystal, and tortoiseshell trinkets. She declined to allow the war to change her habits. "War's so vulgar," Harold Acton heard her say. Acton was one of the few friends able to speak to Nancy about her mother; once, after Nancy had asked in a mocking tone how Her Ladyship was, he suggested she call on her and perhaps even obtain help finding congenial work from one of Lady Cunard's many contacts. But Nancy rejected the idea with hostility. Acton found the feud sad, since the resemblances between the two seemed to him very strong.

Lady Cunard's parties were as sparkling and varied as ever. She entertained generals and politicians as well as writers, musicians, and artistic young men. As for the political tone, "Emerald's salon had an unqualified right-wing bias," writes Lehmann. "The politicians one met there were, with rare exceptions, conservative, the outlook entirely conservative, the prejudices almost at times a caricature of the conventional aristocratic class consciousness, though sustained with a wit and vigour of mind that were delightful to anyone with an ear for dialogue."

By the autumn of 1943 Nancy hit on a new and entirely characteristic project; to produce and edit an anthology of poems by English writers in celebration of France. She was partly inspired by the anthology *Poems for Spain,* produced by Stephen Spender and John Lehmann in 1939; her aim was to make a gesture of admiration toward the resistance spirit that she was sure most Frenchmen, and especially most French writers and intellectuals, felt. She went about the task in her usual fashion; she simply sat down and wrote to all the poets she could think of, some of whom she knew but many of whom she did not, asking them, "Have you a poem to send me connected with France since the war began?" She also placed a request for poems in the *New Statesman* and the *Times Literary Supplement;* and if she happened to run into someone she thought might contribute, she roped them in. She made several new friends through the anthology, which she called *Poems for France;* one was the writer Irene Rathbone, who met Nancy at a PEN club dinner in 1943.

" 'I want a poem from you,' she said.

" 'But, Miss Cunard, I am not a poet. You're mistaking me for someone else.'

" 'I mistake you for no one. I've read a poem of yours. Your only one? What do I care? You can't get out of writing another, and this time for me.' "

Another was a young Francophile schoolmaster, Walter Strachan, who answered one of Nancy's advertisements and found himself meeting her for lunch in the Café Royal. He found her "absolutely charming" and very knowledgeable about French poetry. She was delighted to find that as well as translating French poems himself, he had a great interest in typography. She was eager to help him get his work published; she introduced him to Raymond Mortimer on the *New Statesman,* who took a translation by Strachan of a Péguy poem. Strachan's experience of Nancy revealed a side of her that was to get stronger as she grew older. For people she liked and considered worthwhile, she was always generous with encouragement and introductions.

Eventually, Nancy collected contributions from seventy poets, and the anthology was published by La France Libre, the Free French publishing house, in 1944. (It was published in French. Nancy translated it and republished it after the war.) The quality of the poems varies as widely as the age and style of the writers, who include J. C. Squire, Lord Dunsany, Vita Sackville-West, Hugh MacDiarmid, William Plomer, and Alan Ross. Nancy provided biographical notes on the contributors (describing herself as "Poet and Journalist . . . a convinced believer in French and Spanish spirit and culture") and a statement of intent:

"This volume is a manifestation of our faith in France, our appreciation and love of her people and culture, our admiration for the dynamic, organised force of her resistance—and an earnest of the conviction that our two countries must ever march together."

When Nancy remembered the winter of 1943–44, she thought of *Poems for France* and Norman Douglas.

All of that winter I worked on my anthology of *Poems for France,* in the bed-sitter that could be made so warm and small wonder, for £1.5s—I worked it out—used to go into the electric meter every week. Often you [Douglas] came here after lunch and we brewed some of that delicious coffee. And once there was an enforced case of "where I dines I sleeps"—the last bus gone and the last Tube, with the nocturnal wails of "taxi, taxi" ringing in vain through the blackout all down Piccadilly.

Often à deux that winter, Christmas night is one of the times I think of you frequently yet, in certain moods. There was a little party for you at which Morris had supplied some munificent American whisky and there you sat in my bed-sitter ensconced in all of its dilapidated late Victorian comfort as five or six of us moved and conversed around you. Finally we were left alone. . . .

"Come and sit by me on the sofa."

We sat for hours, I know, our arms linked, talking of the things we would do, later, later. . . . At present we were playing at being in the Wagons Lits—the very sofa could be said to resemble one. We were crossing France towards Italy, and as romantic about it as could be. And why not?

In the spring of 1944 Nancy went down to Dorset to visit two new friends, Sylvia Townsend Warner and Valentine Ackland. The bombing of London had started again, and she had thoughts of finding somewhere in the country for her and Douglas to share. Sylvia Townsend Warner was already a well-known novelist and poet; Valentine Ackland was also a poet and ran a small antique business in Dorchester. They and Nancy had been in touch with one another over Spain, for which they shared strong feelings; they first met in the winter of 1942–43, when Nancy and Morris Gilbert paid a short trip to the West Country. The three women took to each other at once; Sylvia Townsend Warner was captivated by Nancy's style, her "neat, slightly tripping gait, like a water wagtail's," her efficiency when traveling—she would carry her things around in a tartan haversack or a large spotted handkerchief tied at the corners—and her capacity for hard work. Nancy left her ivory bracelets with them for safekeeping and paid them several short visits. "On a desert island, in a jail cell, she would have kept herself spruce, well kept, clean as a cat," Sylvia Townsend Warner recalled. "Her temper was notorious, her life was wilful and erratic—and she was compellingly respect-worthy." As a guest, Nancy had beautiful manners. At meals she would sit

> upright and slightly formalised, conversing agreeably, as a guest should. This frosting of social convention made her peculiarly entertaining, since it coexisted with a wide range of violent opinions and violent language. Even when she was drunk, it persisted, though allargando into solemnity and owlishness. "Nancy, you're tight," "Only a little, darling" flawlessly enunciated. And when an explosion of feeling broke through this habitual bel canto, the effect was formidable.

Nancy found a cottage near the sea at Lulworth that she thought would suit Douglas, but he changed his mind; Sylvia Townsend Warner was secretly relieved. Nancy felt that Douglas needed looking after, but her friends in Dorset were worried about her. "She was thin as a wraith and had a tormenting neuritis in her shoulder," Sylvia Townsend Warner remembers.

> This did not prevent her from walking with great speed and energy over the downs, nor from coming back with such loads of flints in her coat pockets that silhouetted on a skyline, her slender person gave the impression that paniers had been fastened on a cheetah. During the next hour or so, Nancy would be in the bathroom working on the flints with a nailbrush. Then a towel would be spread over her bed and the flints laid out to be admired, examined, graded. This capacity for magpie collecting was one of her prettiest charms. She used to collect beads (and sewed little bags exactly to contain them), shells, small nonsenses.

Nancy could not stay long in Dorset because the second front was building up in the spring of 1944 and nonresidents were forbidden to remain near the south coast. She moved briefly to a pub at Montacute, in Somerset, and then back to London.

The Allied armies crossed the Channel into Normandy on June 6, 1944, and French troops reached Paris on August 25.

Nancy was immensely excited when Paris was liberated, and she instantly decided to get back there as soon as she could. She had been in touch, sporadically, with her good friends the Goasgüens, from the inn at Réanville, and from their careful, semicoded letters, received via the International Red Cross, she knew that the news of her house was not good. German soldiers had been billeted there, and local vandals and collaborators had done some damage. She started looking for commissions that would get her to France as an accredited journalist; meanwhile, she moved again, this time to a flat in Jermyn Street that she found through Aleister Crowley, who had once lived there and was a friend of the landlady. Nancy had known Crowley slightly since the early 1930s and was amused by his reputation for wickedness and black magic; she visited him in the country near Oxford during the war, when he gave her a magic cocktail of a curious blue color and told her he was working against Hitler "on the astral plane."

By the late summer of 1944 Nancy was working on the translation of a book about the French resistance by a friend of hers, Gabrielle Picabia, wife of the painter. (She feared, rightly, that the book would be overtaken by events and not find an English publisher.) Again she was looking around for a job. She was taken on by SHAEF (Supreme Headquarters Allied Expeditionary Forces) as a translator from French, and she worked long shifts at their headquarters in Kingsway, which she found "gruelling. Typing, and broadcasting at dictation speed, all day or all night, I now knew the hurried step of the early morning worker, the muffled, dreary return of an evening." Although the work was uninspiring and she detested being tied to office hours and routine, Nancy was curiously proud to be part of the military machine and to be in uniform. When Kay Boyle and her husband, also in uniform, came to London that winter and met Nancy, "we were proud, the three of us, of the fight to which we were committed. 'How in the world did we get on the side of authority?' Nancy asked."

During the autumn Nancy heard firsthand news of her house at Réanville. Morris Gilbert, in France with the advancing American army, heard one day that Réanville had been liberated. He took his sergeant and a jeep and drove up to Nancy's house. He told her it was a shambles. Long before the Germans had arrived, the mayor, no admirer of the strange foreign woman with the black, Spanish, and communist friends, and the possibly subversive printing press, had ordered the place to be unlocked and did nothing to prevent the looting. Many of Nancy's pictures and objects had been stolen or defaced, and her books and papers were strewn everywhere, in filth and chaos. Gilbert brought back with him some battered copies of the Hours Press edition of Douglas's *One Day*, which he had picked off the top of a carpet of books on the bathroom floor.

Now Nancy thought she knew the worst. She wired to the Goasgüens: "I beg you, take the shovel to it all," and she redoubled her efforts to get to France. By early 1945 she had commissions from the *Burlington Magazine, Horizon,* and *Our Time*, and was also sponsored by the British Council. On February 27, 1945, with her cousin Victor Cunard and her new friend Irene Rathbone to see her off, Nancy, wearing a Russian fur hat and carrying her typewriter, took a night train from Victoria and crossed to France.

Return to France

When Nancy stepped on to the platform of the Gare du Nord, she embraced the large blue-bloused French porter with tears in her eyes and asked him what the occupation had been like. "It was very hard," he told her. She was moved and bewildered by her return to Paris. "I am glad that first day back in Paris over," she wrote in her article for *Horizon*. "I know what Lazarus felt after the tomb. It was terribly painful and somehow I could not think this out, yet wanted to. . . . I walked alone (and have never stopped walking since) down the whole of the Champs Élysées along the Grands Boulevards to the Bourse, glad to be alone, hoping I would meet no one I knew, hesitating on the threshold of what future."

Although for the first few months after her return to France Nancy was busy finding her friends and writing her articles, it became increasingly clear to her and to her friends that she did not really know where, or how, or with whom she was going to live, or what she was going to do. It was to take her four or five years to find a new base and some sort of equilibrium. Among the friends she found in Paris soon after she arrived was Janet Flanner, who wrote to Solita Solano:

Darling Nancy has just been in my room. She looked stunning—something like (in enamel and a bit cracked today, like any museum example, as against yesterday's fresher pastelle powdery version) the exotic old days. When she looked any-

thing but English, she thought, and was willing to use any
continent or strange island to prove it.

Nancy told Janet Flanner she was living on thirty pounds a
month plus whatever she could earn by writing; sometimes
she sold an old skirt or dress for a few francs. Nancy's clothes
had been becoming steadily more eccentric since the mid-
thirties but Janet Flanner thought she looked "lovely . . . a
grey tweed suit, a shirt front of giddy red and Roman stripes
made from a morsel of silk she'd bought for $1 on the streets
of New York, she said, a red hankie in her pocket and an
enormous grey felt hat, very mannish and widebrimmed.
Sandals! And I noted a bandage round one poor frost-bitten
toe."

Nancy's long "Letter from Paris" was published in *Horizon*
in June 1945. Her reaction to what she found going on in
Paris was fervent, unqualified admiration: "The war is not
over, but activity in all things of the intellect and of the arts is
already in its stride, because France is free of the Germans,
because there is an *immense* desire and intention of renewing
all the old links with the rest of the world as soon as may be,
and because this is just characteristic of France's eternal, beautiful force of renewal." She listed some of the new books,
papers and magazines coming out in Paris, several of them
involving such old friends as Aragon and Sadoul, and noted
that "Sartre and Camus have been constantly mentioned to
me as the two outstanding new writers." But "Aragon and
Éluard share about evenly, I should say, the gratitude of
France, as poets, and as leaders."

Despite the endless difficulties of everyday living—shortages, rationing, bad exchange rates, lack of transport and
heating, and the black market (all of which irritated Nancy to
a frenzy)—she found morale in Paris generally high. Nancy's
wholeheartedness would tolerate no qualifications, let alone
criticism. She regarded any hints that the French might have
reservations about their British and American liberators as
distortions or worse. "I know two or three people who have

returned to London from here saying 'The French are furious, they think it's worse than under the Germans, and even preferred them.' These people are either deliberately lying or saw only Fascists and fifth columnists."

She was reluctantly impressed by the exquisite clothes and cosmetics on sale in the boutiques and shops, and she saw "a future of great beauty in all the stuff of adornment." She went to several premieres, including the film *Les Enfants du Paradis,* which she loved and predicted firmly "will be famous," and Sartre's *Huis Clos.* "You will like it very much," she informed *Horizon's* readers. She went around the exhibitions and mentioned in particular one reconstructing the lives of the two and a half million French prisoners in German camps; one of them was Raymond Michelet, her former lover and colleague on *Negro.* She fulminated against the effect of the deportations and wartime food shortages on health, particularly of children and pregnant women. Nothing she saw or heard led her to question her assumption that the spirit of the resistance had permeated the whole country.

"The Germans have massacred, tortured, blackmailed, attacked psychologically and done much more but they have emphatically NEVER dominated the spirit of the men, women and children of France. . . . Everywhere, in every class and religion, the Germans were met with fortitude, with dignity and stupendous self-sacrifice, with the real *noblesse d'âme* of a fine and extremely resurgent people."

Nancy's faith in the French nation was severely shaken, however, when she managed, soon after her arrival, to get down to Réanville. Although she had been warned what to expect, the shock was devastating; she never quite got over it. Her fullest description of the shambles was written nearly twenty years later; what hurt most was that although it was possible to blame the war and the Germans in general for what had happened, most of the damage, and the hatred and contempt that lay behind it, had come from local people, natives of her adopted country, among whom she had lived, she thought, as a friend, for so long.

At first, she simply felt numb. "In a dream I wandered through the shell of my home." Then she started work, clearing and sorting through five years' pillage and squalor. The Goasgüens, at considerable risk to themselves, had at various times crept into the house and removed items more or less at random; they told her that they had tried to salvage everything that had her name on it. Nancy was touched and grateful; their loyalty was some comfort to her. But she had still lost much of what she valued most; her past life had been pillaged and defiled.

What was this in the bath torn away from its fittings? The two stone heads from Easter Island that Alvaro Guevara had given me years after I had printed *St. George,* one of them broken in two (that must have taken some doing). And this, nailed firmly to a window in lieu of glass? The once green vellum covers of Rodker's large and beautiful edition of Ezra Pound's Cantos. . . . Sticking out of some debris was my father's first letter, torn out of a family album, dated in the early 1850s when father was around four. I read, "I am a good boy, I know my letters." On the mantelpiece in the same ravaged bedroom stood a large question mark in red and black cardboard—that had never been mine. Here, flung face down and horrible creased, was my lovely blue landscape by Tanguy . . . it was shot full of bullet holes, ten small, one large. Most of the other paintings and drawings had disappeared although there was still half an abstract, torn roughly across, by the surrealist artist, Malkine, whom I had liked so much. And I saw what looked like a bayonet thrust through part of the portrait Eugene MacCown had done of me in Paris in 1923.

All her valuable oriental rugs had gone, and the chest from Spanish Morocco which had contained the African beadings she had hung in the Hours Press shop; she found a few beads crushed underfoot. "Of the entire collection of African and other primitive sculpture not one single piece remained, and most of the African ivory bracelets had vanished along with the trunk they were in. Georgette [Goasgüen] had picked up some of them in the fields, mostly those thin, disc-like ones that Man Ray had photographed for *Henry-Music.*" Nancy was told that the German troops had put the African sculpture up on the wall near the house and stoned it.

Nancy combed through every inch of the chaos. Georgette Goasgüen told her she was a born scavenger. "Three long days went by raking through fragments in the stillness and peculiar odour of the gutted house." When she had finished, she had collected fifteen large cases and sacks of paper, apart from books. But much of her personal correspondence, and virtually all the papers concerning the Hours Press, had gone. She listed the vanished letters: "gone were those of Arthur Symons, Aldous Huxley, Michael Arlen, Richard Aldington, Ezra Pound, T. S. Eliot, Wyndham Lewis, Robert Graves, Robert Nichols, Ronald Firbank, Roy Campbell, Osbert Sitwell, T. W. Earp, St. John Hutchinson, Iris Tree, Evan Morgan, Clifford Sharp . . . Raymond Mortimer, Geoffrey Scott, John Strachey, Alvaro Guevara, . . . Aragon, Breton, Tzara, Crevel."

The roof had been torn off the printery, but the press itself, though rusty, was intact. "Down the well, I had been told, had been thrown a small sheep to putrefy, books, excrement, an old chintz cover from the sofa and two rifles. All, by now, I thought would be compost." Since she first heard of the extent of the damage she had been telling herself that at least the big round thyme bush at the back of the house would have survived. It had not. This seemed the last straw. "The missing bush seemed to say: 'No more, no more of any of this for you. Don't try to come back.' "

Nancy realized that she could not continue to live at Réanville. The atmosphere as well as the house was ruined for her. She heard all kinds of stories from the village about who had done what; the Goasgüens, disgusted by what had happened, were planning to move away. She decided to fight for compensation and to sell the house.

It was no sense of fatalism that made me accept the sack and loot, the ruin and end of Le Puits Carré. The very word accept

is wrong, for one is not in a position to "accept" or to "refuse" a fact. Do either and nothing will be any different. No
bombs, no artillery, no air raids, no shooting war had there
been just here at any time, but a detestable permanent war
within war of hatred in the village. This is what I realised as
the spate of almost incomprehensible narration rolled for days
over my head.

Nancy lost no time in consulting a lawyer and claiming
compensation for what she had lost; she calculated the total
value as thirty-six hundred pounds, of which twelve hundred
represented the damage to the house and land, fifteen hundred
was for "African artwork," and pictures, books, and furniture
made up the other nine hundred. The case dragged on for
several years, with the authorities presenting counteraccusa-
tions about the Spanish communist refugees she had allowed
to live in the house and arguing about the impossibility of
protecting a foreign subversive's property under the German
occupation. Nancy, it must be said, was less than candid
about some of these allegations. In the end she got nothing;
the case was dismissed for lack of evidence. Nancy resented
this bitterly and was convinced there were political motives
behind the decision. She wrote a furious poem which she sent
to many of her friends:

Death to the intellect, was roared—
These Norman peasants heard the cry
And oped their breeches and let fly.
The Germans only burned the books
And played their war and went away—
The peasants shat another day.

During 1945 Nancy was still involved with Morris Gilbert,
who came over to France soon after she did. They stayed in
small hotels and borrowed flats in Paris; he drove her down to
Réanville more than once and they went to southwest France
together, where Nancy was beginning to think she might
look for a new house. It is clear from letters that they were

seriously thinking of a future together; but Gilbert's work, his ties in America and the fact that when the war was over, his career as a journalist would almost certainly take him back to New York made such plans precarious. Nancy was very attached to him, and some of her friends came to regard this relationship as one that might have induced her to settle down at last; but although she was unhappy—she described the summer of 1945 as "the most incoherent time in my life"— she was, as always, more in the mood for travel and action than for commitment and security. Probably no man, by this time, could have changed Nancy's nature sufficiently to make a permanent relationship possible; and the notion that at the age of fifty she would ever be content to subordinate her plans and movements to someone else's must have seemed highly unlikely. But when Gilbert went back to America at the beginning of 1946, they parted on the assumption that they would be together again before long.

As soon as she could, Nancy left Paris and Normandy for Toulouse, Andorra and the Spanish border. But on the way she stopped in the Dordogne, and it was from Gourdon that she wrote a long letter to Ezra Pound, who by then was in St. Elizabeths Hospital in Washington, D.C., while the debate dragged on as to whether he was mentally fit to stand trial for treason. Nancy had heard that Pound wanted to communicate with her. For her part, she had plenty to say to him. She would have none of the suggestion that he had supported the fascists in Italy out of ignorance or insanity.

"Williams [William Carlos Williams] has called you misguided. I do not agree. The correct word for a Fascist is 'scoundrel.' . . . Fascism is not insanity, unless evil itself, all evil, be insanity (a point that can certainly be argued psychologically and philosophically, *in the abstract*. War is not abstract)."

Nancy's letter reviewed her thirty-year acquaintance with Pound and recalled the good times as well as the bad: his helpful advice on her poetry in 1921; his love of the French countryside, which had stimulated hers; and his liking for

Henry Crowder. "Do you remember how often we were together? Henry loved you—so did I, always, then, and before then up to the last time I saw you in 1928." After that had come his unsatisfactory reply to her questionnaire on Spain in 1937, and a letter informing her that the Ethiopians were "black Jews." "Incidentally," wrote Nancy, "for several years, I thought you were Jewish yourself, Ezra. What could it have mattered, one way or the other?"

Nancy found Pound's support for fascism difficult to grasp because he undoubtedly was the two things she admired most—an intellectual and a fine poet. "I cannot understand how the integrity that was so much you in your writing can have chosen the enemy of all integrity." The only bitterness in what was otherwise a calm and even generous letter came when she described the ruin of her house in Normandy by the "allies of your friends."

She received, in August 1946, a short distracted reply from Pound. It began, "What the blue beggaring hell are you talking about?" He said he wished he had Henry Crowder's address.

This exchange seems to have marked the end of Nancy's contact with Pound. But if she read the *Pisan Cantos,* begun during his imprisonment by the allies in Italy, and published 1948, she may have noticed that both she and Henry Crowder were fleetingly mentioned by name.

Toulouse was the center for exiled anti-Franco Spaniards and their sympathizers; Nancy, who was outraged by the apparent apathy in London and Paris about the Franco regime, found the atmosphere in Toulouse exhilarating. She was still agitating in every way open to her for the Spanish cause; she wrote numerous articles and letters of complaint about the need to carry on the struggle, about Franco's persecution of his opponents, about the conditions in prisons and detention camps; and she bombarded her friends with requests for money, food, and clothes. She was also writing a series of poems, in French, on Spanish themes; one, written when victory in Europe was at last achieved, sums up her feelings:

Un litre de vin pour la Victoire?
Deux doigts de peine pour toute la vie.
Dix litres des peines pour la Victoire
Et pour la vie les restes et lies—
O incomplète, o dérisoire, O Pyrénées de leur oubli.

She spent several weeks in Toulouse and then in Andorra in the summer of 1946 and wrote to Solita Solano: "I am with the Spanish workers for EVER and against their enemies who are and always have been mine. . . . There was love in Andorra, great love, and much of it. Excitement, tragedy, danger, beauty, huge walks, climbing, dawns and nights and WINE and TOBACCO and REAL values." There were also rumors that Nancy was involved in smuggling arms from Toulouse across the border into Spain and that she was learning about explosives.

In Toulouse, she made one new friend in particular who was to remain devoted to her for the rest of her life: a writer and broadcaster, Géraldine Balayé, for whom Nancy was one of the most beautiful, romantic, and brave people she had ever met. They went on long walks together, talking about poetry and the Spanish cause; Géraldine was, like Nancy's other close women friends, a source of affection, admiration, and above all, the continuity and security her nature did not allow her to find with a man. But it was not long before Nancy had found another male lover and traveling companion.

She was back in Paris in the spring of 1947, staying at the Hotel Montana in the rue Saint-Benoît, when she met a young American, William Le Page Finley. She was fifty-one, and he was twenty-four and basically homosexual; but when he saw her having a drink in the Café de Flore one day, he was determined to meet her. He discovered they had mutual friends—one of whom was Brian Howard—and he went to her hotel. "The concierge said she wasn't in at the moment and went on to say, quite gratuitously, that the police had been there a number of times making enquiries. This struck me as odd until I got to know the facts; the French police were keeping an eye on her for so-called political reasons." A few days later he found her in; she was pleased to see him.

> Her looks and charm quite overpowered me. We talked a good deal about people we knew, she showed me a copy of *Negro* and suggested we have lunch. Then she told me about the destruction of her house in Normandy by the Germans, that she intended to sell it and would I like to come with her to see it. We set off for Vernon where we stayed at an hotel and walked back and forth to the ruined house while she was negotiating the sale. The walks seemed endless to me but she never tired walking all the time I knew her.

Finley was good-looking, cosmopolitan and charming, he was interested in poetry and politics; and he had enough money to travel around amusing himself. Nancy was much taken with him, and she was intrigued by his background— partly American, partly Irish, and a dash of red Indian. She took him to England with her for a month and introduced him to her friends, including Sylvia Townsend Warner, Herman Schrijvcr, and Edgell Rickword; he also met her cousins, Victor and Edward. Nancy felt no self-consciousness, much less embarrassment, on this or subsequent occasions, about appearing with a lover so much younger than herself; one friend with whom Nancy and Finley stayed a few days in London remembers how her housekeeper remarked one morning how touching it was to see a mother so devoted to her son—the young man must have been unwell, since Mrs. Cunard had spent the whole night in his room looking after him. Nancy got to hear this story, loved it, and frequently told it to other people. Back in France in the autumn of 1947, she and Finley went south again to Perpignan, Toulouse, and Andorra, where he met several of her Spanish refugee friends; he was struck by how frustrated and angry she seemed over the Spanish situation. When he suggested that they might go together to Mexico, where he had spent part of the war and had many friends, she was enthusiastic. They decided to pick up a boat from Lisbon; it was possible to go through Spain on transit visas. And so, ten years after the Spanish civil war had started, Nancy found herself traveling through the country she now felt more passionately about than any other. She saw traces of bombings: "My heart was dry and hard with hatred as I looked at them . . . and drier yet with despondency at the increasing feeling that nothing will be done by 'the democracies' against Franco's detested regime." They changed trains at Irún, where Nancy plied a porter with cigarettes and wine and discovered to her delight that "No Man of Franco he!" When they arrived in Lisbon, they discovered that boats to Mexico were irregular; they had a month to wait and spent it on a walking tour of the Algarve. According to Finley, the voyage was unpleasant and expensive, and Mexico turned out to be "a disappointment for us both." Nancy sought out her Spanish friends, but apart from Angel Goded, who had started a restaurant where he gave them a fantastic welcome, her encounters with them were not a success. "These people had adjusted to a new way of life," Finley wrote, "and Nancy didn't feel part of it." He went on alone to the United States to see his mother; and Nancy, on her own, became increasingly miserable, angry, and accident-prone. She fell while out walking and spiked her eye on a cactus; the injury was painful and slow to heal. She developed abscesses under her teeth and had to have three extracted. She drank too much, and made angry scenes which alienated her friends. Finally she decided to leave and pay another visit to her cousin Sir Edward, who was now retired and living in Barbados. She had a nightmare journey, traveling as usual as cheaply as possible, and found herself stranded in Panama City, which shook even her confidence. (She told Solita Solano later that to survive alone in Panama City, you really had to be able to look after yourself.)

Her stay in Barbados, too, does not seem to have been as enjoyable as her time there in 1941; if there were more calypsos devoted to her, she did not preserve copies of them, and she found the colonial atmosphere stuffier than ever. She was relieved to find a place on a crowded old troopship sailing to

Europe; by good luck, she was able to share a cabin with Freya Stark, the writer and traveler and good friend of her cousin Victor. Freya Stark found Nancy an admirable companion, interesting to talk to, determined to find time and space to work—she was planning a book about Mexico—and keen to avoid as far as possible the boring rituals of meals at the captain's table. When a young Jamaican girl was found as a stowaway, Nancy became her champion and friend and collected money from the passengers to give the girl a new start.

By the early summer of 1948 Nancy was back in Paris, where Finley rejoined her. Le Puits Carré had finally been sold at a reasonable price to some Parisians who wanted a weekend house. Nancy knew she badly needed a new home: "Lack of a base is very bad for me." she wrote to Solita Solano. "That is my trouble, my difficulty, my preoccupation." Meanwhile, she and Finley decided to spend the summer in Normandy at L'Arche de Nöe, a hotel in Giverny.

There was a small colony of English expatriate writers in Giverny that summer. Two acquaintances of Nancy's, Joan Black and Eda Lord, the novelist, were sharing a house nearby; Malcolm Lowry and his wife, Margerie, were staying with them. Margaret Anderson (who had edited the *Little Review*), her friend Dorothy Caruso (widow of the great singer), Sybille Bedford, and Esther Murphy (who had been married to Nancy's former lover John Strachey) were part of the group as well. Nancy and Finley were frequently at Joan Black's house, where, Finley recalled, "most evenings . . . were very gay with dancing to Radio Andorra far into the night. Malcolm [Lowry] would usually be there dancing about alone with his watered wine." But then a curious incident led to trouble. According to Finley:

One evening at Joan Black's, being rather tipsy, I happened to discover a bottle of gin in a cupboard and told Malcolm and he suggested we take it and go to an empty bedroom and enjoy ourselves. We were finally discovered by Nancy, followed by the other guests, and a disagreeable scene followed. The gin was confiscated and they left us alone. The next morning at dawn, feeling very guilty, we crept out of the house and made for the inn in Giverny picking up a bottle of cognac on the way. We locked ourselves in Nancy's room as it was larger than mine, stripped and went to bed with the cognac. By noon Nancy and Malcolm's wife Margerie were at the door and we refused to open. I said "Can't you understand when two men want to be alone together?" They went below to the dining room and sent up a platter of food. When we finally unlocked the door Margerie got her husband dressed and took him away. Joan Black never forgave me for this incident and I was barred from the house.

While she was at Giverny, Nancy heard that her mother was dangerously ill. Earlier in the year Lady Cunard's health had begun to fail; she had developed a permanent sore throat, and then she caught pneumonia. Although she seemed to be recovering, she was found to have cancer of the throat. Nancy was kept informed about her mother's condition by their mutual friend Tony Gandarillas. He has recalled a strange incident during one of Nancy's postwar visits to London, when he was returning from an evening at the theater with Lady Cunard and James Lees-Milne. Their car swerved to avoid a woman in the road ahead of them; as they looked back, they all realized it was Nancy. Lady Cunard gasped audibly, but no one said anything. Lady Diana Cooper, who had once again, after a gap of many years, been seeing something of Nancy in France (Duff Cooper was Britain's first postwar ambassador to Paris), remembers suggesting to Nancy that since her mother had not long to live, she might now like to see her and that she knew Lady Cunard wanted a meeting. But Nancy wouldn't hear of it. " 'Her Ladyship? You must be mad—oh no, quite out of the question.' " William Finley remembers a telephone call from Lady Diana: "Nancy wanted to know if her mother had asked for her and as she hadn't Nancy decided not to go to her bedside."

On July 6 Gandarillas wrote to tell Nancy that her mother had taken a turn for the worse and that there was little hope.

On July 10 Lady Cunard died. In her will she had asked that Gandarillas should contact Nancy when she died; she had left everything she had in equal parts to three people: Nancy, Lady Diana Cooper, and Sir Robert Abdy.

Nancy did not go to London for her mother's cremation, or to attend the bizarre little ceremony when Sir Robert Abdy scattered the ashes in Grosvenor Square. Finley remembers that Nancy "wept once; the one thing that upset her, she told me, was Sir Thomas Beecham's desertion to marry a younger woman."

If Nancy could not bring herself to mourn for her mother, there were others who did. The *Times* published a glowing obituary on July 12: "Outstanding though her services to the arts were, she could not have achieved half what she did without a social gift which combined gracious sympathy with a salty yet never malicious wit. . . . She had friends in all walks of life. . . . Her like will hardly be seen again in the years ahead and she did much to deserve her place in the social and artistic history of her time." A few days later Sacheverell Sitwell contributed another tribute: "She will be missed and never forgotten, by her friends of three generations. . . . It is dreadful to think one will never feel her light touch again or experience her deeds of kindness." Chips Channon wrote mournfully in his diary: "London society has had a terrible blow. There is only me left. Although I had not seen her so much during the last year, I have nevertheless loved her since the first moment I saw her in 1919 . . . her kindness was proverbial . . . she loved arranging other people's lives: nothing was too much trouble for her. But her heart was lonely. Thomas Beecham had broken it."

One of the many ironies to be found in the complicated, sad story of Nancy's relationship with her mother is that the generosity they shared—along with many other qualities—toward their friends, materially and emotionally, failed them both toward each other. They also shared a fierce pride; but although Lady Cunard, to one or two people close to her, seemed very occasionally to regret the bitter hardening of the breach with her daughter, Nancy never did. If she ever felt remorse for not going to her mother's deathbed, she never showed or spoke of it, although, as the years passed, she was able to write and sometimes speak of her with objectivity and detached appreciation of her gifts. Some of Lady Cunard's friends were outraged that Nancy not only found it apparently easy to accept her mother's legacy but showed a lively interest in getting her due; but to Nancy, who had always blamed her mother for keeping her financially dependent in her youth, it was probably simply a matter of justice being done at last.

For the next couple of years Nancy's main preoccupation was to find herself a house. Her lingering attraction to Normandy was given a further blow by an upsetting incident. One day, when she and Finley had gone to Le Havre to collect a trunk sent back from Mexico, a journalist arrived in Giverny from Paris looking for Nancy. He failed to find her but spoke to one or two of her friends, Margaret Anderson in particular, and made enquiries in the village. The result appeared in a right-wing Paris journal, La Bataille, in August 1948, headlined: "Too Revolutionary to be a Communist, the Rich Heiress has Refused Millions and Nancy Cunard Lives by her Pen in a French Village." It began:

> So who is this woman of uncertain age, with disheveled hair, dressed in old trousers and a cardigan? Her arms are as thin as those of the wretches returning from Ravensbrück, the feet she places on the steps of the village bus show a protruding vein, and her ankle bone looks as if would pierce the skin. And yet there is a sparkle in the eye, a twitch of the mouth . . . yes, it is her. It is the beautiful Nancy Cunard, one of the curiosities of the interwar period, Aragon's egeria from the time when, a poet, he had not yet discovered the eyes of Elsa . . . !

The picture presented by the article could not have offended Nancy more. She was portrayed as a shadow of her former self, a physical wreck, someone for whom the villagers felt pity; but worst of all, the notion that she was the millionaire heiress of the Cunard Line was brought up yet again, together with the story that she had disdainfully rejected this great wealth—and spurned her mother's recent legacy—out of revolutionary principle, preferring to earn her own living by writing. The article also contained jibes at Aragon and the Communist party and hinted broadly that her "scandalous" opinions and actions owed as much to copious drinking as to principle. The fact that beneath this farrago were some uncomfortable grains of truth did not help; the whole episode was another blow to Nancy's affection for France and an unpleasant indication of what some of her friends really thought of her. She wrote furiously to Margaret Anderson and threatened to sue the paper; but the damage was done.

She returned to Paris with Finley, and soon afterward they went down to the Dordogne together to look for a house. Nancy decided to rent a cottage near Souillac as a base, but Finley by this time had decided their relationship could not continue.

> The house was ghastly, no running water, no comforts of any kind and practically no furniture. The prospect of spending the winter there appalled me and I decided I must get away . . . the relationship was beginning to wear thin, for me certainly and I was weary of Nancy's possessiveness. . . . Furthermore I preferred male companionship. There had been many quarrels, drunkennesses and I had fled from her a number of times. I had a friend send a wire from Paris to notify me that my mother was ill. Nancy did not fall for that one, but she realized by then I was leaving. She saw me off at the train station and I never saw her again. . . . I adored her looks, her character, the stories she had to tell but I knew I could not go on living with her. With her I had no life of my own.

Although Nancy had certainly been a little in love with Finley for a time, there is no evidence that his departure was a serious blow to her; but the style and pattern of this relationship seemed ominous to her friends. Finley was disarmingly frank about the problems in their relationship; he felt there was a strong maternal element in her feeling for him, but at the same time she was sexually demanding, although she was certainly aware of his preferences. He did not enjoy her autocratic ways or her tendency to violence when she had been drinking. There were to be other young men, of much less intelligence and honesty, who enjoyed Nancy's charm and style less and what was left of her money and influence more.

About this time, too, Nancy was forced to realize that Morris Gilbert was not going to return from America. She did not really want to go there to join him, although she thought of doing so. Their correspondence trailed away in excuses and failed plans; Nancy kept one of his last letters and covered it with bitter, angry comments. Now in her early fifties she was more alone than she had ever been.

Nancy had to make several trips to London in 1948 and 1949 in connection with the settlement of her mother's estate; the division, though amicable, was complicated, and it was soon plain that Lady Cunard had much less to leave than might have been expected. Eventually, Nancy found that her share of the American capital would bring her in about another three hundred pounds a year. She acquired the two paintings she particularly wanted: S. C. Harrison's portrait of George Moore, and Moore's lovely Manet, *Étude pour le Linge*. Other paintings and furniture she sold in London, and she put the money toward buying and furnishing her new home. She had found what she wanted: an old house, not much more than a barn, on a hillside just outside a hamlet called La Mothe Fénélon, twelve miles from Souillac.

Nancy chose to live in the Dordogne for several reasons. She had loved the area since the mid-twenties; she wanted to base herself within reasonable traveling distance from Toulouse and the Spanish border, and Souillac was on the main railway route; Normandy was ruined for her, and she had begun to feel disenchantment with postwar Paris. She loved both the ancient history of the Dordogne and its gallant record during the occupation. The fact that her chosen village was remote and that her house, even when rebuilt to her specifications, was primitive and inconvenient did not bother her. She intended to travel during the winter and to spend the late spring, summer and early autumn at La Mothe, writing and having her friends stay with her. This was to be the pattern of her life during the 1950s; and to start with it worked reasonably well. Nancy's energy and confidence remained phenomenal; although she grumbled and complained a good deal about the inconvenience and expense of her way of life, it was plain that even now Nancy had no real desire to settle down. Most of her friends, even the most unconventional, had by now found a lasting relationship, in marriage or friendship, or were tied to aging parents or had other family responsibilities. But though Nancy respected such obligations in others—indeed, as her correspondence shows, she was endlessly interested and concerned about her friends' domestic arrangements—she did not regret having no ties of her own. Her age seemed to be no bar to casual sexual relationships; and though the men she would appear with sometimes seemed quite deplorable to her old friends, Nancy herself was never apparently aware either of indignity or of being exploited.

But if her lovers came and went, she was as quick as ever to make new, lasting friends. One of them was the English novelist and film scriptwriter Anthony Thorne. He and his wife were to become among her most reliable sources of hospitality and support. Thorne had heard of Nancy's activities in Harlem and Spain for years; when finally they met at a party in Venice in 1949, where Nancy had gone to attend a PEN Club Congress in the late summer, he was not disappointed. "Her appearance?" Thorne recalled, "A girl once said to me: 'I come into a room and at the end of it there's the most beautiful woman I've ever seen. Then as I get near her I realise it's Nancy Cunard.' Yes, she was raddled and distressingly thin, but the fine bone was there and the fire-blue eyes of a warrior and a smile ready for a quip." Nancy asked Thorne to a party she was giving the following night in an old *palazzo* where she had taken rooms. He remembered how she met all her guests at the landing stage in pouring rain, wearing a plastic raincoat. When she learned that Thorne knew Harlem and had lived for a while in Haiti, their friendship was sealed, though when he took her out to dinner, they had a sudden furious row when she accused him of being "too bloody English." But the next night he found

> a very different Nancy, dressed in conventional "Government House" black satin, though still with barbaric jewellery and the inevitable bandeau across her forehead. It was at a ball given in the Palazzo Rezzonico, to which we paid not the slightest attention, spending the entire night in talking on a balcony. She was thoughtful and sober, pained by memories of an earlier Venice, and suddenly, with the gesture of a priestess, poured a libation of champagne into the Grand Canal. "For Henry," she said.

It was natural that Nancy should be thinking of Henry Crowder; this was her first visit to Venice since they had left there together in 1928. She had had no news of Crowder for years. She described him for Thorne a little later on when she sent him an inscribed copy of *Henry-Music:* ". . . a man you would have loved . . . a man who introduced a whole world to me in 1928, and two continents. . . . A most wary and prudent man, among many other beauties and qualities, who often said: 'Opinion reserved!' Whereas to me, nothing—nor opinion nor emotion nor love nor hate—could be 'reserved' for one instant on the score of things this Man-Continent-People gradually revealed to me about his race and the life of his race."

They left the ball in a gondola, and Nancy tried to engage the gondolier in Spanish-Italian. (Her Italian was the least good of her languages, and never recovered from her immersion in Spanish in the late 1930s.) Her interest was again aroused on this visit to Venice about the gondoliers' problems, their wish to organize themselves and raise their prices, especially when she again met one of the gondoliers she had known in 1928. She promised him to do what she could to help.

Nancy went on from Venice to Rome, and then to Capri to visit Norman Douglas, who had returned to the island in 1946. She found him just the same, he did not seem to her much older or frailer, though he complained about his health. He was comfortably installed in his own part of the beautiful Villa Tuoro, owned by their mutual friend Kenneth Macpherson (whom Nancy had known since 1928 and who was one of her contributors to *Negro*). Nancy and Douglas met for drinks in the cafés, and they took occasional gentle strolls together. She joined the party at the Villa Tuoro for leisurely meals. She asked Douglas to help her write a formal letter to the mayor of Venice, asking permission to attend a council meeting on behalf of the gondoliers; Douglas grumbled crossly at her latest cause, but he wrote the letter for her. Nancy was moved almost to tears when, in answer to her questions about how a projected biography of himself by John Davenport was going, Douglas murmured, "Let them write what they like my dear—let 'em, let 'em."

As she was leaving Capri, she rang Douglas from a noisy café to say a final good-bye. "And, although I could not hear you very well, beyond a detached 'You're off, are you?' The last words of all did seem to have rather a sound of 'Well, ta-ta, my dear, ta-ta . . .' " Nancy and Douglas exchanged letters and cards, but they never met again.

She was settled in her new home by the spring of 1950 and wrote to a friend in Paris, the writer Cecily Mackworth:

Ah but NOW I have a house: Incredibly small and elementary and I adore it and adore this region and know it and shall know it better in time. I have no desire for Paris, and thank God this is 9 hours distant, which keeps away the bores and may not impede the few one really wants to see, who knows? But the house has taken all too much time already, on account of the state it was (and is) in. No sheets, etc. No lavatory, no water. Superb electric light and divine neighbours who load me with gifts, eatable gifts. I wish I had NEVER seen bloody Normandy. Had I lived down here from the start the whole of my life would have been different and I should not have lost everything.

The house was small; there was a kitchen, sitting room and spare room on the ground floor, with narrow wooden steps leading up to Nancy's bedroom, and a tiny attic room above. The kitchen had an old-fashioned wood-burning stove, fed with twigs through the top, on which a pan of water took an hour to boil; the walls were bare stone. Nancy furnished the house mainly from local sales of old furniture, with some cheap modern stuff; only the huge old table from Nevill Holt had survived the sack of Réanville. But she draped the walls with Moroccan tapestries, put green velvet curtains in the window, hung the Manet and the portrait of George Moore in the sitting room, arranged her books carefully, and had a special case made to hold the complete set of her Hours Press volumes. She would put vases of wild flowers and grasses on the shelves, as well as a collection of her latest *objets trouvés*—interestingly shaped stones, old bottles, curiously twisted pieces of wood covered with lichen or crystal-encrusted stones from the river. During the summer she kept a big table outside where she would work and eat. A woman from the village came to clean and cook. There was always a pile of big straw hats for guests.

Among her first and then most regular visitors during the 1950s was Irene Rathbone, who found the place idyllic. She would come in the summer when La Mothe was

> hot, peaceful, delectable. . . . From the spare bedroom on the ground floor of her house one stepped, wearing a dressing gown, straight onto grass; then, at a long, rough wooden table, sunlit at that hour, later tree-shadowed, one sat having coffee. The morning slid by. One tranquilly wrote or read. Nancy, in her room under the roof, typed letters. She had a

vast correspondence and the people she kept up with included
rich and poor, black and white, French, English and Spanish
poets, curators of museums, duchesses, old dressmakers, journalists. The rattle-bang of her machine continued till lunchtime, when down she wafted. We had not seen each other
since the evening before. Dressed by now, I helped to carry
food from kitchen to garden. There was not a great deal of it,
quite enough; and, as always, enough wine. Across the valley
spread the wooded hills.

Carrying a picnic lunch, they went on huge walking expeditions around the countryside, planned by Nancy to include
crumbling châteaux or farmhouses burned out by the Germans, with stops for drinks at small cafés. Nancy seemed
tireless, and "was familiar with every path in the district.
Fields shimmered in the heat: walnuts on a length of road cast
shade. But we were seldom on a road. In my mind I invari-
ably see her moving beside crops, beside pastures, through
woods, moving with that tall grace of hers, that elasticity."
Irene Rathbone found the local people puzzled by Nancy,
but friendly. Her cook could not understand why she liked to
live so simply, when she seemed to have enough money to
afford modern conveniences. When her friend tried to explain—"What she cares about is foreign travel in winter,
supporting at all times good causes, helping distressed friends,
and buying, very occasionally, some small *objet d'art*"—the
cook shook her head.
"It's not normal, her way of life. But we like her very
much."
Nancy's main problem, once she had found her new base,
was that none of her writing projects turned out very well.
She needed to earn extra money, but more than that she desperately needed the stimulus and objective of work. Several
ideas collapsed, partly because she could not achieve what she
planned, partly because publishers, after showing initial interest, lost enthusiasm. Her book on Mexico remained a sheaf of
random jottings; a plan for a book about the Dordogne never
got beyond the early stages; a publisher in London who had

encouraged her to expect publication of a new collection of poems did not like what she sent in, which were her poems on Spain, the war, and the resistance. Eventually she published a leaflet, *Poems for Spain,* in Perpignan in 1949 at her own expense. She managed to get regular translating work from a French firm, Editions Braun, specializing in art history and guidebooks, but this was not what she really wanted to do. For a time she insisted that Spain was all she really wanted to write about, and she planned a long book, or an epic poem; but without encouragement, and with no very clear idea herself of how to give her ideas and experiences form and structure, this project also languished. Nancy never lost interest in her prewar causes, as her correspondence and notes and collection of cuttings on black and Spanish topics prove, but the days when she could simply hurl herself into a project and achieve results had gone, partly because times had changed, partly because she was now living so far from the center of events and was dependent upon letters and newspapers to keep in touch.

She was still writing the occasional article for the ANP or some London publication, but the strength of her former journalism, which was always most effective when she described events firsthand, was missing when she wrote out of her head or from newspaper reports, and her ideas on race or Spain sounded fixed and two-dimensional when restated in the postwar context. She missed the excitement of the thirties and wartime, and the causes and certainties that had seemed so clear then. Nancy liked to proclaim, not to enquire, and gradually even her old friends on magazines or reviews stopped asking her to write for them, and they turned down her proposals.

She began to receive suggestions from publishers and friends that she should write about herself; but the idea of an autobiography irritated her. She wanted to do something more creative and more objective; to exploit her past seemed negative and distasteful.

Nostalgia was inimical to Nancy; she had a strong sense of the past, but no detachment from it. And yet, when she settled down to write a book about Norman Douglas, soon after his death in 1952, she found that she was, half-reluctantly, writing as much about herself as about her subject.

Looking Back:
Norman Douglas

Although Nancy did not see Norman Douglas again after her visit to Capri in the autumn of 1949, they continued to exchange affectionate letters and postcards. She told him she missed him especially during a solitary trip she made to North Africa early in 1951. She had news of him from mutual friends who went to Capri; he was as spirited as ever, still working, but he and his friends knew his health was failing. In the winter of 1951 Nancy spent some time in England and joined in the Authors World Peace Appeal, a petition signed by hundreds of writers, addressed to the governments of the great powers, protesting against the dangers of nuclear war. Nancy never gave up; she sent this manifesto to Douglas, suggesting he might like to sign it. His reply was as characteristic as her action. "I can't write much as I am quite ill and they must do without my signature. (Did such Appeals *ever* do the slightest good?)" This was the last letter she had from him. Ten weeks later he took an overdose of his prescribed drugs and died. He was eighty-three.

Nancy and Douglas had been friends for twenty-five years; she loved and respected him and appreciated the affectionate mock-strictness with which he would deplore her vagaries, emotional and political, and her restless, disorganized way of life. His basic attitude to life—do what you want, and to hell with everything else—had always appealed to her and influenced her; their friendship contained no hint of censure of each other's idiosyncratic morals. It was the discomfort of her way of life Douglas deplored, not her conduct. With his death she lost one of the few remaining fixed points of her life.

When Nancy started thinking of writing a book on Douglas, she saw it as something more than a book of memories, but she never intended it to be a biography. Two friends of Douglas's, and acquaintances of hers, John Davenport and Constantine Fitzgibbon, had embarked on biographies during Douglas's lifetime that came to nothing, partly because of the awkwardness involved in writing truthfully about Douglas's relationships with preadolescent boys. Nancy had no intention of venturing onto such dangerous ground; she wanted, above all, to write an appreciation of Douglas as a writer. She began rereading all his work and planning a series of critical essays. She also started thinking along familiar lines, of a small-scale anthology, and wrote off to some of their mutual friends for contributions. She then hit upon the curious idea of presenting her personal recollections of Douglas in the form of a long, reminiscent letter from herself to him, perhaps because by so doing, she could maintain her own integrity and his and avoid any hint of revelation. All this made the friends she turned to for approval and advice rather anxious, and it caused problems in particular to John Cullen, then working for Methuen, who found himself Nancy's editor. The progress of the book was stormy, with Nancy obstinately clinging to her more peculiar ideas, desperately needing firm guidance but prickly at any criticism. Also, she did not find it easy to settle down calmly to work. She spent the summer of 1952 at home in La Mothe Fénélon, but she had no domestic help and found concentration difficult. She wrote crossly to Solita Solano: "I now also know what I always suspected; that HOME is not the place for work when home is like this: having to think about getting the damn food."

In the winter of 1952 she set off for Italy, taking her half-written book with her. She spent a few days in Florence to see Harold Acton. She would spend the days writing or revisiting her favorite paintings—she was especially fond of the Benozzo Gozzoli frescoes in the Palazzo Ricciardi—and dine with Acton in the evenings. She told him she was hoping that Steve, her policeman friend from Barbados, might be coming to Europe to join her. They discussed the latest news of Brian Howard, who was struggling to cure himself of drink and drugs and to find a settled home; Acton was nervous at the suggestion that he might choose Italy. Nancy told Acton about her problems in trying to interest publishers in her poetry: " 'I've just written a poem . . .' 'You've done nothing of the kind, you've committed a nuisance!' THAT is the lovely attitude of now."

In December she moved on to Rome, passing through Arezzo where she stopped to look at the Piero della Francesca frescoes and made friends with a prostitute, whom she invited to lunch. She was nervous, aggressive, drinking too much, anxious about her work. She found Rome expensive and unpleasant. She set off for Capri, but she could not settle there either and returned to Rome, where she got in touch with the Johnsons, old friends from the Paris of the 1920s. John Johnson, Arthur's son, remembered her staying in a small hotel near the Pantheon.

"La Signorina Coonard?" said the diminutive maid, turning on her heels, and we followed the silent padding of her slippers on the red tiles of an endless corridor. From a room far away a typewriter could be heard drily rapping. The maid knocked at a door. The typewriter was silent. We were within a tiny cubicle. In a corner, on a wire bed, Nancy Cunard lay propped up by cushions, a slice of elephant tusk moulding her forearm, red coral like spaghetti in tomato sauce spiking out round both wrists. On a pair of bony knees perched a Hermes baby typewriter.

"Darlings, how lovely to see you."

We glanced round the cold little bare room which had only a shaft-like window near the ceiling.

"Let's have a drink, I think there must be a glass somewhere. John, be a darling, there on the washbasin." She opened a brandy flask and we passed the tumbler round. . . . It was not our intention to tire her after her journey, but when we suggested leaving her to her writing, she wouldn't hear of it. She carefully rouged her lips, fluffed out her auburn hair and wound across her high square forehead a multi-coloured fishnet of the kind used for shopping bags and sold in tourist souvenir shops. Thus attired she looked the image of 1925 in 1952. Tall and slim, she preceded us down the corridor, bouncing silently on silent blue and white plimsolls.

Nancy and Arthur Johnson stayed up very late talking about the old days in Paris. The next day was Christmas Day and Nancy arrived at breakfast time to spend it with her friends. When she left in the evening, Arthur Johnson said he would walk her home. He reappeared at eight the next morning.

"And where have you been?" my mother enquired.
"Oh, we ended up at the Hotel de la Ville, where Nancy started talking to some Negro women who do a music hall act. They invited us back to their flat."
"And did you take Nancy home safely?"
"No, I put her on a train to Frascati."
"Frascati. Why Frascati?"
"Because that's where she wanted to go."

Nancy had decided that a small town would be a better place to write than Rome. She stayed several weeks in Frascati, working away on her Douglas book in her hotel or in cafés, drinking plenty of the local wine, making friends with waiters and fruit sellers, buying everybody drinks, talking politics and prices and writing letters to her friends. Géraldine Balayé came to join Nancy at Frascati and remembered her one evening scribbling away at a café table with an old newspaper seller asleep at her side, his head resting on her shoulder. One evening, in a drunken rage after a row over a bill, Nancy got into trouble with the police; she was beginning to react badly to anyone in uniform, and she would let fly, verbally and physically, if she was told to calm down.

On one of her visits to Rome she heard something that put her into a hurt rage with one of her oldest and dearest friends.

Harold Acton, she was told, had asked a mutual friend if Nancy was "really working." However innocently the question was put, the implication offended her. She had already been mildly irritated by the picture of the more chaotic side of the Hours Press that Acton had given in his affectionate and appreciative references to Nancy in his *Memoirs of an Aesthete,* which had appeared in 1948. Now she sat down and wrote him an angry letter.

> Well. I see now there is nothing I can do to remove that long anchored fixation of yours, i.e. I am a sort of little Johnny head in the air "giddy goat," "good-timer," "smart society girl" (only fifty six years old and nearly fifty seven) racketting away like mad, who only went to Frascati anyway because of the wine, and who spends a good deal of the time there sitting up till 5 A.M.—drinking alone in her bedroom scribbling tipsy illegibilities . . .

The quarrel was not serious; Acton replied soothingly, and Nancy bore him no grudge, but it was another small blow to her confidence.

In March she went back to Capri again and this time stayed for a month at the Villa Tuoro discussing her book with Kenneth Macpherson. She sent some of it to Otto Theis in England; he wrote back as gently as possible suggesting that she needed to prune the summaries of Douglas's books, build up the personal recollections and reconsider the structure. John Cullen at Methuen said much the same, and Nancy was not pleased with either of them. She was so indignant that she withdrew the book from Methuen; but she continued to work on it in France that summer, and when she went to England in the autumn and consulted Cullen again, she had in fact made some of the changes he had suggested. But the book was still not what he wanted. After much agitation Roger Senhouse, who had known Nancy for years and was a great friend of her cousin Victor, took it on for Secker and Warburg, who published it in August 1954.

Grand Man: Memories of Norman Douglas is a book of about three hundred pages, of which over half consists of Nancy's "Letter to Norman," containing all her personal recollections of him and their times together. This part of the book is by far the best—funny and evocative. The rest is less successful, attempting as it does to combine scholarly annotation of all Douglas's work with Nancy's own views on it. The structure of the book remained peculiar: a chronology of Douglas's life, with comments, is followed by a list of his books, which is followed by an "Essay on Douglas," divided into three parts: "Of His Ways and Character," "Douglas and Italy," and "Some Thoughts on His Writing." Then comes the "Letter to Norman," again in three parts. Then a section called "Appreciation by Several Friends" (Victor Cunard, Harold Acton, Charles Duff, Arthur Johnson, and Kenneth Macpherson). Cecil Woolf contributed a bibliographical note. Last, there is a thirty-page assessment of all Douglas's books in chronological order, by Nancy.

The book revolves around Nancy's loyal and affectionate feelings for Douglas. "It has seemed to me," she wrote in her introduction,

> that such radiant humanism as Douglas' might be recorded (if properly recorded it can be!) as a corollary to the great pleasure one derives from reading his books. . . . What image arises at the mention of Norman Douglas? That of a master of modern prose—a great individualist—a free spirit—a salubrious iconoclast. Is he thought of sufficiently as the man of profound and perfect taste that he was? As the connoisseur who developed out of the youthful scientist and scholar? . . . The innate feeling in him for things fine and true was always expressed with magnificent and arresting lucidity. The opposite drew his masterly lancet stroke. And there was in him to a phenomenal degree that nature [*sic*] force which is *humor*.

Her descriptions of his books are uniformly eulogistic, peppered with random self-questionings and asides. (The most peculiar of these must be when, in discussing Douglas's attacks on formal education in his *How about Europe,* published in 1929, Nancy remarks: "But oh what a contradiction is here! Why did *he* take such pains in educating a number of boys himself?") The descriptions leave an impression of an enthusiastic amateur critic with a passion for her subject that is beyond analysis or organization.

Nancy kept a scrapbook about the preparation and reception of *Grand Man;* she followed every detail of publicity, as well as reviews, with keen interest. She regarded the reviews she received as poor, but in fact they were on the whole positive and kind, though all the critics deplored the peculiar construction of the book. But the book's real quality—its loving evocation of Douglas as a person—was not missed. One or two critics were fierce; her old friend Raymond Mortimer, on the *Sunday Times,* felt bound to point out that "her book is a hotchpotch and the style is desperately slapdash." But on the whole the verdict followed Harold Nicolson in the *Observer;* "There will be more solid books about Douglas, but none will have quite this freshness."

Nancy made quite frequent and regular visits to England in the 1950s. She would base herself in a small cheap hotel or guest house in the Bloomsbury or Fitzrovia area and make expeditions out of London to stay with or near such friends as the Strachans in Bishops Stortford, the Thornes near Hungerford in Berkshire, or Sylvia Townsend Warner and Valentine Ackland in Dorset. She also stayed regularly with her cousin Victor Cunard, who was now living in a fine old house at Pertenhall in Bedfordshire, which Nancy found a source of security and comfort, and where the flat fenland landscape reminded her of Nevill Holt. In London she would sometimes entertain people at the Café Royal, which at that time was still much as it had been when she used to escape there from Grosvenor Square during the First World War.

In 1950 she met a young American, Charles Burkhart, who was living in England while he worked on a thesis on George Moore. He had written to Nancy to ask for advice. They quickly became friends. Burkhart was still in his

twenties, good-looking, sociable, and amusing; he and
Nancy spent much time together on her visits to London,
meeting in Soho pubs or restaurants, seeking out Moore's
old house in Ebury Street, and sometimes traveling out of
London together to pursue their other great mutual interest,
small antique hunting. "We bought vigorously and as cheaply as possible," Burkhart recalled.

> There was always a grand vernissage in our rooms at night
> after our shopping; the first thing was to clean, with warm
> water and soap, and then to display, as in a museum, except
> that we used the floor or the bed, and Nancy's silk squares, a
> cup made of horn, a papier maché snuff box, a model of a
> pyramid, a ruler made of various marbles, wooden beads from
> the South Seas. . . . We drank more whisky and the room
> grew muggier with smoke and the objects grew lovelier, and
> we congratulated ourselves on them at length and made plans
> for the morrow.

On Boxing Day 1953 Nancy organized a small gathering in
the back bar of the Café Royal, where she introduced Burkhart to her old friend Herman Schrijver; the two men became
great friends. About the same time another friend of Burkhart's was appearing at the Embassy, Swiss Cottage, in the
pre-West End run of Sandy Wilson's 1920s musical, *The Boy
Friend*. Nancy wanted to see it, so Burkhart arranged tickets.
"The night we went we'd had a long day of antiqueing, in
Peckham and elsewhere, and arrived chaotically late and dis-
hevelled, to find that the seats arranged for us were directly
behind Princess Margaret. Nancy paid no attention to royalty,
but some little pained attention to *The Boy Friend*. 'Oh no,
darling, the Twenties weren't like that!' " Afterward, at a
party for the cast "she was several times addressed as 'Lady
Cunard' which, in view of her feelings about her mother, was
at least ironic."

Nancy became so fond of Burkhart that she would call him
her "second American"—Henry Crowder being the first,

though as Burkhart said, "between Crowder and my own second rank a great gulf was fixed."

By 1953 Nancy was once again in touch with Henry Crowder. She had had no idea of his whereabouts and no news of him from 1935 till 1947, when word seems to have reached her that he had come through the war and was back in Washington, and working in the U.S. Bureau of Customs. Among the handful of his letters to her that have survived there are two from the 1950s. One, dated October 1953, sounds as if she had just written to him after a long silence.

> Dear Nancy,
> What a pleasant surprise to hear from you. . . . Life for me here in the USA is now following a set pattern. Pretty dull and monotonous but I am living and going through the motions of life without any special interest. . . .

He refers vaguely to Norman Douglas, whom Nancy was writing about at the time, and appears to answer a question she had put to him about Ezra Pound, who was still in the mental hospital in Washington where he had been sent at the end of the war. "I have a sneaking suspicion that Ezra is putting on an act," wrote Crowder, "and that he is saner than most people." The tone of the letter is calm and detached. It ends: "I do hope you are happy and that you are enjoying yourself. As ever, Henry."

When, much to Nancy's sadness, Burkhart decided to return to the United States, she urged him to try to find Henry Crowder; she felt sure they would like each other, and she longed for proper news of him.

In January 1954, she wrote to Burkhart:

> I do wish you would see Henry! What is in your mind about that? I can't feel that you hesitate; there should be no sense of hesitation, believe you me. Henry is, surely, the same great person he ever was, in looks and deportment, and in rollicking humour too. I wish we could have had Henry in that warm little grill, with our Beaujolais. I keep on thinking you would

like him so much, as he, you. And I should ADORE recent news of him in his Coastguards office—indeed—(what an address!)

Later that year she must have sent Crowder a copy of *Grand Man,* and asked him for details about his job and way of life, and told him that she had asked Burkhart to look him up. He wrote back in November thanking her politely for the book: "I have read the book entirely and find it very interesting and informative. . . ." As for how he was living and what he was doing and thinking: "I am a clerk. I handle all outgoing mail of the Coast Guard headquarters. The job is pleasant and the hours of work agreeable. . . . And as for music I believe I am now a better pianist than I have ever been in my life. I devote a great deal of time to the piano, and singing." As for life in general: "I am not happy, and I am not sad." He gave no details of his personal life, but clearly his life was very different from the old days with Nancy. "As for nightclubs—all that is a thing of the past—never cared much for them anyway." He had not yet heard from Burkhart.

Finally, he described, apparently in answer to Nancy's questions, the changes and improvements in the racial situation in the United States. "Things are changing rapidly here in America along the color line. Great and fundamental changes." He mentioned integration in the army, schools, restaurants, theaters, and cinemas. "A lot remains to be done . . . but we are grateful. . . . Still, I would love to see Europe again."

Nancy's next news of Crowder came from Burkhart, who discovered early in 1955 that Crowder had died. He wrote to Nancy to tell her. On April 24, 1955, she wrote back.

And so Henry is dead—
How extraordinary it is to me to think of the way this news comes to me. . . . Do you know that, otherwise, I should *never* have known? . . . Is this what happens when one asks a friend to look for the long-dead past? Pretty obviously, I

should never have seen him again. He might have been dead from 1935 to 1947, for all I knew. Henry made me . . . and so be it. . . . I don't know WHO could think of words, or even thoughts, with which to thank you for writing about this. I am at a loss. . . . All I feel is a kind of stupor, an amazement that YOU should be in this, dearest Charles. It seems, perhaps, connected with the amazement it was for me to know Henry at all—in Venice in 1928—"Introducing America." That covers it. And then, all the rest. . . . I am finishing the litre of "rough red" to your health, amazed, amazed for ever that you, darling Charles, should be the messenger of Henry. Others have loved me more (?), and I, perhaps, others. No, probably not, for me, has this been true. In any case: Henry made me. I thank him.

Some time later, when Géraldine Balayé was staying with Nancy at La Mothe Fénélon, she observed that Nancy received a letter from America that seemed to have upset her. She did not talk about it at first but went off by herself to play some old blues and jazz records on the record player that Géraldine had lent her. Géraldine glanced at the letter, which was lying on a table. It was from Crowder's wife, to whom he had returned after he left Europe. The letter ended on a proprietary note, saying that the writer was Henry Crowder's only true, loving wife. At first, Nancy seemed sad, almost hurt. Later, she was able to laugh about it.

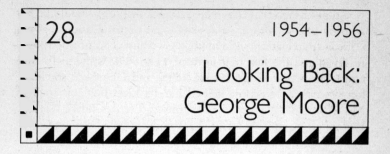

28   1954–1956

Looking Back: George Moore

The summer her book on Norman Douglas was published found Nancy comparatively contented, at home in La Mothe Fénélon, working on a translation into French of Douglas's book about Tunisia, *Fountains in the Sand*. She had a French friend, Gaston Bouchoux, staying with her and helping her with the work. She tackled it with great energy and perfectionism, but when it was finished, despite expressions of interest from several Paris publishers, it was turned down by one after another. However, by this time Nancy had embarked on another book of her own. Encouraged by the praise her personal recollections of Norman Douglas had received, and with the support of Rupert Hart-Davis, who by then had left Cape and set up his own publishing house, she decided to write a book of memories of George Moore. Charles Burkhart also encouraged her, and he was able to help her substantially; in the course of his own research he discovered that Moore's biographer, Joseph Hone, had made copies of several of Moore's letters to Nancy before the war. Nancy was delighted that letters she had thought lost were available after all.

As she started work early in 1955, she remembered how Moore himself had suggested, in 1928, that she should write about her childhood and their mutual affection when she was printing *Peronnik the Fool* at the Hours Press; she felt that she had his blessing in trying to write down everything she could remember about him. At the same time, as with Douglas, she was determined that the mainspring of the book should be her admiration for Moore as a writer; but the realization that her critical appreciations of Douglas's writings had not been well received and the fact that in Rupert Hart-Davis she had a firm editor on whose judgment she relied and for whom she had a long-standing affection helped her to keep her approach to Moore direct and simple. She wrote to Charles Burkhart from Pertenhall in January 1955: "I AM doing a little book on G.M., yes! LITTLE book. If I can get as far as forty thousand words I shall think myself lucky, for I have a sort of small voice in my head saying: 'There is hardly a book's worth in what you have to remember about him.' There will be NO other material in it save what I remember of his ways and of his talk." She was worried, though, that she would find such a book hard to write: "My idea of writing, of really writing and enjoying it, is when the ideas, etc. come so fast that there is barely time to pick up another sheet to put into the typewriter—and then revise, revise, revise. . . . Some kind of fluid is there and oneself merely the transmitter, the canal, THAT is enjoyable."

Nancy wrote her book on George Moore at home in France during the summer of 1955. This time, although she reread many of Moore's writings, she relied almost entirely on her recollections of him, his letters to her and the inspiration she drew from S. C. Harrison's portrait, which she felt was watching her from the wall. As she thought back, she remembered her three locked diaries from 1919 and reread them for the first time.

As it turned out, she need not have worried that she did not have enough to fill a book. She had, after all, known Moore well for over thirty years; and, as the book shows, she had an instinctive confidence in describing his conversation, mannerisms, and the unique relationship that had existed between them. G.M.: Memories of George Moore contains the best of Nancy's writing.

When published, it ran to some two hundred pages, of which just under half described Moore at Nevill Holt during

Nancy's childhood. She showed herself capable, at last, of generous appreciation of her mother; and her account of Moore's role at Nevill Holt shows that she came to realize, looking back, how unconventional a character he was in such a setting. She remembered a middle-aged *enfant terrible* who took a mischievous delight in introducing subversive themes, anti-religious, anti-prudish, anti-imperial, into what was still a highly conventional atmosphere despite Lady Cunard's interest in art and writing. The second half of the book is more fragmented, but there are two clear themes, based on the recurrent topics of conversation between Nancy as a young woman and the aging Moore: her poetry, in which he took a great interest, and her romantic life, which fascinated him. In both areas, her account makes plain, the young Nancy went rather too far for Moore's taste; he was bemused by many of her enthusiasms for modern poetry and painting, and his belief in the varieties and complexities of love stopped short of recognizing homosexual love affairs as anything but unnatural and pathetic. Nancy's account of all this is delicate, affectionate, and funny; she never hits a wrong note.

The one topic she did not feel able to deal with, although she certainly thought of doing so, was the question of whether Moore might have been her father. Nancy kept a letter from Mrs. May Cooper, who had been Moore's nurse at the end of his life, and who wrote to Nancy in 1955 in answer to a request for her memories of Moore. Mrs. Cooper wrote: "He used to talk to me about the most intimate things. I even remember he told me a question you put to him, although sometimes I think he used to imagine things he liked to believe." Nancy wrote underneath this passage: "G.M. saying 'Oh my Lord! Oh my Lord! Never ask your mother that . . .' and then he suddenly burst out laughing but when the great chuckles subsided his mood changed again as quickly, and it was with a sort of dreaminess he said: 'I wish I could think so, Nancy, . . . but I fear not, I fear not.' "

She was also persuaded by Anthony Thorne, to whom she showed a draft of the book, to take out her account of how

Moore, in the mid-1920s, would ask her to let him see her naked and of the occasion when she complied.

Nancy also understandably softened two late episodes with Moore. She included an account of her conversation with him in general terms about color prejudice, but she chose not to discuss Moore's reaction to her affair with Henry Crowder and did not mention how she had written to him to try to explain how she felt. Nor did she reveal how angry she had been at his refusal to let her sell *The Talking Pine*.

By the autumn of 1955 the book was written and Nancy was on the move again. She had decided to write a book on African ivories, a subject that seemed to her far more appropriate and important than a book about herself. She started a notebook, part research notes, part diary; rereading her 1919 diaries had prompted her to try keeping a daily record again. She had a title for her new project, *The Ivory Road*, and planned a series of visits to museums, galleries and private collections of ivories in Europe. She had long wanted to do such a book; she wrote in her diary that it had been in her mind "ever since the end stages of my *Negro* in 1933–1934. A promise to self."

Nancy wrote off confidently to her friends telling them of her new project and set off from La Mothe Fénélon at the end of October. She went first to Toulouse, where she left George Moore's Manet in a bank for safekeeping; she spent a few days in the Grand Hotel, seeing Géraldine Balayé and her Spanish friends.

On November 6 she made a short expedition to Prades to call on Pablo Casals; she spent forty-five minutes with him and found him, at nearly eighty, "round and plump and without a line and looking much younger than I who am not yet sixty." They had an enjoyable talk about Spain: Nancy greatly admired Casals for his decision not to play in Spain while Franco ruled but was horrified to find him reading Orwell's *Homage to Catalonia;* she warned him against what she persisted in regarding as Orwell's "perfidious inaccuracies."

For the next two months Nancy traveled alone by train

through Switzerland, Germany, and Holland, stopping for two or three days in Geneva, Basel, Zurich, Munich, Bern, Frankfurt, Hamburg, Bremen, Cologne, Düsseldorf, Leiden, and Amsterdam. She traveled third class, staying in cheap station hotels. She spent her days visiting collections of ivories and talking to museum directors and collectors, some of whom she had met in the thirties, and her evenings writing notes or letters in her room, or in a bar or restaurant.

Her diary shows that her energy was phenomenal, her spirits mostly high, her interest in her work impressive; but it indicates too that she came to realize that the task she had set herself was colossal, and to wonder, secretly, whether the research needed to do the book properly was really within her capabilities. It also hints that she was lonely. There are notes of interesting conversations with taxi drivers and porters and long talks over drinks with waiters in station buffets; in Hamburg she made friends with a twenty-six-year-old student and stayed up half the night drinking and talking. In Bremen she slipped and fell on "overpolished marble" and bruised herself so badly she could hardly walk. "Did totter down to bar . . . nice talk with page-boy about *wages*." She got into conversation with a middle-aged businessman in the cotton trade and questioned him about German nationalism. The next day she could not get out of bed, so she summoned "the man from the museum" to her room to look through her photographs and papers. A few days later, in Cologne, she was amazingly buoyant again: "a splendid white fog, quite complete, and soon the good sun on the sparkle—as brilliant as Bach's Brandenburg concertos."

In England for the first three months of 1956, Nancy spent most of her time visiting the British Museum and her other favorite collections of African art—in Liverpool and at the small, chaotic Pitt-Rivers museum in Dorset. She kept working away at her ivories book but was never to be able to get her mass of material into shape; there are seven hundred pages of notes and descriptions in her papers and two hundred pages of undigested source material, much of it translated from German.

By the time *G.M.: Memories of George Moore* was published, in September 1956, Nancy was back in France. The reviews were extremely good, especially those by Raymond Mortimer in the *Sunday Times,* Harold Nicholson in the *Observer,* and Anthony Powell in *Punch.* Among the people who wrote to Nancy to congratulate her on the book was Samuel Beckett, whom she had recently seen again after a gap of two decades.

She was immensely pleased when *Waiting for Godot,* which was put on in Paris in 1952, made Beckett almost overnight as famous as she had always thought he should be. She saw the London production in 1955 and liked it so much that she wrote to him suggesting they should meet on her way back to La Mothe in April 1956. He wrote back:

> I am so glad you saw the play and that it wound its way to you, but the French production was more like what I wanted, nastier.
>
> I still have *Negro* snug on my shelves, unlike most of what I once had, and even a few Whoroscopes. . . . I shall not fail to be in Paris round about the 20th and hope you will keep an evening free for me. The dog is duller than ever but its friends know it doesn't mind if they get up and go away. If you are organising subscriptions for your African Ivories, put me down. . . .

After their reunion lunch Beckett wrote to a friend that he found Nancy looking "very wraithy." She wrote to Solita Solano saying that Beckett "looks like a magnificent Mexican sculpture now." During the next few years they corresponded and met occasionally for a meal in London or Paris. Beckett asked after Henry Crowder. (Nancy would have been happy to know that while in hiding in the Auvergne during the war, Beckett used to listen to Crowder's music played on an old upright piano.) When *Godot* was put on in New York in 1956, Beckett wrote to Nancy: "Godot reopening Broadway November with an ALL NEGRO CAST! That's my best news." He also asked her to send him a copy of her poem *Parallax,* if she had one to spare, since he wanted to read it again.

In the autumn of 1956, influenced by the success of the Moore book, the intractability of the ivories project, and in response to the urging of Hart-Davis, Nancy made a serious effort to plan a sort of autobiography. The only way she could bring herself to contemplate it, however, was as a series of portraits of people she had known. The idea of writing anything with herself at the center repelled her; and she was much irritated by the whole idea of the twenties as a fashionable period.

She started a new notebook, a small, cheap blue-covered volume with squared paper. "Begun, this day of rain, Monday, October 29, 1956," it opens "in the café Divan, Gourdon, Lot, France. NOTES for the makings of the MEMORIES BOOK of the Writers and Artists one has known throughout life—Chronologically. ('These fragments have I shored against my ruin.')" She jotted down some possible chapter headings—"Holt and Childhood," "London War Period," "English Twenties," "French Twenties," and made lists of the people who had visited Holt in her childhood.

The next entry in the book is dated December; by then Nancy was back in Rome. She started all over again with a similar plan of chapters and went on to list the people she remembered visiting her flat in the rue le Regrattier in Paris between 1924 and 1927. "It would be a brilliant 'great book of names'—if there had been one," she wrote. "All these things seemed natural to me—to us. Why the smarming over 'The Twenties'? . . . *I do not want to write this book*—as I have clearly told my dear editor. I want to write my book on what I lived—or, if you prefer—'saw' in Spain between August 1936 and the end of 1938. Nobody wants *that,* say editors. . . . *No* autobiography. To what point? Certainly not to mine." Possibly, she thought, she might do it for a huge sum of money, which she certainly needed. Suddenly, after these jerky fragments, comes a passage of great fluency. Nancy realized that she found it almost intolerable to be offered the chance to publish a book she did not want to write, while what she did long to write was rejected.

"A faraway (to me still odious) memory can epitomise my feeling." She described the time when the one thing she wanted was to win the first prize for English literature at Miss Woolf's School, but instead she won two other prizes.

> When you have wanted something, and thought you'd "worked" for it, and then been granted two firsts—in something else. *No.* That is not good enough for me. One wants one's love—and then there appear two other lovers entirely. How odious it is to think of. . . . I knew already then, it seems, that if you don't get what you *want*—(and know you have worked for) *nothing else counts*. Sure, it could count if you are a male, and go into a career—But I am not a male, and I have no career.

Another stumbling block was that Nancy could not distance herself from the past and her friends. To do so seemed like a betrayal of the emotions and ideas they had shared. Nancy never cared for looking back in private, let alone for public consumption. "How much rather would I see (fleetingly, and some of them less fleetingly) the bearers of these names—objects of curiosity to some, of 'virtue' to others—the dead and the alive" she wrote. "I do not want to write this but I will do my best."

As well as the notebook Nancy kept notes and jottings for her memoirs on odd scraps of paper, which she put into a large brown envelope entitled "You, Me and Yesterday." She attempted to write something about the early days of Surrealism, but her thoughts came out jumbled and inconclusive and she abandoned it. One of the only sections she actually wrote was four or five pages about Michael Arlen. She did make a few poignant, revealing notes about herself:

> When of SELF writing: Re the three main things.
>
> 1 Equality of races.
> 2 Of sexes.
> 3 Of classes.

> I am in accord with all countries and all individuals who feel,
> and act, as I do on this score.

Slowly, over the next few years, Nancy persevered, writing separate short essays on some of her writer and artist friends. Eventually, in 1959, she sent a draft to Rupert Hart-Davis, but he felt he had no choice but to tell her it would not do; it was fragmented, lacked direction, and was not sufficiently personal and lively. Depressed and angry, Nancy put the material to one side.

In December 1956, in Rome, a chance encounter brought her intractable past vividly before her. She bumped into Iris Tree, whom she had not seen for over twenty years. They had lunch together in a *trattoria,* filling in the huge gaps of their knowledge of each other's doings, both moved to find their mutual affection still strong. Iris Tree wrote to Lady Diana Cooper about the meeting:

"Seeing Nancy again was sweet but rather terrible—the nymph I remember was still there but concealed, as it were like a mermaid in its scales." Nancy talked confidently to Iris about the ivories book, and about her house in France; but later Iris felt that something was wrong. "I gathered that her days there were lonely, somehow malevolent, bereft of surrounding sympathy or love." They met several times in Rome, and a friend of Iris Tree's, Milton Gendel, who met Nancy with her, was struck by how much they had in common. Both were natural performers, high bohemian in style, original and irrepressible, with a taste for wine and an eye for handsome young waiters. He was impressed by Nancy's brilliant talk, especially about Africa and black culture; and he was mesmerized when a chance remark led her to flare up into an impassioned denunciation of her mother. Nancy and Iris Tree made a plan to meet on New Year's Eve and see 1957 in together, but Iris Tree missed their rendezvous, which she always regretted. They did not meet again.

About this time, when Nancy was entering her sixties,

there are many references in her letters and notes to what was beginning to seem like a semi-permanent state of malaise, if not of actual illness, part physical, part psychological. She had frequently felt ill or exhausted, but this was different; she had started to feel a kind of depression that was new to her. "I am most dispirited," she wrote to Solita Solano. "A thing of the private fibre, due to WHAT? . . . with me it is the ever-recurrent 'nerves' of a life time (by now), or melancholia." She told Solita that she had recently been to Andorra to see a doctor she trusted, who had told her her physical condition was all right, but that her nerves were in a bad state. Nancy suggested an explanation: "It all comes, *as ever,* from those operations in 1921—gland deficiency of some kind." She took tonics and tranquilizers, but nothing really worked. Nancy's nature had always been highly strung and volatile, but her resilience and stamina had also been phenomenal; even when she was very drunk, she had not felt she was losing control. Now she began to wonder.

"When there are certain kinds of crises," she wrote to Solita Solano, "they get into one and something gets a tremble with more rage and indignation than usual, and with apprehension. . . . I am in such a state at the moment."

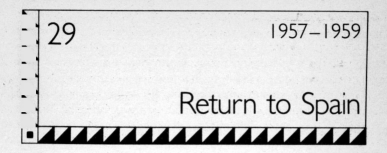

Return to Spain

By the late 1950s an ominous pattern marked Nancy's life. Her health, physical and psychological, was increasingly precarious; but she was by this time more than ever incapable of taking the kind of precautions that might have warded off disaster. Everything she needed, she did not have: her writing was not going well, she saw her real friends infrequently, she ate too little and smoked and drank too much, and she refused to stay in one place and take care of herself. The times she spent at home in La Mothe Fénélon could still be calm and restorative, especially when she had old friends to stay with her; and in London, too, where there were people to look after her, things went fairly well, for a while. But when the visitors went home from France and the weather got colder, and when she had already used up the three months that was all the tax regulations allowed her to spend in England, she would take off, usually alone, and more often than not, to Spain. In her vulnerable state—without a companion except those she picked up along the way, feeling as she did about the Franco regime and spending much of her time drinking in bars and restaurants—it was almost inevitable that she would get into trouble. Possibly, in her personal and political frustration, trouble was what she was seeking.

Not every trip to Spain went badly, however; in the summer of 1957 she met Charles Burkhart and another American friend, Bill Rose, an English professor and Wyndham Lewis scholar, in Madrid; she visited Toledo with them, pointing out civil war battlefields she remembered on the way. Burkhart remembers that despite the intense heat and the evident fact that Nancy was far from well, the expedition was exhilarating.

But the following year, when she went off alone to mainland Spain after a visit to her old friend the painter Jean Guérin in Majorca, things began to go wrong. In Madrid she met a young Spanish photographer of thirty-one; she decided that he was the collaborator and companion she needed for her long-projected book on Spain. They spent some weeks together traveling around the country. Once Nancy was arrested and detained by the police for five hours after causing a disturbance on a train. She drew attention to herself with fierce political arguments in a bar in Barcelona. When they returned to Madrid, the young man was arrested and Nancy was told that her tourist visa, which had almost expired, would not be renewed. She was also told her friend had a criminal record, which she did not believe, though she knew he had been arrested once for possessing a firearm. She flew back to Majorca in a state of fury; the press came to hear of the affair, and stories full of innuendo started to appear in the English newspapers.

"Miss Nancy Cunard, authoress and reputed millionairess, aged 62, had tears of anger in her eyes," one *Daily Mail* story opened.

> "They have refused me a visa!" she cried. "It's monstrous! How can they throw me out when all I did was try to get an innocent man released from prison?"
>
> The ordeal, which has left her looking pale and frail and very indignant, concerns a 31 year old Spanish photographer.
>
> "Brilliant, strange, almost Napoleonic" is how Miss Cunard describes him. . . .
>
> All my questions on reports that they were to have got married were skilfully parried. . . .
>
> She has written to prominent people both here and in England, including an MP. . . .
>
> Her mood suddenly changed. "Let's forget the sordidness. I'll read you some of my poetry." She did. For half an hour at

the airport bar the waiters and I listened to her Spanish and English poems. Then Miss Cunard and I drove into Palma. In search of another photographer.

By the time Nancy reached London in the winter of 1958, she was in a bad way. Luckily, this time she did not have to stay in a hotel; the Thornes had bought a house in Maida Vale, overlooking the canal, with a separate furnished flat that Nancy insisted on taking. "Useless to tell her that the place needed redecorating and that one was longing to get rid of the appalling furniture—no, she must have the flat *at once,* and all I had time to do was to reorganise the heating arrangements, to make sure that those bird bones would be warmed in winter," recalled Thorne. Some of Nancy's acquaintances were not so generous. "People jeered at me. Imagine taking Nancy on as a tenant. You'll regret that, won't you?" Almost at once she became really ill, with blood poisoning from a septic foot, bronchitis, and general nervous collapse. One doctor told the Thornes she was seriously undernourished; but she would not, or could not, eat the food they prepared for her. She detested being made a fuss of, but she did admit she felt dreadful.

Her friends hoped she would not go back to Spain; but she did. In Majorca in 1959 a man she had met briefly the year before, Clyde Robinson, remembered her making great friends with a Palma taxi driver, with whom she would disappear on secret business; then she went to Valencia, talking of organizing protests and raising funds for political prisoners in Franco's jails. After she left, she wrote to Robinson: "When the great day comes, it will be good to be in Spain. I kept on having the feeling when in Madrid last year that everything was perfectly ready for the change, only the spark to set it off was missing. But it is bound to come."

Nancy's collapse was a great deal more imminent than Franco's. In the spring of 1960 she was expelled from Spain, after being jailed for several days in Valencia and Palma. According to a rather incoherent letter she later wrote to Robinson, this was through "no fault or action of mine." She had another young man in tow, this time a twenty-seven-year-old blacksmith called Tomás, but she had to leave Spain without him. She told Robinson she then traveled through southern France "surrounded by Fascism" to Geneva, where she was again in trouble after she threw her passport from table to table in a café and then out of the window. In France on her way to England she was again arrested and badly bruised in a fight with the police, who she claimed knocked her down and kicked her.

She arrived in London on April 20, 1960. The next few weeks were a nightmare for Nancy and her friends. Her control had gone and her mind was cracking. Her tendency to paranoia swelled to insanity. Anyone who tried to calm or restrain her became a fascist spy, especially if they were in uniform. Aggressive, violent, sometimes incoherent, drinking constantly, she roamed London insulting policemen, making sexual propositions to strangers, terrifying the people who would have liked to look after her. Anthony Thorne was away, but he has described what happened when Nancy arrived at their house and found Mrs. Thorne in.

The bell rang after midnight and there was Nancy having a violent argument with a taximan. She had lost her money somewhere and her baggage too—suitcases full of valuable ivories scattered over the stations of London. It was a weekend, and my wife had just enough money to pay the fare, but no tip. "No tip anyway," shouted Nancy. "He tried to have an affair with me, he even pushed my head under the wheel."

She came in with a paper bag full of ham sandwiches which, refusing the offer of other food, she then ate, hurling the crusts into the empty fireplace. At one point she picked up a Fornasetti ashtray, demanding: "Is this supposed to be pretty?" and was about to hurl it after the crusts when my wife stopped her. She had to get Nancy to bed before they were both out of their minds.

"No sheets!" protested Nancy as clean ones were produced. "If you sleep in this bed," my wife said firmly, "you will have sheets." Nancy gave way.

Restless in another bedroom my wife contemplated the possibility of the house being burnt down over her head. (It could have happened, for not long afterwards Nancy showed the familiar and expected signs of incendiarism and on one occasion, in another flat, set fire to her clothes, declaring: "I shan't need these any more!")

In the morning Nancy telephoned to ask who else would give her a roof, intending to make a round of visits in London—and it is interesting to remember the distinguished friends who found reasons why they could not see her.

The truth about Nancy's condition was bad enough, but the rumors that spread about her were even worse. She was said to be carrying explosives acquired on behalf of Spanish revolutionaries; one tale had her leaving a taxi in flames after blasting it with a flamethrower she had kept since the civil war. In another version she set fire to a policeman. Then there were the sexual tidbits: She was said to have thrown her skirt up in a restaurant to reveal that she was naked underneath; and it was rumored that when an elderly porter showed her to a hotel room, she tried to force him to sleep with her.

It does seem as though Nancy's sexuality was as deranged as her mind at this time. When, early in May, she was finally arrested in the King's Road, it was on charges of soliciting followed by drunk and disorderly behavior. She fought the police and threw her shoes at the magistrate, who sent her to Holloway Prison on remand for a medical report.

The authorities had trouble finding friends or relations who would or could take responsibility for her. Her cousin Victor was in London staying at the Bath Club—where Nancy had also made a drunken scene—but his own health was failing, and he was not up to taking charge. The medical report on Nancy from Holloway was unequivocal. She was found to be suffering from a mental disorder aggravated by alcohol; she was probably an alcoholic and certainly certifiable as incompetent. The medical officer described her as incoherent in conversation, elated, verbally aggressive, incapable of looking after herself physically or of managing her own affairs. Her physical condition was poor; she was undernourished and anemic. She was said to be in urgent need of treatment in a psychiatric hospital but in no fit state to make the decision for herself.

The magistrate then ordered Nancy to be moved from Holloway to an East End hospital, Saint Clements, Bow Road. She was there for ten days while certification was being organized. By this time many of her friends had been alerted; Nancy wrote a series of pathetic letters, many of them virtually illegible scrawls, all of them proclaiming her conviction that she had been incarcerated by fascist reactionaries, in league with the CIA and the Home Office. She also wrote to the home secretary, to the prime minister, to Khrushchev, asking them to get her out. Anthony Thorne visited her in Saint Clements.

> It was a dismal place . . . doors kept firmly open . . . and a shuffling procession of people who giggled momentarily, staring at one another.
>
> There was Nancy, lying across the coverlet of her bed, fully dressed and with the usual bandeau across her forehead . . . . There was a negro with her, a young man just arrived from Ghana. Hearing somehow that Nancy was in hospital he had come to see her for the first time, bringing flowers and a photograph of himself. It was gradually beginning to dawn on him what kind of a hospital this was, and I admired the coolness and good sense with which he came to accept the situation. But alas, when she demanded some matches he gave them to her, and she tucked them one by one into the hem of her skirt, like a refugee hiding jewels, and with an expression of cunning that I had never seen on her face before.

She placed his photograph facing out from her room. "There is no point in having a photograph," she said, "unless everybody can enjoy it."

Finally Nancy was certified insane; Roger Senhouse signed the order on behalf of Victor Cunard. Her affairs were placed in the hands of the official solicitor. She was then transferred from the East End hospital to a less depressing institution outside London, Holloway Sanatorium, Virginia Water. She was to remain there for nearly four months.

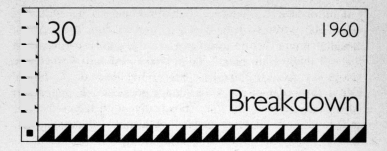

Breakdown

Although it was evident that Nancy had had a mental break-down, several of her friends could not bring themselves to agree that it had been necessary to certify her and take over the management of her affairs. "I never for a moment thought she was insane," wrote Charles Burkhart later, "though she did insane things; maddened, but not mad." To John Banting, one of her symptoms, that she soaked her clothes in the bath, was explained by her preference for clothes with the stiffening removed, and as for her " 'Persecution Mania'—Anyone with her past activities would be a fool not to realise a possibility of persecution even in free England." Louise Theis wrote to the doctors at Holloway Sanatorium after visiting Nancy there early in July: "She was her usual self, except, as is natural with age, more individualistic and contemptuous of authority than ever. But NOT insane! She feels the world has been against her, as indeed it was throughout all her childhood and youth. . . . it was one of the most hideous shocks of my life when I learned she had become a certified lunatic."

Others, just as devoted to Nancy, felt differently. Raymond Mortimer wrote sadly to Janet Flanner at the end of June: "I fear that she is profoundly insane."

Far from wanting to hide her plight from her friends, Nancy continued to write to them from Holloway Sanatorium and to protest against the injustice, as she saw it, of her detention. None of these letters is as incoherent or illegible as those from Saint Clements, but for several weeks they were just as obsessive. "Drink . . . has nothing to do with my case," she wrote to Janet Flanner, "but Fascism has." And a few days later: "Damn Spain and all its doings. It is because of that—(I *think*) I am here." To Sylvia Townsend Warner, she wrote that her confinement "comes by order of the Home Office (by order of the USA) and it goes back, I suppose, to *Negro* and the Spanish War." Gradually, with rest, sedatives, and food and vitamins instead of alcohol to sustain her, Nancy began to improve. Sylvia Townsend Warner heard from the doctors halfway through July that Nancy had made good progress.

From her letters it looks as if the obsession about a fascist plot was superseded by an obsession about Tomás, the young Spaniard she had picked up on her last trip to Spain. He had made his way to France, and by early in July Nancy was in touch with him, urging him to come to her in England, and giving him the names of people in Paris who might help him. She wrote to Janet Flanner, saying "I want him here, with me, as close as can be, FOR EVER" and begging her to lend him money. She told Tomás to go to see Aragon, who would help him to get to England. Her letters at this time are coherent enough, but they reveal a painfully ravaged mind, in which Tomás, the Spanish civil war, and her illness all form part of a nightmare crisis of self-evaluation.

On July 19, 1960, she wrote Janet Flanner a long letter that is the most revealing thing she ever wrote about herself, ill or well, drunk or sober. "To think that it all began today in 1936," she began. "In Spain—I wish I'd seen it—I wish I'd had my fill of blood and bullets before being killed under fire the morning of the day Toledo fell, October 28th 1936. . . . I wish T [Tomás] were 67 not 27, because *then* he would understand better—understand his own country, and me." She went on to write about Angel Goded, feeling that at least something good had come out of her association with Spain: "I . . . the cause of Angel's rich new life in Mexico as father of 6 children who (he tells me) have been taught to bless my name (I wonder what Angel would think of my case? He would recognise it for what it is—unavowedly political—and not drink)."

Then she started to wonder about love, and whether she had ever felt the kind of love for any man that could override all other considerations. "There never was, and there never will be a man of that kind for me—so not being one who wants to go through life entirely alone in every sense and at every hour I have *loathed* my life, all of it, and spit on it, at present, for the future and in the past." But perhaps, after all, certain things had been worthwhile. She recalled *Negro* with pride, and the rescue of Angel and the others from the camps, and her collection of ivory bracelets. But "I do not count the Hours Press; I don't think it was important." And as for poetry—perhaps just a very few lines.

She wondered about the men who had cared for her.

> I don't think anyone has ever loved me save Louis [Aragon]— who did so, I think, entirely all the time we were together. . . . I, on the other hand have truly and entirely loved many. Henry, and Morris, and Louis . . . and several more. So much for love. As you remember Louis line "Il n'y a pas d'amour sans amour malheureux." It seems incontrovertible for me—and perhaps for him. . . .
>
> What else have I been or done that was worthwhile?—Oh for 1 month I wrote the truth about the exodus into France from Spain in 1939.

Finally, she confronts her present situation. "Everything here continues to be absolutely hellish. A convicted prisoner has at least knowledge of the length of his sentence. . . . Not so I. *I am accused of nothing.* . . . It will go down, falsely that NC was a convicted lunatic. . . . The stigma will remain. I do not care what *anyone* thinks, but I do care if this gets in the way of whatever I may yet want to do before I die."

It was not easy for Nancy's friends to know what to do about Tomás. Those who met him were not impressed; he struck them as stupid and venal. For Nancy's sake they kept him happy and in Paris for the time being; the effect on her could have been terrible had she heard from him that her friends were rejecting him. Equally, no one thought it would do her any good if he did turn up in England while she was in the sanatorium. Both Janet Flanner and Aragon lent him money and listened to his hard luck stories when he came back for more. On one occasion he arrived at Aragon's house when only Elsa Triolet was there; since she spoke no Spanish and he no French, communication was impossible. She remembered that Pablo Neruda was in Paris, and she rang him to ask for help; he came over immediately.

Nancy's friends in England did what they could to support and reassure her while she was in Holloway Sanatorium. They visited her, wrote her loving letters, sent her books and anything she asked for; they kept in touch with the doctors and lawyers dealing with Nancy's case in order to make it plain that there were people who cared enough about her to keep a close eye on what happened next so that there would be no question of her being forgotten. In England that was about as far as anyone felt able to go. But in France a more dramatic gesture of solidarity was arranged.

Louis Aragon had heard about Nancy's plight soon after the crisis occurred. He was moved and horrified by the news; and he wrote Nancy a series of affectionate letters, as did Elsa Triolet. Aragon received a number of letters from Nancy, complaining about the injustice being done to her; to some extent, Aragon agreed with her. Her complaint, that she was in effect being held prisoner indefinitely and had been unfairly deprived of her rights, seemed to him not unreasonable. He ascribed her breakdown mainly to alcohol and considered it a temporary illness from which she would recover when she stopped drinking.

The issue for July 24, 1960, of *Les Lettres Françaises,* the communist weekly newspaper edited by Aragon, carried a front-page story headlined: "A Poem by Nancy Cunard; For Life?" "Some strange news has come to us from London," it began, "and a poem. Nancy Cunard is known in France. She has lived here for most of her life, and later on it will not be possible to write the intellectual history of part of this century without discussing her."

The story—which was probably written not by Aragon but by Georges Sadoul, who was on the staff of the paper—described Nancy's career; mentioned her poetry, *Negro,* the Spanish civil war, her support for the French resistance, and *Poems for France;* and emphasized the break Nancy had made with the society in which she had been brought up. "And now," it went on,

> the news has also reached us that in London, in obscure circumstances, Nancy Cunard has been shut up and "certified insane" which, strangely enough in the country of Habeas Corpus, may turn out to be equivalent to a life sentence. If one goes by her letters, and by this poem recently received, everything fits into the overall pattern of a generous life, nothing adds up to mental breakdown. Let it be known in England that Nancy Cunard is not, as she believes, "as alone in the world as a newborn baby" but that in France, in Spain, in Italy, in all South America . . . in all the black world, in America, in Africa, there are men and women who have not forgotten her, and who are waiting to hear the justification for such arbitrary procedures.

The article went on to compare Nancy with other "poets and great spirits" who had suffered in a similar way, mentioning Baudelaire, Strindberg and Nietzsche. "It must be said that, in the case of Nancy Cunard, incarceration falls rather too neatly into place, explaining a life that has been upsetting for received ideas, giving comfort to a society that can now think reassuringly to itself that in the end, it was all a matter of psychiatry."

Finally: "It is not for us to determine the question. But opinion demands to be informed. And seriously. One cannot make a woman like Nancy Cunard disappear, in the middle of the twentieth century, without explanations. And *for life.*"

"All for Life" was the title of the poem, dated Palma, Majorca, February 1960, and printed alongside the article. Not one of Nancy's best, it is a jerky, angry piece proclaiming the writer's belief in the resistance spirit in France despite recent revelations about the other side of the picture. Naturally, Nancy was delighted with the article; she wrote to Aragon to thank him and to tell him that she thought she noticed improvements immediately in the way she was treated.

In the United States Walter Lowenfels also took up Nancy's cause. He wrote an open letter that he sent to friends and sympathizers urging them to write to Nancy and to officials in England and America on her behalf. His account is taken almost entirely from the *Lettres Françaises* article. "Certain circles in England always thought Nancy was crazy, not only for deserting society for poetry but for her love of Negro culture, and what she had done to make it better known and appreciated," he wrote. He recalled how he had heard Nancy say thirty years before in Paris that it was the Foreign Office that had stopped her and Henry Crowder from going to Africa together. The last letter he had had from Nancy mentioned that she was going to Spain in the winter of 1960: "What happened to her in Spain? Everyone knows on which side Nancy's voice was always heard."

It seems plain why Aragon arranged and published the article; he felt that Nancy would be helped by a demonstration of loyalty and affection and that the more pressure for her release, the sooner it would come. One may wonder, however, whether it was really either kind or constructive to give any hint of credence to Nancy's paranoia; it is hard to believe that her hospitalization had more to do with her past activities than with her recent drunken vagaries and mental collapse.

And yet there was clearly a connection between Nancy's rebellious past and her breakdown. Nancy, in 1960, was not a sane woman unjustly certified and institutionalized for political reasons; nor was she someone suddenly stricken with a mental illness that had no relation to her past history. Nancy since girlhood had combined remarkable physical and mental resilience with a tendency to undergo sudden flareups of bodily or nervous ailments. She had spent her considerable resources of energy with abandon all her life, and alcohol became more and more a necessary stimulant and prop to her; she probably literally could not do without it for at least thirty years before her breakdown. At times she probably took other drugs, although there is no evidence that she was ever a habitual drug user. During the postwar years, however, one or two of her friends (Charles Burkhart and Cecily Mackworth among them) occasionally noticed suspicious signs. She had always lived under pressure: from her own nature, the strains she chose to experience, and the palliatives—drink and sex—that she needed. She certainly never regretted the break she made with her mother and her mother's world in 1930–1931, but it was profoundly traumatic; the sense she had then of being persecuted and spied on may have been exaggerated, but it was based on actual events. Nancy was not, in fact, paranoid for no reason; there were times when her activities were of interest to the authorities, especially those concerned with communist conspiracy and anticolonial agitation, and she was kept under observation from time to time; the detectives in Normandy after the war were not figments of her imagination. She knew what prison was like.

It is also relevant that phrases like "she must be mad" had been constantly on the lips of Nancy's mother and her circle from the time when Nancy first began to show signs of wanting to go her own way. Later there were plenty of people—some of whom purported to be Nancy's friends—who really believed that it was a sign of insanity to have a black lover and advertise the fact, or to translate French communist poets and publish the results in London magazines. Nearly always it was the openness—or exhibitionism, some would say—of Nancy's behavior that provoked the accusations of insanity; plenty of people loathe one of their parents, but very few publish a pamphlet attacking their mother in print.

Some recent studies have suggested that women who refuse to conform to a gentle, passive, dependent female stereotype may be especially vulnerable to breakdowns and to diagnoses of insanity. The implication is that society is deeply threatened by such women, who therefore experience hostilities and pressures that are likely to make them react badly or behave in a peculiar manner, and then they are penalized for being different. The fact that Nancy punished herself, most obviously through drink, does not make the relevance of this suggestion to her case less interesting. It cannot be the whole answer, but it may be a part of one.

In many ways Nancy's behavior had not been "normal" for thirty years at least before she broke down. The qualities that made her remarkable—her beauty, intelligence, energy, and courage—had a dark counterpoint. Her drinking, her promiscuity, her aggression, her restlessness had puzzled and frightened the people she cared for most and who cared deeply for her. And she did not slow down as she grew older; the vagaries of a woman of sixty are bound to be less comprehensible and excusable, if excuses are called for, than those of a woman of thirty.

Most of all, perhaps, Nancy could be said to have paid a high price for her freedom from a permanent emotional bond with another person. There were many people who loved her and a few who were able to stay with her in France or have her to stay with them for long enough to calm her down and soothe her physical and emotional aggravations. But they all had homes and ties of their own; there was always a limit. Nancy's letters of the late 1950s and early 1960s are full of outbursts against the remoteness and inconvenience of La Mothe Fénélon and of plans for somehow establishing a base of her own in England. At one time she was thinking of renting a room in a house her cousin Victor might buy; another time it was sharing a flat with Irene Rathbone. Something always went wrong with these plans; and one suspects that behind the mutual regrets lay mutual nervousness. Nancy, by this time, was not easy to live with; she must have known it. She had become, as Sybille Bedford puts it, "the friend one loved, whose arrival one often dreaded."

Slowly, Nancy got better. In July she was able to go out for the day with visitors. Raymond Mortimer and Roger Senhouse took her on a visit to Eton College Chapel. Mortimer wrote afterward to Janet Flanner: "She kept complaining that her presence in a mental hospital was an outrage. A careless observer might easily have believed this to be true, for she talked no obvious nonsense, was never incoherent or frantic, except that almost her first words were 'America has had me sent here.' " Otherwise she was calm and affectionate, and she did not seem to mind the sanatorium as much as he would have expected. "She was the old buoyant, responsive Nancy, delighting in details of the mediaeval frescoes and modern stained glass." The sanatorium itself was not a very cheerful place. Mortimer described it as "a preposterous vast 1870s-ish building in the Loire Château style, a depressing labyrinth with gloomy women muttering to themselves or obsessively picking up tiny fragments on the floor." Other visitors too found Nancy remarkably unaffected by her surroundings, her natural good manners quite restored as she offered them tea and thanked them for their presents of flowers or books. Gradually, her insistence on the plot behind her detention turned into a more rational anxiety about how, having been certified incompetent, she was to get out and resume control over her life.

She kept up a stream of letters, and it is hard to believe that a letter such as one she wrote to William Plomer on July 23 was written by someone certifiably insane. Plomer, who although never a close friend, had known Nancy quite well in the early 1930s and had contributed a poem to *Negro*, sent her a copy of his collected poems. She wrote to thank him and to say how much she like the poems, and to describe her situation.

> I moulder on here. At least doctors and nurses and staff laugh at the "certified insane" business; they know better, for there really are some honest-to-god goofies here, poor bitches. One groans night-long and nips off the heads of pretty flowers and eats them. . . . Another one thinks she is a Countess, and is humoured. She goes about with *bits* of newspapers, pretending to read them. . . . Another one, "the fat girl" screams like

a sedge bird—you never heard such a wail of a cry. . . .
Another one . . . I will not weary you further; nothing interesting, as you see. To find again the real world is to open your
poems. . . .

. . . Back to me a minute. I find from John Banting that he
too was "certified insane" when very young, and de-certified
with the greatest ease.

I find from Charles Burkhart that he knows some man who
has been certified insane *four times*. So that makes me feel better, but I really am in the depths of sadness; the doctor here has
the say of all the wretched people and he is a beastly man, one
of those blessed with total lack of understanding where I am
concerned. I don't know how much longer I have to stay here.

Early in August Nancy was told that she could leave Holloway for weekends to stay with friends, and that if she continued to improve, she could expect to be allowed to leave permanently in three or four weeks' time. She spent a weekend
with John Banting in London, and one with the Theises in
Sussex. On August 17 she wrote a sad, tired letter to Solita
Solano: "The doctors simply will not tell me when I can
expect to leave." She had been expecting Tomás to arrive in
England, but now she was resigned to his awaiting her in
Paris. "On the whole I hope he does not come here."

At the end of August Nancy had another outing with Banting;
they went to a big Picasso exhibition at the Tate Gallery and to
see the Ballet Africain, both of which Nancy adored. The doctors had told her that she could leave in about two weeks, provided she stayed with friends. The Theises offered to have her to
stay with them in their cottage at Battle, in Sussex.

Before she left the sanatorium Nancy had another severe
blow. Her cousin Victor, who had returned to his home in
Venice during the summer far from well, died there on August
28. At least one close friend of his, Nancy Mitford, believed
that the strain of Nancy's collapse and the heartrending letters
she wrote him from the sanatorium hastened his death. Nancy
was stricken by the news. Victor had been her friend since
childhood; although he was often unnerved by her behavior

and dreaded being involved in her battles, he was patient, affectionate, and a source of comfort and protection.

Nancy left the sanatorium on September 10. She was told that in due course, if all went well and she continued to satisfy the doctors, she would be able to approach the official solicitor for the discharge of his responsibilities and the return of her passport. She was prescribed Tofranil and Librium—both antidepressant drugs—and advised to keep off alcohol. She went straight to the Theises, whose affection and confidence were vital to her recovery.

"She arrived wearing an olive green patterned chemise, cheap thick stockings, pale cream moccasins," Louise Theis remembered. "She had taken in the sides of her red suit by herself, but the slit was too far up the back, and the olive green chemise showed beneath the narrow skirt. She had no nightgown. She wore no hat, but carried a number of scarves for head and neck, one a brilliant orange red made of veil-like material from Woolworths. As always she carried a typewriter (new), lots of books, letters and other papers."

For the next three months, Nancy stayed quietly with the Theises, enjoying rest and good food and conversation and, with Louise's help, fitting herself out with new clothes made locally, a new suitcase, fur-lined boots, and a fine new set of false teeth. The Theises' devotion and loyalty to Nancy was all the more striking because they were both getting on in years; Louise was seventy-five and Otto eighty.

Louise Theis's love and admiration for Nancy did not blind her to her faults, and her confidence in Nancy's recovery and sanity did not prevent her feeling anxious about the future. "How I have worked to open her eyes to certain things about which she harbors the deadliest illusions," Louise Theis wrote to John Banting during Nancy's stay.

I thought, inspired, when she was coming here, that I would reform her! I've worked daily with every ounce of brain I still possess to rid her of some of her "spoiled girl" attitudes, her intolerance, her hate—which springs up like a viper in the innocent grass. I think I have made some impression. But I fear it will all go, because her memory is so bad, and she lives so much in the instant. She is one of the few I love with my whole heart and soul, and I feel bitterly disappointed that I have not been able to do more for her.

She has slept well, been warm and free and beloved here, and there has never been a shadow of a shadow between us. . . . She is well, so far as she can ever be well. . . . Sometimes I think she really has learned that she must keep out of Holloway. . . . I do believe, unless her memory lets her down that she will be careful.

Nancy was still corresponding with Aragon. On September 22 *Les Lettres Françaises* carried a short news story that simply said that readers would be happy to learn that Nancy Cunard, whose fate had given cause for anxiety recently, had been released from the hospital. It seems from a letter from Aragon that Nancy had anticipated a more triumphant or vindicatory announcement.

By this time, with Nancy safely out of hospital, Aragon felt able to be somewhat more open about Tomás, who had been to see him again, claiming that the British consul in Paris had dissuaded him from going over to England and asking for more money because he had had to spend what he had been given so far on living expenses. He told Aragon that he wanted to stay in Paris and study French at the Sorbonne and that meanwhile he thought he had found a job in a restaurant. Aragon made enquiries and found that the "restaurant" was a low homosexual bar. He had given Tomás a little money, but as he wrote to Nancy: "This cannot go much further, What is to be done?" Another difficulty was that Tomás insisted that he had no interest in politics and no republican sympathies, which made it, Aragon tactfully pointed out, difficult for him to put Tomás in touch with the people he knew who could help him.

In November the doctor in Battle gave Nancy the necessary certificate stating that he had treated her for several weeks and found her perfectly competent to handle her own affairs. According to Louise Theis, the official solicitor was a model of tact and kindness in his dealings with Nancy, though she remained angry with the lawyers and friends who had put her in his charge in the first place. By mid-December, Nancy was ready to leave Battle. The Theises' remarkable goodness and Nancy's own qualities had made her stay there as successful as it could have been; but they were exhausted. "She is the best possible guest," Louise Theis wrote to Banting, "a miracle of guestmanship—but I need peace and aloneness for a while. I don't think I could have done this for anybody but Nancy. And she has been an angel of tact and understanding. It has been a wonderful experience having her in these peculiar circumstances."

Shortly afterward Nancy left for London. Two or three days later she crossed to France. She went to Paris and found Tomás. They went back to La Mothe Fénélon together.

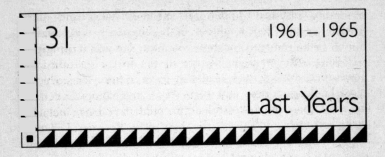

There was not a trace of fear or self-pity in Nancy's nature.
She put her mental breakdown firmly behind her; indeed, she
hardly ever referred to it afterward at all, except to complain
bitterly when she discovered that her enforced residence in
England during 1960 had made her liable for extra taxes. She
swore she would never set foot in the country again. The next
few years had black patches; overall, they could be regarded
as pitiful, even tragic. And yet somehow Nancy's indomitable
spirit was more evident than ever before.

Tomás stayed at La Mothe Fénélon with Nancy until July.
At first she kept up a brave front, telling her friends they were
working together at his writing; she typed stories and the
beginnings of a novel to his dictation. She tried to interest
publishers in Paris and London in his works without success;
the handful of notes and postcards from him that survived in
her papers suggests he was barely literate. By the summer he
had decided to return to Spain. After he had gone, Nancy
confessed to Solita Solano that she was relieved to be rid of
him. "Everything has been horrible to me this year. . . . T,
thank god, went back to Spain. He was beastly here, utterly
different (I hear you laugh) and bored to death, although less
so than I."

Nancy's friends were deeply concerned about her, especially
when they knew she was spending long periods alone—and
with good reason. Her letters—and she kept up an astonishing
rate of correspondence—show that she was battling against

mounting physical disabilities; she was weak and dizzy, coughing badly, hardly able to walk. But she was determined not to be submerged by these troubles; she was writing poetry continually, in particular a long poem that she called *The Visions,* into which she was trying to cram her own story, her feelings about poetry and politics and war. She sent off sections of it as she wrote them to several friends, including Walter Strachan, Solita Solano, and Sylvia Townsend Warner.

Help with the house and cooking was harder than ever to find. Nancy seems to have accepted that her traveling days were over, but she could not remain at La Mothe during the winter months; she would move to a hotel in Toulouse, the Capoul, where at least there was a bar and a restaurant downstairs, and Géraldine Balayé and other friends nearby.

Although it was really as much as Nancy could manage to get herself from La Mothe Fénélon to Toulouse, or to visit friends along the Côte d'Azur, she never quite gave up the idea of another journey. Some correspondence she had in 1959 with George Padmore's widow in Ghana made her toy with the idea of making, at last, a proper trip to black Africa. She wrote a slightly incoherent letter to Clyde Robinson suggesting they should go to Ghana together; but when he sent back some cautious enquiries, she flew into a fury at him for having so unrealistically suggested the trip in the first place.

Around the same time Nancy was corresponding with another old African contact from the days of *Negro,* T. K. Utchay, who had contributed an account of the disillusionment he had experienced as a black teacher surrounded by white missionaries in Nigeria in colonial days. Nancy and Utchay never met; they only knew each other through letters. In 1933 Utchay started his own group of schools in Port Harcourt; he called the first school Cunardia School after Nancy. During the war the school became unpopular with the authorities and was forced to close; but in 1959 it reopened, and Utchay resumed contact with Nancy. He sent her a copy of the brochure explaining how the school was named.

Many have asked me the meaning of Cunardia. The name belongs to Nancy Cunard of England. She is a woman who published a Negro anthology in 1932. . . . To hear that a white man or white woman was in true sympathy with the feelings of the Africans, brought me peace, courage and sanity; and so I named the first school of the Education Missionary Society "Cunardia." . . . The Africans want to honour her for taking their side when the colour war was raging fiercest. She suffered slander, ostracism and loneliness because of us. We simply want to honour her in so little a way. May she be blessed!

In October 1960 Utchay wrote to Nancy, "Today we have got self-government for Nigeria. Cunardia School is firmly established." He also told her that he had named his daughter after her. She must have written back giving some indication that her life was not easy, for in February 1961 he wrote back: "I do not like to hear that you are bothered. Although you have not told me much about it, I know you had sacrificed very much for the cause of the African race, and for that reason the people of your own race turned against you. We do not want you to continue to suffer. Africans will honor you. This is why we have named our school Cunardia. Some free-minded Europeans here call our school Nancy Cunard School. The ignorant ones of your race told me to erase your name from the school!"

Utchay knew that Nancy was not universally regarded as a disinterested benefactor of Africans. He had been urged at one point to denounce his contribution to *Negro* and had refused; later, to his great indignation, he heard a rumor had grown up that he and Nancy must have been lovers. But his admiration did not waver. "You need not be so worried about saying that I had done you too much honour," he wrote. "I want anything for Cunardia or about Cunardia to be superb." During 1961 Nancy had a letter from her namesake, Nancy Utchay, who was fifteen and hoping to be a nurse. Nancy sent the girl a handkerchief and her father a copy of *Grand Man*.

In the spring of 1962 John Banting and a friend arrived in La Mothe Fénélon for a long visit. At first, although he was upset to find Nancy very fragile, the stay was successful. Banting, as well as working on his painting, did the cooking and made sure that Nancy ate. By the summer she had put on a little weight and was able to go for short walks. But, to his great sadness, he found that they were increasingly at odds. Especially after a few drinks, Nancy would seem to want to argue and pick a quarrel. She seemed to him obsessed with the last war—"World Bore II," he was driven to call it. She had come to regard it as a glorious antifascist crusade, and any questioning of its aims or results led to fury. The visit ended badly when Banting's companion became suddenly ill and they had to leave abruptly. Nancy and Banting continued to correspond, but, as he remembered, "things were never quite the same again."

Another of Nancy's troubles at this time was money. Her income of about six hundred pounds a year was not going as far as it had. She had begun to feel weighed down by the possessions she still had at La Mothe, expecially since she was forced to leave the house empty and uncared for when she went away. She started to sell some of her books and smaller drawings and paintings, either directly to friends or through Sotheby's; and in 1961 she asked Herman Schrijver to take charge of selling George Moore's Manet. The painting was shipped to England and put up for sale at Sotheby's with a reserve price of twenty-one thousand pounds; but after it had twice failed to reach the reserve at auction, Nancy decided to withdraw it and wait for a better time. She did not want the trouble or expense of bringing it back to France, and so when Schrijver offered to keep it for her in his flat in London, she was touchingly grateful for his help. Her many letters to Schrijver over this negotiation show her to have been perfectly clear about what she wanted, if sometimes repetitive and forgetful of what had previously been agreed.

In July 1962 Sir Edward Cunard, her other favorite cousin, died. As well as being another sadness for Nancy, his death led to complications and delays in the still uncompleted settlement of Victor Cunard's estate; Sir Edward had been his chief heir. As a result Nancy was in regular and friendly correspondence with some of her cousins on the Cunard side, and in particular with Mrs. Cecilia Dawson, widow of Geoffrey Dawson of the *Times,* and their son Michael. Far from there being any ostracism of Nancy as the black sheep of the Cunard family, her cousins—none of whom knew her at all well—were concerned about Nancy and eager to make sure that she received her share of Edward and Victor's estates. Nancy herself showed no antagonism or reluctance; her main concern was the fate of Sir Bache's silver fox, which Victor Cunard had kept for her, and which she also now wanted to sell, if the terms of the legacy allowed.

In the summer of 1963 Nancy had two new friends to stay at La Mothe Fénélon. They were a young American academic, Hugh Ford, and his wife Thérèse, who had come especially to work with Nancy on another book, an account of the Hours Press. Ford had been corresponding with Nancy since 1961, when he wrote to ask for her help with a book about the poetry of the Spanish civil war. She wrote him a series of lively, informative letters, and he and his wife made a brief visit to La Mothe in the summer of 1962. The Hours Press book began as Nancy's attempt at autobiography and was based on the material Rupert Hart-Davis had turned down in 1959. Nancy had sent what she had written to Walter Lowenfels in New York, and it was his idea that with Ford's collaboration and editing it might make an acceptable book.

When the Fords arrived, they found that Nancy had not been to La Mothe Fénélon since the previous summer. They met in Gourdon, the small town nearby, and went back to the house together. They mess they found was daunting; but between them they cleaned up and put the place to rights. Thérèse Ford had been a nurse and was able to be a great help to Nancy; although she was plainly sometimes ill and nervous, and drank what seemed to the Fords an inordinate amount of rum and rough local red wine, her charm won them completely and her capacity for work was still impressive. With Ford's help she reworked her material and added more until they had produced a simple series of short essays, part reminiscence, part criticism, on each of the authors she had published. Ford was confident that he could find a publisher, perhaps among the academic presses.

"The Prof. is my idea of 'perfect man,' " Nancy wrote to Solita Solano. "So perceptive, just, imaginative too, and very hard working. I love him and Thérèse."

After six weeks, when the time came for them to leave, the Fords were worried as to how Nancy would manage on her own. They had tried and failed to find her regular local help; but they knew Nancy was planning to spend the winter with her old friend Jean Guérin at his villa in Nice, where he had offered to take her as a paying guest whenever she wanted.

All the same, when their train north passed La Mothe Fénélon and they looked up to see the white cloth Nancy used to wave to departing friends from her window up on the hillside, Thérèse Ford felt close to tears.

After a week alone Nancy moved down to Gourdon in September and went into the hospital there for a checkup. It was found that her chest condition had worsened; emphysema was diagnosed. When she came out, she moved into a hotel; it was there that Charles Burkhart and Herman Schrijver found her when they made a quick trip from Paris to see her.

Burkhart was moved and horrified by Nancy's situation and condition. The hotel was new and ugly:

. . . downstairs a salon café of pinball machines, local youth and nervous young proprietor; upstairs, tiny rooms furnished and panelled in raw orange pine. . . . When Nancy was able to leave her raw orange cubicle (where she had an old suitcase or two, as she always did, full of manuscripts or correspondence or ivory, and a bottle of rum, her favourite drink, on the bedside table), she descended and sat in a corner of the pinball salon, writing her letters, drinking rough red, which she would occasionally ask one of the boys to share a glass of, catching her breath between Gauloises. Still writing, but desperate; dazed and bemused with pain and the drugs they gave her at the hospital. . . . [She was] able to walk five steps before she must stop to catch a little breath into her incredibly thin body, able to talk only a minute or two before rage overwhelmed her. She was always like a cat, and her rage was like that of a puma encaged, an ocelot or a cheetah; green eyes blazing like a cat's, she pounded the table weakly and gasped in her fury, "If I could breathe!" Anger at everything, at the food she would not eat—she crumbled up bread and made little balls of it in her plate; at the doctors who were expensive and wrong; at Franco, all Fascism, and the world.

The next day they hired a car to drive to the house at La Mothe Fénélon, which Schrijver had never seen and which Nancy longed to show him. It was raining hard. "La Mothe itself one could hardly enter," Burkhart recalls. "Grass so thick by the gate; the house itself, which I remembered as steeped in the sun and splendidly open and full of air seemed crouched and defenceless in the rain. It was crumbling; the books, precious books some of them, were mildewing; on the mantelpiece where the Manet had sat, there were a few old wine bottles, spider webs, odd rocks, metal or wooden scraps, *objets trouvés* from the days when she could walk; musty sad debris of all that famous and brilliant and energetic life."

Nancy had recently been asked, at Anthony Hobson's suggestion, to write a bibliography of the Hours Press for the *Book Collector*. Burkhart helped her look through her copies of the Hours Press books for details, and they also went through her remaining ivories, which she was thinking of selling.

To Burkhart the whole scene was "a nightmare. The cold and the rain and the pointlessness; but at one moment, when she held a favourite ancient bracelet to her cheek, she crooned something I could not hear and gave me a look of dim, remote ecstasy, as if I would understand."

They left the next day, having been assured that Nancy was herself leaving for Guérin's villa the day after. They both remembered the visit as horrific; Nancy was simply sad that they had not seen her house on a better day.

The winter of 1963/64 and early spring of 1964 Nancy spent with Jean Guérin at the Villa Pomone in Saint-Jean-Cap-Ferrat. Although she was more comfortable there and had the companionship of an old friend, her health and spirits fluctuated alarmingly. She was unsteady on her feet, even when she had not been drinking; she ate less than ever and had trouble sleeping. She enjoyed Guérin's fine collection of classical music records and his small Tibetan terriers; and she made friends with the gardener at the villa, a brown wrinkled old peasant with whom she would discuss life and nature. She decided to call the peasant Adam and put him into a long poem she was working on. Her one consolation was writing; she was working obsessively, as well as writing as many letters as ever. "The only time I don't feel so ill," she wrote to Solita Solano, "is when I get to this machine and compose, and correct, and copy." Her illness and frustration made her quicker than ever to fly into furious, irrational rages; and the news of the death of a friend, such as, inevitably, came more and more often, would put her in a passion. Tristan Tzara, to whom she had been very close in Paris in the 1920s, died in December; when a letter from Hugh Ford happened to arrive around that time containing some questions about Tzara, Nancy wrote him a furious answer. Part of her still felt it was distasteful, or disloyal, to discuss her life, and her friends, for publication. Later she regretted her outburst, and wrote apologetically: "My reaction is always angry at the death of someone I have loved."

But there were better times. She would visit friends nearby, such as Douglas Cooper at Argilliers or Tony Gandarillas at Hyères. At lunch one day Gandarillas could not forbear to tell her that as she walked onto his terrace she looked so much like her mother that he thought he was seeing a ghost. Nancy remained quite calm. "I understand," she said. "I wish she had gone on living, but not with me."

Sometimes she and Guérin would invite friends to the villa for dinner and put on a fancy dress; on Christmas Eve they received their guests dressed as a mandarin and a geisha girl, with the Tibetan terriers prancing at their feet. On her sixty-eighth birthday, in March 1964, she celebrated by going to the opera in Monte Carlo. She still had the power to draw all eyes; when Nancy came into a restaurant, in her leopard skin coat and the usual bright veil across her forehead, her ivory bracelets clacking, everyone looked up. She was deeply wrinkled and desperately thin, and she could look frightening, even grotesque; but her impact was unmistakable.

For the summer of 1964 she went back to La Mothe Fénélon. Irene Rathbone went to stay with her again, although there was barely room, since Nancy had managed to get a woman from Toulouse to live in and look after her. Nancy was too ill to go for walks herself, but she insisted that her friend should not feel tied to the house. She stayed behind and worked on her poems. The weather was beautiful; Nancy's mood seemed gentle and melancholy, though she complained with spirit about the chatter of her housekeeper and the radio she kept on perpetually. When Irene left, Nancy handed her a poem she had written especially for her; it seemed to her friend to capture the mood perfectly of a brief interlude from cold and pain and anxiety.

Her last visitor that year was Géraldine Balayé. When the time came for her too to leave, Nancy insisted on taking a last short walk with her down the hill from the house. "In slippers, her steps slowed by asthma, leaning on my arm so as not to fall, she managed, by a heroic struggle, this short walk; she was hardly able to speak to me, but now and again she stopped and picked up a golden pebble or a twig encrusted with moss." It seemed to Géraldine that Nancy's eyes had a look of sad tenderness as she gazed at her house, the portrait of George Moore, her books, and the view of the walnut trees beginning to turn from green to gold.

32

The Last Journey

The winter of 1964/65 found Nancy staying with Jean Guérin at the Villa Pomone, short of breath, unsteady on her feet, but working away at her long poem and writing letters late at night to all her favorite correspondents. "All my instincts beg of me," she wrote to Walter Strachan, "is to lie in bed, sleep colossally, have a sup brought up on a tray, maunder about, grumbling, have a very strong drink of ROMOLO [rum] and THEN put something on, and get to the typewriter . . . to see 'what I have wrote the night before' copy it out roughly, correct like mad, re-type, like mad. . . . I admire scholars. I do not envy them. I do not ENVY anyone for that matter, I envy and WANT the *time* I want for myself."

She was curiously moved when late one night one of the Tibetan terriers gave birth to a litter of puppies on her bed. Nancy held the dog in the crook of her arm and wrote tender accounts of the incident to her friends. She was distressed and angry when a little later a pile of books disturbed by one of the puppies crashed down and killed it, especially because her own book on George Moore was one of the first to fall. "Bloody books," she wrote to Solita Solano.

On January 7, 1965, she heard on the radio at lunchtime that T. S. Eliot had died. She sat down and wrote a three-and-a-half-page prose poem about him, which she sent to his friend John Hayward. She recalled meeting Eliot at a ball of her mother's in 1922, how he wore a dinner jacket and she a panniered Poiret dress, "gold with cascading white tulle on the hips." She danced with the Prince of Wales ("so polite, lovely face") and observed how brilliantly her mother handled "all this sort of thing." But Nancy was bored, she claimed, until she found herself having supper alone with Eliot and talking about poetry.

When she suggested a "tryst" for the following evening, Eliot agreed. They met at the Eiffel Tower, had plenty to drink and talked for hours. Nancy remembered that they were both engaged to dine with the Hutchinsons, but "I begged you not to get us there, and in the end I won."

As her lines on T. S. Eliot show, Nancy did sometimes feel the need as she got older to look back and recall particular incidents and people; but what she could never bring herself to attempt was a coherent account of her life, feelings, and actions. Her responses were still as direct, personal and immediate in her sixties as they had been in her twenties.

During the night of January 21 Nancy had a fall in her bedroom—she thought perhaps she had tripped on the valance trying to avoid one of the Shih Tzu puppies—and broke her thigh. A doctor could not be found till morning; from eleven p.m. to nine a.m. she lay in agony. She was then taken to a clinic in Nice, operated on immediately, and told she would not be able to walk for about three months.

After two weeks in the clinic she was taken back to the Villa Pomone. She was still in great pain, and, as always, weakness and immobility made her angry and aggressive. That year the spring was late in Nice and the weather cold and stormy. Her host himself was far from well, and the domestic arrangements were complicated; a young man who had been Guérin's companion and factotum had recently married and returned to the villa with his pregnant wife. Nancy's mood darkened. On top of everything else, her medical expenses were high, and she began to worry, not altogether rationally, about money. She wrote to Janet Flanner and Solita Solano asking them if they would consider buying any of her remaining objects of value—a card case she had been given as a wedding present or a cigarette case of Her Lady-ship's. They at once sent a check for several hundred dollars.

As always when things went wrong, Nancy's instinct was to move on. She decided once and for all to sell up in France and move back to England. She wrote detailed letters to Herman Schrijver, among others, begging him to find her a cheap mod-ern ground-floor flat in Brighton. He responded cautiously.

During this black time one piece of news pleased her im-mensely. Hugh Ford wrote to say that the book about the Hours Press they had constructed together in the summer of 1963 had been accepted by Southern Illinois University Press.

By the first week in March Nancy was finding life at the Villa Pomone intolerable; and no doubt her host, for all their long friendship, was finding his guest intolerable too. The pain-killing drugs she had to take, combined with the drink she could not do without, the weakness she loathed in herself, the anxiety beneath the brave plans for moving back from France to England, and her panic about money brought Nancy once again to the edge of insanity. One night she provoked a violent quarrel with Guérin during which she apparently said such appalling things that he asked her to leave.

The next day, half-crazed with rage, pain, and drugs, Nancy put into an old suitcase a few belongings, including some papers and a few of the remaining ivory bracelets, and prepared to go to Paris, perhaps as the first stage of the journey to England. The young factotum took her to Nice station; she begged him to have a last drink with her at the buffet but then quickly became too drunk and weak to move. His wife was about to give birth and he had to leave Nancy waiting for the train alone. He did what he could by making sure she had her ticket and some money, alerting the railway staff and the Red Cross and arranging for her to be carried to a compartment. The details of what happened next are hazy; but somehow Nancy boarded the train, where she drank and raved her way across France on the journey she had made so many times, until, furious at the sight of a ticket collector's uniform, she apparently ate her ticket in front of him rather than do what he asked and give it up.

On the night of March 9, she arrived without warning at the small house shared by Solita Solano and Elizabeth Clark in the village of Orgeval, just outside Paris. It was the eve of her sixty-ninth birthday, and her two friends had been talking of her when they heard a taxi drawing up outside. The taxi driver carried her in and deposited her in an armchair in the sitting room. She had no money on her at all; "Pay him for me, ducky," she instructed Solita Solano. "He's coming back for me in the morning. I shall stay tonight here."

Ten years later, Solita Solano and Elizabeth Clark could not speak of that night without horror and grief. Nancy was skeletally thin, ravaged with pain, and barely coherent. She wanted two things: to write and to drink. They were afraid to deny her the small supply of alcohol they had in the house— some vodka and some red wine—but they refused to send out for more. She smoked incessantly and dropped the lighted ends on the carpet, as if she wanted to start a blaze that would destroy them all. She absolutely refused to go to bed, and when she threatened to spend the night in a wheelbarrow in the garden, they let her stay in the armchair. When she decided she wanted a bath, Elizabeth Clark carried her upstairs and helped her to wash. She listened to Nancy's stream of incoherent talk about her quarrel with Guérin, her suspicions of most of her close friends, and her plans for the future, and she reassured her that the emaciated, half-crippled body in the bath was still alluring. They dared not go to sleep themselves for fear of what Nancy might do, so they brought her paper and pencils and sat with her while she talked and raged and scribbled; sometimes what she said was poetry, sometimes letters to friends in Paris or London who she said would take her in or go traveling with her. She wrote a letter of hatred to Guérin, which she sealed with a blob of red ink to stand for blood and carefully spat on as she sealed it.

It was plain that Nancy needed a doctor and psychiatric

treatment, although she rejected any such suggestion with extreme suspicion and hostility. During the night her friends managed to reach Janet Flanner in Paris by telephone, and they arranged that the taxi due to call for Nancy in the morning would take her straight to a doctor. Next day, though, to their alarm and distress, Nancy announced that she had decided for the time being to stay on with them. Feeling like traitors, but knowing that she must somehow be put under qualified supervision, they told her that they themselves were leaving Orgeval that day. When finally the taxi came, they saw her off, confident that the driver knew his instructions and that Janet Flanner was waiting in Paris. Nancy went, to their relief, quite calmly, but she said as she left: "Well, I don't suppose we shall be seeing each other again."

Nancy did not keep the rendezvous with Janet Flanner and the doctor. Instead, she turned up at the small apartment on the outskirts of Paris where Raymond Michelet was living with a woman companion with whom he had been happily settled for many years. Nancy and Michelet had remained sporadically in touch by letter, but they had hardly ever met since the war. Now, on top of the shock he felt on seeing her in such a condition, Michelet realized with dismay that she seemed to be assuming that he would take care of her, that they would go to England together to live and perhaps collaborate on another book. She looked at his companion with hatred.

For the rest of that day she lay on Michelet's sofa, semidelirious. She would have nothing to do with the two doctors they summoned; instead she demanded that old friends be found and brought to her. Michelet remembered that she particularly asked for Aragon, Sadoul, and Beckett. Michelet contacted Aragon; but this time Aragon and Elsa Triolet had had enough. They did not see what his presence could achieve; Nancy should be in a hospital. Beckett, apparently, was out of Paris.

That night, Michelet reached Georges Sadoul. He and his wife immediately went to help. "A hideous spectacle awaited us," Sadoul wrote later. "Nancy Cunard had lost her reason and was delirious. She had become thinner than a Buchenwald corpse. She weighed no more than 26 kilos. With her broken thigh, she could no longer stand. Stretched out on a divan, half-naked, she was talking incessantly. . . . Her mind had cracked, her beautiful intelligence had clouded over and she hardly knew what to do but insult her best friends, present and absent."

At their wits' end, Michelet and Sadoul tried to decide what to do. Michelet could not handle another night of Nancy, and the Sadouls felt equally unable to take the responsibility. Nancy had revealed that she had a room reserved at a small hotel in the Quartier Latin, one of several she had known for thirty years. It was nearly midnight; nevertheless they decided to take her there, to see that she was safely put to bed and to arrange for medical and psychiatric help the next morning. When they arrived at the hotel, they found that she did indeed have a room reserved on the third floor and that the staff, who knew her well, were prepared to take her. According to Sadoul:

> The hotel had no lift. She allowed Michelet and me to support her as far as the foot of the stairs, but she forbade me, threatening violence, to give her any more help at all, to hold her up, even to touch her. And she began to mount the stairs all by herself. She would sit down on a step, find the strength to heave herself on to the next, then rest there long enough to regain her strength and breath, sometimes as long as ten minutes. This slow ascent must have lasted 90 minutes, perhaps two hours, among the longest of my life.
>
> I was afraid that Nancy might suddenly become violent, that the police might be called, that she might then be taken to an asylum from which we could never retrieve her. But luckily her monologue was no longer one long invective, but more like an almost sociable conversation. From time to time, guests of the hotel would climb the stairs, astonished to see her seated on the steps, with her turban and her leopard skin coat and her ivory bracelets. I explained that she was ill and absolutely in-

sisted on climbing unaided to her room. They went on their way. From time to time she would ask the passers-by whether, for example, they knew Pablo Neruda, and whether they thought he would get the Nobel Prize.

During this atrocious and interminable *End Game* she spoke to me in particular of Samuel Beckett, whom I had forgotten she knew. Was he in Paris? Could she telephone him? Would he come and see her? He was very fond of her. If he had agreed to this request for a meeting, he would have found himself confronted not by the Nancy Cunard he had known, but by one of the heroines he put on the stage, paralysed, buried in sand or in urns, reliving their past in a series of apparently disconnected phrases. "This woman," Nancy would say, speaking of herself in the third person, "has just today had her 69th birthday, and entered her 70th year." Her birthday was long over when at last, around two in the morning of the 12th of March, she reached her little rented room. She refused to allow me to help her on to the divan bed.

Drained and exhausted, Michelet and Sadoul decided that as she was clearly incapable of leaving her room, as she had no money and as they had left strict instructions that she was to be given no drink, they could safely leave her overnight. The next day, they sent a psychiatrist to see her; he found her in such a state of physical collapse that he said there was nothing he could do for her mind until her body had been treated. As soon as he left, Nancy telephoned Michelet and accused him of having sent a police spy to see her and of being himself an agent of the fascists. So was Sadoul, and so were all her other friends. Michelet returned to the hotel; when he got there, he found Nancy had gone; somehow she had managed to get downstairs and find a taxi. Before leaving, she had burnt some of her papers on the floor of her room; the fire was discovered when the hotel staff saw smoke emerging from beneath the door.

Precisely what happened next is not known. At all events the taxi driver turned her over to the police, and the police had her taken to l'Hôpital Cochin. Later, her friends learned that she had regained consciousness and asked for red wine, which she was not given, and writing materials, which she was. She told the nurses she was working on a long poem against all wars. Three days later, on March 16, 1965, alone under an oxygen tent in a public ward, she died.

Epilogue

Through the British consulate, Nancy's friends and then her relations in England learned of her death. A small funeral service was held at the British Embassy church in Paris on March 24; among the handful of people present were Janet Flanner, Raymond Michelet, Douglas Cooper, and the journalist Sam White, who described the occasion for his newspaper, the London *Evening Standard,* as a "sad, lonely farewell to a toast of the Twenties." Nancy's English cousins sent a large wreath of spring flowers. Her body was cremated the next day and the ashes placed in Père Lachaise Cemetery. Two years later, realizing that the remains were unidentified, Solita Solano arranged for a suitable plaque to be put up.

In London and New York Nancy's death was briefly noticed in the press. References were made to her breach with her family, to the Hours Press, and to her work for Negroes. In Paris she was given more space. Georges Sadoul wrote a eulogy for *Les Lettres Françaises,* paying tribute to Nancy's "great heart," "brilliant intelligence," and "strong character." He stressed that she was something more than "an extravagant figure of the crazy twenties," and he suggested that, as well as jazz tunes, "around her shade float Afro-American blues and spirituals, Spanish republican ballads and the immortal rhythms of modern French poetry."

Although Nancy had corresponded with her lawyers about a will and had sent a characteristically eccentric draft to Douglas Cooper asking him to be her executor, she died intestate.

She had wanted her African ivories kept together as a collection and exhibited, but they, with all the rest of her property, were in due course sold. It was found that at her death Nancy had over sixty thousand dollars in American shares, and the sales of her house, the Manet, the ivories, and her books and papers (which she had thought worthless) more than doubled that figure.

For several days after her death, friends in France, England, and America continued to receive her last, often incoherent, letters and postcards.

Appendix I

NANCY AND *THE WASTE LAND*

The facsimile edition of T. S. Eliot's drafts of *The Waste Land* (edited by Valerie Eliot and published by Harcourt, Brace and Faber and Faber in 1971) shows that the third section of the poem, "The Fire Sermon," opened in an early version with seventy lines of couplets in the style of *The Rape of the Lock* by Alexander Pope.

The central character in the passage is Fresca, a spoiled society girl with literary pretensions. She is under the wing of a prominent hostess with musical and artistic aspirations, Lady Kleinwurm, whom she purports to despise. (In another draft passage, the hostess is called Lady Katzegg.) It is tempting—although not flattering—to identify Nancy with Fresca. Eliot's portrait is imbued with powerful disgust for Fresca's sexual avidity and contempt for her poetic dabblings. Intellectual women, he states, are even less interesting than ordinary sluts. Beneath their pretensions, there is the same basic lust. Fresca is described as having grown up soaked in late Victorian sentiment, and then been so overexcited by Scandinavian and Russian literature that a poetic outburst was the inevitable result. When she has nothing better to do, or lies awake at night, she writes mournful poetry. Immature, surrounded by sycophantic friends and nervous critics, she takes herself all too seriously as a poet and turns into a frivolous literary hostess in her own right.

According to a recent critical study of *The Waste Land* (Lyndall Gordon, *Eliot's Early Years* [Oxford University Press, 1977]), "The Fire Sermon" was probably written in 1921, at a time when Eliot, with Pound's encouragement, "overlaid private meditation with documentary sketches of contemporary characters."

T. S. Eliot had met Nancy several times by 1921. Her 1919 diary notes meeting him and indicates that she was excited to make the acquaintance of a poet she admired. Vivienne Eliot, T. S. Eliot's first wife, mentions in her diary for the same year an evening the Eliots spent with St. John and Mary Hutchinson, when Nancy, Osbert Sitwell, and Duncan Grant were also guests.

One further fragment of evidence links Eliot, through his adviser Ezra Pound, to Nancy. One of Pound's comments, scribbled in the margin of Eliot's draft of "A Game of Chess," the second section of *The Waste Land,* is the same quotation from a French critic that Pound used in his letter of advice to Nancy: "Il cherchait des sentiments pour les accomoder *[sic]* à son vocabulaire."

Perhaps the most one can safely say is that T. S. Eliot could have had Nancy in mind when he wrote the passage. Its bitterness might be explained by the contrast between the struggles of Eliot and his wife against illness and poverty, and the affluent, leisured existence of Nancy; not to mention the contrast between the difficulties he and Pound experienced in getting their work into print and appreciated and the ease with which the well-connected amateur, Nancy, found publishers and respectful reviewers for her poems.

Appendix 2

BIBLIOGRAPHY OF HOURS PRESS PUBLICATIONS

1928

Aldington, Richard. *Hark the Herald.* December. 5½ by 7½. 2 pp. 100 hand-set, signed copies, Vergé de Rives. 17 pt. Caslon Old Face. Mary blue wrappers. Title in gold letters on front wrapper. A present to the author; not for sale.

Douglas, Norman, *Report on the Pumice-Stone Industry of the Lipari Islands.* June. 6 by 10. 6 pp. 80 hand-set copies; ordinary commercial paper. 11 pt. Caslon Old Face. Title printed on front. A present to the author; not for sale.

Moore, George. *Peronnik the Fool.* December. 6 by 9. 63 pp. 200 hand-set, signed copies. Vergé de Rives. 11 pt. Caslon Old Face. Title stamped in gold on front, pale blue board covers. £2.

1929

Aldington, Richard. *The Eaten Heart.* Late winter. 7 by 11. 28 pp. 200 hand-set, signed copies, Canson-Montgolfier. 16 pt. Caslon Old Face. Title on front, gilt lettering on green marble paper. £1 1s.

Aragon, Louis. *La Chasse au Snark.* Early winter. 9 by 12. 30 pp. 300 hand-set, signed copies. Alfa paper. 16 pt. Caslon Old Face. Title on front designed and composed by Aragon, in typographical patterns and letterings on dull scarlet paper boards. Also 5 copies, Japan paper; same size, binding. 300 copies at £1 1s. Japan paper copies at £5 5s.

Douglas, Norman. *One Day*. July. 6 by 10. 55 pp. 200 signed copies. Velin de Rives. Monotype. Title stamped in gilt scarlet leather. £3 3s. Also 300 copies; same size, type, Vergé de Vidalon, puce-colored boards. £1 10s.

Guevara, Alvaro. *St. George at Silene*. January. 10 by 13. 4 pp. 150 hand-set, signed copies, Velin de Rives. 16 pt. Caslon Old Face. Title, front and back, endpapers, designed by author. Gray paper, stitched covers. 10s 6d.

Symons, Arthur. *Mes Souvenirs*. July. 6 by 10. 48 pp. 200 signed copies, Velin de Rives. Bound beige cloth boards. £2 2s.

1930

Beckett, Samuel. *Whoroscope*. Midsummer. 6 by 9. 6 pp. 100 signed, hand-set copies, and 200 unsigned copies. Both on Vergé de Rives. 11 pt. Caslon Old Face. Title in black ink on dark red paper; upper cover, white band affixed, stating that poem had won the Hours Press £10 prize for the best poem on "Time." Signed copies: 5s; unsigned: 1s.

Campbell, Roy. *Poems*. July. 7 by 11. 24 pp. 200 hand-set, signed copies, Canson-Montgolfier. 16 pt. Caslon Old Face. Title lettered in gilt on leather spine; Vermilion paper boards, with two drawings by Campbell. £1 10s.

Crowder, Henry. *Henry-Music*. December. 10 by 13. 20 pp. 150 copies, signed by composer. Hard board covers, front and back different, specially designed photomontages by Man Ray. 10s 6d.

Graves, Robert. *Ten Poems More*. Early spring. 7 by 11. 24 pp. 200 signed, hand-set copies, Canson-Montgolfier. 16 pt. Caslon Old Face. Title stamped on dark leather spine. Covers both different, photomontages by Len Lye. £1 10s.

Lowenfels, Walter. *Apollinaire*. Early summer. 7 by 11. 16 pp. 150 signed, hand-set copies, Canson-Montgolfier. 16 pt. Caslon Old Face. Title, stamped gilt on leather spine. Covers, both different, specially designed by Yves Tanguy, printed black on daffodil-colored paper boards. £1 10s.

MacCown, Eugene. *Catalogue of Paintings, Drawings and Gouaches by Eugene MacCown*. Early summer. 6 by 10. 20 pp. 1000 copies. Vergé de Rives. Caslon Old Face Italics. A present to the artist; not for sale.

Pound, Ezra. *A draft of XXX Cantos*. Midsummer. 5 by 8. 142 pp. 200 copies and 10 signed copies (with two copies on real vellum for the author). The 200 copies on Canson-Montgolfier-Soleil Velin. The 10 signed copies on Texas Mountain paper; 200 copies in stout beige linen boards; title stamped in red on spine and upper cover. 10 copies in vermilion leather, with same lettering. Both with initial letters at start of each Canto by the poet's wife, Dorothy Shakespear. Ten copies at £5 5s. 200 copies at £2.

Riding, Laura. *Twenty Poems Less*. Spring. 7 by 11. 40 pp. 200 signed, hand-set copies, Canson-Montgolfier. 16 pt. Caslon Old Face. Title stamped gilt on dark leather spine. Covers, both different, photomontages by Len Lye. £1 10s.

————*Four Unposted Letters to Catherine*. Early summer. 6 by 8. 50 pp. 200 signed copies, Haut Vidalon. Garamond Italic. Title gilt lettering on dark leather spine. Covers, both different, designed photomontages by Len Lye. £2.

Rodker, John. *Collected Poems*. August. 6 by 10. 36 pp. 200 signed copies, hand-made paper, initial lettering by Edward Wadsworth. Title lettered in gilt on dark leather spine. Covers, both different, specially designed montages by Len Lye. £1 10s.

1931

Acton, Harold. *This Chaos*. January. 7 by 11. 32 pp. 150 hand-set, signed copies, Canson-Montgolfier. 16 pt. Caslon Old Face. Paper boards, title lettered in gilt on leather spine. Covers, both different, specially designed abstracts, printed blue, by Elliot Seabrooke. £1 10s.

Aldington Richard. *Last Straws*. January. 6 by 10. 61 pp. 200 signed copies in green suede cloth boards; title lettered in gilt on upper cover; and 300 additional copies in gray-brown paper boards, design by Douglas Cockerell, with printed label on upper cover. Signed copies at £2; unsigned copies at 7s 6d.

Brown, Bob. *Words*. January. 7 by 11. 23 pp. 150 signed, hand-set copies, Canson-Montgolfier. 16 pt. Caslon Old Face. Title lettered in gilt on leather spine. Upper cover designed in letterings by John Sibthorpe. £1 10s.

Ellis, Havelock. *The Revaluation of Obscenity*. Spring. 6 by 10. 40 pp. 200 signed copies. Type and paper unknown to Miss Cunard. Blue leather spine on blue cloth boards. £2.

Howard, Brian. *First Poems*. January. 7 by 11. 48 pp. 150 signed, hand-set copies, Canson–Montgolfier. 16 pt. Caslon Old Face. Title lettered in gilt on dark leather spine. Pale blue paper boards; special designs, upper and lower covers different, by John Banting. £1 10s.

Moore, George. *The Talking Pine*. Early. 8 by 10. A 2-leaf plaquette, 500 copies. Light beige paper covers. Paper and type unknown to Miss Cunard. Not for sale.

Appendix 3

NANCY CUNARD'S WRITINGS

(Contributor), *Wheels: An Anthology of Verse,* seven poems (Longmans, Green. 1916).

Outlaws (Elkin Matthews and Marrot, 1921).

Sublunary (Hodder and Stoughton Ltd., 1923).

Parallax (Hogarth Press, 1925).

Poems, two poems (Aquila Press, 1930).

(Ed.), *Negro* (Wishart & Co., 1934).

(Ed.), *Authors Take Sides on the Spanish War (Left Review,* 1937).

(With George Padmore), *The White Man's Duty* (W. H. Allen, 1943).

(Ed.), *Poems for France* (La France Libre, 1944).

Grand Man: Memories of Norman Douglas (Secker and Warburg, 1954).

G.M.: Memories of George Moore (Rupert Hart-Davis, 1956).

These Were the Hours (Southern Illinois University Press, 1969).

Permission Acknowledgments

Grateful acknowledgment is made to the following for permission to reprint previously published material:

Alfred A. Knopf, Inc.: "I, Too" by Langston Hughes. Copyright 1926 by Alfred A. Knopf, Inc., and renewed 1954 by Langston Hughes. Reprinted from *Selected Poems of Langston Hughes* by permission of Alfred A. Knopf, Inc.

Blond & Briggs, Ltd.: an excerpt from *Brian Howard: Story of a Failure* by Marie Jaqueline Lancaster.

The Book Collector: the bibliography of the Hours Press.

Chilton Book Company, Radnor, Pa.: extracts from *Nancy Cunard: Brave Poet, Indomitable Rebel,* edited by Hugh Ford. Copyright © 1968 by the editor.

Curtis Brown, Ltd.: an extract from *Reminiscences* by Marchioness Curzon. Used by permission of Curtis Brown, Ltd., on behalf of the author.

David Higham Associates, Ltd.: excerpts from *Piracy, The Green Hat* and *Babes in the Wood* by Michael Arlen. Published by the Heinemann Group Publishers, Ltd.

Evelyn Singer Agency, Inc.: excerpts from a letter to Nancy Cunard from Mike Gold.

Granada Publishing, Ltd.: a selection from *Memories of George Moore* by Nancy Cunard. Used by permission of Rupert Hart-Davis/ Granada Publishing, Ltd.

Hamish Hamilton, Ltd., and the New York Times Book Company: an excerpt from *A Life of Contrasts* by Lady Diana Mosley. Copyright © 1977 by Lady Diana Mosley. Published in the United States by Times Books, a division of Quadrangle/The

Notes

Sources

Unless otherwise stated, all of Nancy Cunard's papers from which quotations were drawn for this book—including her diaries, scrapbooks, drafts, notebooks, and all letters written to her—are to be found in the Humanities Research Center, University of Texas at Austin.

Nancy Cunard's letters to the late Miss Janet Flanner and the late Miss Solita Solano are in the Library of Congress, Manuscript Division.

Abbreviations

BPIR   Hugh Ford, ed., *Nancy Cunard: Brave Poet, Indomitable Rebel* (Chilton Book Company, 1968).

GM   Nancy Cunard, *G.M.: Memories of George Moore* (Rupert Hart-Davis, 1956).

HRC   Humanities Research Center, University of Texas.

ND   Nancy Cunard, *Grand Man: Memories of Norman Douglas* (Secker and Warburg, 1954).

SIU   Morris Library (special collection), Southern Illinois University.

TWTH   Nancy Cunard, *These Were the Hours* (Southern Illinois University Press, 1969).

Chapter 1

My account of Maud Burke's background is based on that given by her biographer and friend, Mrs. Daphne Fielding, in *Emerald and*

Nancy: Lady Cunard and Her Daughter (London: Eyre & Spottis-woode, 1968). Published in the United States as *Those Remarkable Cunards: Emerald and Nancy* (New York: Atheneum, 1968). For the early stages of her relationship with George Moore and his writings about her, I have followed the exposition given by Sir Rupert Hart-Davis in his introduction to Moore's letters to Lady Cunard.

p. 22   *Anglo-American society marriage.* Elizabeth Eliot, *They All Married Well* (London: Cassell, 1960).

29   *decoration of the house.* Interview with Mr. D. C. S. Phillips, Nevill Holt School, November 1976.

30   *"Take her away!"* James Lees-Milne, *Ancestral Voices* (London: Chatto and Windus, 1975).

Chapter 2

Nancy described her childhood at Nevill Holt at length in GM.

p. 31   *"a low thing: the lowest."* Quoted by the late Lord Kinross in *Queen* (London), April 16, 1967.

31   *friend had borne a child.* Lord Clark, *Another Part of the Wood* (London: Murray, 1974).

33   *apart from social acceptability.* The visitors book is in the HRC.

34   *her mother's admirers.* Nancy Cunard to Clyde Robinson, 1960 (SIU).

38   *what are children coming to?"* Quoted in Christopher Hassall, *Edward Marsh, Patron of the Arts* (London: Longmans, 1959, and New York: Harcourt, Brace and Company, 1959).

39   *not sympathetic to children.* Interview with Mr. Vere Gosling, April 1974.

Chapter 3

Nancy Cunard's Album Amicorum is in the collection of Mr. Alastair MacAlpine, London.

Chapter 4

Sources include GM, and the late Iris Tree's account of Nancy in BPIR.

p. 49   *ruin her promising daughter.* Interview with Miss Joan Haslip. October 1974.

       their confidence than anyone else." Roy Jenkins, *Asquith: Portrait of a Man and an Era* (London: Collins, 1964, and New York: Chilmark Press, 1965).

50   *praised one of her poems.* BPIR.

52   *fond of Lady Cunard.* Interview with Lady Diana Cooper, January 1974.

       and pretty girls. Diana Cooper, *The Rainbow Comes and Goes* (Boston: Houghton Mifflin, 1958 and London: Hart-Davis, 1958).

55   *She was marvellous."* BPIR.

       I can do as I like." Interview with Lady Diana Cooper, January 1974.

       abject situation of apology." Quoted in Nicolas Mosley, *Julian Grenfell* (New York: Holt, Rinehart and Winston, 1976).

Chapter 5

This chapter is based on Nancy's scrapbook, interviews with and material supplied by John Fairbairn, and an account of her relationship with Sybil Hart-Davis written by Nancy for Sir Rupert Hart-Davis and Mrs. Deirdre Bland.

p. 59   *and you can go.' "* The Marchioness Curzon of Kedleston, *Reminiscences* (London: Hutchinson, 1955).

61   *good things to come."* GM.

66   *never quite lost.* BPIR.

Chapter 6

p. 88   *if ever there was."* ND.

Chapter 7

The descriptions of Nancy are taken from BPIR.

p. 97   *word for Mr. is "Bahr-rohn."* This was pointed out to me by Professor Harry Keyishian of Fairleigh Dickinson University, Madison, New Jersey, who also drew my attention to Nancy's presence in *Piracy* and "Confessions of a Naturalised Englishman." (See his study, *Michael Arlen,* Boston: Twayne Publishers, 1975.)

99   *"his female prototype."* Diana Holman Hunt, *Latin among Lions: Alvaro Guevara* (London: Michael Joseph, 1974).

101   *always been very painful.* Interview with Professor Hugh Ford, May 1974.

Chapter 8

My account of Nancy's relationship with Aldous Huxley is based on Sybille Bedford's biography of Huxley (*Aldous Huxley,* New York: Knopf, 1974), and on discussions with her.

p. 112   *I never saw him again."* Nancy Cunard in conversation with Hugh Ford, 1963.

119   *rooftop in the south of France.* John Jukes Johnson, "Nancy Cunard: Sketches of a Scandalous Friend," *Queen* (London), July 1969.

120   *Englishwoman, Duff Twysden.* Stated by Nancy in a short note about Duff Twysden written for Solita Solano.

Chapter 9

Nancy's poetry scrapbook contains letters about her poetry.

p. 127   *was for me."* GM.

128   *jealous scenes.* Nancy Cunard in conversation with Professor Hugh Ford, 1963.

Chapter 10

p. 133   *great gentleness and delicacy.* Written for her book on George Moore but omitted for fear of scandal. See Chapter 28.

137   *hard day's work."* BPIR.

139   *never to meet Lady Cunard.* Interviews with the late Miss Flanner, May 1974, and the late Miss Solano, March 1975.

142   *in which [she] lived."* Hugh Thomas, *John Strachey* (London: Eyre Methuen, 1973).

144   *gaiety this vulnerability."* BPIR.

p. 145   *wanted to marry again.* In 1926 Sydney Fairbairn was married to Angela Fane. The marriage was, according to their son John Fairbairn, "a notably happy one." Sydney Fairbairn's health never altogether recovered from his experiences in the First World War, and he died in 1943.

Chapter 11

p. 148   *"icy green velvet dress."* BPIR.
149   *drinking red wine.* BPIR.
         African ivory bracelets." BPIR.
         inadequate, or indiscreet." Interview with Louis Aragon, March 1974.
         sexually too demanding. Interview with Raymond Michelet, April 1974.

Chapter 12

John Banting's and Georges Sadoul's descriptions of Le Puits Carré appear in BPIR. Nancy wrote two accounts of the Hours Press: an article for the *Book Collector* of winter 1964, and *These Were the Hours,* edited and with a foreword by Hugh Ford (Carbondale and Edwardsville, Ill.: Southern Illinois University Press, 1969).

p. 159   *Aragon's love for her.* According to Raymond Michelet, a long passage (pp. 36–42 in the edition of *Irène* published by L'Or du Temps, Paris, 1968) that has no relation to the rest of the book is a lament by Aragon at the end of his relationship with Nancy. (Letter from Michelet, October 1977.)
161   *inflicted on her lovers.* André Thirion, *Revolutionaries without Revolution* (New York: Macmillan, 1975).

Chapter 13

In this and subsequent chapters I have quoted from and used information contained in Henry Crowder's unpublished autobiography, written in the mid-1930s with the help of a journalist, the late Mr. Hugo Speck. The typescript is in the possession of Dr. Ernest B. Speck of Sul Ross State University, Alpine, Texas.

p. 162   *everyone else crazy*. ND.

          was speaking of her. Aragon Parle. . . . Interview of Aragon by Dominique Arban (Paris: Seghers, 1968).

167   *Henry Crowder, Jr., was born.* Crowder's autobiography does not mention that he had a child. This information comes from his granddaughter, Mrs. Dolores Finch of Washington, D.C.

171   *beginning of their relationship.* These letters are in a private collection.

Chapter 14

p. 177   *drive in the country.* Nancy Cunard in conversation with Professor Hugh Ford, 1963.

          critical time in her life. Richard Aldington's letters to Bridget Patmore are in the HRC. I am much indebted to Mrs. Carolyn Harris for drawing them to my attention.

186   *he said calmly.* Interview with the late Miss Janet Flanner, May 1974.

          Crowder replied mildly. Interview with Sir Harold Acton, October 1974.

          we hired a piano for Réanville." TWTH.

Chapter 15

Sources for this chapter and Chapter 16 include TWTH and Hugh Ford, *Published in Paris* (New York: Macmillan, 1976).

Chapter 16

p. 201   *to Nancy for her support.* Interview with Mr. André Thirion, March 1975.

          he fell in love with her. Interview with Mr. Raymond Michelet, March 1975.

202   *and gusty talk."* Sir Harold Acton, *Memoirs of an Aesthete* (London: Methuen, 1948).

203   *in her place.* Interview with the late Mrs. Wyn Henderson, November 1974.

207   *straight to the Hours Press.* Interview with Mr. Samuel Beckett, April 1975.

p. 208   *parts of* Parallax. Interview with Mr. Samuel Beckett, April 1975.

          am I doing here?" Interview with Sir Harold Acton, October 1974.

209   *had been an inspiration.* TWTH.

Chapter 17

Nancy's account of her breach with her mother is taken from her privately printed pamphlet *Black Man and White Ladyship*.

p. 212   *around the door.* Interview with Mr. D. C. S. Phillips, November 1976.

213   *Sir Harold has recalled.* Interview with Sir Harold Acton, October 1974.

          rococo Italian tables." Diana Mosley, *A Life of Contrasts* (London: Hamish Hamilton, 1977).

          dissatisfied with me as a lion." Michael Davie, ed., *The Diaries of Evelyn Waugh* (London: Weidenfeld and Nicolson, 1976, and Boston: Little Brown, 1976).

221   *with a young man."* Marie Jaqueline Lancaster, *Brian Howard: The Story of a Failure* (London: Blond, 1968).

222   *what will happen.* This and subsequent quotations from Brian Howard's letters and diaries are taken from Marie Jaqueline Lancaster, op. cit.

226   *black man repelled her.* Interview with the late Sir Robert Abdy, February 1975.

227   *black astrakhan cap."* Interview with the late Mrs. Wyn Henderson, November 1974.

Chapter 18

Raymond Michelet's account of his relationship with Nancy is in BPIR. This chapter and the next are also based on interviews with him.

p. 235   *movement was in progress.* BPIR.

237   *their close friendship.* Interview with the late Mrs. Wyn Henderson, November 1974.

Chapter 19

p. 250   *was all she said.* Daphne Fielding, *Emerald and Nancy: Lady*

Cunard and Her Daughter (London: Eyre & Spottiswoode, 1968).

Chapter 20

p. 255   *into the blind."* Nancy Cunard in a letter to Professor Hugh Ford, 1964.
longing to fight." Nancy Cunard in a letter to Professor Hugh Ford, 1964.

260   *her quick wit."* BPIR.

265   *Disappears from Harlem."* BPIR.
his meeting with her. The late Eugene Gordon wrote the account for BPIR, in which a shortened version appears.

269   *shrug of the shoulders.* Henry Lee Moon writing in the *Amsterdam News,* April 1934.

270   *done to her character.* Interview with Mr. and Mrs. William Patterson, June 1974.

271   *whites must last.* Nancy Cunard, ed., *Negro* (London: Wishart & Co., 1934).

273   *so good a cause.* Interview with Mr. Samuel Beckett, April 1975.

Chapter 21

Sources for this chapter include Professor Hugh Ford's introduction to the edited version of *Negro* (New York: Ungar, 1970), and interviews with Mr. Edgell Rickword, March 1975.

p. 276   *this* is *the format.' "* BPIR.

294   *seriousness beyond question.* Eugene Gordon for BPIR.

Chapter 22

Nancy wrote an account of her friendship with George Padmore and her trip to Russia for Padmore's widow in 1959.

p. 297   *racial and colonial matters.* See James R. Hooker, *Black Revolutionary: George Padmore's Path from Communism to Pan-Africanism* (New York: Praeger, 1970).

299   *would have accepted her.* Interview with Mr. Edgell Rickword, March 1975.

p. 304   *a later American friend.* Nancy Cunard to Professor Charles Burkhart, 1955 (SIU).

307   *matters of this kind."* ND.

Chapter 23

p. 310   *worth fighting for.* George Orwell, *Homage to Catalonia* (London: Secker & Warburg, 1938, and New York: Harcourt, Brace and World, 1969).
loveliest atmosphere going." Martha Gellhorn, *Faces of War* (New York: Simon & Schuster, 1959).

312   *Spanish revolutionary poets.* BPIR.

315   *letters from London."* Pablo Neruda, *Memoirs* (New York: Farrar, Straus & Giroux, 1976).
first publisher of this poem. Nancy herself believed that she published "Spain" first. The leaflet containing the poem is dated April 1937; Faber's version appeared on May 20. However, Auden's bibliographers (Bloomfield and Mendelson, University of Virginia Press, 1972) conclude that Faber published first.

316   *the least Spanish."* Samuel Hynes, *The Auden Generation* (London: Bodley Head, 1976, and New York: Viking Press, 1977).
published later by Faber and Faber." Nancy Cunard to Professor Hugh Ford, 1961.

317   *from the beginning.* Nancy's account of the planning and publishing of the questionnaire comes from letters to Professor Hugh Ford, 1961.

321   *never to get tired.* BPIR.

322   *nor yet again.* Nancy Cunard to Professor Hugh Ford, 1961.

323   *and so did Nancy."* BPIR.

324   *"It did not."* I am grateful to Samuel Beckett's biographer, Mrs. Deirdre Bair, for drawing these letters from Beckett to Thomas McGreevy to my attention.

Chapter 24

p. 331   *wholly desirable fate.* Interview with Mrs. Sybille Bedford, March 1974.

p. 332   *soldiers crossed as well.* Hugh Thomas, *The Spanish Civil War* (London: Penguin, 1965, and New York: Harper & Row, 1977).

338   *were less useful.* Nancy Cunard to Professor Hugh Ford, 1961.

339   *road to Bordeaux."* ND.

Chapter 25

Nancy described her life in London during the war in ND.

p. 341   *enormous dark glasses.* Pablo Neruda, *Memoirs* (New York: Farrar, Straus & Giroux, 1976).

        we all used to meet." BPIR.

        detest this being mentioned." Nancy Cunard to Professor Hugh Ford, 1964.

345   *sat talking with us."* BPIR.

348   *and a blue pencil."* BPIR.

351   *eight on each arm.* BPIR.

353   *unknown to my hostess.* John Lehmann, *I Am My Brother* (London: Longmans, 1960); also in *In My Own Time: Memoirs of a Literary Life* (Boston: Little Brown, 1969).

354   *seemed to him very strong.* Harold Acton, *More Memoirs of an Aesthete* (London: Methuen, 1970).

355   *and this time for me.' "* BPIR.

        encouragement and introductions. Interview with Mr. Walter Strachan, March 1974.

357   *the effect was formidable.* BPIR.

359   *Nancy asked."* BPIR.

Chapter 26

Nancy described the ruin of Le Puits Carré in TWTH. My account of her relationship with William Finley is taken from correspondence with him.

p. 366   *settle down at last.* Interview with Miss Cecily Mackworth, April 1974.

369   *looking after him.* Interview with Mrs. Basil Marsden Smedley, June 1975.

371   *at the captain's table.* Interview with Dame Freya Stark, May 1974.

p. 372   *out of the question.' "* Interview with Lady Diana Cooper,
          January 1974.

377   *scriptwriter Anthony Thorne.* BPIR.

380   *found the place idyllic.* BPIR.

Chapter 27

p. 386   *lovely attitude of now."* Interview with Sir Harold Acton,
          October 1974, and letters from Nancy Cunard to Sir Har-
          old Acton, 1952.
          near the Pantheon. John Jukes Johnson, "Nancy Cunard:
          Sketches of a Scandalous Friend," *Queen* (London), July
          1969).

387   *told to calm down.* Interview with Miss Géraldine Balayé,
          April 1975.

390   *to ask for advice.* Interview with Professor Charles Burk-
          hart, July 1974, and BPIR.

392   *from the 1950s.* Henry Crowder's letters to Nancy are in a
          private collection.
          wrote to Burkhart: Nancy's letters to Professor Charles
          Burkhart are at SIU.

394   *laugh about it.* Interview with Miss Géraldine Balayé.

Chapter 28

p. 396   *THAT is enjoyable.* SIU.

403   *denunciation of her mother.* Interview with Mr. Milton Gen-
          del, October 1974, who also kindly showed me the late
          Iris Tree's letters.

Chapter 29

Nancy described her expulsion from Spain and journey back to England in letters to Clyde Robinson in 1960 (SIU). Anthony Thorne's
account is in BPIR.

p. 410   *series of pathetic letters.* To the late Miss Janet Flanner, the
          late Miss Solita Solano, the late Miss Sylvia Townsend
          Warner, Mr. Norman Sims, Sir Rupert Hart-Davis, and
          others.

Chapter 30

The late Mrs. Louise Theis's letters and description of Nancy's visit are in BPIR. My account of Aragon's reaction to Nancy's situation is based on letters he wrote to Miss Géraldine Balayé.

p. 411   *maddened, but not mad."* BPIR.
         even in free England." BPIR.
420   *hastened his death.* Harold Acton, *Nancy Mitford* (New York: Harper & Row, 1976).

Chapter 31

My account of the Fords' visit to La Mothe is based on interviews with them; Professor Charles Burkhart's description of Nancy at Gourdon is in BPIR.

p. 427   *never quite the same again."* BPIR.
431   *not with me."* Daphne Fielding, *Emerald and Nancy: Lady Cunard and Her Daughter* (London: Eyre & Spottiswoode, 1968).
432   *a twig encrusted with moss."* BPIR.

Chapter 32

My account of the circumstances in which Nancy left the Villa Pomone is based on Daphne Fielding's, who heard about it firsthand. The late Miss Solano, Mrs. Clark and Raymond Michelet all described Nancy's descent on them to me in detail. The late Georges Sadoul's account is in BPIR.

Index

Abbott, Berenice, 140
Abdy, Sir Robert, 215, 226, 373
Abyssinia, 291, 306–7, 353, 367
Ackland, Valentine, 356, 390
Acton, Harold, 135, 154, 186, 204,
    208, 211, 213, 351, 385–86,
    388, 389
  descriptions of Nancy, 93, 202
  Lady Cunard and, 225–26, 250,
    354
  Negro and, 257, 290
Acton, William, 213
Adderley, Peter Broughton, 67–68,
    76, 89
African Notebook (Plomer), 291
Afro-American, 268, 294, 298
L'Âge d'Or (Buñuel and Dali), 218–
    19, 223, 302
Alberti, Rafael, 315
Aldington, Richard, 176–82, 193,
    364
  Hours Press and, 184, 192, 194–
    95, 204, 211, 236–37
  on Nancy, 252–54
Aleixandre, Vicente, 315
"All for Life" (Cunard), 415–16
Allied Newspapers Ltd., 279
Altolaguirre, Manuel, 311
American, 267
American Communist Party, 236
Anderson, Margaret, 190, 371, 374,
    375
Andorra, 368, 369, 371, 404

Anson, Denis, 51
Antheil, George, 235, 256, 288
Antic Hay (Huxley), 111–15, 120
Anti-Jewish League, 218
Apollinaire, Guillaume, 147
Apollinaire (Lowenfels), 206
Arabs, 319, 325–29, 340
Aragon, Louis, 140, 146–53, 218,
    231, 314, 317, 342, 348, 361,
    364, 375, 437
  break-up with Nancy, 161–64,
    175–76, 179, 180–81, 194
  communism and, 152, 183, 290,
    305
  described, 147–48, 194
  Hours Press and, 156–60, 192
  Nancy's breakdown and, 413–
    16, 422
  Triolet and, 175–76, 182–83,
    194, 235
Arconada, César, 336, 338
Arlen, Michael (Dikran
    Kouyoumdjian) "The Baron,"
    94–110, 116, 126, 143, 225,
    325, 402
  Hutchinson and, 96–97
  novels by, 94–95; Nancy as char-
    acter in, 95, 97–109, 119, 120,
    142–43, 265
Armstrong, Louis, 287
Asquith, H. H., 33, 49, 51, 77
Asquith, Margot (Lady Oxford),
    49, 51, 55, 77

Asquith, Raymond, 51
Associated Negro Press (ANP),
    293, 306, 309, 311, 328, 329,
    331, 340, 342, 344, 382
Auden, W. H., 315–16, 317, 318
Auric, Georges, 235
Austin, Alfred, 33
Authors World Peace Appeal, 384
Azikiwe, Ben, 291

Baker, Josephine, 140
Bakst, L. N., 50
Balayé, Géraldine, 368, 387, 394,
    398, 425, 432
Balfour, A. J., 33
Banting, John, 148, 154–55, 204,
    221, 225, 277, 287, 296–97,
    298, 427
  in America with Nancy, 258–63
  Nancy's breakdown and, 411,
    420, 421, 423
  Spanish Civil War and, 315,
    320–23
Baring, Maurice, 123
La Bataille, 374–75
Beach, Sylvia, 130, 189
Beaton, Cecil, 34, 247
Beckett, Samuel, 206–8, 210, 273,
    287, 319, 323–24, 400, 437, 439
Bedford, Sybille, 111, 113, 115,
    330–31, 371, 418
Bedouins, 327–28
Beecham, Joseph, 45–46
Beecham, Sir Thomas, 57
  described, 45–46
  Lady Cunard and, 45, 46–48, 55,
    64, 72, 132, 203, 212, 215,
    216, 227; end of relationship
    between 352, 373
  Nancy and, 47–48, 55, 226–29,
    278
  scandal involving, 46
Beerbohm, Marie, 110–11, 126,
    132, 139

Beerbohm, Max, 43
Bergamín, José, 317
Berry, Walter, 140
Bibesco, Princess, 213
Bird, William, 155
Birkenhead, Baron, 33, 44
bisexuals, 185
Black, Joan, 371–72
Black Man and White Ladyship: An
    Anniversary (Cunard), 245–54,
    261, 265, 267, 311, 318
blacks, see Cunard, Nancy, blacks
    and; Negro
Blackwood, Lord Basil, 33
Blanche ou l'Oubli (Aragon), 148
Blast, 57
Bloch, Jean Richard, 317
Blunden, Edmund, 318
Book Collector, 430
Bouchoux, Gaston, 395
Boyle, Kay, 130, 345, 359
Brancusi, Constantin, 131
Breton, André, 140, 146–47, 148,
    150, 218, 290, 342, 364
Britannia, 22
Brown, Bob, 204, 208, 211
Brown, Sterling, 240, 273–74, 289
Buñuel, Luis, 218
Burke, James, 24
Burkhart, Charles, 390–93, 395,
    405–6, 411, 417, 429–30
Burlington Magazine, 359
Butts, Anthony, 290
Byron, Robert, 226

Calendar of Modern Letters, 276
Calloway, Cab, 287
Campbell, Roy, 204, 208, 364
Camus, Albert, 361
Canto, A (Pound), 192
Cantos (Pound), 211
Cape, Jonathan, 276
Cape publishing company, 276,
    395

Caroling Dusk (Cullen), 289
Carpentier, Horace, 23, 24, 27, 38
Carroll, Lewis, 158, 192
Caruso, Dorothy, 371
Casals, Pablo, 398
Cernuda, Luis, 311
Chambliss, William H., 23
Channon, Chips, 84, 85, 214, 352, 373
Charteris, Cynthia, 33
La Chasse au Snark (Aragon), 158, 192, 205
Chile, 338–41
Churchill, Jennie Jerome, 22; *see also* Cornwallis-West, Jennie
Churchill, Lord Ivor, 213
Churchill, Lord Randolph, 22, 33
Churchill, Winston, 345
Clark, Elizabeth, 436
Cocteau, Jean, 140
Cole, Horace, 53
Colebrooke, A. A., 268, 269, 290
Colefax, Lady, 215
Collected Poems (Rodker), 208
communism, 183, 247, 269, 270, 277, 279, 280, 296–307 *passim,* 374
    attraction of, 296–99
    Communist party membership, 298–99
    fascist threat and, 297
    Nancy's breakdown and, 414, 417
    Negro and, 284, 286, 287, 289, 292, 293–94, 303
    racism and, 271, 284, 297
    Scottsboro Boys case and, 236, 240, 269, 277–80, 286
    Spanish civil war and, 308, 314, 336, 338
    Surrealists and, 152, 235, 290
    World War II and, 346
Confessions (Moore), 86
Connelly, Marc, 239

Cooper, Lady Diana, 55, 127, 128, 213, 214–15, 372, 403
Cooper, Douglas, 431, 441
Cooper, Duff, 51, 64, 127, 372
Cooper, May, 397
Cooper, Sybil, 51
Corey, Mrs. Mabel, 84–85
Cornwallis-West, Jennie, 33, 44
Corrupt Coterie, 51–52, 57, 83
Cotton, Pansy, 43
Coward, Noel, 97
Craigie, John, 75, 83
Craigie, Pearl, 25
Crevel, René, 140, 142, 144, 148, 154, 218, 235, 290, 291, 364
Crisis, 242, 245, 261, 267, 286
Crocker, Mrs. Harry, 27
Crome Yellow (Huxley), 110
Crosby, Caresse, 130
Crowder, Henry, 165–230, 237–44, 258, 398, 400, 413
    background, 166–68
    car accident and, 195, 196–97
    as creative musician, 204, 210, 288, 393
    death of, 392–94
    described, 185–86
    in England, 195–96
    in Harlem, 239–43
    Hours Press and, 186–88, 193–94, 197, 204, 205, 210
    Lady Cunard and, 196, 212–29, *passim,* 250–51, 259, 260
    Nancy on, 378
    Negro and, 210, 238, 242, 281, 282, 284, 285, 288, 292, 293, 303
    notoriety of, 261–63
    in Paris, 183–86
    planned African trip and, 182, 186
    Pound and, 366–67, 392
    on prejudice, 304
    reunited with Nancy, 279–83

Crowder, Henry (continued)
  troubled relationship with
    Nancy, 197–98, 199, 205–6,
    209–10, 222, 224, 230–31,
    237–38, 243–44, 281, 296; end
    of, 299–301; reflections on,
    301–4
  wife of, 167–68, 230, 394
Crowder, Henry, Jr., 167
Crowley, Aleister, 358
Crozier, W. P., 334
Cullen, Countée, 242, 289
Cullen, John, 385, 388
Cunard, Sir Bache (father), 21,
    363, 428
  background of, 21–22
  death of, 143, 145
  described, 19, 28–29, 39, 41
  marriage of, 23, 27–28
  Nancy and, 41, 44, 48, 54, 78,
    87, 102; marriage of, 60, 61
  Nevill Holt and, 28–29, 34
  separation from wife, 45, 47, 50,
    54
Cunard, Sir Edward (cousin), 39,
    83, 84, 126, 165, 169, 179,
    273, 343, 370, 427–28
Cunard, Edward (grandfather), 22
Cunard, Edward (uncle), 21, 22
Cunard, Gordon (uncle), 22, 39
Cunard, Mary McEvers (grand-
    mother), 22
Cunard, Lady (Maud Alice Burke,
    "Emerald"; mother):
  admirers of, 19, 24–27, 33–35, 38
  in Asquith house, 49–50
  background of, 23–24
  Beecham and, 45, 46–47, 55, 64,
    72, 132, 203, 212, 215, 216–17,
    227, 352, 373
  Crowder and, 196, 212–30 pas-
    sim, 250–51, 259, 260
  death of, 372–74, 376
  described, 19, 28, 39, 214; by

  Moore, 25–26; by Nancy, 41,
    247–48; by Miss Woolf, 49;
    by Virginia Woolf, 214
  as hostess, 31–35, 50, 55–56,
    213–16, 433
  marriage of, 23, 27–28
  Moore and, 24–27, 34–35, 40,
    47, 63–64, 80–81, 124, 214,
    215n., 219–21, 236
  at Nevill Holt, 28–40
  new name of, 215
  opposition to Fairbairn, 59–60
  Poniatowski and, 27
  relationship with Nancy, see Cu-
    nard, Nancy, mother and
  separation from husband, 45, 47,
    49
  World War II and, 352–54
Cunard, Nancy:
  adolescence, 47–57
  affinity for undesirables, 280, 377
  African ivory collection, 149,
    171, 185–86, 210, 291, 351,
    356, 363–64, 413, 430, 435,
    442; book about, 398–99, 400,
    403; described, 144, 154, 274
  L'Âge d'Or and, 218–19
  alcohol and, 72, 92, 100, 135,
    144, 177, 185, 325–26, 370,
    375, 386, 387; drunkenness,
    76, 79, 89, 93, 161, 180, 181,
    205, 223, 224, 242–43, 375–76;
    in last years, 427, 428, 435,
    436, 440; mental breakdown
    and, 404, 405, 409, 412, 414,
    417, 418
  Aragon and, 130–64; see also
    Aragon, Louis
  "autobiography" of, 401–3, 428
  autograph album of, 42–45
  avant-garde Paris and, 130–52,
    passim
  birth of, 31
  blacks and, 140, 165–66, 184–85;

Black Man and White Ladyship: An Anniversary, 246–54; cause of, 230, 235–44, 303–4, 348–49, 350–51, 382, 403, 425–26; Crowder, *see* Crowder, Henry; "Does Anyone *Know* Any Negroes?," 245–46; in Harlem, 239–43, 258–64, 267; Negro anthology and, 210, 238, 240, 242, 245, 254; Scottsboro Boys, 235–36, 259–60, 277–78, 279, 286; turning-point conversation concerning, 187–88; in the West Indies, 270–71, 343–44; *see also Negro, and specific individuals*

as character in novels by: Aldington, 252–54; Aragon, 148; Arlen, 94, 97–109, 119, 120, 142–43, 265; Hemingway, 119, 120; Huxley, 111–20, 265; Lewis, 128; Moore, 133–34

childhood, 19, 20, 31, 35–40; effects of, 4–8; end of, 41–48

in Chile, 338–39, 341

communism and, *see* communism

Crowder and, *See* Crowder, Henry

death of, 439–41

debut of, 52

described, 36, 38, 39, 54–55, 60–61, 62, 68, 92–94, 161, 179–80, 233–35, 269, 355; by Acton, 93, 202; by Aldington, 178–82, 252–54; in *La Bataille*, 374; by Burkhart, 430; calypso song about, 343; by Crowder, 302–4; by Flanner, 360–61; by Garnett, 54–55; by Gordon, 266; by gossips, 79–80; by Hobson, 351; by Howard, 315; by Hutchinson, 93; by Johnson, 386–87; by Michelet, 232–33; by Mortimer, 92; by Lady Mosley, 213; by Nancy, 70–90 *passim*, 198–99, 412–13; by Neruda, 311; by Thirion, 161; by Thorne, 377–78; by Tree, 54; by Waley, 50; by Warner, 356–57; by Miss Woolf, 49; by Leonard Woolf, 143–44

diary of 1919, 70–88

Douglas and, *see* Douglas, Norman

drugs (narcotics), and, 221–22, 417

education in Europe, 50–51

fascism and, 405–10 *passim*, 427, 430, 439

father and, 60, 61, 102; death of, 143, 145; relationship with, 41, 44, 48, 54, 78, 87

fear of being alone, 232, 234, 413

finances of, 143, 228–29, 279, 376, 427, 435, 442

Flanner and, 137, 139, 142, 154, 163–64, 250, 360–61

governesses of, 37, 38, 50, 136

Grand Man: Memories of Norman Douglas, 383–93

homosexuals and, 185, 221, 224

Hours Press and, *see* Hours Press

illnesses of, 70, 89, 202, 223, 225, 299–300, 370; in later years, 404–7, 425, 428–40 *passim*; mental breakdowns, 404–23, 435–40; operations, 100–3, 231, 234, 404

inheritances, 143, 373, 376, 428

as journalist, 309–13, 331–36, 350–51, 358, 359, 382; inability to find work as, 339, 340, 346, 348

last years of, 424–32

lesbians and, 184, 219, 397

libel suit by, 279

Cunard, Nancy (*continued*)
"liberator" of, 65
loyalty of, 138
marriage of, 58–69; ending of, 68–69, 70, 73, 81–82, 89, 145; foundering of, 61–69; sex and, 62
in Mexico, 342
Moore and, 47, 73, 78, 82–83, 86, 128–29, 132–34, 139, 148, 376, 380; death of, 236; as father figure, 35–37, 42, 150, 219–21, 226; *G.M.: Memories of George Moore,* 395–400; Hours Press and, 157–58, 160, 184, 191–94; poetry and, 50, 56–57, 63–64, 73, 123–24, 126–27, 132; portrait of, 376, 380, 396, 432
mother and, 19–20, 52, 55, 81, 87, 102, 124, 127, 131–32, 139, 151, 152; Arlen on, 106–7; Beecham and, 47, 55, 203; breach between, 212–29, 236, 245–54, 259, 260, 290, 296, 352–54, 372–74, 403, 417; childhood and, 31, 38–41; Crowder and, 196, 212–30 *passim,* 250–51, 259, 260; death of, 372–74; living together, 72–77, 86, 89–90; marriage and, 59–61; Miss Woolf on, 49
at Nevill Holt, 31–47
new relationships and, 75, 85
as 1920s woman, 91–94
1923 and, 130
"Now Lies She There" and, 252–54
Outlaws and, 102, 121–24, 135
Parallax and, 141–42
patriotism and, 347
as patron, 130
Poems for France and, 354–56
as poet, 63–64, 66, 71, 72, 78, 85, 121–29, 135–37, 289–90, 386, 425, 432, 433; doubts

about, 190; Moore and, 50, 56–57, 63–64, 73, 123–24, 126–27, 132; mother and, 57, 64, 124; Pound and, 124–26; reviews of, 123–24, 137, 141–42; World War II and, 348, 354–56, 365, 382
pornography and, 159
in postwar France, 360–83; at Réanville home, 362–65, 369, 371
primitive art collection, 201, 363
as publisher, *see* Hours Press
Le Puits Carré and, 153–56, 362–65, 369, 371
questionable parentage of, 19, 35–36, 78–79, 397
rejection of marriage, 69
reputation of, 79–80, 92, 98
sex and, 62, 201, 269; casual, 92, 111, 118, 173, 185, 377; Crowder on, 302–3; demanding nature of, 149, 177, 376; homosexuals and, 221, 224; mental breakdown and, 408, 409, 417; Michelet on, 231–35; nymphomania, 233–35
Solano and, 137–39, 142, 154, 163–64, 250, 360
Spanish civil war and, *see* Spanish civil war
Sublunary and, 135–37
Surrealism and, 182
Tree and, *see* Tree, Iris
in the West Indies, 270–71, 343–44
Wheels and, 53, 63–64
White Man's Duty, The and, 348–49, 350
World War I and, 58–69 *passim,* 91; aftermath of, 76
World War II and, 345–59
writing projects of, 381–404; *see also* Negro

Cunard, Sir Samuel (great-grandfather), 21–22, 143
Cunard, Victor (cousin), 39, 57, 99, 140, 175, 179, 187, 273, 278, 351, 359, 371, 388, 389, 390
    Nancy's last years and, 409, 410, 418, 420–21, 428
Cunardia School, Nigeria, 425–26
Curzon, Lady, 59
Curzon, Lord, 59, 77
Cust, Harry, 33

Dada, 131, 135, 140, 146–47
Daily Dispatch, 279
Daily Express, 149, 247
Daily Mail, 406–7
Daily Mirror, 258, 260–61
Daily News (Moscow), 306
Daily Telegraph, 137
Daily Worker (London), 292
Daily Worker (New York), 293
Dali, Salvador, 218
Davenport, John, 379, 385
Davis, Beale, 76, 86, 99, 248
Dawson, Cecilia, 428
Dawson, Geoffrey, 428
Dawson, Michael, 428
Death of a Hero (Aldington), 177
Delano, Luis Enrique, 311, 341
del Carril, Delia, 341
del Vayo, Alvarez, 329
de Massot, Pierre, 132
Derain, André, 140
Desborough, Lady, 55
de Walden, Lord Howard, 43
Diaghilev, Sergei, 50
Dial, 125, 126, 190, 194
Diary of Society as It Really Is (Chambliss), 23
"Does Anyone *Know* Any Negroes?," 245–6, 261
Doolittle, Hilda, 176
Douglas, Archie, 324

Douglas, Norman, 65, 134–35, 140, 162, 186, 190, 257, 273, 291
    death of, 383, 384
    described, 134, 389
    as father figure, 150
    Grand Man: Memories of Norman Douglas, 383–93
    Hours Press and, 157, 184, 191
    last meeting with Nancy, 379
    Spanish civil war and, 318, 320, 331, 334
    in Tunisia, 324–29
    World War II and, 346–50, 355–56, 357
Douglass, Frederick, 285
Dreiser, Theodore, 286, 293
Du Bois, W. E. B., 242, 286, 294
Duchamp, Marcel, 132
Duff, Charles, 309, 389
Dufferin, Lady, 213
Duggan, Mrs. Alfred (Lady Curzon), 59
Dunsany, Lord, 355

Earp, Tommy (T. W.), 56, 79, 110, 126, 127, 364
Eaten Heart, The (Aldington), 192, 195
Eden, Anthony, 353
Edward VII, King, 33
Edward VIII, King, 352, 434
Ehrenburg, Ilya, 338
Eiffel Tower restaurant, *see* Tower restaurant
Eliot, Montague, 37, 43
Eliot, T. S., 79, 125, 176, 276, 318, 364, 433–34
    The Waste Land and, 126, 141, 207
Elkin Matthews and Marrot, 121
Ellington, Duke, 287
Ellis, Amabel Williams, 137
Ellis, Havelock, 139, 211

Éluard, Paul, 146–47, 148, 218, 235, 361
Emmet, Robert, 24, 36
Empire News, 278–79
Ernst, Max, 148, 150, 218
Esther Waters (Moore), 25
Ethiopia, 291, 306–7, 353, 367
Eton *College Chronicle*, 57
Étude pour le Linge, 376, 380
Eyeless in Gaza (Huxley), 119

Fairbairn, Ian, 58
Fairbairn, Steve, 58
Fairbairn, Sydney, 58–69, 79, 83, 87, 114
   marriage to Nancy, 60–61; ending of, 68–69, 70, 73, 81–82, 89, 145; foundering of, 61–69
Fargue, Léon-Paul, 140
fascism, 150, 296, 347, 350, 362, 366–67
   Nancy and, breakdown of, 405–10 *passim*
   Spanish civil war and, 308–39 *passim*
Felipe, León, 313
Finley, William Le Page, 368–76
Firbank, Ronald, 364
Fitzgibbon, Constantine, 385
Flanner, Janet, 140–44, 186, 340, 342, 360–61
   Nancy, Solano and, 137–39, 142, 154, 163–64, 250, 360–61
   Nancy's breakdown and, 411, 412, 414, 419
Ford, Ford Madox, 155
Ford, Hugh, 428–29, 431, 435
Ford, James W., 287, 294, 298, 306
Ford, Thérèse, 428–29
Forster, E. M., 318
Foster, Maud, 46
Fountains in the Sand (Douglas), 326, 395

Four Unposted Letters to Catherine (Riding), 204, 206
Franco, Francisco, 308, 309, 313, 324, 331–36 *passim*, 367, 370, 398, 405, 407, 430
   see also Spanish civil war
Friede, Donald, 276
Futurists, 57

Gandarillas, Tony, 196, 372, 373, 431
García Lorca, Federico, 311, 315
Garnett, David, 54, 189
Garvey, Marcus, 270–71
Garvin, J. L., 124
Gellert, Lawrence, 264–65, 288
Gellhorn, Martha, 310
Gendel, Milton, 403
Georges, Yvonne, 132
Georgia Nigger (Spivak), 286
Germans, 338–59 *passim*, 362, 381
Gervasito (Spanish refugee), 329–30
Gilbert, Morris, 347–48, 351, 356, 359, 365–66, 376, 413
Glenconner, Lord, 56
Glyn, Elinor, 37, 94
G.M.: Memories of George Moore (Cunard), 395–401
Goasgüens (innkeepers), 358, 359, 363, 364
Goded, Angel, 310, 311, 336, 338, 370, 412–13
Goffin, Robert, 287
Gold, Mike, 293
Gollancz publishing company, 276, 319
Gordon, Eugene, 265–66, 294, 306
Gordon, Taylor, 259, 361, 267, 269–70, 285, 293
La Grande Gaité (Aragon), 164
Grand Man: Memories of Norman Douglas (Cunard), 383–93, 426
Graves, Robert, 123, 189, 204, 206, 364

Green Hat, The (Arlen), 94, 101, 103–9, 142–43, 266
Green Pastures (Connelly), 239
Gregory, Lady, 34
Grenfell, Billy, 51
Grenfell, Imogen, 213
Grenfell, Julian, 55, 67
Guérin, Jean, 198, 406, 429–36
Guevara, Alvaro "Chile," 56, 65, 66, 79, 86, 99, 192, 194, 363, 364
    portrait of Nancy, 87, 88, 90, 113
Guggenheim, Peggy, 130, 140
Guillen, Nicolás, 270, 289, 314, 344

Hamnett, Nina, 127, 132
Hark the Herald (Aldington), 194
Harlem, 239–43, 377, 378
    Nancy in, 239–43, 258–64, 267
    Renaissance, 240
Harrison, Austin, 85
Harrison, S. C., 376, 396
Hart-Davis, Deirdre, 65, 66, 89
Hart-Davis, Rupert, 65, 66, 67, 89, 148, 275–76
    as Nancy's publisher, 395, 401, 403, 428
Hart-Davis, Sybil Cooper, 51, 64–69, 73, 86, 89, 143, 276
Hayward, John, 433
Héloïse and Abélard (Moore), 127, 157
Hemingway, Ernest, 119, 120, 155, 190, 322–23
Henderson, Gavin, 213
Henderson, Wyn, 195, 203, 208, 211, 214, 227, 231, 237, 252
Henry-Music (Crowder), 210–11, 288, 364, 378
Herald Tribune, 192
Hiler, Hilaire, 235
Hitler, Adolf, 297, 308, 324, 340, 341, 344, 353, 358

Hobbes, John Oliver, 25
Hobson, Anthony, 351, 430
Hobson, Geoffrey, 351
Hodder and Stoughton publishing company, 135
Hogarth Press, 140–41, 189
Holloway Prison, 409–10
Holloway Sanatorium, 410–23
Home to Harlem (McKay), 257
homosexuals, 185, 221, 224, 243, 248, 320, 368, 397, 422
Hone, Joseph, 395
Horizon, 359, 360, 361
Hours Press, 172, 183, 189–211, 380, 388, 413, 430
    accomplishments of, 211
    aims of, 190
    Beckett and, 206–7
    book about, 428–29, 435
    closing of, 211, 236–37, 245
    Crowder and, 186–88, 193–95, 197–98, 204, 205, 210
    described, 201
    Douglas and, 157, 184, 192
    establishment of, 155–61
    finances of, 191
    Henderson and, 208, 211, 231, 237
    material for, 192, 195
    Moore and, 157–48, 160, 184, 191–94
    move to Paris of, 197, 198, 200
    Pound and, 190, 192, 194, 206, 211
    series of books produced by, 192, 204, 206, 211
How about Europe (Douglas), 390
Howard, Brian, 204, 208, 211, 221–25, 243, 245, 249–50, 368, 386
    Spanish civil war and, 315–19, 324, 330–31
How Britain Rules Africa (Padmore), 298

Hughes, Langston, 240, 242, 285, 289, 293, 314, 320
Huis Clos (Sartre), 362
Humby, Betty, 352
Hunter, Mary, 33, 45, 124
Hunting of the Snark, The (Carroll), 158, 192
Hurston, Zora Neale, 285
Hutchinson, Mary, 74, 93, 110, 434
Hutchinson, St. John, 66, 71, 74, 77–78, 80, 85–86, 110, 127, 364, 434
  on Arlen, 96–97
Huxley, Aldous, 110–20, 127, 265, 318, 364
Huxley, Maria Nys, 110, 111, 117, 118

Intellectuals Alliance, 341
Intellectuals Committee, 337
International Brigade, 313, 321
International Labor Defense, 236, 269, 278
Irène (Aragon), 159
Ivy, James, 286

James, Henry, 19, 33
jazz, 53, 287
Jeune Fille Sophistiquée, 131
Jews, 348, 353, 367
John, Augustus, 53, 65, 66
Johnson, Arthur, 386, 387, 389
Johnson, John, 386–87
Jolas, Eugène, 207
Jones, Chris, 281
Jouhandeau, Marcel, 181
Joyce, James, 202–3

Kenyatta, Jomo, 291
Khrushchev, Nikita, 410
Kisling, Moise, 140
Koestler, Arthur, 314
Kokoschka, Oskar, 139

Kouyoumdjian, Dikran, see Arlen, Michael
Kreymborg, Alfred, 290
Ku Klux Klan, 263, 264

Lady Chatterley's Lover (Lawrence), 119, 159
La France Libre publishing company, 355
la Rochelle, Drieu, 140
Last Straws (Aldington), 211, 237
Laurencin, Marie, 140
Lavery, Lady, 213
Lawrence, D. H., 117, 178
League of Nations, 306, 329, 340
League of Patriots, 218
Leavis, F. R., 276
Lees-Milne, James, 372
Left Review, 319–20
Leginska, Ethel, 33
Lehmann, John, 347, 353, 354
lesbians, 184, 218
Les Enfants du Paradis, 362
Les Lettres Françaises, 414–15, 416, 422, 441
Lester, Ada, 291
Lett-Haines, Arthur, 278
Lévy (printer), 155–60, 192–93, 201
Lévy-Bruhl, Lucien, 272
Lewis, Wyndham, 56, 57, 65, 73, 128, 135, 176, 202, 226, 364, 405
Liberator, 257
Lindsay, Jack, 189
Littérature, 146
Little Review, 190, 198–99, 371
Locke, Alain, 240, 293
London Daily News, 141
London Evening Standard, 441
London Times, 351, 373, 428
London Venture, The (Arlen), 94
Lord, Eda, 371
Lovers of Aurelay, The (Moore), 78

Lowenfels, Lilian, 205
Lowenfels, Walter, 130, 204, 205, 208, 210, 288, 416, 428
Lowry, Malcolm, 371–72
Lowry, Margerie, 371–72
Lye, Len, 204

McAlmon, Robert, 128, 130, 139, 140, 189–90, 202
McCarthy, Joseph, 289
MacCown, Eugene, 128, 130, 132, 135, 137, 139, 141, 142, 206, 363
MacDiarmid, Hugh, 355
McEvers, Bache, 22
McGreevy, Tom, 207, 208
Machen, Arthur, 318
McIntosh, Alastair, 87
McKay, Claude, 204, 257–58, 273
Mackworth, Cecily, 379, 417
Macpherson, Kenneth, 287, 379, 388, 389
McVickar, Jim, 89–90
Malkine, Georges, 201, 363
Mallarmé, Stéphane, 192
Manchester Guardian, 137, 141, 331, 334
Mandeville, Consuelo Iznaga, 22
Mandeville, Viscount, 22
Mann, Heinrich, 317
Manners, Lady Diana (Cooper), 33, 43, 51–52, 53, 56, 58, 60
Mano, Guy Levis, 211
Margaret, Princess, 391
Marsh, Edward, 33, 38
Massingham, H. W., 124
Matheus, John Frederick, 286
Matthews, Ralph, 287
Maugham, Somerset, 33
Maxwell, Elsa, 84, 173
Melchett, Lord, 66
Memoirs of an Aesthete (Acton), 388
Memoirs of My Dead Life (Moore), 34–35

Mercati, Countess Atalanta, 109
Messel, Oliver, 172
Mes Souvenirs (Symons), 192
Methuen publishing company, 385, 388
Mew, Charlotte, 123
Mexborough, Lord, 30
Mexico, 338, 342, 370
Meynell, Francis, 33, 189
Michelet, Raymond, 225, 231–38, 243, 246, 258, 281, 362
  on Nancy, 232–33
  Nancy's death and, 437–39
  Negro and, 245, 255, 271–74, 283, 284, 291, 297
  Surrealists and, 201
Mills, Florence, 287
Miró, Joan, 150
Mitford, Nancy, 420
Modernist movement, 146
Moffat, Curtis, 86, 87, 126, 127, 132
Moffat, Iris Tree, 86–87, 93, 111, 126, 127
  see also Tree, Iris
Moffat, Ivan, 127
Mond, Henry (Lord Melchett), 66
Montagu, Ivor, 317
Moore, George, 34, 214
  described, 25, 78
  Lady Cunard and, 24–27, 34–35, 40, 47, 63–64, 80–81, 124, 214, 215n., 219–21, 236
  Nancy and, see Cunard, Nancy
Moore, George Gordon, 53
Moors, 314
Morgan, Evan, 56, 61, 110, 364
Morgan, Louise (Theis), 141–42
Mortimer, Raymond, 92, 132, 141, 144, 355, 364, 390, 400, 411, 419
Mosley, Cynthia, 142
Mosley, Lady, 213, 214–15, 353
Mosley, Sir Oswald, 117, 142, 213, 215, 353

Moss, Geoffrey, 318
Mouchoir de Nuages (Tzara), 131
Mummer's Wife (Moore), 86
Murphy, Esther, 371
Murry, John Middleton, 117
Mussolini, Benito, 306, 307, 308, 326

NAACP (National Association for the Advancement of Colored People), 236, 242, 286, 293, 294
Narcisa (Spanish refugee), 329–30
Nation, 123, 124
Nazi-Soviet Pact, 338, 340
Negro (Cunard), 210, 238, 240, 242, 245, 255, 400, 412, 413, 415, 425, 426
    aftermath of, 296–98
    banned in West Indies, 294, 343
    communism and, 284, 286, 287, 289, 292, 293–94, 303
    described, 283–91
    making of, 255–74; black reaction to, 261, 267, 269–70; in Boston, 265–66; in Harlem, 258–65; lack of plans for, 255, 272; Michelet and, 245, 255, 271–74, 283, 284, 291, 297; payment for contributions to, 273–74; publicity and, 259–64, 267; scope of, 255–56; in the West Indies, 270–71
    private response to, 293–94, 303
    publication of, 275–95
    public response to, 292, 293, 294–95
    Russian interest in, 305–6
Negro Welfare Centre, 350
Negro Welfare League of London, 280
Negro Worker, 297
Neruda, Pablo, 310, 311, 315, 317, 339, 341, 414

Nevill Holt, 212, 336, 380, 390, 396–97
    described, 20–21; by Nancy, 31–32
    guests at, 32–35
    Maud at, 28–40
    Nancy at, 31–47
New Masses, 293
New Negro, The (Locke), 240
New Statesman, 123, 141, 276, 292, 348, 354, 355
New Times, 309, 351
New Yorker, 137
New York Times, 292
News Chronicle, 351
Nichols, Beverly, 214
Nichols, Robert, 87–88, 110, 325, 364
Nicolson, Harold, 84, 213, 214, 353, 390, 400
Nigger Heaven (Van Vechten), 242
"Now Lies She There" (Aldington), 252–54

O'Brien, William, 24
Observer, 124, 390, 400
One Day (Douglas), 184, 192, 359
Orioli, Pino, 135, 190
Orwell, George, 310, 314
Our Time, 346, 348, 359
Outlaws (Cunard), 102, 121–24, 135, 276
Outlook, 141, 142
Oxford, Lady, *see* Asquith, Margot
Ozanne, Marie, 51, 70–72, 79–80, 86
Ozanne sisters, 50–51

Padmore, George, 291, 297–99, 305, 306, 425
    White Man's Duty and, 346, 348–49, 353
Panama, 370
Pankhurst, Sylvia, 309

Papafiou, Douglas, 280
Parallax (Cunard), 141–42, 189, 208, 400
Parsons, Alan, 52, 83
Parsons, Viola Tree, 52
Patmore, Bridget, 177–82, 194, 207
Patterson, William, 269–70, 278, 305
Payne, John, 243, 287
Pedroso, Regino, 289
PEN club, 354, 377
People, 343
Peronnik the Fool (Moore), 157–58, 160, 184, 192, 193, 194, 395
Picabia, Gabrielle, 358
Picasso, Pablo, 149, 150
Pickens, William, 242, 293
Piracy (Arlen), 94, 95, 97, 101, 102
Pisan Cantos (Pound), 367
Pius, Pope, 39
Pizer, Dorothy, 346
Plaquette of Poems, A (Tree), 192
Plomer, William, 290, 291, 355, 419
Poems for France (Cunard), 354–56, 415
Poems for Spain (Cunard), 382
Poems for Spain (Spender and Lehmann), 354
Point Counter Point (Huxley), 116–18, 265
Poiret, Paul, 83–84, 85
Poniatowski, Prince André, 27
pornography, 159
Pound, Ezra, 56, 57, 136, 140, 155, 176, 177, 178, 202, 257, 318, 364
  as fascist, 350, 366–67
  Hours Press and, 190, 192, 194, 206, 211
  insanity and, 366–67, 392
  on Nancy's poetry, 125–26
  Negro and, 273, 291
Powell, Anthony, 400

Probable Music of Beowulf (Pound), 192
Le Puits Carré, 153–55, 362–65, 371
Punch, 400

Radiguet, Raymond, 140
Ralli, Ted, 79, 89
Rathbone, Irene, 354–55, 359, 380–81, 418, 432
La Révolution Surréaliste, 147
Ray, Man, 131, 132, 140, 164, 204, 210, 218
Reynolds, Mary, 132
Ribbentrop, Joachim von, 353
Richter, Hans, 46
Rickword, Edgell, 123, 316, 346, 369
  Negro and, 276–77, 281–84, 290
Riding, Laura, 189, 204, 206
Roaring Queen, The (Lewis), 128
Robeson, Paul, 258–59, 260, 261
Robinson, Bill "Bojangles," 287
Robinson, Clyde, 407, 425
Rodker, John, 140, 142, 144, 189, 190, 206, 208, 363
Roosevelt, Franklin Delano, 345
Rose, Bill, 405
Ross, Alan 355
Roumain, Jacques, 289
Russell, Bertrand, 87
Russia, 284, 290, 336, 338, 349
  Nancy in, 305–6
  Nazi-Soviet Pact, 338, 340
  World War II and, 344, 346, 348
Rutland, Duchess of, 33, 43, 51
Ryan, Frank, 321–22

Sackville-West, Vita, 38, 43, 318, 355
Sadoul, Georges, 148, 153–54, 164, 176, 200–1, 218, 231, 235, 290, 415
  Nancy's death and, 437–39

Saint George at Silene (Guevara), 192, 194
St. Helens Orchestral Society, 46
Salvo for Russia, 348
Sartre, Jean-Paul, 361, 362
Scanlon, Bob, 219, 288
Scarth, Miss (governess), 37, 38
Schomberg, Arthur, 286, 293
Schrijver, Herman, 351, 369, 391
  Nancy's last years and, 427, 429–30, 435
Scott, Geoffrey, 111, 364
Scottsboro Boys case, 235–36, 240, 248, 259–60, 269, 270, 277–81, 286
Scrutiny, 276
Seabrooke, Elliott, 204
Secker and Warburg publishing company, 388
Seizin Press, 189
Selassie, Haile, 291, 306, 307
Sender, Ramón, 317
Senhouse, Roger, 388, 410, 419
Sharp, Clifford, 77, 87, 364
Shaw, George Bernard, 319
Shaw, Walter, 198
Sibthorpe, John, 208
Simpson, Wallis, 352
Sitwell, Osbert, 53, 55, 134, 364
Sitwell, Sacheverell, 134, 373
Sitwell brothers, 56, 63, 66, 128, 213
Sketch, 127, 128, 192
Sliwinski, Jan, 132
Smith, Eleanor, 318
Smith, F. E.(Baron Birkenhead), 33, 44
Smith, Homer, 305
Smyth, Ethel, 46
Soft Answers (Aldington), 252
Solano, Solita, 368, 370, 371, 385, 400, 404
  Nancy, Flanner and, 137–39, 142, 154, 163–64, 250, 360–61

Nancy's last years and, 420, 424, 433–37, 441
"Sonnets to Aurelia" (Nichols), 87–88
Sotheby's auction gallery, 427
Soupault, Philippe, 140, 146, 148
South, Eddie, 165, 167, 288
Southern Illinois University Press, 435
Southern Road (Brown), 289
South Wind (Douglas), 65, 134, 135
"Spain" (Auden), 315–16
Spain, 405–8
Spain at War, 309
Spanish civil war,
  aftermath of, 367–68, 369–70, 377, 382, 398; Nancy's breakdown and, 405–23 *passim*
  aid to victims of, 330–31, 336, 367
  communist purge during, 314
  end of, 338–39
  in Madrid, 320–23
  manifesto by writers and poets on, 316–20
  Orwell on, 310
  poems inspired by, 312, 314–16, 323–24, 382
  refugees from, 329–38; camps for, 334–36; French treatment of, 336–38
  reporting on, 309–13, 331–36 from front lines, 312–13
  significance of, 308–9
  toll of, 332
Spanish Newsletter, 309
Spectator, 137
Spender, J. A., 77
Spender, Stephen, 317
Sperry, Beth, 27
Spivak, John, 286
Squire, J. C., 355
Stark, Freya, 371
Steve (Trinidadian policeman), 344, 386

Story Teller's Holiday, A (Moore), 67

Strachan, Walter, 355, 390, 425, 433

Strachey, John, 137, 142, 364, 371

Stulik, Rudolf, 73, 83, 95, 96, 98, 195, 217

Sublunary (Cunard), 135–37

Sun Also Rises, The (Hemingway), 119

Sunday Chronicle, 279

Sunday Times, 390, 400

Surrealism, 131, 140, 150–52, 154, 158, 159, 182, 200–1, 257, 402
   L'Âge d'Or and, 218–19
   communism and, 152, 235, 290
   founding of, 147
   women and, 150

Swettenham, Frank, 43

Swingler, Randall, 319

Symons, Arthur, 139, 192, 364

Talking Pine, The (Moore), 236, 398

Tanguy, Yves, 204, 218, 363

Taylor, Jack, 288

Tennant, Edward Wyndham "Bimbo," 56, 58, 63, 67

Ten Poems More (Graves), 206

Theis, Louise, 346, 411, 420, 421–22, 423

Theis, Otto, 142, 186, 195, 275, 346, 388, 420, 421

Thirion, André, 161, 164, 175–76, 200–1, 218, 290

Thomas, Dylan, 347

Thomas, Hugh, 332, 335

Thompson, Louise, 269–70

Thorne, Anthony, 377, 390, 397, 407, 408, 410

Those Barren Leaves (Huxley), 115–16

Three Weeks (Glyn), 37

Thynne, Lord Alexander, 34

Tichenor, Frederick, 24

Tichenor, Mrs. Frederick, 35

Times Literary Supplement, 123, 137, 141, 276, 354

Tomás (photographer), 406, 412, 420, 422, 424

Too Weak (Eliot), 37

Tovalou, Prince, 197

Tower restaurant (Eiffel Tower restaurant), 73, 74–75, 83, 86, 95–96, 98, 111, 131, 136–37, 144, 195, 217, 434

Traité du Style (Aragon), 160

transition (magazine), 207

Tredegar, Lord, 56

Tree, Felicity, 51

Tree, Sir Herbert Beerbohm, 52

Tree, Iris, 64, 93, 111, 126, 127, 139, 192, 364, 403
   marriage of, 86, 87, 132
   teen-age years with Nancy, 52–55, 56

Trefusis, Marjorie, 74, 75, 77, 99, 127

Triolet, Elsa, 175–76, 183, 194, 200, 235, 305, 374, 414, 437

Truth, Sojourner, 285

Tubman, Harriet, 285

Tunisia, 324–29

Tunon, Gonzales, 315

Turks Croft, 77–81

Turner, Nat, 285

Twenty Poems Less (Riding), 206

Twysden, Duff, 120

Tzara, Tristan, 140, 218, 314, 317, 342, 364
   Dada and, 131, 135, 147
   death of, 431

Ubac, Raoul, 235, 273

Ulick and Soracha (Moore), 133–34

United States, 235–42, 257–65, 268, 370

Utchay, Nancy, 426

Utchay, T. K., 425–26

Vail, Clotilde, 132, 140
Vail, Laurence, 140
Van Vechten, Carl, 240, 242
Verlaine, Paul, 192
Victoria, Queen, 22
Vile Bodies (Waugh), 213
Visions, The (Cunard), 425
Vogue, 140
Voice of Spain, 309
von Warlich, Reinhold, 33
Vorticist movement, 57, 73

Waiting for Godot (Beckett), 400
Wales, Prince of, 352, 434
Waley, Arthur, 50
Walrond, Eric, 237
Walton, William, 128
Ward, Mrs. Dudley, 87
Warner, Sylvia Townsend, 356–57, 369, 390, 412, 425
War Story, A (Aldington), 204
Washington, Booker T., 285
Waste Land, The (Eliot), 126, 141, 207
Waugh, Evelyn, 120, 213, 318–19
Week-end Review, 85
Wells, H. G., 318
West African Students Union, 350–51
West Indies, 244, 268, 270–71, 343–44, 370
W. H. Allen publishing company, 349

Wheatley, Phillis, 285
Wheels (Sitwells), 53, 63–64, 110, 121
White, Sam, 441
White, Walter, 242
White Man's Duty, The (Cunard and Padmore), 348–49, 350
"Whoroscope" (Beckett), 206–7, 400
Wilde, Dolly, 132, 179
Williams, William Carlos, 93, 140, 155, 242, 285–86, 293, 366
Windsor, Duke of, 352, 434
Wishart & Co., 276, 277, 295
Woolf, Cecil, 389
Woolf, Leonard, 141, 143–44, 189, 190
Woolf, Miss (teacher), 39, 49, 402
Woolf, Virginia, 141, 189, 190, 214
Words (Brown), 211
World War, I, 57–69 *passim*
    aftermath of, 76, 91, 146
World War II, 338–59, 427
    Germans in France during, 362, 381
    in London, 345–59
    "phony" war, 338–39, 340
Wyndham, George, 33

Yeats, W. B., 34

Zukofsky, Louis, 290